HIPPOCRATES ASSAILED

The American Health Delivery System

Gerhard Falk

University Press of America,® Inc.
Lanham • New York • Oxford

Copyright © 1999 by
University Press of America,® Inc.
4720 Boston Way
Lanham, Maryland 20706

12 Hid's Copse Rd.
Cumnor Hill, Oxford OX2 9JJ

Library of Congress Cataloging-in-Publication Data

Falk, Gerhard
Hippocrates assailed : the American health delivery system / Gerhard
Falk.
p.   cm.
Includes bibliographical references and indexes.
1. Medicine—United States. 2. Medical care—United States. 3.
Medicine—United States—History—20th century. 4. Medical
care—United States—History—20th century. I. Title.
RA395.A3F337 1999 362.1'0973—dc21   99—30669 CIP

ISBN 0-7618-1433-7 (cloth: alk. ppr.)
ISBN 0-7618-1434-5 (pbk: alk. ppr.)

♾™ The paper used in this publication meets the minimum
requirements of American National Standard for Information
Sciences—Permanence of Paper for Printed Library Materials,
ANSI Z39.48—1984

Acknowledgements and Dedication

I want to thank my son Clifford Falk for the many hours he spent proofreading and setting up this manuscript.

This book is dedicated to the memory of my brother Erich Falck and to the six million who were murdered because they were Jews.

Table of Contents

Hippocrates Assailed-The American Health Delivery System

Part Two

Preface

The American health delivery system is the most important issue facing the American people at the end of the twentieth century. This has become so important an issue precisely because American medicine has become so successful.

Prior to the 1940's this was not the case. Beginning then, however, and largely because of the advances in science and medical knowledge gained from the experiences of the second World War, rising expectations have created a gap between that which can be done and that which most Americans want the health delivery system to give them.

This gap between reality and expectations is the substance of all social problems. Thus, death is not a social problem because it cannot be defeated. The weather is not a social problem because it cannot be changed. However, illness and longevity are social problems because we believe we can have an influence on them and change them. Poverty is also a social problem because in America we believe it can be alleviated, a belief not shared in all the world.

The cost of delivering the best "high tech" medical care to all Americans is at the root of the discrepancy of what can be done and what will be done for American patients. Erstwhile, all that could be done for sick persons was not so expensive that it could not be applied, at least to the majority of those seeking help. However, the ever changing developments in chemistry, technology and medicine have made each potential cure so expensive that the over-all cost of giving everyone everything is threatening to overwhelm all other budgetary considerations in the American community. Therefore rationing of medical care for various groups of citizens has already been instituted by some states and is most likely to occur in all of the country in the immediate future.

How such rationing of medical care shall be achieved and how it can be equitably administered is one of the principal issues now facing the

American community. All of this must be confronted even as the various health delivery systems are changing rapidly from their traditional settings into a future environment not yet entirely visible.

It is the purpose of this book to review all of these changes and to explain to the reader the nature and content of the institutions seeking to fulfill the Hippocratic Oath at the end of one century and at the beginning of another.

Introduction

In this book I have shown that the changing status of the medical profession, the rise of health maintenance organizations and the introduction of government into the American health delivery system is threatening to change medicine from a profession into a business. This threat has in turn provoked the "accountability revolution" particularly as costs in the health care area rose immensely during the last quarter of the 20th century.

This has already led to the rationing of health care in some states and will undoubtedly lead to rationing of health care in all states.

The great changes in health care during the 20th century were first and foremost the product of the development of anti-biotics in the 1940's. Great changes in medical education were also responsible for the alteration of the medical profession in this century as was the emphasis on specialization which has dominated American medicine for a century.

Demands for more patient-responsive treatment has resulted in far more sensitivity to patient anxiety and feelings on the part of the medical profession. Even as the profession is making these accommodations the threat to patients now comes from Health Maintenance Organizations who are accused of putting profits ahead of the needs of the sick.

In face of these changing conditions in the health delivery system, medical education seeks to uphold the Hippocratic Corpus which always emphasized the needs of the patient before any other consideration. Therefore, medical education at the end of the century is returning to the training of general family practitioners and reducing the interest on specialization heretofore promoted. Lecture style classes are giving way to more "hands-on" education in medical schools permitting medical students to be more active learners rather than passive receivers of information. In addition, the introduction of the social and behavioral sciences into the medical school curriculum has produced a more caring attitude on the part of physicians than was true when physicians concerned themselves only with the bio-chemical aspects of illness.

Because health maintenance organizations have insisted on cost-containment in treating patients, a problem based education and means of assessment has developed in medical schools and in teaching hospitals. Therefore the daily life of the American physicians has been changed to meet the demands of patients, HMOs, government and public opinion.

One of these changes has been the recent entrance of large numbers of women into the profession. Women now constitute about one fifth of all American physicians and their numbers are ever rising. Therefore, medicine is becoming a gender-equal profession after having traditionally been an almost all male profession. Another change with which American physicians must now deal is the discrepancy between rising expectations and rising costs both created by even more sophisticated technological advances. The consequent introduction of health maintenance organizations into the decision making process has impinged on the professional responsibilities of physicians as has the more aggressive behavior of patients and their "patients'-rights" organizations. These pressures have led some doctors to suffer "burn-out" and retire early or enter into a different occupation altogether. This feeling of "burn-out" has been particularly visible among surgeons.

Surgery has a somewhat different history than medicine. Constantly confronted with the consequences of violence, surgery was at one time regarded as a barber's trade. During the past century, however, surgery gained tremendous prestige particularly as surgery became the very epitome of an autonomous profession and as recent advances in surgery have included transplant surgery and robot technology. This autonomy is now being challenged by the HMOs even as ethical issues and patient's rights pressures are also impinging on surgery. Heretofore entirely dominated by white men, minorities and women now seek to enter this lucrative occupation even as more men than ever enter nursing, heretofore staffed entirely by women.

Nursing is also a changing profession. While nurses at one time worked only at the direction of doctors and as employees of hospitals or visiting nurses associations, nurses are now becoming autonomous as nurse-practitioners. That development has been fostered by the policy of the Federal Governments' Medicare who are now reimbursing nurses for services at one time rendered only by physicians. The Federal Government now has five programs subsidizing health care. In these circumstances the nursing profession is seeking greater political power in an effort to attain equality with doctors of medicine and psychotherapy, which nurse practitioners are now also entering.

Psychotherapy was of course never limited to the medical profession. Freud repeatedly emphasized that medical training is only one of several forms of professional education useful in becoming a psychotherapist. Therefore, nurses, religious counselors, social workers and psychologists are engaged in psychotherapy today. That therapy rests on trust between the patient and his therapist, hence precluding any breach of the "boundaries" existing between the therapist and his/her patient. Therapy, whether emotional or physical, often rests on the availability of drugs normally dispensed by the pharmacy profession. Together with the drug industry, pharmacy has been very successful in alleviating pain and increasing life expectancy. That success has led pharmacy to increase its educational requirements so that the doctorate has become the only degree awarded by American schools of pharmacy. This is taking place even as health maintenance organizations are doing all they can to reduce the costs of drugs under conditions that place pharmacists into the middle of the struggle to help patients and yet keep costs at a minimum.

Health maintenance organizations have not yet affected dentistry and other non-medical health delivery systems such as podiatry, and optometry as much as they have affected medicine and pharmacy. These professions are however of the greatest importance to the American people. Dentistry, a very old occupation, is now a high-tech profession. More and more women are entering these professions and the numerous "alternative medicines" which have developed into major industries during the last twenty years of the 20th century.

The presence of women into the realm of physical exercise and nutrition is more traditional than their presence in medicine and dentistry. Because obesity is one of America's greatest health hazards, a good deal of pressure has developed in the media to promote exercise among the American population. About 22% of Americans follow that dictum so that health clubs and gymnasiums are now found everywhere as is advice on dieting.

In sum, medicine, surgery, nursing, pharmacy, psychotherapy, dentistry and nutrition constitute the foundation of the American health delivery system.

The several health delivery professions, the hospital, the mental hospital and the nursing home are the institutional supports of the American health delivery system. This was not always the case. Prior to the discovery of penicillin medical practice was severely limited and hospitals were dangerous places because the patients were generally infected and could not be cured. Today, hospitals are efficient organizations capable of some of the most remarkable scientific achievements of the century. Cost containment, however, has deprived many patients of the opportunity to take advantage of the facilities hospitals have to offer so that patients are forced to accept "role exit" even as the government is proposing to federalize a "Patient's Bill of Rights" already in effect in several states.

A considerable medical bureaucracy has developed as a "high-tech" approach to illness has become universal in America. This has been a great boon to many patients but has not affected the most common of American health problems, mental and emotional illness.

While mental hospitals were at one time as popular as other hospitals, this is no longer the case. Many states have closed a number of their mental hospitals as cost-conscious insurance companies and health maintenance organizations demand the reduction of expensive hospitalization. The consequences are that many mentally disturbed persons are jailed, particularly because so many disturbed persons are involved in the illegal use and distribution of drugs.

A "revolving door" form of treatment has developed in connection with the effort to hospitalize patients on a short-term basis only. In part this "revolving door" point of view has been fostered by those who oppose psychiatric hospitals in principle and by the effort to reduce the stigma attached to being a "mental patient."

The 21,000 American nursing homes also house a number of disturbed and mentally ill patients, particularly those numerous old Americans who suffer from one or another form of dementia. As life expectancy increases, more and more Americans are subject to Alzheimer's disease and other forms of mental decline.

Not all who have these problems are cared for in nursing homes. There are several other alternatives to nursing homes which are, however, very expensive. Included in these alternatives are home health care, retirement communities and other facilities.

It is therefore no idle speculation to believe that the next century will see ever more Americans being treated at home or in out-patient facilities and that hospitalization will occur in only few and exceptional cases. It is further certain that medical care will be rationed in the future because all cannot be served by everything that is available. This in turn will lead to great debates and political struggles over who will or will not benefit from the technological revolution still in progress at the outset of another millenium.

That revolution in biological knowledge now includes the mapping of the federal human genome project that seeks to map each of the 100,000 genes that determine every physical characteristic in the human body. That government sponsored project has a number of rivals among private researchers who serve the pharmaceutical industry. Evidently, pharmaceutical manufacturers will earn untold fortunes if they can be first to patent the outcome of this research.

Forecasting inherited diseases will become routine in the next century. This is possible because of the ever greater capacity of geneticists to use genetic tests to identify inherited ailments before birth or thereafter. Such tests raise the issue of whether children, yet unborn, who have defects should be aborted. This is a tremendous ethical dilemma. In addition to screening for genetic illness, parents can now also pick a child's sex and may in later years be able to predetermine looks and intellect.

Altering genes to cure or inhibit diseases is certainly possible and will be carried out in the 21st century as will "cloning" or replicating animals and humans, a method already carried out in the case of a sheep named "Dolly". Richard Seed, a physicist, believes he can clone humans within a few years.

Genetics will also be used to cure cancer and other diseases heretofore most deadly. Finally, the genetics revolution has already led to a revival of the old controversy concerning eugenics which was so horribly misused by Nazi doctors in the 1940's.

In view of those dreadful experiments it is unlikely that anyone will soon want to "improve" the human race by genetic means. Nevertheless, these new and ongoing discoveries will alter all human life on this planet radically and create a world those living now can hardly imagine.

Chapter I

American Medicine - An Overview at the End of the Century

I

Before the introduction of anti-biotics in the 1940's and 1950's, American medicine relied on all those traditions which had been in use since the days of Hippocrates (460 B.C.E.-377 B.C.E.), a Greek physician of the 5th Century B.C.E. who has been called "The Father of Medicine." This label has been attached to Hippocrates because he is generally credited with writing descriptions of disease processes and intricate case studies. Added to this collection known as The Hippocratic Corpus is the philosophy of the Hippocratic school of thought which included the well known Hippocratic Oath. That oath is a declaration of professional medical ethics developed over the years by many physicians in addition to Hippocrates. The principal message of that oath is that the physician will act in the interests of his patients at all times, that he will not betray the trust of his patients and that he will "abstain from whatever is injurious."[1]

The Hippocratic Oath, in one form or another, is still administered to new graduates of medical schools to this day. Therefore we seek to examine whether the oath is still valid in end-of-the-century America even as "managed care" has become the principal means of health delivery services in the United States today (1999).

II

In November 1997, Dr. Arthur Caplan, Director of the Center for Bioethics at the University of Pennsylvania, outlined some shortcomings in the American health care system. Included in that list, according to Caplan, is the need for privacy, for confidentiality, for continuity, for accountability and commitment to the sick. Evidently, this well known medical ethicist was of the opinion that these characteristics of an organized health delivery system were either absent or in danger of being ignored by the health delivery system as practiced in the United States at the end of this century.[2]

Now anyone old enough to remember the manner in which American physicians have cared for their patients in the past, and unaware of the recent trends in "managed care" would find it astonishing that privacy, confidentiality, continuity and accountability would even need mention by an "ethicist." For prior to the rise of the Health Maintenance Organizations, it was simply assumed that these features of the doctor-patient relationship were guaranteed by the physicians oath and community standing. Further, it was assumed that the less well would get the most attention from the local doctor because they needed it. Yet, recent developments have divorced the patient so far from his physician that Mark Smith, M.D., chief of the California Health Care Foundation told managed care executives at a recent meeting that "People are scared of you." Smith referred to 24 hour limits on hospital maternity stays; the 'gag clause' prohibiting doctors from speaking to patients about the range of treatment available to their patients and the huge corporate bonuses handed to HMO executives. These issues are now acute and important because 77% of all Americans were already members of Health Maintenance Organizations at the end of 1997 and many more continued to join each day so that it is certain that HMO's are here to stay.[3]

It is no doubt significant that in 1993 51% of Americans were members of HMO's and that in 1988 only 29% were members. In the course of twenty years, membership more than doubled.[4]

Consequently, during the last ten years, the health delivery system has careened like a drunken sailor from a system in which large payments tempted doctors to do too much to a system in which fixed payments tempt doctors and hospitals to do too little.

Premiums for health care have also risen considerably. Nevertheless, while in the 1980's premiums rose nearly 19% a year, premiums have been less inflationary in the 90's than in earlier years. For example, in 1996 insurance premiums only rose 2.5%.[5]

As premiums rose both corporate employers and individual employees were unwilling and unable to pay these ever greater amounts. Premiums rose, of course, because doctors and hospitals used high-cost tests and procedures and sent the bills to insurance companies who paid without question. Finally, the premiums became so great that a depression era idea, prepaid health plans, appeared to be the answer to the health care inflation.

The first such pre-paid plan was called "Kaiser Permanente" which was founded in California in 1933. This plan employed salaried physicians for labor union members and was therefore denounced as socialist by every state medical society. Similar plans came to be known as Health Maintenance Organizations during the Nixon administration in the 1970's. From about thirty such HMO's in the 1970's they have grown to over 1,500 of whom 83% are for profit, earning huge salaries and bonuses for their executives and immense dividends for their shareholders.

Nevertheless, the income and profits of HMOs are not necessarily assured, nor are HMOs as secure as is widely believed. Thus, "Kaiser Permanente" lost $50 million in 1997 even as credit rating agencies downgraded its debt. Similar problems are now being experienced by the other HMO giants, not only because of increased health care costs, but also because consumers, doctors and legislators are beginning to regulate these companies more and more.

For example, shares of Aetna, Inc., as well as U.S. Healthcare and Oxford Health Plans, Inc., declined at the end of 1997. Of these, Oxford lost more than 75% of its stock market value since October of 1997. Such losses were also experienced by PacifiCare Health Systems, Inc., CIGNA Corp. and Prudential Insurance Co. [6]

Because these HMO's are a for-profit business they evidently seek to keep costs down and limit access of their subscribers to procedures which patients may need in order to recover. In short, HMO businessmen now stand between the patient and his doctor. Lists of cheap drugs are given doctors who are told they cannot prescribe anything else. These plans also have committees which review patients' records and decide what the plan will or will not cover.

One of the consequences of this attitude by the HMOs has been State investigations and fines against HMOs who engage in an unacceptable disregard for quality of care. Thus, the State of Texas sued "Kaiser" for skimping on coverage so that that insurance company had to pay a $1 million penalty in order to settle that lawsuit. [7]

Throughout the nation legislatures are writing laws dealing with HMOs. Alone in 1997, nineteen states passed comprehensive managed care laws. All told, states passed 182 laws in 1997 to deal with HMOs.

One of the most objectionable practices of the HMOs have been physician's "gag" clauses which prohibit doctors from telling patients about treatment that may be available but is costly. In Connecticut the toughest HMO law provides that patients and doctors may consult outside reviewers to investigate an HMOs denial of care. Texas even passed a law permitting patients to sue Health Plans for malpractice. All of this is the consequence of a general belief among Americans that Health Maintenance Organizations seek only to say "no". In short, HMOs enjoy little public confidence, whatever their motives.

Recently, Sen. Edward Kennedy of Massachusetts favored the enactment of a Federal consumer "Bill of Rights", which had already been proposed in 1995 by the National Committee for Quality Assurance. Now, President Clinton's Advisory Commission on Consumer Protection and Quality in Health Care has decided to adopt that "Bill of Rights". That commission also evaluated numerous health plans and ranked these HMOs with special emphasis on preventive care such as mammograms and immunization.

Although some of America's largest employers, such as General Motors and Xerox offer their employees a choice of membership in National Committee for Quality Assurance Accredited HMOs, about 43% of all American employees aren't offered insurance through work. This means that about 40 million Americans were uninsured at the beginning of 1999.

There can be no doubt that the years since HMOs have become the principal method of financing health care have also been the years during which the erstwhile doctor-patient relationship, celebrated by such television dramas as "Chicago Hope", has almost ceased to exist.

One exception to the effort to corporatize American medicine is The Association of American Physicians and Surgeons. This association was founded in 1943 and is dedicated to the "free market" practice of medicine. The membership is only 4,174 and is therefore puny compared to the American Medical Association. This association has testified before Congress, written books and newspaper articles and insisted that they are doctors and not "providers." Members of the association will not accept third party payments and have successfully challenged a number of government policies affecting health care, such as the erstwhile prohibition forbidding old people to pay for extra medical help beyond Medicare.[8]

Although a few physicians are willing to fight the encroachment of corporations and government on the profession, this has not been true of the American Medical Association. Hence, more and more bureaucrats are telling doctors how to run their practice so that experienced doctors are leaving the profession as they are faced with decreasing incomes, the strictures of insurance companies, huge malpractice insurance premiums and the demeaning status reductions practiced by government agencies and insurance companies.[9]

First, this is true because in the past doctors earned their income on a fee-for service basis. Hence, every time a patient visited the doctor that visit represented an income. Since the rise of the HMOs however, doctors lose money when a patient visits them. The reason for this is the "capitation" policy of the HMOs. This means that the plans usually pay each doctor a fixed sum each year. Presently, (1999) that sum is about $150.- per patient per year. Consequently, doctors keep the entire amount if a patient does not visit them but finds that the entire sum is soon wiped out if a patient needs extensive help and that it is even possible that a doctor has to pay out of his own pocket for patients whose needs are extensive. Therefore, "capitation" leads to an inevitable reduction in the care any patient will receive.

In addition to "capitation", HMOs have yet another arrangements. This is the bonus system. Here doctors continue to bill for services rendered but receive a bonus if they limit expenses. These bonuses can reach $100,000.- a year. Furthermore, HMOs make it clear to doctors that unless they spend a minimum they will be put out of business. Nevertheless, doctors' incomes averaged $195,000 a year in 1996. Since the HMOs are so recent an innovation it is not now (1999) possible to compare outcomes of patient treatment with the former fee-for-service system. In any case, there is no evidence as of 1999 that the overall health of Americans has been affected one way or the other by the HMO revolution. Nevertheless, many people fear that ultimately health care will be sacrificed to money and that the long range consequences of the HMO system are bound to be negative.

For health care providers, whether physicians, social workers, psychologists, dentists or others, the HMO development has also meant an enormous and confusing involvement in tremendous amounts of paper work. Doctors generally see patients who are enrolled in one of 20 to 30 HMOs. Each of these insurance providers has different forms, papers, rules and regulations. Worse, doctors must now call an 800 number and get permission from someone who may or may not have a medical education to use a treatment after first telling the insurance employee his diagnosis. This loss of independence is perhaps the most galling aspect of the most recent developments in the doctor-patient relationship. Thus, doctors are forced to answer to those they deem uninformed as to why a patient has not yet been discharged from a hospital or why the "provider", at one time called "doctor", is prescribing one medicine and not another which may be cheaper.[10]

Consequently, profits in the health care industry had become so immense that the president of Aetna U.S. Health Care was paid $4.9 million in 1996 even as these corporations shifted their resources to their stockholders and away from patient care. In 1997 the profit of Aetna declined which may have come about because of excessive compensation and excessive profit taking by stockholders.

Since the United States is the only "developed" country in the industrial world which does not guarantee medical care to every citizen, there are 40 million "working poor" who have no coverage because they cannot pay the premiums. Certainly, the uninsured cannot expect that corporate share holders and executives will come to their aid.

There are those who believe that physicians should be paid a salary so that any incentive to order too much or too little care will be removed from the doctors' consideration. Such an arrangement limits the erstwhile autonomy of every doctor considerably and thereby tends to reduce the social prestige of doctors as well. That the HMO arrangement has already done this is exhibited by the manner in which corporate HMOs refer to physicians. Instead of calling them doctors they call them "providers" a term also used for social workers, dental hygienists and anyone else whom the insurers pay. Doctors dislike 'this term intensely as they view it as a significant signal of the status reduction to which the profession has become subject during the decade ending in 1999.

III

Health care reform is not a new proposal in 1998. In fact, in 1991, when Harris Wofford, a social work professor, won the election to Senator from Pennsylvania by making health care an issue many politicians predicted that the Presidential election of 1992 would also focus on that topic. They were right in making such a prediction since the Clinton campaign of that year made a great deal of health care reform. In fact, almost the first thing President Clinton did on achieving the presidency was to develop a plan for health care reform. Largely because of sexism related to the fact that the commission on health care reform was chaired by the First Lady, i.e., Mrs. Hillary R. Clinton, those proposals failed to pass Congress.

The principal reason for President Clinton's proposals was and is that the U.S. health care services are "a mess." This estimate is commonly believed by the American public although it is unfair and remote from historical reality to overlook that at one time the American health delivery system did work.[11]

This is specifically visible in looking at the period directly following the second World War. At that time the U.S. faced a shortage of health care personnel. Thus, in 1950 there were 290,000 physicians in the United States. That constituted 141 physicians for every 100,000 in the population. In 1990, there were 590,000 physicians in this country and that constituted 234 physicians for every 100,000 in the 1990 census population. In the year 2000 it is expected that there will be 726,000 physicians in the United States. That will mean that there will be and almost are already, (1998) 271 physicians for every 100,000 in the American population. Similarly, a deficiency of acute care general hospital beds was alleviated as the acute care hospital beds rose from 3.3 per 1,000 population in 1950 to 4.5 per thousand in 1980. Evidently, then the most acute health care problems were all corrected and dealt with efficiently in the decade after the Second World War with the consequence that health care outcomes also improved.

Largely, the introduction of anti-bacterial drugs, the increased knowledge of the action of hormones, the war time developments in the area of blood replacement and other fluids and the increasing effectiveness of surgery increased life expectancy and also increased expectations of the general public concerning the efficiency and competence of medical practice. This, however, led directly to the discrepancy between the ideal of curing all illness and demands for immediate scientific action in case of every illness, and the reality that bio-medical sciences cannot deliver cure-alls at once but can only progress slowly by means of trial and error and the gradual growth of knowledge.[12]

As we have seen, health care outcomes improved during the decade after the Second World War because of the incorporation of scientific advances into medical practice. After that war, the medical schools of the United States attempted to continue the scientific advances gained during the war. Numerous foundations also sought to participate in the effort to place medicine on a scientific footing. However, directly after the war most universities were spending their money on educating millions of veterans who had just been discharged from the armed services. Foundations, too, were overtaxed in view of the immense requests made of them. Therefore, federal government appropriations for scientific research were activated by politicians who were pressured by citizens and scientists to fund such research.[13]

This means of supporting medical advances, unlike involvement in insurance schemes, seemed popular, safe and non-controversial to the politicians. Therefore, financial support for health research was funneled into and through the National Institute of Health without opposition from the American Medical Association which was too busy fighting national health insurance. Hence, expenditures for health research increased from $12.9 billion in 1950 to $40.7 billion in 1965.[14]

In that year the 1965-1966 congressional session of Congress enacted a good deal of health care legislation by means of amendments to the Social Security Act. These amendments included Medicaid and Medicare legislation as well as maternal and infant care and children and youth projects under Title V of that Act.[15]

Since then, the most striking consequence of American health care success has been the reduction in mortality from heart disease and strokes. All of this was possible because the deficiencies of the immediate post World War II era could be alleviated by expanding the knowledge base and increasing access to medical care through Medicare and Medicaid. It seemed therefore that these early successes could be continued indefinitely. However, now, at the end of the century it turns out that these successes were only temporary because the at-risk population has increased dramatically while the costs of medical care have skyrocketed.

This increase is illustrated by the expenditures for health care services as a proportion of gross domestic product from 4.5% in 1950 to over 14% in 1996. This three-fold increase could not be sustained by philanthropic contributions. Therefore, erstwhile volunteer hospitals became for-profit hospitals even if they did not admit this publicly. Economists, administrators and financiers took over from doctors thereby achieving the "monetarization of medical care" as Ginzberg called it. [16]

As costs increased and public and private health insurers became the principal support of our health maintenance program, hospitals began to shift the cost of uninsured patients to those who have insurance, thus burdening the insurance companies and hence the premium payers. Anxiety over costs increased as the occupancy of hospital beds decreased. Thus, at the end of the 1990's hospital beds are only two thirds occupied. This did not lead to a decrease in hospital bed capacity but rather led to considerable competition among hospitals to fill their beds. Physicians were recruited to bring patients into hospitals even as patients with pre-existing conditions were denied insurance coverage while every effort was made to enroll only healthy individuals who would not use the available services and therefore cost less. [17]

The outcome of all these trends is that medicine is now in danger of becoming a business instead of a profession. This trend endangers physicians and other health care providers unless four recommendations by Relman are given some credence. These are first, that all citizens, including the poor, are assured access to services, second, that health care costs are contained at a reasonable level; third, that more is done to prevent disease since we are presently only spending 4% of health care resources on such prevention and finally that research support be increased from the present 1% of health care expenditures to a far greater sum because research is the foundation of change and advances in medicine. [18]

Such an increase in research support depends of course on the political climate in which requests for such support must be made.

Since this issue is in turn related to the failure of the United States to enact a national health insurance program as is true in all other Western democracies and elsewhere, we turn now to the reasons for that failure. An understanding of the reasons for this neglect will also permit comprehension of the failure to adequately support research.

A number of commentators have attempted to analyze the reasons for our unwillingness to include National Health Insurance in our social security structure. The first of these reasons has been the attitude of the medical profession towards national Health Insurance. That profession, principally represented by the American Medical Association, has always claimed that their professional autonomy could not tolerate government interference in the professional judgments of physicians. National Health Insurance was therefore portrayed as an infringement on that autonomy. This attitude did not preclude that government was expected to build hospitals and to endow research. Hence, the Hill-Burton Act and the National Institutes of Health were both allowed to grow and prosper. Nevertheless, government, in view of the AMA was not to challenge professional autonomy by promoting national health insurance. [19]

During the 1930's, when public health care was first proposed as a possible part of the Social Security Law, physicians actively opposed such a plan because they saw themselves as private businessmen and wanted no interference by government. This despite the fact that physicians did not earn much money during the 1930's. Thus, the average income of physicians in 1933 was only $3,088.- a decline from 1929 of 43% in income. [20]

Sociologists recognize however, that then as now physicians were regarded by Americans as having considerable social prestige. Therefore, then as now, physicians identified themselves with the elite in American society. This was particularly true in small town America as it existed in the 1930's and beyond. Koos has shown that this need to be accepted as a member of the small town elite, most of whom were businessmen, precluded physicians from supporting national health insurance even when the income of physicians in the 1930's would have given physicians every reason to lend their support to such a scheme. [21]

Physicians, until at least the 1950's, also claimed that the poor needed no insurance because they, the doctors, would take care of the poor without charging a dime. This was generally true even if the humiliation of the poor most assuredly accompanied such "free" treatment. Moreover, private foundations often financed the most expensive treatment. Thus, these private charities generally helped cover the cost of treatment in an "iron lung" which was the only means by which polio victims could survive before the discovery of the Salk vaccine in the late 1950's. This dreaded disease, polio, was also fought by the National Foundation for Infantile Paralysis, which was founded by the most famous of polio patients, i.e. President Franklin Delano Roosevelt.[22]

It is, however, not only the American Medical Association which has opposed government sponsored health insurance. Corporations and labor unions have also opposed mandatory national health insurance. Corporations were always opposed to such a scheme because they did not want to pay the premium costs. Labor unions were always opposed to national health insurance because they wanted health insurance to be part of the negotiated benefits the union would provide its members to the exclusion of non-members. This procedure gave union leaders a greater opportunity to demonstrate to members how beneficial membership is even if non-union members were left uncovered by insurance altogether. [23]

This attitude of indifference to the well-being of others indicates a rather cruel and callous attitude in a nation which is largely compassionate and thinks of itself as helpful and charitable. The evidence for the charitable concern of Americans for each other is best illustrated by the numerous social insurance plans adopted during the Franklin D. Roosevelt administration in the 1930's. Yet, even these originally modest proposals concerning old age pensions and unemployment insurance were at that time bitterly opposed by big business and other interests. [24]

Among these "other interests" was Blue Cross, a newly formed private health insurance company which succeeded in convincing the public that the poor received free medical care in any hospital and that the rich could afford to pay for their own medical care. Therefore, argued Blue Cross, only the middle class, and not the rich or the poor, needed insurance coverage which they, Blue Cross, were ready to provide. Blue Cross claimed that the middle class did not want to accept charity and hence would not be willing to accept free medical care in a hospital. Since the middle class could not afford to pay medical bills out of their savings, it seemed reasonable to Blue Cross promoters that only their insurance could provide the middle class with financial protection against illness and that all governmental and other public efforts would violate American traditions and expectations. Said Louis Pink, president of Blue Cross in the 1930's: "The average man, with the average income, has pride. He is not looking for charity; he is not looking for ward care. He wants the best attention for himself and his family....Yet, out of his savings he is very seldom prepared to meeting unexpected sickness or accident expenses." [25]

These and other arguments succeeded well and permitted Blue Cross to enroll 39 Blue Cross plans by 1939 with over 6 million subscribers. Ten years later, Blue Cross had enrolled 31 million subscribers by extensively advertising that there was no reason to provide national health insurance since the private sector had already resolved the issue. Since union contracts provided more and more employees with private health insurance it seemed to the middle class that the need for government sponsored health insurance was not there. All of this overlooked, of course, that innumerable Americans had no health coverage at all. However, the middle class had no self interest in demanding government sponsored health insurance while the poor were ignored and given neither sympathy nor credence.[26]

Thus, Blue Cross succeeded in deflecting the middle class from any demand for government intervention in the providing of health insurance.

Between 1963 and 1965 Congress debated Medicare. That government sponsored insurance permits retirees to buy health insurance at a cost affordable to all those whose income had declined even as their health needs had increased. Testifying before Congress concerning the Medicare proposal at that time was the then Secretary of Health, Education and Welfare, Anthony Celebrezze. He claimed that "People over sixty-five use three times as much hospital care, on the average, as people under sixty five." [27]

The entire argument of Celebrezze in favor of Medicare was that anyone younger than 65 was insured privately by his employer, or was young enough to borrow money and pay it back. That argument ignored, of course, that millions of Americans did not then have any health insurance, a condition which continues to this day.

Opponents of Medicare worried then, and now, that citizens might believe that access to medical help is a right. Therefore, the proponents of Medicare argued that the recipients did of course not have a right to health care but that Medicare, as a part of the Social Security Act would be paid for by patients' premiums. Thus, Medicare did not open the door to yet additional government sponsored health delivery programs. Consequently, to this day (1998), the poor still do not have health insurance coverage because politics dictate that only the middle class and those wealthier than that are entitled to health insurance. Hence, those high on the ladder of social stratification have so far done as little as possible for those who have no money, no power and no political influence.

IV

Before Alexander Fleming (1881-1955) discovered the antibacterial action of penicillin in 1929, the fear of infectious diseases permeated the practice of medicine. Kenneth Williamson, a hospital administrator before the introduction of sulfa drugs and penicillin recalled that :"Any infection, the slightest infection, ...especially if it were a blood stream infection, became a great source of concern to physicians because of the limitation of what they could do about it. It was very different from today's atmosphere."[28]

That limitation continued until World War II when penicillin was first used together with the additional advances provided by Selman Waksman (1888-1973) who coined the word "anti-biotics" upon winning the Nobel Prize in Medicine for his discovery of streptomycin. It is therefore no exaggeration to claim that prior to 1940 medicine was a limited art and hardly a science.

In the 1780's, there were two physicians in England who recognized the nature of contagion and who tried to persuade their colleagues that physicians themselves were the carriers of contagious diseases from one patient to another. Thus, a Scottish doctor Gordon and a Dr. White of Manchester, England both argued that childhood fever was contagious. Both were ignored and scorned by their colleagues.

The American, Oliver Wendell Holmes, (1841-1935) repeated these arguments one hundred years later but was not ignored, but scorned and "refuted" by the leading obstetrician of his day, a Dr. Charles Meigs who found it additionally necessary to ridicule Holmes contention that physicians should separate "post-mortems" from deliveries.[29]

In 1861, the Austro-Hungarian surgeon Ignaz Phillip Semmelweiss (1818-1865) was ostracized because he had published The Cause, Concept and Prevention of Childbed Fever. In this publication Semmelweiss showed that physicians who scrubbed up in chlorine water and used a nail brush before seeing a patient reduced mortality rates from childbed fever among mothers and children. Semmelweiss had come to that conclusion because he noticed that such fever was less prevalent when mid-wives delivered a baby than when doctors did the delivery. Yet, in his day, hardly any physician was willing to take his advice.[30]

Charles Rosenberg, no doubt the foremost historian of American medicine, has shown how nineteenth century America continued to live with the traditions of "two millenia" in medicine. Those traditions included the view that the body is a system interacting with its environment and that disease or health "resulted from a cumulative interaction with its (the body's) constitutional endowment and environment circumstances." It was further believed, during all the years prior to scientific medicine, that illness resulted from the failure of the body to maintain its equilibrium. Thus, "equilibrium" was viewed as synonymous with health and disequilibrium with illness."[31]

In the nineteenth century and before, American and other physicians had no diagnostic tools other than their personal experience. Therefore a theory of "intake and outgo" served as an explanation for all diseases. Accordingly, physicians attached great significance to perspiration, defecation, urination, menstruation, bleeding and pulse. Drugs were used before the rise of scientific medicine but they were not viewed as dealing with any one specific disease but rather were seen as dealing with the entire system at once. Patients reported the appearance of these various bodily excretions to their doctors who evaluated these reports relative to the color or shape of such excretions. Fevers were common and were treated with mercury and antimony. It was common to bleed patients and to give the diuretics (to pass urine) as well as emetics (to vomit) and cathartics or a laxative. Evidently, pre-scientific medicine was based on the belief that disease needs to be expelled from the body by these means. Since most people recovered most of the time despite these measures, this form of medicine was believed to be efficient. Finally, nineteenth century medicine and medicine in earlier days, was embedded in the family and the community. Sick people stayed at home and were seldom admitted to a hospital. The course of an illness was considered unpredictable because it was thought that some forms of disequilibrium could not be righted so that death became inevitable in those cases. Therefore, there was also a good deal of spiritual explanation for illness and death. Few Americans saw any inconsistency between rational explanations and religious explanations. If drugs failed, this proved the ultimate power of God and was accepted as realistic and predictable. Hence, it was assumed that nature would take its course, that physicians could do little to alter the course of nature and that each person had a vital power needed to be helped by the physician but which determined the outcome of an illness in any event. Since it was as commonly known then as now that no two persons had the same constitution or emotional condition the Boston Medical and Surgical Journal editorialized correctly that "no two instances of typhoid fever or any other disease, are precisely alike." [32]

Despite all the obstacles which ignorance and prejudice put in its way, there were a few physicians in earlier years and of course many in our own century who sought to challenge the view that illness is a whole-body experience. Thus, there gradually developed categories of therapeutics and their application to various diseases. Pellegrino has listed these therapeutics and the years in which they were first discovered. It is significant that Pellegrino's list includes only two items dating from the 18th century but fourteen from the nineteenth century. The two therapeutic agents attributed to 1753 and 1785 respectively were lime juice, to be used to deal with scurvy, a deficiency of vitamin C and digitalis to counteract heart failure. In the nineteenth century quinine was isolated, chloroform was synthesized, a diphtheria antitoxin became available and a tetanus anti-toxin came into use. There were other discoveries in the nineteenth century to help the sick and practice medicine.[33]

Thus, the middle and the end of the nineteenth century saw some great scientific improvements and the constant advance of empiricism. However, many physicians resisted these new efforts and denounced the Paris Clinical School and other proponents of laboratory based medical practice. That practice was due to the development of "the laboratory revolution" in medicine in the second half of the nineteenth century. That revolution produced the work of Louis Pasteur (1822-1895), Joseph Lister (1827-1912) and Robert Koch (1843-1910). They created the science of bacteriology and thereby made it impossible to further ignore the role of germs in disease. In fact, the installation of laboratories in the hospitals and medical schools and offices of doctors was the means by which medicine became scientific.[34] These laboratories led to the development of bacteriology which is now, (1999) the foundation of Western medicine. This does not mean, of course, that there have not been challenges to the germ theory of disease. Thus, the belief that germs are the only and singular cause of illness is now being challenged. Therefore, recent research has focused on the human immune system as a possible additional source of disease. Furthermore, sociological factors have recently been reviewed as possible causes and/or cures of diseases. Among these are the emotional state of the patient and the social environment in which the patient lives. This new emphasis is the product of the emergence of new illnesses such as AIDS and the failure to cure such old diseases as cancer.[35]

Thus, questions have now been raised about the germ theory and its application. Among these is of course the old question: "Why is it that not everyone exposed to germs and bacteria becomes sick?" and "Why are some viruses such as herpes and AIDS more virulent than before?" and "Why are some new strains of bacteria developing precisely because we are using anti-biotics?"[36]

Nevertheless, nothing sets modern medical practice more apart from its antecedents anywhere than its therapeutic effectiveness.

Because of that effectiveness, medicine as practiced at the end of the twentieth century has become specialized. Physicians have now become masters over a limited domain of techniques and therapeutics which are growing at an enormous rate so that no one can do more than specialize in a narrow area of concern. Several consequences of that specialization have therefore appeared. One is the use of the hospital, where the equipment needed to deal with many of these therapeutics is available. In fact, unlike earlier centuries, hospitals have now become the center of the physician's interest and activities. Furthermore longer and longer education is now needed to learn a specialty and more complex scientific language is used to describe the specialties practiced. Medical students are therefore selected on the basis of their scientific ability and interests so that care of the patient, the patient's feelings and fears and the family anxiety about illness has been largely ignored by physicians in the past fifty years because these aspects of illness and recovery are viewed as less than honorable issues and concerns and are held to be not proper interests for a scientist-physician. Thus, some specialists are so engrossed in their therapeutics that they overlook the patient as a whole and concentrate only on their own area of expertise. [37]

Twentieth century medicine has relied more and more on the laws of biology, physics and chemistry. Explanations for disease other than those based on these sciences are viewed with disdain at the turn of the century. Hence, the values and interests of patients have been given less and less credence by physicians whose only concern is the scientific evidence and not the patient's state of mind or attitude. This means that doctors and medical students have largely ignored the need to make decisions on the basis of the scientific evidence as well as the patients' wishes and moral views. Furthermore, doctors know less and less about the lives of their patients and vice versa. Hence, when doctors meet patients, strangers meet one another. The only link between the doctor and his patients is therefore their mutual belief that the doctor has the ability to deal with the patient's complaints. Patients, of course, have also accepted the view that science can cure all their ills and have additionally invested the doctor with the status of a wonder-worker who masters science and can and should use every scientific instrument known to bear on the patient's complaint. When patients believe that this has not been done they often feel cheated and disappointed. Lacking the doctor-patient relationship which was the cornerstone of treatment in earlier years, patients are now willing to sue doctors for not using every conceivable scientific method in dealing with their illness or the illness of their loved ones. It is assumed by many Americans that there is a drug for every discomfort and that drugs are the cure-all for everything from alcoholism to xenophobia. [38]

Therefore it has become necessary at the turn of the century to find some means of distinguishing valuable health care from the useless waste of resources. Wolf has called this new concern "The Accountability Revolution."[39]

V

This "Accountability Revolution" concerns quality assessment. This means that hospitals, doctors offices and Health Maintenance Organizations are now open to public scrutiny and therefore permit patients and others to know the quality of competing health care providers so that patients can make a choice. Therefore, this new approach to health care includes the view that not only the physician, but the patient himself, can decide what treatment is to be used in his specific case. It is of course true that since the days of Hippocrates, as we have already seen, physicians have been obliged to at least not worsen the patient's condition. Today, however, that Hippocratic requirement has been augmented by licensing, disciplinary proceedings, institutional accreditation, negligence litigation, peer review and long-term care credentialing.[40]

In addition, patient involvement has produced a considerable concern with the ethics of health care. The word ethics is related to the Greek word ethos meaning custom. Sociologists recognize three kinds of customs. Folkways, mores and laws. Mores are those customs which are not optional like folkways, but are also not part of the written code of law. Hence mores are expectations which members of a group have of one another and which cannot be violated with impunity even if they are not part of law. Ethics refer to such mores. Therefore, evaluating the ethical conduct of health care providers has become widespread during the past ten years. In New York State, for example, The New York State Education Department includes an Office of the Professions which distributes literature encouraging patients to verify the licenses of 600,000 individuals practicing in 38 professions in the state. The Office of the Professions also invites consumers to complain about those engaged in professional misconduct. In New York that is defined as incompetence and negligence; failure to provide records on request; practicing under the influence of drugs including alcohol; being sexually or physically abusive; practicing beyond the scope of the profession; abandoning or neglecting a patient in need of immediate care; performing unnecessary services and charging for work not done. Included in the literature of the Office of the Professions is a Consumer's Bill of Rights.[41]

No doubt lists such as the one above strengthen the position of the patient vis-a-vis his doctor or other health care providers. However, such literature also tends to provoke innumerable complaints against every physician and other provider by a considerable number of people who are anxious to file law suits, are jealous of their doctors income, dislike a providers religion or ethnicity; seek publicity for themselves and a host of other motives. Therefore any effort to evaluate the ethics of a professional needs to include the probability that innumerable complaints will be filed with the State Education Department for all the reasons already listed. This means that doctors, i.e. physicians can no longer make decisions concerning a patient's health based only on the scientific evidence gathered by the doctors. Instead, physicians must now also consider how every move they make will look to the State Education Department and whether the treatment they prescribe is "politically correct" or will lead to a law suit.

Ethics and regulations concerning professional practices can also be applied to organizations which deliver health related services. Therefore, hospitals and health maintenance organizations can be judged by the standards provided by the New York State Education Department or the equivalent bureaucracies in other states. The problems arising from these efforts to place professionals under the scrutiny of numerous bureaucracies are however generally overlooked. Among these problems is first, the reduction of autonomy for physicians and other health professionals. Fearing constant threats from dissatisfied patients, cost conscious insurance companies, lawyers and others, it becomes necessary for health care providers to practice "defensive medicine." This means that everyone in the health care professions must use every possible technique proving, if dragged before courts, investigators, prosecutors and lawyers, that the doctor or other provider has done everything possible to give the patient every treatment known. That, however, is very expensive. Therefore, a doctor who seeks to protect himself finds that he runs afoul of the insurance companies who don't want to pay for every test, every treatment and every procedure known to the provider. Consequently, health care providers, caught between lawyers, bureaucrats and insurance companies are truly "between Scylla and Charybdis."[42]

The belief that every patient has a right to every possible technique which may alleviate his complaint involves the issue of whether health care is a right or a privilege. Those who argue that it is a right overlook that such a "right" depends on the willingness and ability of someone else to give such health care as may be required. It is of course generally agreed that every human being ought to have whatever health care he needs. The problem of how to provide this has divided

Americans for some time. Sloganeers like to deal with this issue by proclaiming that doctors need to be altruists who treat everyone, regardless of ability to pay and that the common good requires universal health care. That implies however, that someone, i.e. physicians and other health care providers, have the obligation to give such care. The arguments in favor of patients' rights are first, that illness attacks everyone, whether rich or poor, male or female, young or old. However, everyone does not agree on the nature of health care needs. For example, abortion is viewed as a need by many women but is abhorred by its opponents. Young women are of course in need of obstetrical care, a need not felt by older women or by men. Similarly, dental care is not considered vital by the young, but is considered vital by the old. There is then a difference between needs and wants which is hard to define. Therefore, someone has to make that distinction. This dilemma leads directly to the involvement of government which is called upon to promote "patients' rights" and thereby define the obligations of the health care profession. President Clinton has urged Congress to pass federal legislation insuring the rights of patients. This would mean that quality standards would be promulgated by a federal bureaucracy which would demand that every American health plan include these standards. President Clinton's proposal is called "The Health Security Act".

That act, if it becomes law, would rely on "managed competition." This means that health plans would compete with one another on the basis of quality and cost. The Department of Health, Education and Welfare would issue "report cards" under that proposal, informing consumers regarding the quality of each plan. Consumers would then "vote with their wallets" concerning the competing plans.[43]

. Included in the proposed "Health Security Act" is a Patient's Bill of Rights. New York already has such a "Bill of Rights" which includes the right to receive competent professional service; the right to verify the credentials of licensed professionals; the right to receive explanations of the services being offered; the right to refuse any service; the right to know what records are kept and the right to have access to such records and keep them confidential; the right to file complaints with the State Education Department; the right to be treated with courtesy and the right to know the consequences of choosing various service options.[44]

Granted that all of these rights should devolve on every citizen we are nevertheless faced with the problem of giving maximum health care to everyone. There are some who abuse their bodies and are perpetually ill by reason of alcohol or other addictions. There are others who are in need of considerable medical resources because of their age, their inherited condition or an unusual and costly illness. Since maximum health care for everyone would use up the entire community budget were it to be permitted, there are those who believe that rationing of health care is the only solution to this dilemma. Such rationing has already been adopted by the Oregon Health Plan effective in 1994. That plan lists 696 condition-treatment pairs of which 131 conditions are not covered by Medicaid because of their poor prognosis, cost and duration. Therefore, chronic illness is most assuredly eliminated from treatment as are AIDS sufferers and the old.[45]

Another dilemma which imposes itself upon the health delivery system is the need of physicians and other health professionals to maintain their independence of judgment and their need to control the outcome of treatments they deem necessary. Surely, when regulators, insurance clerks and bureaucrats of every kind dictate how a doctor should proceed and practice then the most talented will leave the profession. Hardly any doctor will tolerate becoming a pawn among politicians, insurers and lawyers so that a patient-doctor relationship can no longer exist. Furthermore, it is unrealistic and borders on the ridiculous to expect doctors, dentists and health care professionals in general to work for nothing. The need to be paid is obvious. The need to command a respectable prestige may be less evident but it too is an aspect of compensation which doctors expect. If government clerks are permitted to outguess the professional judgment of doctors, if insurance company employees, even with a medical education, are allowed to continue to dictate diagnoses and treatments then reasonable people will not attend a medical school since the practice of the profession becomes impossible when others interfere. The loss of dedicated professionals to various pressure groups can best be estimated if we contemplate the immense benefits which professional medical researchers have bestowed on all of us during the past half century.[46]

VI

Medicine has made immense strides in the past fifty years. These advances have been mainly produced by the vast amounts of money spent on biological research. Examples of these advances include the development of numerous vaccines against various bacterial and virus infections, the use of hormones to treat endocrine disturbances and most recently, the mapping of the human genetic system. While it is indeed true that the cost of all this research is immense, it is evident that the cost of not doing such research is far greater. Consider alone the savings which resulted from the discovery of an anti-polio vaccine by Dr. Jonas Salk in 1953-1954. That discovery has saved an enormous amount of money in the production and maintenance of iron lungs and other devices and methods to treat polio sufferers. At one time there were huge costs associated with the treatment of tuberculosis. That came to an end when at the beginning of this century Robert Koch (1843-1910) discovered the bacillus causing that disease. Now (1999) AIDS has become an epidemic which hopefully will yield to biological research as well. Likewise, the cost of kidney machines, pacemakers and transplant techniques together with expensive coronary care units could all be saved if we could prevent the diseases these devices now alleviate. The same is of course true of cancer.[47]

Finally, we must now spend a great deal of money on caring for patients with incurable or terminal diseases. Again, it would be more efficient and cost less if we could focus on prevention rather than treatment in these situations as well.[48]

The cost of medical care has of course risen more and more as the capacity to cure numerous diseases has increased far beyond the expectations of those who were patients or practiced medicine before 1975. Several factors have contributed to the rise in the cost of health care since then.

One of the most important causes of increased health delivery costs has been the rise in wages and salaries for ancillary (anculus Latin for servant) workers in hospitals. Interns, residents, nurses, orderlies, receptionists and a host of other hospital employees were at one time ill paid, overworked and exploited. During the past thirty years, however, all this has changed. Hospital workers have a far higher standard of living than before 1969. This rise in income for hospital workers became possible because hospitals are receiving income from Medicare, Medicaid and numerous private insurance companies. Another reason for increased hospital costs has been the acquisition of expensive machines for such procedures as dialysis. Often, these units were already available at near-by hospitals, but were acquired additionally by hospitals who sought to increase their prestige or promote the convenience of their physicians. Such duplication together with an expansion of hospital bed capacity has sometimes exceeded the needs of a community and therefore burdened the hospital budget with unnecessary costs. Finally, the third party payment system has increased costs dramatically. That system has allowed hospitals and doctors to undertake costly procedures and increase their charges by billing insurance companies. Therefore, patients were never really confronted with the true costs of medical care.[49]

Not only have patients for years not known the true cost of medical care, but government also has not been able to do much about such a rise in costs. This is so because at the time Congress agreed to

Medicare and other public programs, doctors and hospitals had secured concessions from Congress prohibiting government from controlling costs. These increases in health care costs to government can be seen in the following statistics: Thus, the government's (taxpayers') share in health expenditure jumped from 26% to 37% between 1965 and 1970. This means that government spent $10.8 billion on health care in 1965 and $27.8 billion in 1970. In 1992, the governments share of health care expenses had risen to a phenomenal 44.9% which constituted $71.4 billion.[50]

The total health care bill for the American people in 1996 was $1.035 trillion. This is expected to rise to $2.133 trillion in 2007 as the Balanced Budget Act of 1997 slows down government spending on health care and doctors and pharmacists bills rise together with an anticipated increase in health insurance premiums of over ten percent in the decade ending in 2007.[51]

In terms of Gross National Product, i.e. the cost of everything produced or serviced by the United States, health care costs have risen rapidly in this country since 1960. In that year medical services accounted for 5% of GNP. In 1990 this had risen to 12.2%. A further rise since then will lead to an expenditure of 15% of GNP for health care in 2000.[52]

These expenditures accrued principally because doctors were earning immense incomes. For example, in the 1970's the average gross income of cardiac surgeons exceeded $500,000 per year. That had risen even further in the 1980's so that this author was told by a cardiac surgeon that he earned $1 million per year in the 1990's shortly before his retirement. [53]

All of this came about because the people of the United States had always acceded to the demands of private physicians and to hospitals and insurance companies. However, the ever increasing costs could not be ignored forever so that in 1970 Dr. Paul M. Ellwood, Jr., a Minneapolis physician met with officials of the Department of Health, Education and Welfare and there coined the phrase "health maintenance organization." The HMO's Ellwood proposed were to follow the Kaiser plan. Therefore President Nixon called on Congress to create 1,700 HMO's by 1976 so that doctors and hospitals would no longer benefit from illness but from health. This proposal did indeed come to pass and has resulted in the great proliferation of HMO's at the end of the century. Nevertheless, HMO's have not proved to be the solution to the health care "mess" we have had to confront these twenty years. Therefore, other solutions have also been tried.[54]

VII.

In 1989 the Oregon State Legislature passed three pieces of legislation mandating the rationing or prioritizing of health care in that state for Medicaid patients. This plan became effective in 1994. The purpose of that legislation was to eliminate costly services which did not provide adequate benefits. Subsequently a Health Services Commission was appointed which issued a list establishing three categories of care labeled essential; very important and, valuable to certain individuals. Seventeen sub groupings were also established within these major categories. The Plan also lists 696 condition-treatment pairs of which 131 conditions are not covered by Medicaid because of their poor prognosis, cost and duration. The first category of treatment concerns conditions which are seen as acute and fatal so that treatment can prevent death and promote full recovery. An example would be acute appendicitis. The second category, very important, deals with treatment for non-fatal conditions which will return the patient to a previous state of health. Hip replacement or cornea transplants are examples. Finally, the third category were treatments which would not extend life and would not return the patient to health and recovery. Here are listed treatments for the end stages of cancer or AIDS. In sum, the Oregon plan seeks to ration health care on the basis of health outcome.

A number of ethical issues have arisen in connection with rationing of health care. Among these is the failure of the plan to include technologies which reduce pain and disability even if they do not prevent imminent death. The Children's Defense Fund also argued that the Oregon Plan does not protect children sufficiently. Subsequently, the plan covered 60,000 children and their mothers who had no coverage at all. The blind and the disabled were also denied care in the original proposal although that too has been alleviated since then. Most important, of course, is the issue of exclusion.[55]

Rationing has exposed several common myths about the American health care system. These are listed by Kaplan and include that the United States is second to none in health care. This is patently false since we are 17th in the world in infant mortality and first among those who cannot pay for health care at all. Another myth is that cost cutting leads to a "death sentence" for some patients. This has not happened and is underscored by the observation that several European countries have less expensive health care systems than the United States and score better on most health indicators. A further myth is that interference with the doctor-patient relationship must have disastrous consequences. This argument is offset by the excessive use of all resources at any expense which was the principal method of treatment for so long before HMO's, capitation and other cost saving methods came into use. A fifth myth is that the American people will not allow health care to be rationed. This is of course not true since obviously, the poor are the subject of rationing everywhere as they must depend entirely on the emergency rooms of hospitals to receive treatment because they can neither afford private fee-for-service treatment or insurance premiums. [56]

In sum, then, we have seen in this chapter that there are three problems which affect American health care at the end of the 20th century. These are affordability, access and accountability.

Summary

The rise of health maintenance organizations and the changing status of the medical professions during the past twenty years has introduced government into the area of health maintenance. Medicine is threatening to become a business and not a profession. This threat has in turn provoked the "accountability revolution", particularly as costs in the health area rose precipitously during the last quarter of the 20th century. The outcome of these developments may well be the rationing of health care across the United States, a method already adopted by Oregon.

NOTES

1No author, "The Hippocratic Oath: A Basis for Modern Ethical Standards," JAMA The Journal of the American Medical Association, Vol. 264, No. 17, pg.2311.

2National Association of Social Workers, "Caplan Addresses Managed Care and Ethics," *Update,* Vol. 22, No. 5, November 1997, pp. 1-3.

3Susan Brink and Nancy Shute, "Are HMOs the right prescription?" U.S. News and World Report, October 13, 1997, p. 60-64.

[4]Gabel, J., Liston, D., Jensen G., Marsteller, J., "The Health Insurance Picture in 1993: Some rare good news," *Health Affairs,* Vol. 13, No. 1, 1994, pp. 330-334.

[5]Brink and Shute, *op.cit.,* p. 60.

[6]George Anders and Ron Winslow, "Turn for the Worse: HMOs' Woes Reflect Conflicting Demands of American Public," *The Wall Street Journal,* Vol. 122, Sec. A, December 22, 1997, p. 1.

[7]*Ibid.* p. A1.

[8]Brigid McMenamin, "Crusader," *Forbes,* March 9, 1998, p. 102.

[9]Charles Krauthammer, "We're losing our experienced doctors," *The Buffalo News,* January 12, 1998, p. C3.

[10]*Ibid.,* p. C 3.

[11]Julius B. Richmond and Rashi Fein, "The Health Care Mess," *JAMA,* Vol. 273, No.1, January 4, 1994, p.69.

[12]Alvin W. Weinberg, "Biomedical Policy: LBJ's Query Leads to an Illuminating Conference," *Science,* Vol. 154, November 1966, p. 619.

[13]Edward B. Drew, "The Health Syndicate: Washington's Noble Conspirators," *The Atlantic* Vol. 220, No. 75, December 1967.

[14]Robert Hanft, "National Health Expenditures," 1950-1965" *Social Security Bulletin,* Vol. 30, No. 3, February 1967.

[15]Weinberg, *op. cit.* p. 69.

[16]Eli Ginzberg, "Monetarization of medical care." *The New England Journal of Medicine,* Vol. 310, 1984, pp. 1162-1165.

[17]John B. McKinlay and J.D. Stoeckle, "Corporization and the social transformation of doctoring," *The International Journal of Health Services,* Vol. 18, 1988, pp. 191-205.

[18]Albert S. Relman, "The Future of medical practice," *Health Affairs,* Vol. 2, 1983, pp. 5-19.

[19]James Morone, *The Democratic Wish,* New York, Basic Books, 1990.

[20]Isidore Sydney Falk, C. Rufus Rorem and Martha D. Ring, *The Costs of Medical Care,* Chicago, The University of Chicago Press, 1933, p. 3.

[21]Earl L. Koos, *The Health of Regionville*, New York, Columbia University Press, 1954.

[22]"Man-made Cures," in *The Random House Encyclopedia*, James Mitchell, Editor, New York, Random House, 1990,

[23]Paul Starr, *The Social Transformation of American Medicine*, New York, Basic Books, 1982.

[24]Arthur M. Schlesinger, Jr., *The Coming of the New Deal*, Boston, Houghton Mifflin Co., 1959.

[25]Rothman, David J. "The Public Presentation of Blue Cross, 1935-1965". *Journal of Health Politics, Policy and Law*, Vol. 16, 1992, pp. 672-693.

[26]Starr, *op.cit.*, p. 298 and p. 327.

[27]U.S. Congress 1964:28

[28]Nancy Tomes, "Oral History in the History of Medicine," *The Journal of American History*, Vol. 78, No. 2, September 1991, p. 609.

[29]Oliver Wendell Holmes, "The Contagiousness of Puerperal Fever," *New England Quarterly Journal for Medicine and Surgery*, in *Medical Classics*, Vol. 1, No. 3, November 1936, p. 213.

[30]William J. Sinclair, *Semmelweiss; His Life and His Doctrines*, The University Press, Manchester, 1909.

[31]Charles E. Rosenberg, "The Therapeutic Revolution: Medicine, Meaning and Social Change in Nineteenth-Century America" in Morris J. Vogel, Ed., *The Therapeutic Revolution*, Philadelphia, The University of Pennsylvania Press, 1979, p. 5.

[32]No author. Editorial, "Routine Practice," *The Boston Medical and Surgical Journal*, Vol.108, January 11, 1883, p. 827. In Rosenberg, *op.cit.*, p. 19.

[33]Edmund D. Pellegrino, "The Sociocultural Impact of Twentieth Century Therapeutics" in Morris J. Vogel and Charles Rosenberg, Eds., *The Therapeutic Revolution*, Philadelphia, The University of Pennsylvania Press, 1979, p. 248.

[34]Nichlas Jardine, "The laboratory revolution in medicine as rhetorical and aesthetic accomplishment." in: Andrew Cunningham and Perry Williams, Eds., *The Laboratory Revolution in Medicine*, New York, Cambridge University Press, 1992, p. 304.

[35]Thomas Block, *Milestones in Microbiology*, Washington, American Society for Microbiology, 1975.

[36]Richard Knox, "Drug Resistant Virus has AIDS Implications," *The Boston Globe*, February 1, 1989.

[37]Lewis Thomas, "On the Science and Technology of Medicine," *Daedalus*, Winter, 1977, pp. 37-38.

[38]Pellegrino, *op.cit.*, 260.

[39]Susan M. Wolf, "Quality Assessment of Ethics in Health Care: The Accountability Revolution," *American Journal of Law and Medicine*, Vol. XX, No. 1, Summer 1994, p. 105.

[40]Jay Katz, *The Silent World of Doctor and Patient*, New York, The Free Press, 1984 pp. 93-94.

[41]Johanna Duncan-Poitier, *You Have the Right to Competent Professional Services*, Brochure issued by The New York   State Education Department, Albany, N.Y. (No Year) p. 3.

[42]Troyen Brennan, "Quality of Clinical Ethics Consultation," *Quality Review Bulletin*, Vol. 18, 1992, p.4.

[43]Robert Pear, "Panel Endorses Alternative To President's Health Plan," *The New York Times*, March 24, 1994, p. A 18.

[44] Johanna Duncan - Pointier, *op.cit.* p.4

[45]Richard Conviser, Margaret J. Rotondo and Mark Loveless, "Predicting the Effect of the Oregon Health Plan on Medicaid Coverage for Outpatients with HIV," *American Journal of Public Health*, Vol. 84, No.12, December 1994, pp. 1994-1995.

[46]Outka, George, "Social Justice and equal access to health care," in Stephen Lammers, ed., *On Moral Medicine*, Grand Rapids, William B. Erdmans Publishing, 1987, pp. 634-638.

[47]Lewis Thomas, "AIDS: An Unknown Distance to Go, " *Scientific American*, Vol. 259, 1988, p. 152.

[48]*Ibid.* p. 347.

[49]Paul Starr, *The Social Transformation of American Medicine*, New York, Basic Books, 1982, pp. 379-419.

[50]Victor R. Fuchs, *Who Shall Live?*, New York, Basic Books, 1974, pp.92-94. See also, Otto Johnson, Ed., *Information Please Almanac*, New York, Houghton Mifflin Co. New York 1997, p.76.

[51] Lurie McGinley, "U.S. Health Costs Are Expected to Double by 2007," *The Wall Street Journal*, September 15, 1998, p. A2.

[52]Robert M. Kaplan, *The Hippocratic Predicament*, New York, The Academic Press, 1993, pp. 18.

[53]Benson B. Roe, "The UCR Boondoggle: A Death Knell for private Practice?" *New England Journal of Medicine*, v. 305, July 2, 1981, pp. 41-45.

[54]New York Times, February 19, 1971.

[55]Kaplan, *op.cit.* pp. 6-8.

[56]*Ibid.*, p. 16.

Chapter II

The Political Development of Twentieth Century American Medicine

I

American medicine is based on a number of developments here and abroad which have altered its entire content and structure. Among these are both scientific findings and social changes. Included in the scientific findings which radically changed American medicine was the work of Joseph Lister. In 1865, Joseph Lister, a British surgeon was roundly denounced by his fellow surgeons for promoting "antisepthis". That term implies a method of defeating infection in wounds and consists of the use of chemicals which cleanses such wounds. Lister also followed Semmelweiss in insisting on the cleansing of the hands and clothing of physicians and midwives before assisting women in the birth of children. Yet, Lister's work was eventually accepted and became standard procedure for all surgeons.[1]

In 1895 Wilhelm Conrad Roentgen discovered X rays and thereby opened the door to the diagnosis and therapy of a number of diseases. It wasn't until 1900 that endocrinology was first developed so that the term "hormone" was not coined until 1905. In 1921 the Canadian doctors Frederick Grant Banting and Charles R. Best isolated the hormone insulin for the treatment of diabetes. Cortisone was introduced in 1940.

Because anti-biotics were not available until after 1940 immunology was used to control bacterial diseases such as diphtheria, tuberculosis and tetanus. Since then, human genetics and molecular biology have become important methods of dealing with disease. Most recently, artificial organs, transplants and dialysis have become procedures effective in heretofore unreachable diseases and physical failures.

The opening of the Johns Hopkins Medical School in Baltimore in 1893 is seen by some as another great advance in the development of American medicine as known today. (1999). This was important not only because that school recruited some of the best medical faculty then known, but also because that school admitted women to the study of medicine for the first time. That was indeed a radical political move at that time and led eventually to the introduction of women into medical schools as a matter of course.

Although Johns Hopkins University had appointed an outstanding faculty at the end of the nineteenth century, that was surely not the case in other medical schools. In fact, the status of American medical school faculty was regarded of so poor a quality at the beginning of the 20th century that the executive director of the Carnegie Foundation, Henry S. Pritchett, asked the psychologist Abraham Flexner to study the quality of medical education for that foundation. That study led to the famous "Flexner Report" in 1910. Flexner had studied 155 medical schools in the United States and Canada and concluded that the requirements for admission, the curriculum and the libraries were utterly inadequate.[2]

Flexner's "report" was called Medical Education in the United States and Canada. In that report Flexner makes the oft cited comment that "the physician must first of all be an educated man; this is required by his position in the community and his relations with the family and the community."[3]

From this comment and from many of the other writings of Flexner we can reasonably conclude that Flexner was interested in both the scientific training of the physician and in his education in the humanities and social sciences. There can be no doubt that eighty nine years after Flexner his insistence on the technical competence of physicians has been largely fulfilled. Medical students and their professors are certainly wedded to a scientific education and to a scientific approach in treating patients. However, the recommendation that physicians should have a well-rounded education including the humanities was abandoned by the 1930's as medical school departments offered more and more courses in the sciences and in specialties. Consequently no time was left in the curriculum of medical schools for sociology, psychology or ethics. Instead, internships were firmly established by universities and hospitals. While earlier medical education included work with clinical professors and general practitioners that practice was abandoned in favor of introducing students to full-time medical researchers and scientists who then became the students role models. It is therefore not surprising that in

1910, at the time of Flexner's study, not a single course in medical ethics was taught in any American medical school.

Since then the introduction of medical sociology into some medical schools during the 1950's and 1960's has changed the curriculum somewhat. At that time, medical ethics were viewed as belonging to the province of the sociologists although medical ethicists have developed their own specialty since then.[4]

As we have already seen, funds for medical research increased immensely between 1947 and 1997 because the Federal Government provided over two-thirds of the money. This increase in funding was applied to education as well as research so that the number of medical schools operating in the United States had risen from 87 in 1967 to 127 by 1993. These schools have emphasized research to such an extent that patients have been disregarded and their needs forgotten and overlooked particularly since the curriculum in medical schools has so far dealt exclusively with science and technology. This was and is an attitude quite contrary to the Hippocratic concept of dealing with the whole patient.[5]

At the end of this century, however, the ideas of Flexner concerning "medical humanism" are once more coming to the forefront. This is largely true because patients have become vociferous in demanding more attention from their doctors. Therefore doctors are now (1999) called upon to be sensitive to the patient's needs as a person. Hence the relevant disciplines needed to educate medical students to that requirement are sociology, psychology, communication skills and ethics. In addition, emphasis must also be put on the physician who is, hopefully, adjusted, mature and caring.[6]

By caring is meant that the physician has the ability to communicate that illness, suffering and death unite all human beings. This is very important in American society because we, more than any other people, seek to alienate the ill and the sick from the well and seek to hide death in particular from those not immediately affected. Therefore, the physician, the nurse and other members of the health delivery "team" need to understand the meaning of illness to each patient and treat the patient in his interest. This kind of attachment is frequently lacking in American physicians because many of them believe that scientific objectivity cannot exist simultaneously with the kind of involvement just outlined. Several objections have been made to the demand for more subjective, compassionate involvement by physicians. First is the objection that competence, not compassion, is important. Physicians often believe that nurses, social workers and the family can deliver enough "humanism" and that they need not duplicate the efforts of the family. Other physicians argue that the personality of some doctors permits them to be humane physicians while others have a personality which will not allow this and that education cannot teach a doctor to alter his personality. Most doctors are also of the opinion that their patients are satisfied with them and that nurses, social workers and others who complain about cold, distant and withdrawn doctors are exaggerating and are only interested in smearing the medical profession. [7]

In 1978, Daniel H. Funkenstein published a study he carried on for nineteen years from 1958-1976 concerning the values and interests of medical students. He found that medical students can be divided into two groups, i.e., the "bioscientific" and the "biosocial." Funkenstein used these labels to indicate that those students who had, for the most part, majored in science and were competitive, were generally not interested in people as individuals. Those whom Funkenstein classified as "biosocial" however, had usually majored in a social science, were less competitive and enjoyed interpersonal relations. [8]

Evidently, there is a cleavage between those who may be said to have some compassion and those who view the patient only at a distance and as objects. Therefore the inclusion of the humanities or the social sciences as parts of the medical schools' curriculum and the teaching of ethics has now (1999) become widespread and is aimed at three objectives. These are, learning the skills of ethical analysis and moral choices; increasing the student's awareness of the ethical issues in clinical decisions and helping the student to understand the structure and origin of his own value system. Evidently, medical students will also have to confront death and dying and therefore the limits of scientific medicine. This confrontation with death underscores the importance of care where cure is no longer possible. [9]

II

The history of American medicine can be understood only in a broad social and political context. This means that medical history is also social history and that the view that medical history is only the history of scientific progress is deficient. The deficit of such a purely scientific history lies in the failure of the medical establishment to write their history "from both sides of the bed." An adequate history of medicine should include the experiences of patients as well as practitioners so it can be revealed how status inequalities affect health care. Furthermore, health care is mostly delivered by the "average" doctor and not by great researchers. Therefore, the experiences of ordinary practitioners as a group tell us more about the history of medicine than a recital of the great scientific discoveries or a list of Nobel prize winners in various medical areas.[10]

Even the direction which medicine and medical research takes is seriously influenced by factors other than developments in science. It has been demonstrated that those who support medical research and medical charities influence the direction and shape of medical services because doctors recognize that they can attain lucrative practices if they interact positively with those volunteers who support hospitals and medical schools.[11]

Charles Rosenberg has shown that social class has always entered into the life of hospitals both in the nineteenth century and in our own. He demonstrates that hospitals are a microcosm of the world outside and that an examination of patients' diaries and interviews exhibits the hierarchies included in hospital society.[12]

Race, ethnicity and gender also influence health care so that the poor and hence, blacks, experience far less attention to their needs than is true of the rich, whites and men. Thus, the poor are mainly dependent on the emergency rooms of hospitals for all their medical care while the wealthy can continue to experience a fee for service situation which is furnished them by doctors devoted to their income. In short, social position determines health care. Since sex and gender are the most important statuses we occupy, it is not surprising that the experiences of women in health care are a good deal different than the experiences of men.

Traditionally, and now, paternalism has been the hallmark of health care. Since professionals have a monopoly of medical knowledge and skills they of course control which information to divulge to the patient and what to keep hidden. Added to this professional advantage is the use of technical language as a means of keeping the patient "in the dark." Therefore it is possible for a doctor to disguise information, to suppress it altogether or to deny the risks attached to surgery or the use of medicines. Since "knowledge is power," it is evident that those who can deny patients the information they need to control their own health are in fact controlling the lives of patients.[13]

The issue of control has been at the forefront of women's issues since Betty Friedan published The Feminine Mystique in 1963. That book depicted a problem many women had at that time and that still influences the health of many women today. Friedan called it "the problem that has no name" and defined it as the failure of women to define themselves and be defined in terms of their own work instead of their relationship to their nearest male relative, i.e. their father, husband, son or boyfriend. This attitude has been very much reflected in traditional medicine so that only scientific and technological methods are generally applied to patients' complaints while the emotional is ignored. This has been far more damaging to women than to men. Furthermore, the negative outcomes of technological methods for women have received little attention. An example is the use of intra-uterine devices such as the Dalkon shield and the injection of depo-Provera, both contraceptive methods. Also, the excessive use of forceps deliveries, episiotomies and Caesarean sections has shown a considerable neglect of women's needs and their failure to control their own bodies. At this writing, (1999) this has changed somewhat as more and more women are insisting that they have control over the natural process of giving birth.[14]

Because sex and gender, as well as social class, determine health care the expansion of access to health care has been a long and bitter dispute in America. This dispute is best illustrated by the fate of the Wagner-Murray-Dingell bill which led to so much controversy in the 1940's and 1950's. That bill sought to make medical care "free" by financing it through a federally administered system of social security taxes. That proposal failed in Congress and led, as we have seen, to an ever expanding private insurance program. That program was mainly financed by employers and therefore did not reach that ever increasing segment of the population whose members were over sixty-five and retired. In the 1960's the political struggle concerning Medicare erupted again as it did in the early part of the Clinton administration in the 1990's.

That struggle lasted five years beginning in 1961 when Senator Clinton Anderson and Representative Cecil King introduced legislation addressed to the medical needs of retirees receiving Social Security pensions. The bill called for the provision of ninety days of free hospital care, some nursing home care and virtually no physician's services. The bill was strongly supported by the Kennedy administration but ran headlong into opposition from the American Medical Association. Leonard Larson, M.D., then president of the AMA said at the June 1961 meeting of the AMA House of Delegates: "The medical profession is the only group which can render medical care under any system.......it will not be a willing party to implementing any system which we believe to be detrimental to the public welfare." Evidently, the AMA was threatening to boycott the proposals under the King-Anderson bill.[15]

The attitude of the AMA House of Delegates and their erstwhile president makes it appear that the AMA is a unified, monolithic group who "speak with one voice." This may be true whenever the power of the profession is threatened. However, internally, the AMA is very much divided and its politics are indeed as confrontational as anywhere else. Primarily, the profession is divided into specialists and general practitioners so that specialists battle the generalists and also each other.

There are several reasons for the development of specialists within the American medical establishment. The first is of course the ever increasing accumulation of knowledge which makes it impossible for any doctor to know more than a limited amount of content and a limited number of techniques. This is true of all human knowledge at the end of the 20th century and will become ever more so in the next century. A second reason for the increasing division of medicine into numerous specialties was the increase in urbanization in the United States. Thus, in 1940 56.6% or 74.4 million Americans were living in cities. In 1960 69.9% of all Americans, or 125.3 million people were living in cities. In 1970 74.2% of American residents lived in urban areas and by 1980 this figure had grown to 166.9 million or 73.7%. In the Census year 1990 the urban population stood at 187,051,543 or 79.6 % of the population of the United States, a number which increased to 79.8% in 1994.[16]

This increase in the proportion of city dwellers in America over fifty years had a direct effect on the growth of medical specialties. Evidently, a specialist could not earn a living in a rural area where he would attract only a few cases in his specialty each week or month. In a large city, a specialist can expect to earn a good deal of money as the number of patients is considerable and is augmented by those who live in rural areas who have no specialists and often no doctors.[17]

Finally, medical students are impressed by the prestige, income and social honor which devolves upon specialists. Professors of medicine are generally specialists who refer to the general practitioner in condescending terms such as "he provides medical care within the limits of his competence", or " he refers to other physicians those patients who have problems beyond his competence," or " "his practice gives emphasis to the frequent and commonplace ailments." Another aspect of the low status which devolves on family and general practitioners at the behest of specialists are the restrictions on staff privileges imposed on generalists by hospitals.[18]

A number of political difficulties have arisen within the medical profession because of the great specialization now in vogue. The first of these is the question of jurisdiction. There are a number of specialties which overlap so that it becomes difficult to decide whether a patient should see one specialist or another. For example, there are operations which could be performed by a general surgeon or a neurological surgeon or a plastic surgeon. Thoracic surgery may compete with cardiac surgery and gynecology with internal medicine.

The outcome of the battles between specialists is that restrictions of all kinds are imposed on doctors so that the patient is no longer the issue but the income of the numerous specialists ranks ahead of the needs of those who are ill.[19]

These restrictions are particularly contentious because most hospitals function under a "closed staff" rule which automatically bars any physician not on the hospital staff list from practicing in that hospital. This means that a license to practice medicine does not assure a doctor of privileges in any hospital. Consequently, the politics associated with gaining hospital privileges will determine whether or not a physician can earn a livelihood and how much he can earn. Kerr L. White makes this statement: "The matter of hospital privileges, however, is not related to medical competence alone. The views of the physicians already on the staff with respect to need for physicians of any kind may be either positive or negative factors in deciding the fate of specific applicants." [20]

It is evident that hospital privileges are restricted not only to assure quality care for patients but chiefly to restrict competition. Thus, several specialty boards require that the applicant for certification be a citizen of the United States. A number of boards also want the applicant to submit letters of reference from board certified specialists. This obviously makes it possible for board certified practitioners to eliminate potential competitors. Other arbitrary rules are also used to limit competition. Thus, some boards "reserve the right to limit the number of candidates to be admitted to any examination." Likewise, some boards use confidentiality as a means of limiting competition in that they refuse to divulge examination results to the applicants or include in their by-laws phrases to the effect that "the findings of the board are subject to its discretion and are final." These limitations can of course be used to restrict the entry of members of minority religions, ethnic groups and women from the specialty and can also be used to eliminate anyone against whom board members have a grudge for any reason.[21]

Traditionally, foreigners, religious and ethnic minorities and women have been the target of such eliminatory practices more than men. When, however, the Woman's Medical College of Pennsylvania became co-educational in 1970 that indicated that women physicians believed at that time that their struggle to win equality with men in the profession was close to ended. In fact, women were not accepted everywhere in medicine as late as 1970 and are still not entirely welcome in all medical specialties in 1999. Nevertheless, the name of the erstwhile Woman's Medical College was then changed to the Medical College of Pennsylvania. By 1980 74% of the faculty of that college were women and 40 percent of the students in that medical school were men.[22]

These gender differences at the end of the 20th century are a reflection of the entire history of gender discrimination in the medical profession. For example, during the period 1920 to 1930, when the number of female law students doubled and the number of female Ph.D.'s doubled, the female enrollment at medical schools rose only 16.7% even while the male enrollment in medical schools rose fifty-nine percent. Thus, until the 1960's the number of women in medical schools fluctuated between four and five percent.[23]

As late as 1946, after the second world war, 41.7% of available internships and 34.2% of available residences were still closed to women.[24]

At the end of 1997, 40% of all the medical students in the United States were women This, however, should not be interpreted to mean that total equality between the genders exists in end-of-the-century American medicine. This is visible by inspecting the income of physicians. Thus, in 1997 male family physicians earned more than $131,000 while female practitioners in the same year earned only $112,000' a difference of 15%. Even child specialists experienced such a difference. Thus, male pediatricians earned $137,000 in 1997 and women specialists in child medicine earned only an average of $120,000.[25]

There are many female doctors who believe that these differences in income are the result of the "old boy network" which, some say, still dominates medicine at the end of the '90's and which has not been sufficiently challenged by women in the profession. There are still many female doctors who believe that only someone who can be "one of the boys" can succeed in medicine. This belief is based on the experiences of female medical students and female physicians ranging all the way from sexist remarks to sexual harassment. Yet, male physicians actively deny unequal treatment accorded to women in the profession because men have taken their privileges for granted for so many generations that these privileges have actually become invisible to those who benefit from them.[26]

The evidence is therefore, that a higher income, and not a concern for competence, is the principal reason for discrimination against women and the restriction of certification of specialists. That such restrictions by specialty boards are financially motivated is also revealed by the practice of such boards to carefully evaluate whether an applicant has done much work other than his specialty. The argument before certification is granted is that only a doctor who has done almost exclusive work in his specialty has the necessary skills to qualify as a specialist. However, after certification has been granted, specialty boards do next to nothing to enforce the rule that specialists must stay with their specialty. Specialists who work in areas other than their specialty are rarely reviewed and seldom restrained because income is involved. [27]

III

Specialization and the insistence on a scientific approach to disease to the exclusion of the social and psychological dimensions of the patient's feelings has altered the relationship between the doctor and his patients considerably during the past twenty five years.

That relationship has been altered by several circumstances which have modified the American doctor's position and that of the patient because American culture has changed. An excellent example of such a change is the erstwhile assurance that the doctor-patient relationship must always be confidential. The Hippocratic Oath includes this: "...whatever things I see or hear concerning the life of man, in my attendance on the sick or even a part thereon, which ought not to be noised abroad, I will keep silent thereon, counting such things to be as sacred secrets." In the days of the one-on-one simple doctor-patient relationship, this oath provided no problem. Today there are specialists, ward rounds including an entire entourage, paramedical groups such as physiotherapists, dietitians and occupational therapists and social workers. In addition there are compensation claims brought before the Social Security Administration and other boards. Lawyers are involved in many of these claims. The lawyers, in turn, have secretaries and other personnel. Hence, confidentiality is hardly possible.

Specialization has also led to a communication barrier between doctors and patients. Patients are now sent to several specialists. none of whom have ever seen him before or expect to see the patient again. Teams of doctors see each patient and each specialist deals with only a small segment of the patient's concern. Hence, no one physician is responsible for talking to the patient about his condition as each specialist either assumes the others have already spoken to the patient or as each specialist views himself as a scientist whose prestige is endangered by becoming involved with a patient's concerns. Specialists are also in a great hurry to make as much money as possible and therefore are seldom willing to talk to a patient when that time could be spent seeing another patient and improving the doctors income. In short, it costs the doctor money to speak to a patient or it costs him the good will of his employer if he works for a Health Maintenance Organization. Dr. James Means has observed that "the most conspicuous change in the behavior of the doctor is that nowadays he is usually in such a hurry that he is less accessible and less communicative." [28]

The introduction of the patient's opinion of the medical profession has also altered the doctor-patient relationship. An early English study reported in The Lancet in 1961 illustrates this trend. This study reports the findings of a political and economic planning group which investigates the patients' opinion of their doctors. During the thirty seven years since then, numerous such studies have been carried out in England and in the United States and have revealed that "consumerism" has come to affect the doctor-patient relationship greatly. [29]

"Consumerism" is best defined as the social movement seeking to protect the rights of consumers. In England and the United States that has been expressed in the passage of a Patient's Bill of Rights such as the one adopted voluntarily by hospitals in New Jersey in the early 1970's. The rights protected by New Jersey include the right to be free of discrimination; the right to be introduced to any health care provider by name in addition to the use of name badges; the right to receive confidential treatment; the right to obtain a copy of medical records; the right to provide informed consent; the right to refuse medical care with the knowledge of the consequences; the right to decline participation in medical research or with medical or health care students; the right to be informed of the facility's policies and procedures regarding the withdrawal or withholding of life support; the right to transfer care from a practitioner or facility; the right to be provided with appropriate medical follow-up and nursing support upon discharge and the discharge appeals procedure; the right to receive a copy of the hospital's billing rates and an itemized bill, and the right to be provided with assistance with application for health insurance payment, public assistance and charity care. Even the right of a deaf person to receive the means to communicate and the right of a non-English speaking person to be provided with an interpreter is included in that law. [30]

The New Jersey "Patient's Bill of Rights" is of course much more than an effort to protect the patient from neglect or mistakes by doctors and hospital employees. Such a "bill of rights" and others like it are recent developments mainly limited to the United States and England. However, complaints about doctors are not new. Hawkins quotes Benjamin Franklin who reputedly said that "God heals and the doctor takes the fee" and Voltaire whose usual venom includes this comment: "Doctors are men who prescribe medicines of which they know little to human beings of which they know nothing." Hawkins also cites the thirteenth century lawyer, priest and scientist Roger Bacon (1214-1292) who wrote an essay De Erroribus Medicorum including the comment "Medical men don't know the drugs they use, nor their prices."[31]

In our day complaints against the medical profession have taken the form of litigation which, some say, has become an American mania as everyone sues everyone. It has been suggested that "if your son does not do well in college, sue the obstetrician for brain damage at birth." That comment may appear to be an idle sarcasm until we look at the rise in litigation against doctors during the past thirty years. Thus, claims rose from one per hundred doctors in 1960 to 4.3 per 100 insured doctors in 1970 to 7.8 claims per 100 in 1976 and reached a phenomenal rate of 18.3 claims per one hundred insured physicians in 1986. Since then, the rate of claims has declined slightly. The cost of these claims is huge. Thus, in 1983 medical liability insurance cost $2.5 billion. From there it rose to $7 billion in 1988 and then declined somewhat in real dollars during the 1990's. All told, medical liability insurance accounts for 1 percent of health care in the United States.[32]

This rate of litigation and its costs are at least in part the consequence of the failed relationships between doctors and their patients. For reasons already shown, in recent years doctors have been unable to create trust between themselves and their patients. Moreover, many patients do not understand the limits of medicine's power to cure and therefore hold unrealistic expectations of the medical profession.

In any event, in view of the rising criticism of the medical profession and the "liability crisis", programs of quality assurance led to a new era of self regulation in the medical profession. This was launched with the publication of "Agenda for Change" by the Joint Commission on Accreditation of Healthcare Organizations in 1987.[33]

In addition, however, various legal remedies have been suggested to protect patients from the "pain and suffering" inflicted on them by incompetent or careless doctors while also protecting the medical profession from unreasonable litigation. The best example of such legislation is the California Medical Injury Compensation Recovery Act of 1975. That law limits the amount that may be collected by a medically injured party to $250,000. As a consequence, malpractice insurance costs have stabilized in California. Most important is that there has been no public objection to this limitation which makes physicians more comfortable than in states where unlimited litigation is possible.

A number of proposals have been suggested to deal with medical liability. One of these is the "no-fault" system. This would, however, free physicians from the consequences of their actions and would reduce the security patients could expect from doctors whom they do not know and who may not be able or willing to know them.[34]

Hospitals, no less than doctors, have been affected by both the passage of "Patients' Rights" legislation and by litigation. This has of course led to increased costs of managing hospitals. To combat these costs some hospitals have resorted to recruiting medical super stars to provide them with income. Such a super star can sometimes swing a large number of "cases" from one hospital to another and thereby improve the income of one hospital to the detriment of another hospital, usually in the same area. Another source of income for hospitals during the 1990's has been ambulatory (*ambulare*: Latin, to walk) care. This refers to laser surgery, ophthalmology procedures, urology procedures, plastic surgery, and MRI scanning.[35]

The arrival of "managed care", first in California and since 1991 in all of the United States has created an entirely new relationship between hospitals and their doctors and patients. "Managed care" is a euphemism for fixed price revenue so that hospitals are likely to find that 65%-75% of their income has been set in advance by the use of Diagnostic Related Groups. These DRG's serve to allow a hospital a lump sum in advance for the care of a patient with any diagnosis. The hospital, having been paid in advance, will of course earn a profit if the patient is discharged before the DRG money is exhausted. Therefore DRG's represent a real danger to patients who are discharged too soon and have not fully recovered.

Older Americans are now a major segment of customers in U.S. hospitals. Therefore, Medicare, the government health insurance for those over 65, is providing some hospitals with 75% of their patients. This has led some hospitals to convert their underused beds to extended care units and/or to buy nursing homes.[36]

All of these developments underscore the introduction of consumerism into the health delivery system while also creating a diffusion of responsibility for the welfare of the patient. As we have already seen, the doctor-patient relationship which erstwhile gave the doctor the whole responsibility for the patient's fate and which was compensated by the trust of the patient in his doctor, is gone. Managed care, diagnosis related groups, health maintenance organizations and numerous state and federal bureaucracies have depersonalized and atomized the responsibility for each patient so that a truly anomic scene faces those among us who become ill and need help.

Traditionally, physicians and others insisted that the cost of care should not be relevant to treatment decisions. This is another way of saying that physicians had at least given lip service to the proposition that they should deliver care without regard to the patient's social standing. This view has been supported by the almost universal insurance coverage of patients and the consequent ability of both patients and doctors to shift the cost of treatment to a third party. This cost shifting opportunity has led many physicians to deal with medical uncertainties. An example is an illness known as anorexia nervosa. This is indeed a dangerous and severe illness which consists of refusing food and is found among adolescent girls in middle class families. This condition demonstrates the influence of culture on disease and is therefore not necessarily subject to medical intervention. Such conditions can also exist in other circumstances which would be mainly the province of psychiatry.[37]

A further example of the influence of culture on medical outcomes is the legal position of doctors and hospitals. That legal position is partly responsible for the high technological standards adopted by the medical profession after 1970. This came about as more and more doctors were sued for not using every possible technique and for failure to use even the most remote methods in case of an adverse treatment outcome. All told, economic considerations, ethics and legal issues have led physicians to deliver expensive resources to patients, particularly because these resources were paid by third parties. Expenses have therefore not been a consideration for either doctors or patients. We have seen earlier that the U.S. now spends about one trillion dollars a year on health care. That constitutes about 14% of our Gross National Product. Because of this great cost patients find that their treatment is dictated by insurance companies and that their perspective is substantially ignored even as the Patients' Rights movement is gaining more and more momentum.[38]

In view of the ever increasing pressure on physicians to consider patients' rights, insurance companies' costs, health maintenance organizations directives and government regulations in treating their patients, many doctors have concluded that they cannot "keep the needs of their patients foremost in mind when every interaction is laden with adminstrative burden and fraught with legal peril." An excellent example of the burden which government and insurance companies have placed on practicing physicians is this excerpt from a letter by a physician practicing internal medicine in the Washington D.C. area. Citing the "Health Insurance Portability and Accountability Act of 1996", Dr. Jody Robinson writes that "enforcement responsibility (of that act) will rest with 450 FBI agents hired specifically for this purpose. The new regulations, issued by the Health Care Financing Administration, are so heavy handed that it is clear that they have little or nothing to do with the care of the patient."[39]

Robinson shows how the enormous burden of documenting every minute detail of contacts between patients and doctors robs the patient of the time normally available to the doctor in evaluating symptoms, making a diagnosis or treatment plan, explaining the problem and writing a prescription. [40]

In addition to government regulations, doctors and other health care providers are also vicitmized by the corporate health care system. That "system" earns $952 billion a year by treating patients like an "industrial commodity", a phrase used recently in a manifesto published in the Journal of the American Medical Association by 2,300 Massachusetts doctors. These doctors accuse the corporate health care "providers" of forcing the medical profession to deny patients the advantages of the numerous advances in medical and surgical technology now available, such as injections to stop heat attacks, plastic lenses to help the blind, genetically engineered tests and many others.

Physicians say that Health Maintenance Organizations are a scheme to redistribute income from physicians to corporate executives who earn vastly more than any doctor ever earned. HMO's are also accused of caring only about the "medical-loss ratio" which is defined as "that percentage of yearly revenue allotted to patient care."[41]

In view of this massive intrusion of government and business interests into the medical profession, it can be predicted that the role of the physician will be quite different in the America of the next century than it has ever been before. In addition to the consumerism and government interference, physicians will also face competition from other health care professionals. Nurse practitioners are already claiming that they can do everything a physician can. Respiratory therapists and radiological technologists with four years of higher education also compete for patients. The competition has already become severe because these health care deliverers can now bill directly. Previously, only physicians could bill the patient or the insurance company. Now, however, these ancillary providers can do so also and therefore cut into the physicians income. Now (1999) there are about 140 physicians for every 100,000 Americans. It is estimated, however, that at the end of the decade 2001-2010 there will be 280 physicians for every 100,000 Americans. That rise in the number of doctors will surely increase competition for patients, reduce the doctors' prestige and income and place the patient "in the driver's seat", particularly because of the ever increasing demand for accountability and "patients' rights."[42]

IV

One of the most unforeseen consequences of the new developments in the political and economic situation of medicine is the loss of power and prestige at one time associated with academic medicine. That power has now (1999) been curtailed because cost control has become the overriding issue in medical care. Prospective payments to hospitals has led to a constraint on the teaching of fellows and residents and the "capitation" payments to doctors has threatened the fee-for-service provisions of the faculty practice plans.

The Diagnostic Related Groups payment method to hospitals has shortened the stay of patients in hospitals and has therefore made clinical teaching more difficult. Furthermore, the income of teaching hospitals has been threatened because there are more empty beds as a result of the DRG's. Furthermore, academic medicine suffers from several flaws of its own making.

As a consequence of the changes concerning medical practice already reviewed, academic medicine is no longer in the dominant position it occupied in the 1950 - 1990 decades. This is the outcome of the failure of academic medicine to become involved in the prepaid comprehensive care movement which has now engulfed health delivery. Community hospitals no longer need to pay much attention to academic or teaching hospitals because the doctors who have been trained in such hospitals become independent and take their business to the community hospitals and not to the teaching hospitals whence they came. Finally, it should be obvious that academic medicine has no control over for-profit health care corporations.[43]

Several conditions contributed to the decline of power and influence of academic medicine over the profession. First among these was and is the practice of the National Institute of Health to fund individual researchers and not institutions. The consequence of that practice has been that researchers and other full time faculty members often received all or a large part of their salary from the "soft money" of the NIH. That left these faculty independent of the universities and some faculty to leave one university for another and take their money with them. Hence loyalty to any university was lost in favor of loyalty to the National Institute of Health.

The power structure within a university's medical school was also affected by these research grants. Those departments which have the most money have most of the influence on decisions within the medical schools so that a hierarchy of influence has developed in medical schools depending on the amount of outside money collected. Since departments with a humanistic attitude, such as family medicine, do not attract nearly as much money as those with purely scientific interests, reform of medical education in favor of the patient has been delayed or rejected.

There are in most large American cities so called "teaching hospitals." These hospitals are often associated with a university. The fiction is that the "teaching hospitals", like any university department, is part of the university and controlled by the university administration. That however, is not the case. "Teaching hospitals" are really autonomous because their income is derived from providing clinical services and not from teaching. This is the main difference between "teaching hospitals" and any university department. The hospitals have an income independent of the university and the university needs the hospital more than the hospital needs the university. It is therefore a mistake for a university to make a hospital part of its structure because such an assumption is a fiction and cannot work.

Finally, academic medicine has failed to recognize that the costs of teaching, research and patient care are not inseparable. This meant that academic medicine was not prepared for the arrival of the Health Maintenance Organizations whose interest is financial and not clinical. Consequently, academics in medicine did not recognize that health maintenance organizations would not give the academics any credence until it was too late. Now that HMO's are firmly established they are in a position to decide whether the doctor can treat a patient at all, what kind of treatment can be used and who may deliver the treatment. Hence, managed care has made academic concerns become meaningless as have the concerns of patients.[44]

Linda Peeno, M.D. has described the dilemma facing anyone seeking to help a patient gain access to needed medical help and the desire of the HMO management to save money at all costs. Peeno has been medical director of an HMO and worked in other capacities for that HMO at an earlier time. She describes how an increase in hospital admissions, an increase in outpatient surgery and an increase in emergency room admissions became a topic of contention at board meetings as officers and board members looked at "the numbers". "Getting our numbers lower, cutting costs as much as possible and denying everything we could," says Dr. Peeno, was the only interest the board of directors expressed. They had no interest in the patient or his care. She goes on to show that dropped admissions and days in the hospital, controlled access to expensive X-rays, limited hysterectomies, C sections and tonsillectomies were forced upon the profession and their patients.

Peeno further writes that employees of the HMO of which she was medical director complained to her that she was approving too many procedures and spending too much money so that those who expected bonuses from the HMO's success resented the approval of medical procedures which Peeno judged to be reasonable and vital. "Despite all the talk about quality and outcomes, the overriding concern in managed care companies is avoiding expenses."[45]

HMO' s create incentives for practitioners to deny care. These incentives reduce health care costs. One such example is the well publicized California case labeled Fox vs. Health Net. In that case an enrollee, Fox, was diagnosed with breast cancer at age 38. Health Net refused to pay for a bone marrow transplant so that Fox was forced to wait for fund-raising from friends and relatives before she could undergo the procedure. Fox subsequently died and her husband sued the HMO for refusing to provide the treatment under the enrollment plan. A California jury ordered Health Net to pay $89 million in damages to Fox's survivors as compensation for emotional and physical suffering on the deceased and her survivors.[46]

Truly bizarre is the case of Jacqueline Lee who fell off a 40 foot cliff in the Shenandoah Mountains while hiking in 1996. She was flown to a Virginia hospital by helicopter with a fractured skull, arm and pelvis. Her HMO, Optimum Choice, Inc. refused to pay the hospital on the grounds that the hospital failed to get "pre-authorization." Only after being fined by the Maryland Insurance Commissioner did the HMO finally pay some of the hospital charges in 1998.[47]

This example, and many more, once more focus on the principal issue we seek to discuss in this book. That issue is the treatment of the patient within the promises of the Hippocratic Oath to do no harm but to act in the interest of the patient at all times.

Summary

This chapter continues the overview begun in the first chapter. It is evident that health delivery and the medical profession have been profoundly altered since the 1940's when anti-biotics first became available. Since then, medical education has also changed in favor of scientific training and to the exclusion of the "humanistic approach." Specialization has become almost universal in American medicine although at the end of the century a minor effort is under way to respond to patients demands for a more patient-responsive health delivery system. While these accommodations are being made by the medical profession, the threat to patients' well being now comes from the Health Maintenance Organizations who have been charged with an almost exclusive interest in profits to the detriment of the patient.

In view of these conditions it remains the purpose of medical education to continue the traditions of the Hippocratic Corpus. How that is accomplished shall therefore be the subject of our next chapter.

NOTES

[1] Allen B. Weisse, *Conversations in Medicine: The Story of Twentieth Century American Medicine in the Words of Those Who Created It.* New York, New York University Press,1984,pp. 1-2.

[2] *Ibid.*, p. 7.

[3] Abraham Flexner, *Medical Education: A Comparative Study*, New York, Macmillan, 1925, p. 86.

[4] John Duffy, *From Humors to Medical Science: A History of American Medicine*, 2nd Ed., Urbana, The University of Illinois Press, 1993, pp. 276-279.

[5] *Ibid.*, p. 283

[6] Edmund D. Pellegriono, *The Reconciliation of Technology and Humanism: A Flexnarian Task 75 Years Later*, in Charles Vevier, Ed., *Flexner: 75 Years Later: A Current Commentary on Medical Education*, New York, University Press of America, 1987, p. 82.

[7] *Ibid.* p.86.

[8] Daniel H. Funkenstein, *Medical Students, Medical Schools and Society During Five Eras: Factors Affecting the Career Choices of Physicians*, Cambridge, MA., Ballinger Publishing Co., 1878.

[9] *Ibid.* p. 99.

[10] Judith Walzer Leavitt, "Medicine in Context: A Review Essay of the History of Medicine," *American Historical Review*, Vol. 95, No. 5. December 1990, p.1473.

[11] *Ibid.*, p. 1476.

[12] Charles E Rosenberg, *The Care of Strangers: The Rise of America's Hospital System*, New York, Basic Books, 1987.

[13] M.C. Lovell, "The politics of medical deception: challenging the trajectory of history" *Advances in Nursing Science*, Vol. 2, No. 3, 1980, pp. 73-86.

[14] L. Teri, "Effects of sex and sex-role style on clinical judgment." *Sex Roles*, Vol.8, No. 6, pp. 639-649.

[15] Frank D. Campion, *THE AMA AND U.S. HEALTH POLICY SINCE 1940*, Chicago, Chicago Review Press, 1984, Chapter 15.

[16] Glenn W. King, *Statistical Abstracts of the United States 1997*, Washington, D.C., The Bureau of the Census, 1998, p. 39.

[17] Gerhard Falk, *A Study of Social Change in Six American Institutions during the Twentieth Century*, Lewiston, N.Y., The Edwin Mellen Press, 1993, p. 32.

[18] Citizens Commission on Graduate Medical Education, *The Graduate Education of Physicians*, Chicago, The American Medical Association, 1966, pp. 37-38.

[19]Elton Ryack, *Professional Power and American Medicine,* Cleveland and New York, The World Publishing Co., 1967, p. 210.

[20]Kerr L. White, "General Practice in the United States," *The Journal of Medical Education,* XXXIX, April 1964, pp.337-338.

[21]Walter Gelhorn, *Individual Freedom and Government Restraints,* Baton Rouge, Louisiana State University Press, 1956, p.127.

[22]Regina Markell Morantz-Sanchez, *Sympathy and Science: Women Physicians in American Medicine,* New York, Oxford University Press, 1985, p. 350.

[23]Patricia M. Hummer, *The Decade of Elusive Promise, Professional Women in the United States,1920-1930.* Ann Arbor, Research Press, 1976, pp. 143-148.

[24]Hulda Thelander, "Opportunities for Medical Women," *Journal of the American Medical Women's Association,* Vol. 3, February 1948, p, 67.

[25]Lisa Kalis, "Salary Report," *Working Woman,* Vol.22, No.1, January 1997, pp. 31-33 and 69-76.

[26]Frances K. Conley, "Gender Stereotyping and the Medical Profession," *College Science Teaching,* Vol. 24, No. 1, September-October, 1994, pp. 17-21.

[27]Retake, *op.cit.,* p. 226.

[28]Clifford Hawkins, "Changing Doctor-Patient Relationships: The Causes," *Contemporary Review,* Vol.25, No. 1484, September 1989, p. 146.

[29]No author, "Patients and Consumers: Wants and Needs." *The Lancet,* Vol. 1, 1961, pp. 927-928.

[30]Melanie H. Wilson-Silver, "Patients' Rights in England and the United States of America: *The Patient's Charter* and the New Jersey Patient Bill of Rights: a comparison." *Journal of Medical Ethics,* Vol.23, 1997, pp. 213-220.

[31]Clifford Hawkins, "Changing Doctor Patient Relationships: The Effects" *Contemporary Review,* Contemporary Review, Vol. 255, No. 1484, p. 183.

[32]Mary-Jo Del Veccio Good, *American Medicine: A Quest for Competence,* Berkeley, The University of California Press, 1995, Chapter One, p. 11.

[33]*Ibid.,* p. 13.

[34]Robert D. Utiger, "Praise Reform and Start the Litigation," *The New England Journal of Medicine,* Vol. 329, No. 23, December 2, 1993.

[35]Russell C. Coile, Jr., *The New Medicine: Reshaping Medical Practice and Health Care Management,* Rockville, Md., Aspen Publishers, 1990, p. 7.

[36]*Ibid.* p.10.

[37]Joan Jacobs Brumberg, *Fasting Girls: The Emergence of Anorexia Nervosa as a Modern Disease,* Cambridge, Mass., Harvard University Press, 1988.

[38]E. Haavi Morreim, "Redefining Quality by Reassigning Responsibility," *American Journal of Law and Medicine,* Vol. XX, No. 1 and 2, Summer 1994, p. 86.

[39]Jody Robinson, "I'm a Doctor, Not a Paper Pusher," *The Wall Street Journal,* April 1, 1998, p. A18.

[40]Ibid., p. A 18.

[41]Ronald J. Glaser, "The Doctor Is Not In," *Harper's Magazine,* Vol. 296, No. 1774, March 1998.

[42]No author, "New Doctor Roles for 21st Century" USA Today, Newsletter Edition, Volume 118, No. 2531, August 1989, p. 11.

[43]Robert H. Ebert, "Medical Education at the Peak of the Era of Experimental Medicine," *Daedalus,* Vol. 112, No.5, Spring, 1986, pp.76-77.

[44]*Ibid.,* p.80.

[45]Linda Peeno, "What is the value of a voice?" U.S..News and World Report, Vol. 129, No.9, March, 1998, p. 40.

[46]Lee Ann Bundren, "State Consumer Fraud Legislation Applied to Health Care Industry," *The Journal of Legal Medicine,* Vol. 16, No. 1, March 1995, p. 159.

[47]David S. Hilzenrath, "Some HMO's get tight-fisted about paying bills," *The Buffalo News,* March 31, 1998, p. E 2.

Chapter III

The Education of Physicians: Scientific Specialists or Humanitarian Healers?

I

Medical education, like all education, lays the foundation for those experiences which dictate the nature of a professional or work life for those who practice it. This means that the "truths" learned in school influence us to such an extent that it is an axiom of education that we expect what we have been taught to expect and that we fail to see or view with hostility what we were not taught or were taught to disdain.

Surely one of the principal lessons learned in the medical schools of the United States during the past fifty years has been that specialists are important, prestigious and deserving of a high income and that generalists and therefore practitioners of primary care and practitioners of family medicine are viewed as inconsequential.

As we have already seen, Abraham Flexner, who made the basic recommendations for American medical education in 1910 proposed that both scientific and humanistic education be included equally in the curriculum of any medical school in the United States.[1]

While one part of that recommendation was indeed carried out, the second part, the recommendation to give physicians a well rounded education in the humanities was ignored during the eighty nine years since Flexner made his "report." This becomes visible if we look at any class schedule of almost any medical school in the United States in 1998. Here we find an array of courses on such important subjects as Recent Advances in Pathology, Clinical Biology, Pathophysiology, Cardiology, Pulmonary Diseases, Renal Diseases, Allergy, Rheumatology, Infectious Diseases, Gerontology, Ontology-Hematology, Gastroentorology, Pulmonary Diseases, Ambulatory Care,

Clinical Pharmacology and a great deal more depending on the medical school and its resources. [2]

This curriculum and others indicate that at least traditionally the basic sciences were "rammed down the throat" of every medical student. That traditional view has considered medical students as resentful children and has infantilized them despite the fact that most medical students are high achievers who have, however, become the victims of the self fulfilling prophecy. [3]

The infantilization of medical students has had some unfortunate consequences for students intent on learning their profession. Thus, a recent national survey of the working conditions of medical interns revealed that not only young medical students but older residents are victimized by unnecessary stress over and beyond the need to learn. This survey revealed that medical students and residents are the victims of wide-spread abuse. Sexual harassment, discrimination, alcohol and substance abuse and falsifying medical records by staff physicians are only some of the problems 93% of medical students and residents have seen and experienced as reported in that survey. [4]

This kind of conduct by professors and senior residents does not invalidate the need for a scientific curriculum. On the contrary. The scientific curriculum is admirable, necessary and crucial in providing students with the training and information they will need and which will be required of them. In fact, American patients, who generally lack scientific training, have become convinced that their scientist-doctor can deal with any and all of their complaints. It is therefore believed that the application of science to any ailment will lead to prompt and immediate cures for everything that bothers anyone. Such beliefs, fed by unrealistic television "shows" which are entertaining but untrue, place doctors into the uncomfortable position of having to "deliver" on promises which they did not make but which popular opinion demands of them. Moreover, some patients who suffer from conditions that are life threatening tend to imbue their doctors with powers which doctors reject because they know their limitations and the limitations of their science while their patients are generally ignorant of all of this.

An excellent example are the encomiums which regularly devolve upon Dr. Keith Black who removes 250 brain tumors a year from patients at the University of California at Los Angeles medical center. Dr. Black is one of only 50 brain-tumor specialists in the United States. Because of his exceptional skill in removing tumors from the brain Dr. Black has undoubtedly rescued numerous patients from certain death or at least paralysis. Consequently he has to listen to such exclamations as "You are God" which are truly perilous. Such patients and their families would like Dr. Black and other doctors to "play God" and tell them they can cure anything and that the patients will never be sick again. Evidently, such beliefs and attitudes are fed by a misunderstanding of the nature of science, the restricted efficacy of medicine and the limitations of human understanding.[5]

This adoration of specialists, together with the large income specialists earn is evidently very influential in providing medical students with incentives to become specialists and avoid the lesser income and the stigma of practicing family medicine or general internal medicine. However, there are those who predict that a decline in the demand for specialists is now in progress and that generalist physicians will be and should be more in demand. This shift in physicians utilization from specialists to generalists was recognized by Congress when it established the Council on Graduate Medical Education in 1986 to provide subsidies and guidance on issues related to the physician work force.[6]

This Council has proposed that the proportion of physicians completing training in internal medicine, general pediatrics and family medicine be increased from 30% to 50% in the near future. The Council has also proposed that the number of training positions available to international medical graduates be reduced from 35% to 10% at U.S. medical schools. This proposal would reduce the total number of residencies from 24,000 each year to 18,000 with particular emphasis on reducing the number of foreign physicians.

At present the differences between the medical education received in various disparate countries are still great enough to force foreign doctors to learn a number of American techniques and ideas not known by them. However, it is proposed that international standards become the norm in training doctors in primary health care. To achieve this, five recommendations have been made by Abrahamson. These are informing medical teachers around the world of responsibilities of doctors at the primary health care level; establishing "umbrella authorities" who will coordinate health care manpower, plans and priorities; establish co-ordination boards who will link together all the medical schools in a country and in turn in the world; review the powers given to medical councils and regulatory bodies with a view to focusing their decisions on the populations health needs and furnish medical schools with enough money so that they can improve the present relevance of their medical education for the population living now. [7]

These proposals are augmented by the request that the number of physicians completing primary care would rise by 34 percent each year even as the number of medical students in a specialty would be reduced by half.

All this is of course having a considerable impact upon the academic medical centers in this country because the federal government has for decades given these medical centers so much support. [8]

One anticipated consequence of increasing the number of physicians trained only in primary care is that it will make access to such doctors easier. Since the number of doctors graduating each year is small, it would still take a long time to reach the goal of having 50% of doctors generalists and the other half specialists. [9]

The reason for the successful eighty year effort by American medicine to increase the number of specialists lies in the explosion of knowledge in the basic biomedical and life sciences in this century. This has meant that medical schools devoted themselves exclusively to scientific education to the neglect of the social and humanistic studies which, as we have seen, were one of Flexner's proposals in his first "report" in 1910. Now, (1999) however, more and more patients are demanding that they be treated as whole persons and not as "cases" and that their social and emotional needs be given at least some weight by the medical profession. [10]

Consequently, medical education is undergoing considerable examination with regard to a more "caring" approach to health services in the future. Andrew Wallace, the dean of Dartmouth Medical School believes that "The Thing That Really Matters Is That We Care" and writes that a "liberal education is the best foundation for sustaining the values of our profession and for cultivating the kind of doctors our country needs most." Such doctors are best found by introducing diversity into medical schools so that the student body represents the racial, demographic and economic diversity of the nation. Diversity also means that medical students ought to include women and men with a diversity of interests from poets and athletes to butterfly collectors. Wallace also urges medical schools to emphasize learning instead of instruction so that students learn how to ask questions and find the answers. "The goal," says Wallace, " is learning, not instruction." [11]

The need to keep learning and to care is not only due to the demands of patients but also to the increases in life expectancy world wide which scientific medicine has achieved. Labeled the "health transition" by some writers this means that life expectancy world wide has attained age 60 and is a good deal longer in such "developed" nations as the United States. The differences in life expectancy between the "developed" and the under-developed nations lies not in the potential ability of medical sciences to even out the life expectancy of the poorer nations with the richer nations, but in the quality of life issues which consist of poverty, poor sanitation, malnutrition and war all of which are social issues and hence the province of those whose care about such conditions. [12]

Because more and more physicians care about social issues, the social sciences are getting more and more attention from medical school faculties. In addition, more and more physicians recognize the relationship between biology and behavior. For example, there is an evident connection between prosperity and health, between early childhood development and illness and between the functioning of the immune system and psychological health. Meanwhile, molecular genetics is showing that there may well be a biological basis for alcoholism, substance abuse and depression.

McLeoud and McCullough have listed a number of areas in the behavioral and social sciences which could be included in the curriculum of the medical schools in this country. These are sociology, child growth and development, gerontology, medical anthropology, psychology, social ethics, health economics and political science and environment and occupational health. Furthermore, McCloud and McCullough conclude that in the light of the behavioral sciences chronic diseases will be better understood than heretofore. This refers not only to long term care but also to community based care. [13]

Since the study of community is the province of sociology it is not surprising that medical sociology has been introduced in numerous medical schools in this country. This means that sociology is taught at about three quarters of the 127 American medical schools. In England there are 34 medical schools of whom 32 teach medical sociology. Many other countries also include sociology in the curriculum of medical schools. These sociology courses concern the patient's and the physician's social and cultural background and the influence of that background on health care. [14]

The uses of sociology in medical education have chiefly been in the area of the doctor-patient relationship with particular emphasis on medical interviewing. Human development has also been given some prominence in the area of medical sociology while education in the social aspects of illness has received a good deal less attention. Aging has become an important aspect of medical education. Together with class, ethnicity and gender these aspects of the human condition affect the health of any person and of large populations and are therefore the concern of medical sociology. All this has been recognized by the Association of American Medical Colleges in their report entitled *Physicians for the Twenty First Century*. [15]

In the 1960's the revolt of students against the Viet Nam war and the effort of women to gain gender equality led to a greater interest in the rights of individuals in all phases of American culture and social life.

Therefore, American medicine also began to promote a more sociological attitude towards the patient as an individual. It was during the 1960's that "the total patient" or "the patient as a person" first became a popular phrase in the medical profession. Hence, medical education introduced the idea of "human values" and began to stress that "most illnesses derive from societal causes."[16]

In addition to these benefits of the sociological approach there is yet another advantage to the teaching of medical sociology to aspiring physicians. That is the introduction of theoretical sociology as a means of understanding the patient. One aspect of theoretical sociology which can be of great help to medical students is a recognition of "labeling." "Labeling" refers to the manner in which so-called "deviant" behavior is interpreted by observers. Hence, someone "labeled" as mentally ill may well have been given that "diagnosis" because the person so affected refuses to play a traditional role or challenges established authority. No doubt the film One Flew Over the Cuckoo's Nest illustrates how a person who fakes mental illness is nevertheless regarded as mentally ill because it may suit an authoritarian nurse or administrator to force a very much sane prisoner into that role. Similarly, sociology can contribute a good deal to a medical student's understanding of death and dying and to the relationship between the social environment and issues of health and illness.[17]

Social stratification is undoubtedly one of the best researched and understood areas of sociological knowledge. Therefore sociologists are in a position to make medical students aware of the hierarchy existing in the medical profession itself. Evidently, specialists rank at the top of the medical hierarchy, general physicians rank second in that status system and non physician medical clinicians such as nurses are ranked third. Because psychologists and some social workers do independent clinical work they too receive some recognition in the medical hierarchy. At the very bottom of this arrangement are sociologists and other social scientists such as anthropologists who have no independent practice and who are all lumped together in the view of medical personnel as "behavioral scientists."[18]

In addition to medical sociology, medical schools have also begun to teach medical ethics. In fact, "medical ethicists" are now employed in a number of American and foreign medical schools. In July, 1983 a conference concerning medical ethics was held at Dartmouth College. That conference involved ten participants who were all recognized as world leaders in medical ethics education. These ethicists formulated a list of goals to be attained in the area of medical ethics by medical students. However, they recognized that medical students come to medical school with a set of moral convictions which need not be taught in medical school because the character of the students has already been formed. However, the ethics that must be taught in medical school have a great deal of bearing on the patient-doctor relationship and it is in this area that the principal amount of teaching must be done. Empathy, sympathy and insight into the patient's feelings are areas which have been neglected almost entirely by doctors in an effort to keep these sentiments from interfering with scientific objectivity.

Another area of interest to medical school ethicists has been the recent discovery that some medical researchers present false information to financial sponsors of medical research in order to guarantee themselves the kinds of results which will assure the funding of their projects in the future. This is indeed an ethical issue as well as an economic one since many medical researchers support themselves on "soft money" only and have no other income.[19]

In order to teach ethics and humanities to medical students it is necessary to overcome a great deal of resistance to such subject matter among medical students. Medical students as well as physicians are generally interested only in pragmatic information which will allow them to cure the patient of a physical illness. Little credence is generally given by an overwhelming number of medical practitioners to social science, humanities and/or philosophy. Therefore it is important that this kind of information is taught in a clinical setting involving live cases currently available and related to the students own experience.

Ethics also include the wishes and background of the patient. Keeping that in mind, it is vital that medical students recognize that Americans of various cultural backgrounds may view as ethical or unethical ways of thinking or doing which are contrary to American majority practices. One such area in which the ethics of one group may well clash with the ethics of another has to do with death and dying. There are those who believe that a patient suffering from a terminal illness should not be told that he is dying. There certainly are cultures whose members believe that one should lie about such a fatal prognosis and that it is immoral to tell a patient that he cannot recover. Thus, there are sub-cultures in this country among whom it is impossible to tell a patient or his relatives "bad" news. Among these minorities, concealment is regarded as the only legitimate manner of dealing with such "bad" news even as the majority of Americans think that a patient should be told exactly where he stands with regard to his health. Physicians ought to know how to deal with such an ethical dilemma which seriously questions whether absolute truth telling is the answer for every patient whose life is threatened.[20]

Yet another issue which ethicists should discuss with medical students is whether the preservation of life is always and in all circumstances the only choice a physician can make. The success of scientific medicine in prolonging life may well be a "two edged sword" in some cases in which the patient may well be kept alive by the use of every device available even if the life so prolonged is not worth living. Such a choice will have to be made by almost all doctors within the limitations of their own beliefs. [21]

These beliefs are of course distinctive with each participant in the doctor-patient-family relationship. Hence these subjective beliefs and values influence how the physician himself will react to any situation that may arise during the patients treatment. Failure to understand that the patient and his family may have a different set of values than the doctor will result in the development of communication barriers between patients and doctors. Therefore a program in medical sociology and in medical ethics will tend to remove such value barriers and to help families, patients and doctors to make the best possible choices respecting the welfare of the patient.[22]

Before an understanding of another person's values is possible it is of course necessary that a medical student recognize his own values or preferences for a course of action. To do so it is suggested by Amado that medical students organize a values journal. Such a journal, it is believed, helps students recognize who they are, what their social and professional roles are and what their expectations are. Likewise it is suggested that patients also develop a values journal so that a dialogue between patients and their physicians can result in compromise rather than confrontation in case of a dispute. This is particularly important when patients demand the use of expensive resources and unrealistic treatments which physicians cannot or will not grant. Such disputes have for years resulted in innumerable and expensive law suits and/or the transfer of the patient to another physician. Hence, the development of shared values and shared expectations between doctors and patients should resolve many of these disputes even though the medical school can only teach medical students and not the general public.[23]

Ethics are also involved in the issue of abortion. That issue has been bitterly fought for many years and is usually labeled a dispute between the supporters of "freedom of choice" and the advocates of "pro-life" positions. The question is: "How can an ethicist teaching at a university medical school deal with that issue when he must be aware that every medical school class includes students adhering to either of these positions?"[24]

Yet another example of an ethics conflict is the product of the inevitability of the rationing of medical resources which is already a reality in American medicine at this time (1999). The resolution of disputes concerning such resources cannot be postponed. Therefore medical students need to learn how to discover which values they share with their patients and their families so that health care policies applied on an individual basis can, in general, reflect a common consensus. Such an effort was made by the Georgetown University Medical Center from July 1992 to July 1994. During that time medical students were exposed to discussions concerning the ethics of cost control in medicine; brain death and related states and the assessment of competency. In addition "competency and consent," "confidentiality," "justice and medicine," "withholding and withdrawing," and "do not resuscitate" requests were also discussed. The results of these discussions appeared very favorable indeed. Ninety-six percent of students found the discussions very stimulating and eighty-eight percent found these discussions very useful. These ethics sessions improved the medical students knowledge of the content of the Hippocratic oath and the outcome of several legal cases revolving around medical ethics. Most important is that the confidence of medical students improved a great deal as their knowledge of ethics increased.[25]

II

Over the many years that the medical education system has developed in this country it has attained a position of trust among the American people whose health and lives are dependent on it. It is therefore a truly revolutionary and even shocking experience for many doctors and their patients that this system, so long regarded as sound and reliable is suddenly confronted by a severe threat to its existence. That threat is called "managed care" and refers to the literal "take over" of the American health delivery system by those who seek to reorganize American medicine on a "business first" basis. It should be understood, however, that the forerunners of "managed care" have been with us since the 1830's when employers, religious orders, physicians and various communities first attempted to make health care more accessible to the poor and allow communities more involvement in the organization of these services.[26]

Medical education in the United States was controlled from the beginning by physicians who wanted to separate poor patients from rich patients. Furthermore, physicians traditionally had little interest in the chronically ill including the mentally ill. Therefore, physicians associated with the early plans and systems were systematically excluded from medical education and from organized medicine generally. Hospitals generally did not accept the patients of doctors associated with health plans so that these plans were forced to buy or build their own hospitals. Group practice was also unwelcome among medical educators. Consequently, medical educators made outsiders of these organizations.[27]

The exclusion of some of these managed care plans can well be justified by the evidence that there are plans which have no conscience and are solely interested in profit. There are, however, other plans whose management does in fact exhibit a considerable degree of social responsibility. Furthermore, medical educators need to recognize that managed care, in one form or another, is becoming the dominant method of health care delivery in the United States and therefore cannot be avoided. Nevertheless, both teaching hospitals and health care plans are staffed by those who view the other with suspicion. Thus, medical educators accuse all managed care plans as "money grubbing, socially irresponsible, profit mad, care rationing bullies," while the managers of these plans paint most teaching hospitals as wasteful, arrogant and self-serving.[28]

Numerous allegations concerning medical schools and medical education have appeared in the literature in recent years. These include the charge that medical schools are producing an oversupply of physicians because applications to medical schools have risen by 43% between 1988 and 1995; that medical students are led to create a glut of specialists and an insufficient number of generalists; that medical researchers are using public money to develop privately owned patents on new medical discoveries; that medical researchers received money to study AIDS but instead used the money for another purpose. It is further charged that such researchers experiment on the poorest Americans with new techniques and drugs which are not available to the same persons who were used for such experiments once the drugs are perfected because the poor, of course, cannot pay.[29]

These criticisms, whatever their merit, cannot serve as cause to abandon university based medical education. Instead it needs to be recalled that the reasons for university based medical education can be listed as several propositions which may not be found in practice but which are the theoretical foundation of the alliance between universities and medical schools. These propositions are that medical education is a public service as are all medical activities; that change in science is so great and so rapid that apprenticeship cannot adequately train a doctor; that medicine requires education in both the biological and social sciences and that this is available only within a university; that Medical education is a slow and difficult process which is rewarded by increased knowledge and not profits and market shares; that universities are wedded to differences in opinion and expression of widely divergent views which therefore leads to education in values and attitudes not available outside a university and that clinical education in particular and medical education in general is costly, financially inefficient and slow. This is not tolerated in a profit driven setting and must therefore remain within the university. It is of course true that in Europe universities and medical schools have been allied since the Middle Ages and that this association has been most productive in America as well during the past one hundred years.[30]

One consequence of the association of medical schools with universities is the number of applications received by American medical schools. Because so many undergraduate students become aware of the presence of medical schools on the campus of their own university the interest in pursuing a career in medicine is enhanced. This became most visible during the decade ending in 1998 when more than 47,000 applications were received by American medical schools as compared to only 27,000 in 1988. This increase in applications to the profession is particularly surprising in view of the great changes which medical practice is undergoing at the end of the century. Financial risk has now shifted from the insurance companies to the so-called "providers" i.e. physicians who receive a set fee for each patient. Groups of patients, not individuals, are the interest of the so-called "health care delivery networks" as primary care physicians are valued more than specialists by these managed care conglomerates. Hospital care is now (1999) being reduced in favor of walk-in clinics (ambulatory care) so that physicians have less autonomy, more regulations and less and less interest in a solid doctor-patient relationship.[31]

These changes in the profession have led to major changes in the curricula of American medical schools. Among these changes are reduced numbers of lectures to passive students; increased numbers of small group discussion sessions and problem based learning situations. That includes opportunities for medical students to talk to hospitalized patients, to be present in operating rooms and to benefit from clinical based education instead of using the old animal based methods involving laboratory dogs. Students can therefore ask questions of practicing physicians and surgeons and gain a "hands on" experience from the beginning of their medical school education.[32]

Because of the "hands-on" education now practiced at many American medical schools performance-based assessment methods must now be used in such schools. These performance based assessments have pushed aside the traditional multiple choice tests which were factually oriented but by no means as realistic in providing students with opportunities to exhibit problem solving skills. These forms of assessment, now in use about 35 years, have included patient-management problems in which a brief description of a patient's situation is followed by history-taking, a physical examination and laboratory scenes. All of these experiences are however based on simulations and not on actual patient contacts.

The University of Oklahoma Department of Medicine has used techniques of simulated patients to teach interviewing skills to senior medical students. According to a study by Harmon and Vanetta, this role playing has been most successful and has resulted in a 30% saving of faculty time and a considerable improvement in interviewing skills by the participants. [33]

Computer based simulation has also been in use for some years and is expected to become quite common in the near future. A third method of assessment, oral examinations, are indeed the oldest methods of assessment in use for hundreds of years. While these examinations are still in use in England and elsewhere, they were eliminated from the United States licensing examinations in the mid-1960's. [34]

Although performance-based assessments resemble reality, these examinations are nevertheless only simulations and therefore it should be assumed that examinees do not behave in assessment situations as they would under real-life conditions. In any event, however, the traditional method of reading faculty prepared handouts without gaining any realistic experience concerning real patients has been generally given up by American medical schools.   Students now read about patient's cases in the medical literature and present their findings to other students and to faculty preceptors. Now students also read primary sources while the old fashioned memorization method has also been abandoned. Traditionally, anyone blessed with an excellent memory would excel although medical students never said a word for the first two years of their training. Now, students talk a great deal, work together and evaluate medical literature. Hence, the application of knowledge in a patient setting is now stressed in medical school so that activity and not passivity has become important. All of these changes are reflected in the newly revised Medical College Admissions Test which now requires students to read passages and apply knowledge instead of merely memorizing. Integration, application and analysis of knowledge have thus replaced rote learning although a background in biology, physics, general chemistry and organic chemistry are still important prerequisites for admission to medical school. [35]

The immense growth of information in all areas of human knowledge and in particular in the area of medical education confronts medical educators with the need to make choices within the information overload now available. All this needs also to be taught within the framework of "managed care" and the great emphasis on cost containment. Medical students must now learn how to treat a patient during the course of an illness with these limitations in mind. In addition, the issue of generalist/specialist physicians needs to be re-examined in medical schools at the end of the century. Surely, the deprecation of general practice and the enticement of greater incomes earned by specialists have in the past driven almost all medical students into becoming specialists of some kind. However, generalists are now needed more than specialists particularly because there is a glut of specialists in the profession at the end of the 1990's. Finally, medical schools need to adjust to the entrance of a greater number of women and so-called minorities into the profession.[36]

Until the mid-1960's medical students were almost always white men. Thirty years later, at the end of the 1990's more than 40% of all medical students are women and a large contingent of such students are not of European descent. It had been thought that the entrance of so many women into the medical profession would result in a more patient friendly environment in the profession. Whether the current effort to include a greater emphasis on the "humanities" in medical school is the product of the greater participation of women or whether it is the consequence of the same attitude changes which admitted more women in the first place will forever be a matter of speculation. In earlier years, before the "Flexner report" of 1910 led to the absorption of most proprietary medical schools by colleges and universities, there were a considerable number of women in medical schools and in the profession. However, during the sixty years after 1920, women were rare in the medical field so that their current admission into the field is a reversal of a trend that had become so traditional and entrenched that even at this late date, 1999, women physicians are still a curiosity, if not a rarity.[37]

It is surely beyond dispute that the ultimate goal of medical education is the health and care of the population. Therefore such changes as those already discussed are defensible on the grounds that they improve the health delivery system now in use. Further changes in the health delivery system may even include the movement of health delivery teams from the hospital to the community in such a fashion that the physician will become only one member of such a team. In such an anticipated community based health delivery system health delivery may well begin in the factory, school or home and not in the hospital.

III

In 1993 the World Summit on Medical Education, meeting in Edinburgh, Scotland declared that a number of reforms were needed in medical education. These reforms, said the World Summit, should include relevant educational settings; a curriculum based on national health needs; emphasis on disease prevention and health promotion; life-long active learning; competency based learning; medical teachers trained as educators; integration of science with clinical practice; coordination of medical education with health care services; balanced production of types of physicians; multiprofessional training; continuing medical education and selection of entrants to medical schools for non-cognitive as well as intellectual attributes.[38]

All of these suggestions can only be put into practice if the financial resources necessary for their implementation are made available to teaching hospitals. This is an issue which has been debated for years but has become particularly acute since the emphasis on hospital cost containment became prominent after 1972. Health maintenance organizations and insurance companies have claimed that graduate medical education leads universally to longer stays in the hospital and that therefore teaching hospitals cost them too much. These profit driven organizations hold that the cost differences between teaching and non-teaching hospitals are caused by expenditures in teaching hospitals for non-essential and unwarranted practices. However, it must be clear even to the most money oriented insurers that the practice of medicine would come to an end in this country if no medical education and no teaching hospitals were available here. Indeed, there are some costs attached to teaching hospitals which non-teaching hospitals need not face. For example, there are indirect costs such as floor space devoted to conference rooms, larger medical libraries and support for teaching hospitals. In addition, teaching hospitals usually also include nursing education and continuing education for staff physicians. Because of their academic efforts, teaching hospitals also require more technical support for patients with extraordinary problems which are referred to teaching hospitals and not to those lacking these resources. Evidently, the presence of patients needing specialized care leads to greater costs. It is also well known that teaching hospitals receive more patients with few resources and hence with a more common history of bad debts. Since 1983, Medicare has reduced the support of indirect costs to hospitals by 30 percent as Diagnostic Related Groups prepayments have not included consideration of these expenditures.[39]

Some efforts have been made to develop international standards for medical education. These efforts are motivated by the belief that medical training and ability to care for patients should be independent of place. Nevertheless, various national commissions have made recommendations concerning medical education in the United States with a view to the special problems encountered in this country relative to the health delivery system in vogue here. The lead in these efforts has been taken by the Council on Graduate Medical Education established by Congress in 1986 and charged with the task of recommending federal and private sector efforts to deal with physicians workforce needs. That Council has recommended that the American medical education system graduate one half of its participants into primary care practice.[40]

In 1997-98, 66,748 students were enrolled in American medical schools. 14,114 medical students graduated from U.S. medical schools that year.[41] It is anticipated by the American Medical Association that 4,800 international medical graduates will enter into the physician supply. Hence the Council on Graduate Medical Education has recommended that first year positions be set at 19,300 to include those graduating from foreign medical schools. Because it is anticipated that one half of these graduates will enter general or family practice, only one half will become specialists if this scenario can be carried out. Therefore the number of specialists will decline particularly if pay equality for primary care physicians is built into the system. Unless that is done physicians will continue to gravitate toward specialties no matter what the education system attempts to do to increase the number of medical students seeking a residence in general medicine.[42]

There is then nearly unanimous agreement that the American medical education system turns out too few generalists and too many specialists. It may be that normal market forces will correct this imbalance. That, however, is unlikely. Therefore the Association of American Medical Colleges seeks to appoint a politically independent national commission responsible for limiting residency positions in accordance with estimates of future needs. At the end of the twentieth century American graduate medical education has evidently become too large and too expensive as indicated by the pressure on Congress to reduce the funds so far appropriated under Title VII of the Public Health Service Act.[43]

The costs of educating medical students are of course considerable. In a review of studies spanning twenty years, Jones and Korn found that estimates of such costs vary immensely. Thus, one study estimated the cost of one year of medical study to be only $11,175 while another study placed the cost at $100,000 per student per year. Of these costs, in 1998 students payed tuition and fees at public medical schools of about $8,500 per year while private medical schools charges ranged from $17,000 per year to an average of $25,000 per year. [44]

In any event, the immense differences in these estimates are the outcome of several ways of accounting for such costs. According to the Institute of Medicine, these costs can be divided into instructional costs and total educational resource costs. Instructional costs are further divided into marginal share costs and proportionate share costs which makes reference to joint activities with the university and/or hospitals in the education of medical students.

Generally, instructional costs include faculty time spent in teaching, preparation for teaching and student evaluation and administrative activities directly related to teaching. In addition, instructional costs involved office space, student affairs, curriculum development and scholarships for students. Finally, library resources, computers, campus security and administration all are directly related to the education of a doctor.[45]

Without becoming entangled in the intricacies of accounting it is evident that a variety of methods can be used to calculate the expenses relating to a medical education and that therefore numerous estimates, all honestly calculated, can be presented.

However, Jones and Korn were able to reconcile differences in nine studies of annual per-student medical education costs and came to the conclusion that the range of expenses is no less than $72,000 and more than $93,000 in 1996 dollars.[46]

IV

One of the aims of President Clinton's effort to overhaul the nation's health care system in 1993 would have been a series of reforms designed to cut spending and to influence the training and education of medical students to achieve better skills and different attitudes of physicians. Among these changes is of course the need for physicians to work effectively in the "managed care" environment now defeating the private practice tradition in medicine. This will mean that physicians will have to deal with prevention strategies such as nutrition and exercise and will also have to learn to work with teams of "care givers" who are not necessarily physicians. This massive effort to reshape the entire health industry failed when Congress refused to pass the reforms proposed by Hillary Rodham Clinton and her more than 400 advisors in 1993.[47]

Those reforms would have included limits on medical costs by directing patients to family doctors and away from expensive high-tech medical centers; the development of "health alliances" designed to select health insurance options for whole regions and academic medical centers for treatment only available in academic settings; phasing out payments to teaching hospitals for indigent patients as these patients would come under the new health plan; the expansion of the National Institutes of Health that focus on disease prevention; a plan to limit to 50% those medical students receiving training in specialties; new financing to permit minorities and low-income students to attend medical, dental and nursing schools; a doubling of federal programs to support the training of physician's assistants and nurse practitioners and a plan to train doctors outside of hospitals in conjunction with other health care professionals, mainly nurses.[48]

Nurses with master's degrees and 500 hours of clinical training have succeeded in establishing themselves as nurse-practitioners in many American communities and are therefore competing with doctors for the income derived from patient care. The principal impetus for this development has been the demand by managed-care plans that low cost methods be used to treat patients. Meanwhile the proportion of medical graduates planning careers in primary care has more than doubled since 1991 when only 14 percent of such graduates were interested in general practice. It appears therefore that managed care plans do not view medical education as necessary to deal with most patients and that the day may well come when all doctors will be specialists while nurses will administer all primary care. At Texas A&M professors are already teaching nursing students and medical students at the same time. Since nurses have only one year clinical training while doctors have five years training it seems that either nurses are not truly prepared to do the work of doctors and are performing in a pseudo-medical fashion only because they cost less, or that medical schools are unnecessary and that nurses are cheaper substitutes for doctors *ipso facto*.[49]

The employment of nurses as primary care givers and other recommendations of the Council on Graduate Medical Education are augmented by the views of some private organizations interested in Health Care delivery and medical education. Most prominent among these private organizations is the Robert Wood Johnson Foundation.

In 1992 the Robert Wood Johnson Foundation issued a report which sought to widen the settings in which medical education takes place. The report suggests that in addition to the traditional hospital setting, nursing homes, ambulatory offices and hospices also be used as teaching areas. The report also seeks to alter the examination of students from outside test makers to the interests of the faculties actually teaching medical students. Finally, the report asks that an "authority" be appointed to oversee curriculum changes in medical education. Furthermore, the report recognizes that patient behavior plays a major role in many illnesses and that therefore behavior changes are critical in health promotion and disease prevention. The Robert Wood Johnson commission supports the view that a dichotomy between psychosocial and biological factors in an illness is untenable.[50]

Two years after this report was issued, the Robert Wood Johnson Foundation distributed grants to 14 medical colleges in the United States to support the training of primary care doctors. These grants, amounting to $947,000 each enabled these medical schools to introduce a number of new programs including a fourth year elective on evidence-based medicine, epidemiology and community medicine. In addition, medical schools used these grants to increase the number of primary care residents at university residency sites. [51]

Although the numerous "reports" and "recommendations" which have recently developed have had some influence they have been mainly academic exercises and administrative paper pushing   Recently, however, a new "problem-based" approach to medical education has taken hold in some medical schools and hospitals. This problem based approach invalidates the erstwhile lecturing and listening method so common and so traditional for so many years. One such "problem based" program is in New England. This program has already had practical effects and real results and is more than just a theoretical reform of medical education. This program enrolls students who volunteer in the Emergency Rooms of hospitals. These students gain real experience in caring for patients, conduct research for doctors who have no time to do so themselves and relieve the overworked staff by helping in numerous situations. Included in this program is the Yale-New Haven Hospital, the Bridgeport Hospital and the Lincoln Medical Health Center in the Bronx, NY. Comments by students who work in the emergency rooms include "....the emergency room is unlike anything I have ever seen. It's just an incredible experience from the minute you walk in until you leave," and "at this stage you take a lot of biology and chemistry classes and it is easy to lose sight of what you are doing all this for.........but working in the E.R. reminds you why you want to be a doctor." [52]

Another example of a "problem based" learning experience in medical schools is the McMaster University program used in Hamilton, Ontario, Canada. Two methods of teaching - learning were developed there. First, students were placed in small tutorial groups and second, students were taught to investigate real problems that might arise in the treatment of real patients. Students were given access to patient records and were then asked to determine a patient's medical problem and devise treatment. Both the University of New Mexico and the Harvard University School of Medicine instituted similar programs. At Harvard the program was called "The New Pathway." Numerous other medical schools have adopted similar methods.[53]

Recognition that disease and illness cannot be exclusively treated by chemical means has become quite general at the end of the century so that it is not surprising that some doctors are now willing and ready to teach that what is needed is an "integrated" medicine. Dr. Andrew Weil of the University of Arizona's College of Medicine has introduced a Program of Integrative Medicine there. This program refers to "bolstering the body's resistance by living in a healthy way." Weil criticizes conventional medicine and argues that plants and food, rather than toxic pharmaceuticals, should be used to treat illness. Weil does not seek to discard conventional medicine because he recognizes that conventional medicine is important in emergencies when the body is too injured to heal itself. The main complaint about Weil's approach is that he recommends treatments which have not been tested. Consequently he has been accused of being a "snake oil" salesman. Nevertheless, some H.M.O.'s and the State of Washington require that doctors become acquainted with "alternative medicine" and have sent their physicians to the University of Arizona to study with Weil.[54]

These examples of problem based medical education as developed in New England, in Canada and in Arizona are only a few examples of the many changes which have occurred in medical education and in the profession over the twenty five years ending in 1998. It is therefore worthwhile to discover whether these changes have brought about attitude changes among medical students and physicians. To that end a study of professional attitudes of physicians is instructive as is a study of student satisfaction with the Medical School learning environment.

A number of studies have been conducted since the 1950's concerning the medical school's learning environment. These studies have shown that students' progress toward becoming physicians and toward their interest in various specialties is very much influenced by the students mood, satisfaction and psychological well being. Students are very much affected by mistreatment or by humane interaction with their professors and that in turn is reflected in the fashion in which students treat each other. In fact, a study by Simmons and Cavanaugh suggests that a caring professional school environment may be one of the strongest predictors of a student's ability to care for patients. This means that those students who believed that faculty cared for them and were concerned about their education were positively affected in their ability to offer compassionate care to their patients.[55]

Another study of medical students' attitudes was conducted during a period of twenty- five years ending in 1997. This study, conducted by Barney, *et al* sought to uncover the internalization of professional attitudes in a sample of physicians. Such internalization of professional attitudes are demonstrated in the doctor-patient relationship and are linked to values and norms or expectations of conduct. The specific expectations studied had to do with empathy, which is defined as the ability of the physician to understand the way the patient feels and understands the way in which the patient understands. Such a definition does indeed impose a considerable burden on the doctor. The example used by Barney is illustrated by the choice of two possible statements a physician might make relative to a patient's condition. Thus, the doctor could say "you have a 75% chance of survival," or he could say "your chances of dying are 25%."

Compared to such issues as prestige of the profession or economic rewards or opportunities for research, it is evident that the twenty five year study reveals again and again that help for patients outweighs all other considerations of the physicians studied by Barney *et al.* This finding may well be the consequence of the introduction of the social and behavioral sciences into the medical school curriculum during the past quarter century. That, however, is not conclusively proved because it is possible that those who study medicine in the first place seek to be of help and have a good deal of empathy for others *ipso facto.*[56]

In view of the currently diminishing prestige of physicians and the leveling off of doctors income, it is evident that the mythological model of rich doctors, an all powerful AMA and "the best medicine in the world" is giving way to reality. That reality for a young medical student consists of a $70,000.- debt and the prospect of being a life-long employee instead of enjoying personal, professional autonomy. Under these new circumstances only those would want to be engaged in the practice of medicine whose principal commitment is to service and to healing the sick and to be of help.[57]

Community-based medical education is therefore one means by which students are promptly introduced to the experience of providing primary care to patients. This has become necessary because most medical care now occurs outside hospitals. Furthermore, because insurance companies have instituted the Diagnostic Related Groups method of paying hospitals a lump sum for each patient, patients have such a short average stay in hospitals that students cannot learn very much from patients whom they can hardly meet because the patients are discharged almost at once. The time patients stay in the hospitals are simply too short to give students sufficient opportunity to gain clinical exposure.

In Scotland there is a well developed community based medical curriculum which requires students to spend one afternoon in community based teaching. The whole effort here is to allow the student physician to see the patient as a whole person in the "wider social and personal perspective." This kind of education permits the eventual general practitioner to look after people, not disease. Students who are engaged in community based medical education see their patients in several stages of their lives and therefore work well with a large variety of people. In contrast, the modern hospital with its scientific specialization sees only the disease of the moment and cannot deal with the meaning of disease for the patient at hand. If fact, in the traditional super-specialized hospital hardly anyone even considers who the patient is or what the patient may feel. No doubt there are exceptions, here and there, so that some specialists also concern themselves with the whole person. However, the general practitioner will in any event be more likely to meet those whose complaints are not specific and classifiable in terms of traditional diagnoses but who need help of a general nature even if it is only the opportunity to complain. Therefore, in general practice and in clinical care an empathetic manner will allow a positive relationship between doctor and patient which clinical skills alone can never produce.

Community- based medical education then consists of seeing patients at home. The practice of seeing patients at home is as old as Hippocrates and was long practiced in the United States and elsewhere. It was only the rise of the scientific hospitals which reduced home visits by doctors to patients because it was evident that hospitals have the diagnostic equipment which doctors cannot carry around in their medical bags. Now, however, students are encouraged to make such visits and to spend as much as 90 minutes with a patient depending on the nature of the patients condition. [58]

Yet, even as community based medicine is introduced to students it cannot be overlooked that clinicians need to assimilate a good number of facts. In the past the sole criterion of success for a medical student was that he could recall large numbers of such facts so that a good memory was the prerequisite attribute needed by a medical student. This requirement has really not diminished. Hence the recent emphasis on "deep processing" does not mean that this newer approach is an alternative for the learning of clinical facts. It is, instead, an addition to the curriculum and not a substitute. [59]

This is illustrated by events at Stanford University Medical School, which show how change of the medical school curriculum may proceed in one medical school but serve as an example to others, particularly since Stanford University has a great deal of prestige in the academic world. Thus, medical education at Stanford traditionally had students study anatomy, physiology, biochemistry and histology the first semester. That initial course was followed by two years in the hospitals and wards and clinics of the former Cooper Medical College in San Francisco, which later merged with Stanford University. Together with the teaching of human anatomy this 2x2 model has endured for years even as a continuing struggle over the kind of doctor the school wanted to produce has led to innumerable curriculum changes over time.

V

There are 1,025 teaching hospitals in the United States. These hospitals have traditionally produced the needed physicians for this country. In recent years, however, health care organizations have warned that the nation has too many doctors. One reason for this increase in residents trained at these hospitals has been that teaching hospitals get as much as $100,000 from Medicare for each resident trained. This means that in fiscal 1996 the government paid more than $12 billion to U.S. teaching hospitals for graduate medical education. Therefore, Congress has expanded a program first available only in New York State which gives teaching hospitals across the country the opportunity to reduce the number of residents they train by paying these teaching hospitals to eliminate some residencies altogether. This program became available in July 1998. Since teaching hospitals have become accustomed to rely on government funding for their residency programs they have so far been reluctant to reduce the number of residencies. The transitional funding for residency reduction will therefore allow teaching hospitals to move towards the goal of reducing the number of doctors in the U.S. even as it is anticipated that the Medicare Trust Fund will have a $600 billion deficit by 2002.[60]

The great cost of the residency programs is further increased by the practice of teaching hospitals to over bill Medicare. Applying the False Claims Act to such practices, the Department of Health, Education and Welfare has audited numerous hospitals to ascertain whether or not physicians at such hospitals had submitted false bills. Evidently, these hospitals billed the government for the treatment of patients by senior doctors when in fact the treatment was delivered by medical residents.[61] This audit resulted in the agreement of the University of Pennsylvania hospital to settle charges by paying $30 million to Medicare for overbilling and the imposition of a fine of $12 million on the medical school at Thomas Jefferson University.[62]

Because fraudulent practices were so wide-spread the Association of American Medical Colleges complained to Congress about these audits and succeeded in having the House pass legislation suspending such audits. Even as the Senate was still debating this issue, the Health Care

Financing Administration penalized two more hospitals on fraud charges.[63]

It may surprise many that the medical profession would be accused of such practices or that doctors would be interested in gaining income by illegitimate means when heretofore it was assumed that doctors had the option of working when and wherever they pleased. However, the fraudulent practices uncovered by the Health Care Finance Administration may well be the product of the great change in the financial opportunities for doctors which managed care has brought about. While primary care physicians are still very much in demand and their initial earnings are about $100,000 a year these changes have affected specialists the most.[64]

In fact, in some specialties the compensation for new hires is dropping. These difficulties affect anesthesiologists, radiologists and otorhinolaryngologists (ear, nose and throat doctors) more than any other specialists. General surgeons and heart surgeons are also having problems finding well-paid positions, particularly in favored metropolitan areas. As a result more and more doctors have been willing to move to under-supplied rural areas where the pressure of managed care is either absent or not very strong.[65]

As the demand for highly trained specialists is decreasing and young doctors find that they are unemployed, the training programs keep producing a constant stream of such new specialists just the same. This is truly devastating to those who have spent a decade in training only to find that there is nothing for them. This is particularly true of those doctors who work directly for hospitals in large urban and sub-urban areas. The result of this job shortage has been that some doctors are practicing elective surgery which is not covered by health plans but is based on a fee for service arrangement. [66]

The Council on Graduate Medical Education has estimated that by 2000 there will be a surplus of 125,000 specialists and a modest shortage of about 20,000 generalists. In part this oversupply of doctors is the result of the admission to the United States of "international" medical graduates of whom about three quarters remain in the United States after graduation. Therefore the Council on Graduate Medical Education recommends drastically reducing the number of international medical graduate residents.

Summary

While medical education had heretofore emphasized the training of specialists, the current effort is to educate more general practitioners. This change has been accompanied by abandoning the old lecture style education for a more "hands-on" education permitting students to be active rather than mere passive receivers of information. The introduction of the social and behavioral sciences into the medical school curriculum is the consequence of a more caring attitude by physicians for their patients than was the case when doctors concerned themselves only with the biochemical aspects of an illness.

Many of these changes can be traced to the concern for cost-containment promoted by managed care organizations who seek to prevent illness. Hence a problem based education and means of assessment have developed in medical schools and in teaching hospitals even as government, health maintenance organizations and insurance companies seem to have converted the medical profession into a business. The consequences of these many changes in the medical profession for the profession itself and the expectations of the American public are the subject of our next chapter. That will concern itself not only with the daily activities of American physicians but also with some portraits of the individuals who have devoted themselves to healing the sick and who have sworn with Hippocrates "by Apollo the physician, by Aesculapius, by Hygeia and all the gods and goddesses..........I will keep this oath and stipulation."[67]

NOTES

[1]Abraham Flexner, *Medical Education: A Comparative Study*, New York, Macmillan, 1925 p. 86.
[2]State University of New York - University at Buffalo, *Graduate Professional Class Schedule*, Buffalo, New York, Fall 1998, pp. 66-67.
[3]Kathryn M. Hunter, "Eating the Curriculum," *Academic Medicine*, Vol.72, No. 3, March 1997, p. 169.
[4]Steven R. Daugherty, "Learning, Satisfaction and Mistreatment During Medical Internship," *Journal of the American Medical Association*, Vol.279, No. 15, April 15, 1998, pp. 1194-1199.
[5]Michael D. Lemonick, "The Tumor War," in *Heroes of Medicine*, Edward L. Jamieson and Barrett Seman, Eds. New York, Time Special Issue, Vol. 150, No. 19, Fall 1997, pp. 46-48.
[6]John Z. Ayanian, "The Prospect of Sweeping Reform in Graduate Medical Education," *The Milbank Quarterly*, Vol. 72, No. 4, December 1994, p. 705.
[7]Peter J. Blizzard, "International Standards in Medical Education or National Standards/Primary Health Care-Which Direction?" *Social Science and Medicine*, Vol. 33, No. 10, 1991, pp. 1168-1169.
[8]*Ibid.*, p. 706.
[9]J.A. Kindig, J.M. Cultice and F. Mullan, "The Elusive Generalist Physician: Can We Reach a 50% Goal?" *Journal of the American Medical Assoication*, Vol. 270, 1993, pp. 1069-1073.
[10]S.M. McLeod and H.N. McCullough, "Social Science Education as a Component of Medical Training," *Social Science and Medicine*, Vol.39, No. 9, 1994, p. 1367.
[11]Andrew G. Wallace, "Educating Tomorrow's Doctors: The Thing That Really Matters Is that We Care," *Academic Medicine*, Vol.72, No. 4, April 1997, pp. 253-258.
[12]*Ibid.*, p. 1368.
[13]*Ibid*, p. 1371.
[14]K.B. Wells, "The behavioral sciences in medical education and practice." *Journal of the American Medical Association*, Vol.60, 1985, pp. 493-495.
[15]Stanley Muller, "Physicians for the Twenty- First Century: Report of the Project Panel on the General Professional Education of the Physician and College Preparation for Medicine," *Journal of Medical Education*, Vol. 59, Part 2, 1984.

[16]L.A. Falk, B. Page and W. Vesper, "Human values and medical education: From the perspective of health care delivery," *Journal of Medical Education,* Vol. 48, 1973, pp. 152-157.

[17]Bernice A. Pescosolido, "Teaching Medical Sociology through Film: Theoretical Perspectives and Practical Tools," *Teaching Sociology,* Vol. 18, No. 3, July 1990, p. 340.

[18]Gerard J. Hunt and Jeffrey Sobal, "Teaching Medical Sociology in Medical Schools," *Teaching Sociology,* Vol. 18, No. 3, July 1990, p. 320.

[19]Shimon M. Glick, "The teaching of medical ethics to medical students," *Journal of medical ethics.* Vol. 20, No. 4, December 1994, p. 241.

[20]*Ibid.,* p. 243.

[21]Malcolm Parker, "Autonomy, problem-based learning, and the teaching of medical ethics," *Journal of Medical Ethics,* Vol.21, No. 5, October 1995, pp. 305-310.

[22]Rivka-Grundstein Amado, "Values education: a new direction for medical education," *Journal of Medical Ethics,* Vol.21, No. 3, June 1995, pp. 174-178.

[23]H.S. Miles, "Informed demands for non-beneficial medical treatment." *The New England Journal of Medicine,"* Vol. 325, 1991, pp. 512-515.

[24]Raanon Gillon, "Case studies and medical education," *Journal of Medical Ethics,* Vol.22, No. 1, February 1996, pp. 3-4.

[25]Daniel P. Sulmasy and Eric S. Marx, " Ethics education for medical house officers: long term improvements in knowledge and confidence," *Journal of Medical Ethics,* Vol. 23, 1997, pp. 88-92.

[26]H.H. Evans and C.A. Fergason, "Medical unversities and academic health centers: lessons of history," *Academic Medicine,* Vol. 71, 1996, pp. 1141-1142.

[27]Emily Friedman, "Managed Care and Medical Education: Hard Cases and Hard Choices," *Academic Medicine,* Vol. 72, No. 5, May 1997, p. 327.

[28]*Ibid,* p. 327.

[29]G. Annas   "Baby Fae: the 'anything goes' school of human experimentation" in G. Annas , *Judging Medicine,* Clifton, N.J., Humana Press, 1988.

[30] Gert H. Brieger, "Why the University-based Medical School Should Survive: A Histroical Perspective"
Academic Medicine, Vol 72, No.5, May 1997, pp.363-364.

[31]Carol L. Elam, Edwin D. Taylor and E. Nelson Strother, Jr., "Preparing for Medical School and the Medical Profession: Advice to

Advisors" *National Academic Advising Association Journal,* Vol. 16, No. 2, Fall 1996 p. 34.

[32]Henry Heimlich, "Advances in Medical Education," *Resource Video,* Physicians Committee for Responsible Medicine, 1997.

[33]Susan M. Harmon and Jerry B. Vannatta, "Senior medical students learn as simulated patients," *Medical Teacher,* Vol. 17, No. 1, March 1995, p. 31.

[34]David B. Swanson, Geoffrey R. Norman and Robert L. Linn, "Performance Based Assessment: Lessons from the Health Professions," *Educational Researcher,* Vol.24, No.5, June-July 1995, p. 6.

[35]Elam, *op.cit.* p. 35.

[36]Carol C. Nadelson, "Medical Education: A Commentary on Historical and Contemporary Issues," *American Journal of Psychiatry,* Vol 153, No. 7, July 1996, Festschrift Supplement, p. 3.

[37]*Ibid.,*p.3.

[38]Ahmed Okasha, "The Future of Medical Education and Teaching: A Psychiatric Perspective," *American Journal of Psychiatry,* Vol 154, No. 6, June 1997, p. 80.

[39]I. Steven Udvarhelyi, Terry Roseborough, Richard Lofgren, Nicole Lurie, and Arnold M. Epstein, "Teaching Status and Resource Use for Patients with Acute Myocardial Infarction: A new look at the indirect costs of graduate medical edducation." *American Journal of Public Health,* Vol 80, No. 9, September 1990, pp. 1099-1100.

[40]Council on Graduate Medical Education, *Fourth Report: Recommendations to Improve Access to Health Care through Physicians Workforce Reform.* Rockville, Md., U.S. Department of Health and Human Services, 1994.

[41] Barbara Barzansky, Harry S. Jonas and Sylvia I. Etzel, "Educational Programs in U.S. Medical Schools, 1997-1998," *Journal of the American Medical Association,* Vol.280, No.9, Septembr 2, 1998, p. 805.

[42]Fitzhugh Mullan, Robert M. Politzer, Sandy Gamlet and Marc L. Rivo, "Balance and Limits: Modeling Graduate Medical Education Reform Based on Recommendations of the Council on Graduate Medical Education," *The Milband Quarterly,* Vol.72, No. 3, September 1993, p. 395.

[43]David Altman and Jordan J. Cohen, "Problems and Promises: The Potential Impact of Graduate Medical Education Reform," *The Milbank Quarterly,* Vol. 72, No. 4, December 1994, pp. 719-722.

[44]E. Ginzburg, M. Ostrow and A.B.Durka, "*The Economics of Medical Education,* New York, Josiah Macy Foundation, 1993; L.S. Valberg,

M.A. Gonyea, D.G. Sinclair and J. Wade, *Planning the Future Academic Medical Centre.* Ottawa, Canadian Medical Association, 1994. Also see: The Association of American Medical Colleges, *American Medical School Admission Requirements, 49th Edition,* Washington, D.C., 1998, p. 52.

[45]Robert F. Jones and David Korn, "On the Cost of Educating a Medical Student," *Academic Medicine,* Vol. 72, No.3, March 1997, pp. 201-208.

[46]Ibid., p. 207.

[47]Edward H,. O'Neill, "Academic Health Centers Must Begin Reforms Now," *The New York Times,* Vol. 40, September 8m, 1993, p. A 48.

[48]Scott Jaschik, "Health - Care Changes Would Transform Medical-School Financing and Curricula," *The New York Times,* Vol 40, September 29, 1993, p. A24.

[49]Katherine S. Mangan, "Some Medical and Nursing Schools Declare a Truce and Start to Work Together," *The Chronicle of Higher Eduction,* Vol. XLIV, #17, December 19, 1997, p. 8.

[50]Robert Q. Marston and R. M. Jones, *The Science of Medical Practice: Medical Practice in Transition,* Princeton, The Robert Wood Johnson Foundation, July 1992.

[51]Penny Singer, "Grant Helps to Ready Primary Care Doctors," *The New York Times,* Vol. XIV, WC p. 10.

[52]Richard Weizel, "A Test of Mettle in a Real-Life E.R.," *The New York Times,* July 27, 1997, Sec.13, p8.

[53]David N. Aspy, Cheryl B. Aspy and Patricia M. Quinby, "What Doctors Can Teach Teachers about Problem-Based Learning," *Educational Leadership,* Vol. 50m No.7, April 1993, p. 22.

[54]Larissa Mac Farquhar, "Andrew Weil, Shaman, M.D.," *The New York Times Magazine,* August 24, 1997, pp.30-31.

[55]Simmons, P. and Cavanaugh, S., "Relationships among childhood parental care, professional school climate and nursing student caring ability," *Journal of Professional Nursing,* Vol. 12, 1996, pp. 373-381.

[56]Joseph A. Barney, Janet Fredericks, Marcel Fredericks and Patricia Robinson, "Internalization of Professional Attitudes of Physicians: Implications for Health Care," *Education,* Vol. 117, No. 4, Summer 1997, pp. 530-539.

[57] Eric J. Cassell, "A Dilemma for Medical Education Reform: Form versus Content," *The Milbank Quarterly,* Vol. 72, No.4, December 1994, p.716.

[58] David Snadden and Donald Mowat, "Community-based curriculum development: what does it really mean?" *Medcial Teacher,* Vol. 17, No.3, September 1995, pp. 298-302.

[59] Carl W.R. Onion and Peter D. Slade, "Depth of information processing and memory facts," *Medical Teacher*, Vol. 17,No.3, 1995, p. 307.

[60] Paulette Walker Campbell, "U.S. Will Pay Teaching Hospitals to Reduce the Number of Residents They Train," *The Chronicle of Higher Education*, Vol. XLIV, Number 2, September 5, 1997, p. A 51.

[61] Kurt Eichenwald, "Some in Congress Seek to Curb Inquiry Into Fraudulent Billing by Teaching Hospitals," *The New York Times*, Thursday, July 3, 1997, p. A 14.

[62] Jeffrey Selingo, "Suit Seeks to Halt Audits of Teaching Hospitals," *The Chronicle of Higher Education*, Vol. 44, November 7, 1997, p. A 34.

[63] Paulette Walker Campbell, "Senators Are Dubious of House Plan to Suspend Audits of Teaching Hospitals," *The Chronicle of Higher Education*, Vol. XLIV, No.10, October 31, 1997, p. A45.

[64] Brad Burg, "What Jobs are out there now? Which jobs will there be tomorrow?" *Medical Economics*, September 25, 1995, pp. 171-174.

[65] *Ibid.*, p. 173.

[66] Elisabeth Rosenthal, "Young Doctors Find Specialist Jobs Hard to Get," *The New York Times*, April 15, 1995, Sec. I, p. 1

[67] The Hippocratic Oath.

Chapter IV

The Practice of Medicine - The Physician in Action

I

In 1998 the American Medical Association published a statistical summary concerning the professional characteristics of American physicians. In that year, 48% of the 737,764 American physicians were younger than 45 years of age. 35.4% of doctors were then more than 45 years old but had not reached age 65. The oldest doctors, aged 65 or more numbered 122, 469 or 16.6 percent of physician manpower in the country.

At that time the race and ethnicity of 64% of physicians was known to the American Medical Association who identified 79.5% as white. 81.4% of men and 71.3% of women belonged to that group. Evidently, more non-white women than non-white men had entered medicine at that time. Black physicians were then 2.9% of all physicians and 4.6% were Hispanic. Another 10.4% were of Asian/Oriental heritage and 2.6% not in any of the categories listed. Twenty one percent of physicians were female in 1997-98. (154,930). Women as well as men were more often engaged in internal medicine than in any other specialty. This was true of 18% of women and 21% of men. Pediatrics, or the care of children, occupied 15% of female doctors but only 9 percent of male doctors. This means that pediatrics ranks second in frequency of interest among women physicians and fourth among men. Family practice ranked second among male doctors and third among female doctors. The greatest discrepancy between the sexes concerning medical practice is however visible in the area of surgery. General surgery is the third choice in frequency among men but ranks tenth among women. There are several specialties, such as cardiovascular diseases which ranks ninth among men but is practiced so infrequently by women that it does not appear on a chart listing the twelve most frequently practiced medical specialties.

In 1998 the ratio of physicians to the total population was 278, up from 1960 when there were 142 physicians for every 100,000 in the American population. It is remarkable that the proportion of inactive physicians has increased from 5.9% to 9.8% in the years since 1970.[1]

A review of the income of physicians reveals that as late as 1998 the average income of women family practitioners was $116,147 or 86% of male family practitioner's average income. Male internists earned an average of $140,000 as of February 1998 while women internists earned only $119,998 or 86% of male income in that specialty. An even greater gender discrepancy in earnings exists in the field of ophthalmology. Here female doctors earned an average of $162,254 in 1997-98. That is only 73% of male earnings in ophthalmology which averaged at that time $221,663.-.A similar discrepancy is found in neurology where female earnings were an average of $118,171 or 73% of male earnings which were, on the average, $161,893. The highest female earning as a proportion of male earnings in all of medicine is earned by female psychiatrists. Women in that specialty earn an average of $125,600 or 94% of male earnings of $133,710.-. Some other earnings of medical specialists are: male orthopedic surgeon $317,201, female orthopedic surgeon $227,443 or 72% of male income; male diagnostic radiologist, $293,910, female diagnostic radiologist, $234,820; male anesthesiologist $248,235, female anesthesiologist $195,930; male general surgeon, $227,671; female general surgeon, $205,191 or 90% of male income; male obstetrician-gynecologist, $233,941, female obstetrician-gynecologist $200,380; male dermatologist,$190,627, female dermatologist, $160,404 and male pediatrician, $136,200, female pediatrician, $118,955. In sum, women doctors earn about 85% of the earnings of men in the profession. In general, in 1998 American women earned 76% of male income.[2]

The principal reason for this income disparity lies in the need of women to concern themselves with the supervision of children and their households. Evidently, women work shorter hours than men in order to accommodate these responsibilities. Furthermore, women doctors are younger than male doctors because the entrance of women into the medical profession in large numbers is a recent development. Thus, only 15% of male physicians were under age 35 on December 31, 1995. On that same date, 31% of female physicians were under age 35. Similarly, only 27% of male doctors were aged 35-44 at a time when 38% of female doctors had attained that age. However, among those over 55 and over 65, male - female ratios were the reverse. Male doctors over 55 constituted 15.2% of all male doctors and those over age 65 were 19.5% of all male doctors. Only 6.5% of female doctors were older than 55 at the end of 1995. This plainly indicates that the majority of women in medicine have not practiced long enough to reach the highest salaries earned by men. We can therefore anticipate at least some closing of the gender gap in the area of compensation when more women will have gained more experience in the next decade. (1999-2008).[3]

These professional characteristics should of course be augmented by a look at the social characteristics of physicians. Such information is not readily available although Fredericks and Mundy published the results of a ten years study of such characteristics in 1976. This revealed that in that study the occupations of the fathers of doctors were primarily semi-professional and technical. 17 % of doctors had fathers who were also doctors while 25% were from homes in which at least one parent was either a doctor, a lawyer an engineer or a member of another profession.[4]

According to that study physicians believe that knowledge of a technical kind is most important. The ability to establish rapport with patients, regardless of social class background, is held as next important to technical knowledge. However, doctors with an upper class background were consistent in their view that race, ethnicity, education, religion and social class were not important even while doctors from a middle class and poor background found these characteristics to be very important. Despite the fact that the majority of doctors come from relatively comfortable families, most of them had to depend on their wives' income, on loans and on "externships" at local hospitals to finance their way through medical school. Other findings concerning the impact of social class on physicians were that doctors looked upon the medical profession as having the highest prestige rating of any occupation in the United States. This is of course entirely true as evident from the inspection of any Occupational Prestige Scale as published by the General Social Surveys of the National Opinion Research Center at intervals reaching into the 1990's. While the second place in these surveys of occupational prestige has sometimes resulted in a tie shared by professors and lawyers, physician has always been first by a considerable distance from the prestige of the second rated occupations. Doctors have generally held a prestige score of 86 while lawyers and professors have achieved a prestige score of only 74 or 75 on a scale giving shoe shiners an occupational prestige score of nine.[5]

In view of the considerable influence money and income have on social prestige in this country it is interesting to compare the salaries paid executives of health maintenance organizations to those of doctors already reviewed. One such example is the compensation paid the chief executive officers of three Health Maintenance Organizations in Buffalo, N.Y. in 1996. The CEO of Independent Health in 1996 in Buffalo, N.Y. was paid $515,336; the CEO of Community Blue, $213,695 and the CEO of Health CarePlan/Choice Care, $366,557. [6]

II

Nothing could be further from the truth than the view that the medical profession has betrayed its oath. On the contrary. That betrayal was conducted from the outside and forced upon American physicians by circumstances they did not create. If that is true than we would be encouraged to seek elsewhere the cause of the current dilemma facing patients and practitioners alike at the end of this century. However, as we have already seen in our initial overview in this book, the cause of all the discomfort concerning health delivery at the end of the 20th century lies in the scientific revolution and not in the machinations of any group of ill intentioned manipulators, be they insurance executives, doctors, politicians or advocates of "patients' rights."

It is therefore the thesis of this book that culture lag in the form of rapid advances in medical research and slow advances in the reorganization of health delivery is the underlying cause of the general misgivings, complaints and disputes which influence current conditions in the medical profession. Culture lag is a sociological concept relating to social change. Accordingly, "inconsistencies in a cultural system, especially in the relationship between technology and non-material culture" are the nature of culture lag. An excellent example of culture lag is the ability of the medical profession to keep patients alive by means of organ transplants, heart pumps and artificial respirators without knowing what the responsibilities of family members and doctors are towards such patients. [7]

This ethical dilemma did not exist before the advent of the most recent methods of insuring bodily survival for the very ill and the very old. Therefore, medical ethics has become an even more important issue than it had always been. Because the practice of medicine is described as a profession it is tempting to relegate that practice into the same categories which apply to others trained in a form of specialized knowledge. Thus, airplane pilots, accountants, systems analysts and computer programmers and a host of other providers of occupational services like to call themselves a profession. The practice of medicine, however, relies on more than only technical knowledge. Medical practice involves giving a bodily service to others. That service focuses on the welfare of the recipient and therefore is permitted only those who have achieved a medical education and have demonstrated their competency by means of examination and graduation and licensing. In addition, however, ethical conduct concerning self-advertisement, fee demands, respect for patients, confidentiality and absolute honestly are a basic demand which physicians have at all times supported. That support has come from professional organizations such as certifying boards who have also functioned as a quasi border police providing protection from invasion of the medical profession by unqualified outsiders. Because heretofore only licensed members of the medical profession were allowed to deliver any of the procedures included in the corpus of medical knowledge, it was relatively easy to protect doctors from competition and therefore it was also a simple task to insure the ethical standards demanded of the profession. The great dilemma that faces doctors now is that their income and prestige are no longer assured. The profession has lost its monopoly on servicing the patient even as nurses, chiropractors, medical technicians, physician's assistants and a host of others lay claim to medical expertise and compete for income and social standing with doctors.

Ethics, however, constitutes a significant part of what it means to be a professional and it is in this area that doctors incur an obligation unknown elsewhere. That obligation is trust. While in commercial transactions the buyer can inspect or test the product he is about to buy this is not true of patients. Patients have to rely on the competence and integrity of their doctor who, unlike commercial providers, cannot guarantee the outcome of treatment no matter how diligent he may be. Furthermore, individualism has a great deal of influence on the doctor-patient relationship. The manner, attitude, skill and experience of a doctor is always a matter of personal background with direct and serious implications for the patient. It is, however, precisely this individual pattern which distinguishes the medical profession from other occupations not only because patients have to deal with the doctor's particular personality but also because their decisions can make the difference between life and death. That is certainly not the case in any other profession.[8]

Death is of course as much hidden from the American public and those living in other technological societies as is birth. Because almost all American deaths occur in hospitals and not at home few Americans are prepared to witness death and to deal with it either on the part of others or themselves. Obviously, medical students on first becoming exposed to suffering and dying view this process with compassion and are often offended at the equanimity of veteran doctors concerning death. Since it is however essential that doctors not become emotionally involved with patients if the patient is to benefit from the doctor's competence, the medical student becomes desensitized to death as he proceeds into the profession of medicine. Coombs reports that a number of mechanisms are used by doctors to manage their feelings and make the death experience more tolerable. One such method is to objectify the treatment of the sick and dying and thereby avoid the tension impending death arouses. This is also true of using humor. There are also those doctors who try to keep away from dying patients because they cannot tolerate death. This means that some doctors ignore the patient because of their own fear. There are also some hospital procedures which make it easier for doctors to cope with death. For example, it is expected of every available physician in a hospital to rush to a room designated as "code red" to participate in a "last ditch" effort to save the patient. Thereafter, all doctors responsible for the patient discuss his "case" after his death to discover what might have been done to prevent death. All this helps doctors live with the trauma that the death of a patient causes and with the additional anxiety that the death of others arouses in those who know that when "the bell tolls it tolls for thee." No doubt, there are some doctors who believe that they can defeat death at every turn as that is their mission in life. However, as the years progress older doctors cannot fail but recognize that the "god complex" is unrealistic and that they cannot save everyone.[9]

The Judicial Council of the American Medical Association has summarized the responsibilities of physicians relative to the terminally ill. Their statement holds that while the social commitment of the physician is to prolong life and relieve suffering one of these obligations may conflict with the other. Therefore the AMA advises that "Where the observance of one conflicts with the other, the physician, patient, and/or family of the patient have discretion to resolve the conflict." This means that a physician may not intentionally cause death but that he can permit a terminally ill patient to die by withholding treatment.[10]

It is therefore important for the dying and those they leave behind that doctors, social workers and psychologists learn a means by which death can be accepted and the pain of the dying eased. One such method is called "Guided Imagery" as practiced by Tess Taft a Syracuse, N.Y. social worker. Accordingly Taft seeks to find a "guide" to help the dying patient in her journey to death. This consists of imagining a beautiful place in which her ancestors are waiting for her. Using "palliative and comfort care" the dying can be helped by having their families surround them either at home or in the hospital. It is recommended that the family and friends ask the dying person if he is in pain. It is important that they believe the dying and it is important to do something to alleviate such pain. This can generally be done only by a professional. However, additional care consists of hugging one's loved ones, and to have photographs taken. Many dying patients are also helped by reaching for the sacred. Once the dying person has entered a coma, *Guided Imagery* is used to permit each family member to recall a special story about the loved one who has just died. [11]

Added to the burden of doctors concerning the inevitability of death is the most recent effort on the part of some physicians to induce death among those hoping to die soon. These are patients who seek to benefit from assisted suicide, a practice approved by the voters in Oregon in 1994 and upheld by the U.S. Supreme Court on June 26, 1998. Because politicians and others are uncomfortable with permitting assisted suicide in their state the alternative of failing to prosecute or convict doctors who do so has become the preferred choice of prosecutors. In that connection it is useful to review the survey on the subject of doctor assisted suicide conducted by the New England Journal of Medicine in 1994. That survey shows that a large number of doctors say that they cannot decide whether a patient has less than six months to live, a decision demanded by the Oregon law. In addition to this dilemma other problems arise in connection with doctor assisted suicide. One of these problems is the possibility that some old patients seek to commit suicide, not because of their physical condition, but because they fear becoming a burden on their families. There is also no certainty that someone is "terminally ill." All of this makes the campaign of Dr. Jack Kevorkian in favor of doctor assisted suicide so controversial. Even as some are adamantly opposed to doctor assisted suicide the federal appeals court in San Francisco ruled that there is a constitutional right to die. The sum of these considerations concerning death and dying is that death and dying confronts every doctor with an ethical dilemma which no one individual may want to decide alone. Therefore, collegiate groups help doctors deal with that and other ethical issues in their practice. [12]

Because these various collegiate bodies which seek to regulate the profession of medicine have only limited legal power they depend very much on the collaboration of the members of the medical profession. Therefore these organizations cannot enforce altruism nor abolish the interest in economic advantage and competition which must of necessity invade the profession. This then is the paradox which exists in the medical profession in end-of-the-century America. Ethics are considered of the greatest importance by the profession but there is no one available to enforce ethics. [13]

One reason for this inability to enforce ethics is that ethics or moral philosophy are areas of opinion which cannot be stated with scientific certainty. Nevertheless, the German philosopher Immanuel Kant (1724-1804) closed the door to most speculation concerning ethical conduct by the publication of his dictum: "So act as to treat humanity, whether in thine own person or in that of any other, in every case as an end withal, never as a means only." This statement is known in the English language as Kant's categorical imperative distinguished from his hypothetical imperative to the effect that there are aspects of ethics or the good which are contingent on our desires. For example, we may work hard at our occupation because we seek income and wealth. Hard work may therefore be viewed as good and ethical as long as we value the outcome. We can, however, abandon the objective and be as lazy as we like. The categorical imperative, however, is a dogma which prohibits the conversion of people into things and the motivation to gain material advantage for oneself at the expense of the dignity of man. The categorical imperative further demands that all human beings shall be treated as equals and that the actions of each person shall at once become the law for the entire community in which the actor lives. Hence the categorical imperative further admonishes that we should "act only on that fundamental rule of conduct which you can at the same time want to become a universal law."[14]

It is of course unrealistic to believe that physicians will act only on the basis of the categorical imperative. The hypothetical imperative intrudes at once if we consider that a doctor may well give a patient a treatment that prevents the family from suing him even if that treatment is not really needed to cure the patient.

Campbell, Gillet and Jones have listed four leading maxims as the "cornerstones of medical ethical thinking and behavior." These are that all medical decisions and actions should be guided by the intention to do good and no harm. That of course is the core of the Hippocratic oath. Further, Campbell, Gillet and Jones propose that respect for the autonomy of the patient be always observed. This refers to the patient's right to choose. Third, these ethicists hold that medical services must be provided with justice. They mean by "justice" the equal distribution of medical services to the poor and the rich without respect to religion, race, ethnicity, sex etc. The fact is, of course, that the rich live longer than the poor precisely because medical help is far more and better available to those who can pay a lot than those who cannot pay at all. Finally, these three authors view it as an ethical obligation for practitioners to dispense their services with the least waste of time and for no more money than is necessary.[15]

Trust in the doctors expertise, skill and ethics mean that patients must, in any doctor-patient encounter, surrender part of their autonomy to the physician. This is always difficult and sometimes galling to the patient who is normally accustomed to maintaining an adult status and unaccustomed to being infantilized. A common example of the effort of medical personnel to infantilize the patient and thereby insure a "superior" status for themselves is the practice of calling a patient by his first name. Other methods are the distribution of open hospital gowns which reveal the patient's backside, addressing the patient as "we" and speaking about the patient to his relatives in his presence without addressing him. That kind of conduct is principally reserved for old people who constitute about one half of the patients seen in hospitals and doctors offices.[16]

Ethics concerning patients are only one dimension of the ethical concerns of the medical profession. The other dimension is the conduct doctors owe one another. Because it was heretofore assumed that physicians would act according to ethical principles it is surprising to outsiders and often to physicians themselves that unethical and even immoral conduct exists among them. However, as competition for income and social standing increase the number of unethical manipulations within the profession also increase. Payment for "professional services rendered" is, and should be, an important motivation for any form of service and is certainly no less so for the profession of medicine.

At the end of this century (1999), that payment is derived mostly from the U.S. federal government. In fact, the taxpayer is the largest single payer in the health care system. Unlike most European countries and Canada, the United States has not given government the power to organize the delivery and maintain the quality of medical care. Instead, American physicians are, at least theoretically, independent professionals. Traditionally, physicians in America have worked on a fee-for-service basis and have cherished the "doctor-patient" relationship which has been sanctified in such legends as "Marcus Welby, M.D." and "Dr. Kildare." Despite these legends, however, the American doctor is now almost entirely dependent for his income on group medical prepayment plans including Medicare. Because the average age of Americans is increasing and the old are receiving more health care and also more expensive services the cost of Medicare will grow faster in the 21st century than the gross domestic product. In view of the support which government, i.e., the taxpayer must give these programs the shift from private fee-for-service arrangements to the present health maintenance system will be and already is a major $760 billion annual expenditure in the federal budget[17].

This shift of the cost of medical services from the private to the public sector did not come about suddenly nor without antecedent events. In fact, the early 1930's saw the first proposals for risk-sharing plans as a means of insuring those who were suddenly confronted by illness if not catastrophe. Thus it came about that the staff of the Committee on Economic Security, which developed the background leading to the Social Security Act of 1935, prepared a statement on national health insurance at that time. That committee proposed a scheme which underlies all insurance plans. That scheme is, that risk can be pooled so that "each family carries an average rather than an uncertain risk." [18]

Both in 1950 and in 1960 the U.S. government once more acted in behalf of those who could not otherwise afford health care. In 1950 the federal government allowed state and local governments to make payments to private insurance companies on behalf of welfare recipients. In 1960, the government, under the Kerr-Mills bill made federal grants to the states to pay for medical care to the old on welfare. This was followed by the Medicare program in 1965. Accordingly, the government pays the medical bills of the old and private insurance companies provide health insurance for everyone else not on welfare. Because the costs of Medicare kept rising Congress passed the Health Maintenance Organization Act in 1973 which was designed to forestall expensive care by limiting the frequency and length of hospitalization. Since however efficiency and reduced quality of care both cut costs it has been impossible so far to discover whether savings are the consequence of the first or the second alternative. We can test which of these alternatives is the most defensible by recalling that the federal government also supports the Medicaid program. That program is designed to help the indigent receive medical treatment. It is therefore of interest to note that Medicaid pays, on the average, only 47% of private fees or 73 percent of Medicare fees. Consequently only 34 percent of physicians participate fully in the Medicaid system, 26 percent do not participate at all and 40% participate occasionally.

Obviously, then, the profit motive is a major consideration in providing health care so that it is reasonable to conclude that the same motive applies to Medicare. Hence the poor receive less care than the wealthy so that we can conclude with confidence that the reason for the savings induced by the Health Maintenance Organization Act is not efficiency but a lesser level of care.[19] Evidently, then, physicians are profit maximizers. If the government lowers the reimbursement for the poor, physicians will not raise prices for privately insured patients but will instead see fewer of the poor. [20] In 1995 the Physician Payment Review Commission reported that an increasing number of states had promoted managed care for Medicaid patients because of real or perceived inefficiencies. It is therefore reasonable to expect that increases in fees would bring more physicians into the Medicaid program. This, it has been argued, would shift the site of the patients treatment from hospital emergency rooms and outpatient departments to physician's offices, thus offsetting the higher fees paid to physicians. Gruber *et al* investigated this proposition. In view of a substantial increase in doctor's fees in Tennessee they found that there were indeed physician participation increases. They also found that there was at that time a drop in hospital admissions. However, Gruber *et al* found little or no drop in outpatient or emergency room use. However, they were unable to attribute this drop to the new physician fee policy. It is of course possible that physicians' offices are more suitable for the kind of treatment which is usually administered in emergency rooms and outpatient clinics.[21]

If that is the case, then it would be of interest to know whether the poor have as much access to physicians offices as to out-patient departments. This issue has been studied by Hogan *et al* who found that "generally, it takes a beneficiary in a Medicare managed care plan longer to schedule an appointment with a physician (than) with the outpatient department. Furthermore, beneficiaries of Medicaid are far more likely to use public transportation to get to their doctor than is true of those not on Medicare. Waiting periods for Medicaid beneficiaries are generally longer for those who do not have supplemental private insurance than is true of those who have only Medicare. Those entitled to both Medicaid and Medicare experience longer waits in doctors' offices than any other group of insured beneficiaries.[22]

III

Waiting in doctors' offices is now commonplace (1999). There was a time, however, when physicians made house calls, a practice which had been almost abandoned by the end of the 1960's. That small group of patients who still receive house calls are almost all very old and very sick. According to a study published in 1993, fewer than one percent of American patients received a house call in 1997. This is true despite the fact that Medicare pays about $20.00 more for a house call than for an office visit. Several reasons for so great a decline in that time honored practice may be listed. First among these, however, is the doctor's reliance on technology which they cannot carry in their black bags. Particularly, younger doctors are trained to rely more heavily on laboratory medical tests than was true of the older generation. There are those, however, who argue that a doctor who makes a house call can gain a more complete picture of the patient "by seeing ....whether the person has food in the refrigerator or a ramp up the front steps." No doubt such observations would be most beneficial to the patient if the application of medical producers were still related to treating the "whole person." That however, is hardly the case in 1999. Instead, physicians had largely lost their autonomy at the end of the 20th century and have instead become middle-men between patients and insurance companies and health maintenance organizations.[23]

Traditionally, the concept of professional autonomy has referred to the right of professional self direction. Among physicians this has meant autonomy over the content of their medical practice. However, because of the aforementioned pressure by insurance companies to control costs at any price the profession of medicine has recently adopted a set of "clinical guidelines" designed to improve the quality of medical care and to ultimately preserve some autonomy over treatment even though these guidelines diminish that autonomy somewhat. Elliott Freidson, whose book The Profession of Medicine was a pioneer study in this area argued in 1994 that "professionalism is being reborn in a hierarchical form in which everyday practitioners become subject to the control of professional elites."[24]

These professional "elites" are often professional organizations who have declared themselves willing to deal with insurance companies demands in order to preserve at least a modicum of autonomy. However, many doctors feel themselves and their patients betrayed by insurance companies intervention leading to a decline in doctors' morale so severe that some doctors have given up medical practice altogether rather than be subject to these strictures. [25]

A recent study, conducted by the Medstat Group and JD Power and Associates and New England Medical Center discovered that 7 in 10 doctors are opposed to managed care. More than 46% of doctors contacted in that study said they often think about leaving clinical practice. The researchers asked the opinion of 30,000 doctors in more than 150 health plans and found that 55% would leave a health plan because of quality of care issues, one half would leave a health plan because of the manner in which the plan's employees treat doctors, 41% would leave because of the administrative requirements of health plans and 40% would leave because of the reimbursement policies of health plans. Other complaints concern getting help with denied claims appeals, paperwork, getting paid, and needing authorization from health plans and insurance companies for tests, procedures, referrals, hospital stays, and admission.[26]

In view of the manner in which health maintenance organizations and insurance companies have dealt with doctors, some doctors have organized labor unions and other organizations charged with the responsibility to defend doctors against the encroachments of the governments and the insurance industry. One such effort is under way in New Jersey where Dr. Anthony Tonzola has organized a union of surgeons seeking to bargain collectively with the insurance companies active in that state. Dr. Fred Nahas is leading a group of about 200 doctors, also in New Jersey, who seek to be represented by the United Food and Commercial Workers Union. These doctors want to be represented in negotiations with AmeriHealth, a local HMO whom Dr. Nahas accuses of practicing medicine without a license. The House of Delegates of the American Medical Association has also adopted a resolution calling on doctors to engage in collective bargaining. Another group, called The Ad Hoc Committee to Defend Health Care of Cambridge, Mass. charges that "canons of commerce are displacing dictates of healing, trampling our profession's most sacred values."[27]

Likewise, in early 1999, the Service Employees International Union pledged to spend $1 million to organize physicians. Since 35,000 doctors were already organized at that time it appeared that the money would be well spent.

"I can see the time coming when we're not simply independent business owners ......but just workers," said Dr. Lawrence Koning of Corona, California, and added: "Doctors are being fired, they are being cut back, they are told what to do and how much to make .....we have no power." Dr. Koning is a member of the Union of American Physicians and Dentists. [28]

Other efforts at collective bargaining for physicians have succeeded in New York City where the United Salaried Physicians and Dentists have organized several hundred members and where the Doctors Council of New York represents hundreds of attending physicians employed by city agencies, hospitals and clinics. Similarly, unions and associations of doctors have developed in Florida, Arizona and the District of Columbia.

For many years, the National Labor Relations Board has interpreted labor law in the Untied States to prohibit doctors from organizing unless they are employees of hospitals, clinics or health care plans. Some 20,000 doctors have done so. However, doctors who work independently now argue that they are in effect, employees of the managed care companies who dictate everything from treatment and specialists to the fees doctors can charge. According to the doctors, "We're held hostage by these companies. They restrict care that doctors see as necessary.....and then say:' If you don't agree, you won't get any patients because we control all the patients.'"

This is countered by the insurance companies who claim that doctors seek to unionize to force health care plans to pay them more and drive costs higher than the health care plans now allow. [29]

This dispute leads to the conclusion that at least some physicians are facing the facts of late-century medical practice and recognize that medicine is now practiced more as a salaried trade and less as a profession. This has become true because health maintenance organizations routinely interfere in the decision making function of doctors who have always prided themselves on making decisions strictly on a scientific basis. [30]

It is of course possible to dispute the claim of doctors that medical decision making is based only on medical knowledge and scientific understanding. In fact, a number of non-medical factors have always influenced medical decision making. Surely some of these factors include the age, sex, race, ethnicity and kind of health insurance of the patient. In addition, personality, individual assertiveness and the physical appearance of a patient make a difference in the treatment a patient receives. The characteristics of the doctor himself also influence the decisions a doctor will make. For example the sex of the doctor makes a good deal of difference in the way a patient will be treated because patients tend to display different attitudes towards female doctors than male doctors.

Thus, a recent study discovered that 77% of female physicians had experienced sexual harassment during their career. This is an important finding because it is usual to claim that sexual harassment is the product of unequal power relationships in which women, having less power, will be subject to the unwanted advances of powerful men. However, sexual harassment of female doctors by male patients hardly qualifies in that category. Hence, the work by Schneider and Phillips in this regard is significant in that it contradicts the view that power relationships are necessarily associated with such conduct. Schneider and Phillips report that sexual harassment of female physicians can be divided into "generic" harassment of the sort encountered by all women everywhere and doctor/patient harassment which is unique to that relationship. Among "generic" harassment episodes reported to Schneider and Phillips by their respondents are: calling a doctor "girlie;" pinching a doctor's behind; kissing the doctor 'good-bye'; asking the doctor for a date; "looking the doctor 'up and down", or making such remarks as "I don't know how your husband can keep his hands off you."

Sexual harassment which would not normally affect other women is however experienced by doctors. For example, complaining about penile or testicular pain for the sole purpose of having a woman examine their genitals even when the patient had no pain; making remarks about a doctors breasts; making anonymous 'phone calls to the doctor to engage in erotic comments and others. In addition, female doctors often feel threatened by male patients even if no sexual situation is in evidence. Thus some drug addicts will demand drugs or hostile male patients will make female doctors feel vulnerable even if the hostility is not specifically directed against them. This can involve patients who say that in general they hate women or who admit that they have beaten their wives or girlfriends. In sum, it is evident that female medical students would benefit if this issue were discussed and they became the beneficiaries of advice on how to deal with such conduct in light of the need for a doctor to make decisions based on the patient's needs regardless of his behavior. [31]

Sex is of course not the only factor which influences the treatment of patients and the decision making process by the doctor. Age, race, ethnicity, personality and even the setting in which patients are seen are also influential in the decision making process. The evidence for the view that extra-medical factors influence decision making concerning medical conditions has been presented by McKinlay *et al.* Contrary to the belief that doctors act only on the basis of the patients symptoms and the probability that disease is present, these researchers found that "non-medical factors, ranging from the patient's physical appearance to the organizational setting in which medical care is delivered, may have as much influence on medical decisions in some areas as the actual signs and symptoms of disease."[32]

The patient's age can also have a considerable effect on the doctor's diagnosis. It is far more likely that an old patient complaining of chest pain is suspected of having a cardiac problem than would be true of a young patient. Hence physicians have a tendency to over diagnose heart disease in old patients while under diagnosing this disease in younger patients and to even perceive the complaint of chest pain to be psychogenic. In addition, many people, including doctors believe that old people are not amenable to life style changes. Hence, doctors are less likely to tell an old patient than a younger patient to stop drinking or smoking.

These outside influences on the diagnoses doctors make concerning patients are widespread. There is, however, one more outside influence upon the diagnosis made by doctors. That outside influence is managed care, a system of health delivery care presently agitating the entire medical profession and millions of patients who believe that their income and the health of patients is adversely affected by this recent development. [33]

Because of wide-spread dissatisfaction with managed care Congress will undoubtedly seek to meet the objections of its constituents to the perceived or real abuses of which managed care has been accused everywhere. Critics of managed care complain that patients do not have sufficient access to doctors and that patients cannot appeal the unfair decisions of managed care organizations whose sole interest appears to be financial and who are so calloused that patients have died because health maintenance organizations and/or insurance companies would not pay for their needs. As a consequence of these complaints President Clinton has called for a Federal Patient's Bill of Rights and numerous members of Congress have introduced legislation seeking to curb the abuses of insurers.[34]

IV

It is popular, in 1999, to presume that all physicians are adversely affected by the growth of health maintenance organizations in their communities. However, Simon, Dranove and White have shown that the growth of health maintenance organizations does not always have a negative effect on medical practitioners. Instead, their research shows that specialists have suffered a relative decrease in earnings in areas where managed care has grown rapidly and that primary care physicians have increased their income in those same areas. This indicates that managed care is changing the emphasis of American medicine from specialty to primary care.[35]

In 1993, 70% of all American physicians were specialists. Since specialists are more expensive than primary care physicians it is evident that the cost of relying on so many specialists is a good deal greater than reliance on a generalist. Therefore, insurers and employers are making more and more decisions concerning the type and conditions of care received by patients. While in the past patients with generous insurance policies would use specialists without knowing the cost or caring about the cost, insurance companies seek to avoid the use of expensive specialists so as to reduce costs. Therefore, capitation has come into use as yet another method used by managed care organizations to reduce the cost of health care. Capitation is payment for services on a per member per month basis. For example, a "provider" will be paid $4.00 per month per patient for all the managed care organizations patients. These capitation payments are made from a variety of managed care organization's to hospitals, long-term care facilities and physicians. In view of the ever growing managed care in this country it can be expected that capitation will become the principal avenue of payment to so-called "providers", as managed care corporations like to call physicians. It is noteworthy that the ascendancy of the business world over the medical profession is loudly proclaimed by the entrepreneurs of the health delivery industry not only by dictating to doctors what diagnosis they may discern, what treatment they may prescribe and how long they may see a patient, but also by robbing them of their cherished title of "doctor" and calling them "providers" instead. This change in labels is largely the consequence of the entrance of non-physicians into the medical area. Thus, nurses, social workers, lab technicians, physical therapists and a host of others are now engaged in the treatment of patients and are collecting compensation from managed care. These non-doctors also provide some care to patients and so the HMO management lumps M.D.' with all these other occupations into one term, "provider." [36]

In recent years, and earlier, alternative site providers have also developed within the largesse of the health maintenance organization. Among these sites are homecare companies; skilled nursing facilities, extended care facilities, rehabilitation facilities, outpatient clinics, surgical centers, diagnostic centers, orthotic and prosthetic providers, laboratories and treatment centers. [37]

 The use of cheaper primary care physicians is another means by which health maintenance organizations reduce costs. For one, primary care physicians are used as "gatekeepers" whose approval patients need before asking an insurance company to pay for a specialist. Consequently, the employment opportunities and income of primary care physicians has received a boost from the health maintenance organizations. This move to primary care physicians is further supported by the tendency of relatively healthier individuals to enroll in managed care. Furthermore it is evident that as primary care physicians deliver more services the need for specialists declines and a surfeit of specialists results. This means that a decline in specialists' incomes follows the decline in the volume of their patients. Another consequence of the decline in income suffered by some specialists is the tendency of younger practitioners to move to areas where there is a market for their services such as small towns and the open country. [38]

In an exhaustive study of the issue of the growth of managed care and doctor's incomes it was found that the income of generalists went up and that of specialists either grew a lot less than that of generalists or went down. Thus, radiologists, anesthesiologists and pathologists saw a definite decline in their income across the United States between 1985 and 1993 from an annual growth rate of 4.14% in '85 to a rate of only 0.14% in '93. Meanwhile, and during that same period, the annual growth rate in income of primary care physicians went up from 1.20% to 4.78% in one year. Similarly, a true decline in the rate of increase from 3.33% to 2.35% among specialists occurred during the years

1985-1993. As specialists earn less, primary care physicians earn more. Hence, it is debatable whether these changes will finally lead to a true saving in overall medical costs or whether the distribution of income in favor of primary care will lead to no more than a redistribution of the physician supply towards general practice. [39]

A good indication of the size of a physician labor force is the ratio of physicians to the total American population. In 1993 that ratio was 199.6 active physicians for every 100,000 population. This meant that at that time the nation needed to produce 14,644 physicians each year. 10,348 of these physicians were needed to replace losses due to retirement or for other reasons. The additional 4,296 physicians were needed each year in order to keep the ratio of 199.6 to 100 thousand because of population growth. However, during the years 1990-1994 the yearly average of newly certified physicians amounted to 20,655. Therefore, the physician workforce should have been downsized by 6,011 each year to keep the 1993 ratio intact. This also means that only about 18,500 medical students should have been trained during those years when in fact 24,000 were accepted to medical schools each year from 1990-1994. [40]

It is therefore not surprising that the Council of Graduate Medical Education has recommended a twenty percent reduction in the entrance of new doctors into the profession. That recommendation is based on the assumption that approximately 200 physicians for every 100,000 in the population is sufficient to cover the health needs of Americans. Death and retirement ordinarily reduce the physician work force by 2% each year. However, the need for new physicians must also include anticipated population growth. The Bureau of the Census has estimated this anticipated population growth. From this we can conclude that the medical system will need 9,698 new specialists each year until 2020 if we are to maintain the 1993 physician-to-population rate for non-primary care physicians of 133.2 per 100,000 population. 6,853 of these new specialists would be needed to cover exiting doctors and 2,845 will be needed to cover population growth. Therefore, the annual certification of 14,527 reveals that a reduction of 32% in non-primary care physicians is now in order.[41]

To maintain the 66.8 primary care physician to 100,000 population ratio current in 1993 a total of 4,946 new primary care physicians would be needed each year until 2020. Of these 3,495 are needed to replace those who exit from the system each year and 1,451 are needed to cover population growth. However, an annual average of 6,128 new primary care certificates have been issued from 1990 to 1994. Therefore, downsizing by about 19% or 1,182 doctors would be indicated if the 1993 ratio were to be maintained. In sum, eighty percent of the downsizing should occur in the non-primary care area and only 20% in the primary care areas. [42]

An analysis of 29 specialties indicates that some specialties need far more downsizing than others while eight sub-specialties out of 29 did not need any reduction if the present ratio of physicians to population is to be maintained. These eight are: family practice, general practice, pediatrics, allergy, endocrinology, hematology-oncology, urology and radiology.

In addition to the oversupply of new medical graduates in the United States there are some other reasons for this sudden glut of doctors in this country. One of them is the admission of foreign doctors to the United States. This comes about because only about 1,600 of the 2,500 foreign medical students in America at any one time return to their native country. Hospital downsizing in view of managed care has also reduced the number of job opportunities for doctors, particularly pathologists and others who must work for hospitals and cannot practice alone. Changes in state laws regarding the supervision of laboratories by personnel without medical training and the entrance of nurse-practitioners into the health delivery system have also reduced opportunities for doctors. [43] It remains to be seen whether the success of the health maintenance organizations in assigning patients to nurse-practitioners instead of doctors will lead to a yet further degradation of health delivery from nurse-practitioners to practical nurses or personnel trained in only one procedure and otherwise devoid of any education. In the words of Dr. Mark V. Spadaro of Brooklyn, N.Y. "This is the start of the health maintenance organizations (going) down the path of depriving patients of their right to see primary care physicians and the use of less trained nurses in their place which is..........an insidious way for managed care to lower costs and drive up profits." [44]

Despite the belief that market forces and managed care will *ipso facto* correct workforce problems, it appears unlikely that this belief is realistic. The growth in the number of physicians has now continued for fifty years (1999) without reference to the ever growing glut of medical specialists or the need for primary care physicians. This growth has also been immune from the influence of population expansion or its limits. Furthermore, the geographic maldistribution of American doctors has not been influenced by the need to staff rural areas and stay out of big cities.

It is true, of course, that statements from the most important national medical organizations have addressed the issue of the mismatch between supply and demand in the medical arena. However, no national policy has yet been developed to deal with this problem. Such a policy must be based on the need to maintain the current ratio of about 200 physicians for every 100,000 in the population. To do so it will be necessary to reduce the number of physicians overall by 29%, including a reduction of one third in non-primary care specialties and a twenty percent reduction in primary care. Managed care proponents seek even greater reductions in that they call for downsizing by 43% overall. This is to be achieved by reducing non-primary care by 52% and primary care by twenty -nine percent.[45]

To make certain that the mismatch between primary care physician supply and need is overcome and that those in rural areas, who have little access to physicians are supplied in the future several steps need to be taken. These will have to be realistic efforts instead of efforts which rely on "market forces." Such "market forces" have not worked in the past and will not work in the future. Instead, it is recommended Medicare reimbursement policies be changed. Currently, Medicare rewards those hospitals which have a high level of residency. Furthermore, teaching hospitals have sought to increase their revenue by increasing ever more expensive medical treatments and enhanced clinical services. This has also led to the recruitment of medical school faculties in the subspecialties which yield the most profit. Numerous other policies have also created barriers to a reduction of forces in the health delivery system. [46]

Therefore the nation should follow the lead of New York State which has implemented the recent Graduate Medical Education Demonstration, which will reduce New York residencies by 20% to 25% in the next six years, i.e. by 2003. This includes funding medical schools directly so that they will be less dependent on clinical revenues. That would result in a lesser effort to specialize and recruit an excess of specialty faculty to produce ever more unemployable doctors. It will result in a reduction of the recruitment of sub-specialty faculty and therefore reduce the number of graduates in sub-specialties. Furthermore, the uneven payment of primary care physicians as compared to specialists should cease, thereby evening the supply of generalists with specialists Finally, and most important, the country needs to increase funding for the National Health Service Corps which seeks to distribute doctors to traditionally undeserved areas.[47]

Because the rewards of living in cities appear so much more attractive to most doctors than life in rural areas the unequal distribution of doctors in the United States has been an issue since the middle of the 19th century. That unequal distribution results not only from failure to recruit doctors into rural areas but also from the inability of many rural areas to retain doctors already located there. It has been shown that retention depends on integration into a community and integration is defined as development of security, freedom and identity of place. This is another way of saying that a decision to locate is not the same as a decision to remain there because the decision to locate is made from outside the community while the decision to remain is made from within the community.[48]

Hence, the physician's self-concept is not only very much involved in his decision to practice in one place or another but is also involved in the manner in which a physician practices and how he interacts with his patients. George Herbert Mead is generally recognized as the first American scholar to understand the importance of the self as our inward consciousness. He showed that the self, together with the social or outward aspect of consciousness, constitutes our whole personality or identity. Mead further showed that the self is perpetually changing as our experiences change.[49]

Human behavior is not only determined by personality but also by community or the social structure in which it develops and lives. This view has been part of sociological concepts since Ferdinand Tönnies described Gemeinschaft und Gesellschaft over one hundred years ago. Since then it has been agreed that community includes a diverse set of activities and interests as lived within a locality or place.[50]

Evidently, then, the view physicians have of themselves is constructed by their personalities, their communities, and their "cultural matrices" including their immediate family and their friends.   An excellent example of the consequences of that interaction is the effect of the socio-economic background of the physicians upon their perceptions. Thus, those physicians who grew up relatively or absolutely poor may well be expected to have a better understanding of their communities' poor than someone who has never experienced deprivation. This does not mean, however, that there is a necessary correlation between endemic poverty or wealth and sympathy for those now in need. In fact, there are those among the erstwhile poor who shrink from any association with those now poor and seek to associate themselves only with the financially successful. Furthermore, there is a great deal of evidence that some very wealthy or "aristocratic" persons consider it their duty to help those less fortunate than they are themselves. The career of Richard Nixon illustrates the former and the career of Franklin D. Roosevelt illustrates the latter contention.[51]

A supportive family and the encouragement of role models are also important in the development of a physician's personality and approach to his patients. Role models are generally older physicians, particularly medical school teachers, who influence the manner in which physicians approach their responsibilities. From their experiences in medical school physicians generally develop a "medical personality" in addition to their primary   personality. This new "personality" comes about because the physician's master status becomes that of "doctor" so that, upon graduating from medical school, that master status overwhelms all of the doctor's other roles such as son, husband, father, church member or tennis player. This means that the attitudes and social relations of a physician are supported by the view the community has of doctors and the view the profession has of its members. That in turn determines the numerous roles a doctor must fulfill in his community. A role is distinguished from a status in that a role is the sum of our obligations while a status is the sum of our rights and privileges. How we carry out these roles is largely determined by the influence of the profession upon its members and that influence largely dictates the values of a doctor. [52]

As could be expected, a study by Cutshin found that doctors unanimously value making an improvement in a patient's health. In addition, some doctors value service to the poor or education or family life. Those doctors who were consequently secure in their identity felt comfortable as people with definite identities always do. It is this sense of security which allows some doctors to be most compassionate and empathetic towards their patients.[53]

V

Physicians need two sets of skills to be successfully engaged in patient care. The first of these skills may be called the "scientific-technical." That skill is taught in all colleges and medical schools and is essential for the treatment of any disease. The second skill needed by all physicians may be called the "socio-emotional." This second feature of a physician's skill is demonstrated by compassionate-empathetic behavior and depends *a priori* on the emotional health of the doctor himself. Thus, numerous studies have shown that compassion, empathy and altruism correlated positively with self esteem and a sense of responsibility for others, personal functioning and social competence. [54]

It is of course well known that we are normally much better equipped to be positive towards those who resemble us in values, attitudes, demeanor and social background and that we are generally negatively disposed towards those who differ from us. This common social fact is easily accommodated by anyone who is not a care-giver. Among physicians, however, this is a problematic condition since physicians must always treat people who differ from them in almost every aspect of socialization and hence personality. In addition, doctors are often confronted with diseases they despise or reject. AIDS is one example of such a disease but the well known "social diseases" can elicit equal rejection by physicians. In addition, however, physicians are likely to react to the reward structure in their profession and/or hospital. Scientific/technical skills are most rewarded in almost all American hospitals while compassionate-empathic behavior usually goes unnoticed. Hence, patients in the so-called "best" hospital are generally depersonalized and dehumanized. That attitude in turn leads to the internalization of these rewarded ascriptions so that physicians, seeking to be successful and make a positive impression on their colleagues will invest in scientific research and continuing education to gain recognition in the profession. This does not mean that physicians who are well versed in science and technology are therefore unsympathetic to their patients. It does mean, however, that the rank order in American hospitals is determined by scientific and/or technological skill and, of course, political skill leading to administrative responsibilities generally unrelated to medical or surgical competence. In fact, it is evident that most medical administrators cannot cure diseases or conduct surgery of any kind and have lost all interest in patients or their welfare. As is so common in all large bureaucracies, those who administer seldom retain any understanding of the primary functions of the organization they say they serve. As they run from meeting to meeting in a ritualistic fashion, hospital administrators generally become self serving ritualists without any interest in or influence upon the welfare of hospital patients.[55]

In view of all this it is not surprising that many primary care physicians, and especially family physicians, feel inferior to specialists and "high-tech" doctors of any kind. We have already seen that this attitude is taught to students by medical school professors despite the evidence that the costs of medical care have risen so dramatically in the last forty years precisely because American medical schools have trained too many expensive specialists. Residents and medical students not only hear from their professors that "you are too smart to go into primary care," but 70% of them are also assigned in inpatient and emergency room environments. Very few, i.e., less than 10% spend any time in community clinics or health maintenance organizations.[56]

Yet, the public view of doctors is one of respect and admiration derived from the belief that doctors are empathic in a fashion that is best featured by family practice. There are of course many doctors who are indeed humanitarians and whose motives include the sincere wish to be of help. In any case, it is certain that all human beings have many motives with respect to all of life's conditions and that benevolence does not exclude a wish to earn money or collect the admiration of others. In fact, prestige, status and income are all three a principal motive for the continuing willingness of many college age people to undergo the hardships and tribulations necessary to become a doctor and then to continue in the profession for a lifetime. Evidently, the rewards of practicing medicine such as the opportunity to interact with people, the feeling of accomplishment, the interesting and challenging work and the independence and responsibility that are included in the practice of the profession are offset by some negative aspect of practicing medicine which are generally unknown to the public or are given little credence in popular perception.[57]

A leading liability faced by doctors and other health providers are problem patients. Problem patients may be divided into those who may be called "challenging" patients and those who are clearly "abusive".

Those who can be called "challenging" include, first and foremost, patients who are driven by fear. Surely almost anyone facing death, or the death of a loved one could become emotional and even angry at that situation. Some patients direct their anger at death upon the doctor or his staff. Other angry patients exhibit annoyance because they feel they have lost control over their lives or that they cannot meet the costs of treatment. Such patients are reacting to a situation and should not be seen as personal threats or as abusive despite their sometimes irrational conduct. It is also necessary to understand that the same behavior may annoy one doctor but not another. For example, so-called "historians" who recite their entire medical history and all their grievances over the years are terribly annoying to some doctors. There are also patients who are socially isolated and who call the doctor's office constantly, not because they have a medical condition, but because they cannot tolerate their isolation. Such patients annoy some doctors but are understood by other doctors and are fruitfully referred to social workers or regularly called by receptionists or nurses so that they can rely on at least one human contact at intervals. Some doctors view such contacts as treatment and make these arrangements as part of their responsibility towards those patients.[58]

There are also so-called "head injury" patients. These are people who call or visit with the same complaints over and over again. Some of these patients are indeed unable to remember their previous calls because they suffer from memory problems. This is undoubtedly very frustrating to some doctors. Yet, those patients who truly suffer memory lapses also feel frustrated by their inability to gain the attention they think they deserve.

There are also patients who do not follow treatment plans or those who insist on referrals to specialists they do not need. There are patients who routinely use the emergency rooms of hospitals and there are those who change physicians all the time because they are never satisfied with any diagnosis or any treatment. There are also those patients whose extreme anxiety problems can create havoc in a medical office or a hospital by their questioning every member of the staff over and over again about the same issue. Finally, there are patients with exactly the opposite problem. These are patients who do not comply with treatment that they should receive because they don't make necessary appointments or break existing appointments even as they risk their health and well being. These are some of the "challenges" with which doctors must generally deal every day. There are, however, also "abusive" patients and they can indeed be labeled "patients from hell."[59]

Such patients consistently abuse the staff verbally and sometimes physically. Verbal abuse is of course disruptive while physical abuse may indeed be criminal. Disruptive behavior also includes threats of violence although not carried out; sexual advances without physical contact; excessive failure to appear for appointments such as missing six appointments in a year; intentional misrepresentation of a patient's true identity and misuse of services to the point that the staff can no longer provide care. Truly criminal behavior includes non-consensual physical contact of an aggressive and/or sexual kind; threats of committing bodily harm; behavior that endangers staff or patients or otherwise jeopardizes the safety of the doctors office; forgery or alteration of prescriptions or theft of prescription forms or drug related conduct and damage to or theft of property belonging to patients, the doctor or the facility.[60]

Nevertheless, it can be demonstrated that the recently noticed declining status of physicians is related to the "scientific/technical" attitude of doctors and the impersonal relations to patients which are its consequence. There are doctors who are so impersonal that they make no effort to learn the names of patients, remember their faces or interact warmly. All this contributes to public alienation and obviously destroys the trust and feelings of intimacy that were once the backbone of the profession. This lack of trust is particularly enhanced by the inability of many doctors to communicate in a pleasant manner with patients and their families. This failure to communicate is even more painful when bad news must be told to patients and their families. According to a recent survey "many doctors appear cold and rushed, make rude comments and ...fail to answer questions when discussing diagnoses and treatments for serious conditions." Despite the widespread belief among patients that doctors are frequently unavailable and unsupportive, doctors themselves generally believe that they are supportive. Others say that families who need support should see a social worker or psychologist and not a physician.[61]

All this contributes to the disenchantment of the public with doctors, a disenchantment that is furthered as well by the high cost of medical care which some attribute, justly or not, to the perceived excessive fees charged by doctors for their services. It is however interesting to note here that many Americans also claim that teachers earn too much.

Another reason for the decline in the prestige of physicians may also be the increase in public knowledge about medicine. This "knowledge" is probably spurious in most instances. Nevertheless, doctors and other professionals can hardly expect that public ignorance will give them a shield behind which they can hide from criticism. This willingness to criticize and "second guess" doctors is easily demonstrated by looking at the many malpractice suits routinely filed against doctors everywhere.

It has been estimated that in the U.S. at least one in four doctors will be sued for malpractice every year. Those doctors who practice in high risk specialties will be sued even more often. Very few of these claims actually reach court. In fact, 75% are dropped and of those remaining up to 95% are settled out of court. Nevertheless, such litigation has a considerable impact upon doctors, including those who have not been sued.[62]

This eagerness to sue is in part driven by greed and the expectation that doctors' insurance companies will pay huge amounts to the complainant. There are, however, other reasons for the greater and greater volume of litigation to which doctors are now subject. Major among these reasons is the preoccupation of the media with medical issues. The constant barrage of medical information broadcast by television and radio has led many people to believe that they can define medical competence. Traditionally only physicians determined medical competence. Now, however, medical competence is not only defined by grade school children and their elders, but also by corporate business interests who dictate the conditions of medical practice and decide who can or cannot practice.[63]

The consequence of the constant litigation which doctors must endure has been the decline of a good deal of the harmonious relationship between patients and doctors and a shift of boundaries as to who controls medicine. The issue of the changing position of physicians in American society has become a matter of so much debate because self-regulation of the medical profession is now being challenged by law, government and business. Malpractice trials are therefore an indication of the legal challenge to the concept of self-regulation. Such trials and their consequences force the medical profession to defend its standards of competence before a jury of lay persons leading to the sanctioning or disapproving of professional standards by people who are not physicians. In addition, court actions cause physicians to abandon certain practices or to adopt other practices in order to protect themselves from further litigation. Thereby, outsiders determine medical standards indirectly but forcefully. Therefore the threat to the profession by litigation is far less financial than it is existential. This is true because malpractice insurance, although very expensive, protects physicians from financial ruin. However, the current assault on their self-regulation contests the very meaning of medical practice.[64]

In 1992 the American Medical Association and the Council of Medical Specialty Societies published their "Medical Liability Project." This project demonstrates that physicians who have been sued find that experience to be personally humiliating and degrading. Physicians blame the legal profession for the current "liability crisis" and experience a loss of control over their professional affairs. Physicians also view malpractice suits as arbitrary and are particularly alarmed at the idea that lawyers and patients who have no medical expertise are entitled to overrule their judgment. Doctors generally believe that the proceedings in a courtroom are in no way related to the realities of a medical practice. To doctors malpractice suits are a game favoring lawyers and their income and have no relationship to actual malpractice. Hence doctors see the law as a threat because malpractice suits remove them from their "territory" and place them at the mercy of people who don't want to know anything about medical practice but seek only to profit from unjust accusations. Physicians also regard legal findings of professional medical incompetence as usually unjust because they know that medicine is not an "exact" science and that the outcome of even the most competent treatment is not entirely predictable. As a result, physicians have rejected high risk patients and refrained from high-risk procedures lest they be sued. This means that fear of litigation rather than the best possible practice may determine the kind of treatment a patient receives from his doctor. In sum, physicians challenge the legitimacy of the law in attempting to regulate their profession. Therefore, the American Medical Association has recommended that malpractice complaints be taken out of the courts and that these complaints be heard by an agency involving physicians themselves. [65]

This recommendation arises not only from the effect of litigation on the medical practice of doctors who have been sued but is also considerable on doctors who have not been sued. These consequences have been called "defensive medicine" and can be segregated into positive or negative defensive procedures. Positive defensive medicine consists of the use of diagnostic or therapeutic measures which are designed to protect the doctor from being sued but which are otherwise of no importance. Negative defensive medicine consists of withholding procedures which might be medically justified but which include a risk of failure and hence represent a cause of possible litigation. Several studies have shown that doctors who have been sued keep more meticulous records, including less pertinent information or information which is spurious. About 62% of doctors who have been sued order diagnostic tests for "protection" even if such tests are not clinically needed and 49% of doctors were unwilling to see patients who represent a high degree of risk of litigation. Many physicians who have been sued have retired early and discouraged their children from practicing medicine. [66]

A study entitled "The Harvard Medical Practice Study," discovered that the most frequently sued specialty is obstetrics. According to that Harvard study seventy-three percent of gynecologists and obstetricians have been sued. Therefore, numerous obstetricians have entered a different specialty while family doctors are often eliminating the obstetrical part of their practice so as to avoid the excessive insurance costs associated with such a practice. [67]

Medical accidents are a frequent cause of malpractice litigation. The most frequent type of error made by doctors is misdiagnosis (30%), followed closely by errors in prescribing and finally errors in treatment. Doctors commonly blame their own profession for the high rate of litigation because the profession has overstated the expectations patients have of their doctor. Lawyers are also blamed for the excessive amount of litigation now common in the U.S.A.. In addition, some doctors blame the media because the media generally portray those cases which come to court in terms antagonistic to the interests of the medical profession. Finally, doctors blame the public, i.e., patients who are unwilling to take responsibility for themselves and seek to sue for the sake of suing and making money.[68]

Since doctors are as likely to blame others for their mistakes as much as anyone else it is refreshing to learn of the recommendation of Dr. Albert Wu of Johns Hopkins University School of Public Health in Baltimore. Dr. Wu suggests that doctors admit their mistakes and so inform patients. Dr. Wu reports that his study showed that only one fourth of all American doctors admit their mistakes or tell families and patients about them. Dr. Wu believes that such honesty helps the patient who can therefore seek extra treatment as well as compensation for injury. He also believes that patients who have been told the truth will have greater faith in their doctor thereafter. While these sentiments may well be exemplary and ethically superior, insurers believe that "urging doctors to admit their mistakes is asking them to commit professional suicide." That comment is supported by the evidence that "every word you utter is an admission that can be used against you in a court of law."[69]

IV

The phrase "burnout" has been used by Maslach which Sonneck and Wagner investigated among physicians by using the Maslach Burnout Iventory. Maslach has identified at least 15 connotations of the term "burn out" which she lists as follows: 1. A syndrome of emotional exhaustion, depersonalization and reduced personal accomplishment. 2. A progressive loss of idealism, energy and purpose. 3. A state of physical, mental and emotional exhaustion. 4. A syndrome of inappropriate attitudes towards clients and self. 5. A state of exhaustion, irritability and fatigue that decreases the worker's effectiveness 6. To deplete oneself and exhaust one's physcial and mental resources. 7. To wear oneself out doing what one has to do. 8. A malaise of the spirit. A loss of will. 9. To become debilitated and weakened because of extreme demands on one's physical and mental energy. 10. An accumulation of intense negative feelings leading to withdrawal from situations where such feelings are generated. 11. A pervasive mood of anxiety leading to depression and despair 12. A process in which a professional's attitudes and behavior change in negative ways 13. An inadequate coping mechanism used by an individual to reduce stress. 14. A condition produced by working too hard for too long and 15. A debilitating psychological condition resulting from work related frustrations.[70] Those who suffer from these conditions seek to minimize their social contacts and retreat to "their own four walls", reducing their contacts with others to a minimum. Yet more significant signs of "burnout" are feelings of failure and lack of power. These beliefs are associated with the opinion that the "burnt out" doctor lacks recognition for all his work, that he is insufficient in his ability to do his work and that he is required to do an overload of work which he cannot accomplish. [71]

Among doctors "burnout" is marked by a particularly high score on depersonalization. This undoubtedly explains the large number of complaints by patients that their doctor is not interested in them but only in their disease.

Those who are "burnt out" as well as those who reach old age must or will want to retire. This is true among physicians as well and therefore raises the same issues in that profession as retirement does among all Americans. The problem that assails almost all who are retired is the all-American status problem directly influenced by occupation. Because our work supplies us with our "master status", our identity and our self-respect depend on the source of our income. We have already seen that physicians rank first among all American occupations according to the numerous surveys of the National Opinion

Research Center. Therefore, physicians are even more at risk when faced with the transition to retirement and death which everyone else must also confront. Many people, but especially retired doctors, need to assure themselves of a continuity of self-esteem when the judgment of others designates them as "over the hill." Signs of this altered status are of course unavoidable. The doctor's alma mater (nourishing mother) asks that he remember his medical school in his will while friends, relatives and acquaintances remark "how good you look." Shortly before his death President Dwight Eisenhower remarked that there are three ages of men. Young, middle aged and "how good you look." [72]

Work is the measure of worth in the eyes of American society. Therefore physicians, having viewed themselves as superior to everyone else, run the risk of judging themselves as inferior and useless because they are retired. It is reasonable but nevertheless unfortunate and destructive to abstract the view from the loss of high working status that someone retired and not working is therefore worthless.

Normally it is recommended that we all have absorbing "hobbies" long before we retire so that we can retire to something instead of retiring only from our accustomed work. Indeed all too few heed this advice. Among physicians, however, this is exceptionally difficult because they work so many hours that it is unlikely very many doctors have time to develop a hobby during their working life time. [73]

There are large numbers of retired persons who volunteer at various tasks in hospitals, social service agencies and other voluntary organizations. There are also a good number of retired persons who work for a minimum wage at jobs also staffed by adolescents such as bagging groceries or pumping gas. This gives the retired an extra income and "something to do." Retired doctors, however, cannot normally tolerate the immense status loss such work would entail and therefore cannot use these usual means of alleviating their ennui. That word has been translated to mean approximately boredom but is derived from the Latin word *in odio* meaning hate. Self hate for lack of work is emphasized by boredom and lack of respect and therefore becomes particularly threatening to retired physicians who were accustomed to long hours and an excess of subservience from a host of sycophants and others. It is therefore vital and profoundly important that physicians as well as everyone develop a skill other than their usual occupation which they can use to maintain that level of self-respect and interest which they need in order to live more and more years of retirement at a time when life expectancy is increasing steadily and work is becoming more and more reduced to electronic devices and computerized standards. Failure to make such personal arrangements can become life threatening as demonstrated by the fact that suicide occurs so often among the members of the medical profession that the number of physicians who take their own life in the United States "is equivalent to an entire graduating class of a medical school."[74]

Summary

There are about 737,000 doctors in the United States of whom 21% are women whose income is distinctly less than that of male doctors. The social background of doctors tends to be upper-middle class although the profession includes practitioners originating in all social classes.

At the end of the twentieth century technological advances have increased the costs of medical care immensely and raised expectations beyond the ability of the medical profession to meet these demands. This has created a number of ethical dilemmas for physicians whose status has eroded as business interests in the form of health maintenance organizations have impinged on the professional decision making power of the profession. Furthermore, sex, age, ethnicity and race of patients has influenced that decision making feature of medical practice as has the conduct of patients. Patients have become more aggressive in their relationship to doctors and have engaged in extensive litigation which, together with many other job pressures, have resulted in an increase in the "burn-out" phenomenon and early retirement by some physicians. These pressures are not evenly distributed among all doctors because the numerous specialties in which physicians engage create quite different forms of work and lifestyle among them. Most distinct among all medical specialties is surgery which has a somewhat different history than any other medical practice and which we will therefore explore in the next chapter.

NOTES

[1] American Medical Association, *Physician Characteristics and Distribution in the U.S.1997-1998.* Chicago, 1998, p.vi.

[2] Lisa Kalis, "Salary Report," *Working Woman,* Vol.23, No.2, February 1998, pp. 39-41.

[3] Rudoph, *et al op.cit.,* p.44.

[4] Marcel A. Fredericks and Paul Mundy, *The Making of a Physician,* Chicago, Loyola University Press, 1976, pp. 12-19 and pp. 139-146.

[5] National Opinion Research Center, *Cumulative Codebook: General Social Surveys.* Chicago, 1991.

[6] David Fink and Annemarie Franczyk "Area HMOs", *Busienss First of Buffalo,* May 19, 1997, p. 58.

[7] William F. Ogburn, "Culture Lag as Theory," in William F. Ogburn, *On Cutlure and Social Change,* Chicago, University of Chicago Press, 1964, pp. 86-95.

[8] Thomas H. Marshall, *Class, citizenship and social development,* New York, Doubleday, 1965, pp. 158-179.

[9] Robert H. Coombs, *Mastering Medicine,* New York, The Free Press, 1978, pp. 260-262.

[10] Society for the Right to Die, "The Physician and the Hopelessly Ill Patient," New York, *Society for the Right to Die,* 1985, p.87.

[11] Lori B. Ruhlman, "A Bridge, A Hand, A Guide," *Health Care News of Central New York,* Vol.6, No. 7, Julu 1998, p. 1.

[12] *The Economist, Vol. 338, No. 7957,* March 16th, 1996, pp. 34-35.

[13] H. T. Englehardt, Jr., "National health care policy: the moral issues." *American College of Surgeons Bulletin,* Vol. 78, No. 4, pp. 10-14.

[14] Immanul Kant, *Fundamental Principles of the Metaphysics of Morals,* T.K. Abbott, Translator, Bobbs Merrill, Indianapolis 1949, p. 55. The German version of this book is: *Grundlegung zur Metaphysik der Sitten.* The original German phrase has been restated in American English by the author.

[15] Alastair Campbell, Grant Gillett and D. Gareth Jones, *Practical Medical Ethics,* New York, Oxford University Press, 1992.

[16] Ursula A. Falk and Gerhard Falk, *Ageism, The Aged and Aging in America,* Springfield, Charles Thoams, 1997, pp. 45-65.

[17] Robert Pear, "Panel Finds Medicare Costs Are Underestimated by U.S.'" *The New York Times,* June 3, 1998, p. A 21.

[18] Edgar Sydenstricker and Isidore S. Falk, "Public Provisions Against the Economic Risks Arising Out of Ill Health, " *Preliminary Reports,* Washington, D.C., Committee on Economic Security, 1934.

[19]Thomas W. Reilly, Steven B. Clauser and David K. Baugh, "Trends in Medical Payments and Utilization 1975-1989," *Health Care Finance Reivew Annual Supplement*, 1990, pp. 15-33.

[20]Mark H. Showalter, "Physicians Cost Shifting Behavior: Medicaid versus other patients." *Contemporary Economic Policy*, Vol. 15, April 1997, p. 83.

[21]Jonathan Gruber, Kathleen Adams and Joseph P. Newhouse, "Physician Fee Policy and Medicaid Program Costs," *The Journal of Human Resources*, Vol. 32, No. 4, Fall 1997, p. 634.

[22]Mary Hogan, Franklin J. Eppig and Daniel R. Waldo, "Access to Physicians," *Health Care Financing Review*, Volume 17, No. 2, Winter 1995, pp. 243-248.

[23]Associated Press, "Doctors' Reliance on Technology Is Bringing House Calls to an End," *The New York Times*, December 18, 1997, p. A22.

[24]Elliott Freidson, *Professionalism Reborn: Theory, Prophecy and Policy*, Chicago, The University of Chicago Press, 1994, p.9.

[25]Debra Galant, Organized Medicine: Dr. Anthony Tonzola Thinks a Doctor's Union Is the Way to Keep H.M.O.'s From Calling All the Shots," *The New York Times*, January 25, 1997, Sect. XII, p.41.

[26] No author, "Managed Care," *Medical Economics*, Vol.75, No. 22, November 9, 1998, p. 24.

[27]David Whitford, "Now the Doctors Want a Union," *Fortune*, Vol. 136, No. 11, December 8, 1996, p. 32.

[28] No author, "Union aims to organize physicians," *Buffalo News*, March 2, 1999, p.A1.

[29] Peter Eisler, "Care, control at center of unique labor dispute," *USA Today*, December 7, 1998, p. 1.

[30]*Ibid.*, p.43.

[31]Margaret Schneider and Susan P. Phillips, "A Qualitative Study of Sexual Harassment of Female Doctors by Patients," *Social Science and Medicine*, Vol. 45, No.5, September 1997, pp. 669-667.

[32]John B. McKinlay, Deborah A Potter and Henry Feldman, "Non-Medical Influences on Medical Decision Making, " *Social Science and Medicine*, Vol.42, No. 5, March 1996, p 773.

[33]*Ibid.* p. 774.

[34]Lizette Alvarez, "Nasty, Costly Battle Shapes Up Over Changing Managed Care," *The New York Times*, June 3, 1998, p. A21.

[35]Carol J. Simon, David Dranove and William D. White, "The Impact of Managed Care on the Physician Market Place, *Public Health Reports*, Vol. 112, No 3, May 6, 1997, pp. 222-230.

[36]Alison Cherney, *The Capitation & Risk Sharing Guidebook,* Chicago, Irwin Professional Publishing, 1996, p. 3.

[37]*Ibid.* p. 17.

[38]*Ibid.* p. 223.

[39]Ibid. p.229.

[40]B. Jerald McClendon, Robert M. Politzer, Evelyn Christian and Enrique S. Fernandez, " Downsizing the Physician Work Force," *Public Health Reports,* Vol.112. #3, May/June 1997, p.235.

[41]Bureau of the Census, *Population projections of the United States by age, sex, race and Hispanic origin:1995-2050. Current Population Reports P25-1130* . Washington, D.C., Government Printing Office, 1996.

[42]McClendon, *et al, op.cit.* p. 235.

[43]*Ibid.* p. 237.

[44]Mark V. Spalato, "Nurses, Beware," *The New York Times, October 5, 1997,* Sec. IV, p. 14:6.

[45]Jay Weiner, "Forecasting the effect of health reform on U.S. physician workforce requirement," *Journal of the American Medical Association,* Vol. 272, 1994, pp.222-230.

[46]Jolinn L., Jolly P. , Krakower, J.K. , Beran R.L., " Review of U.S. Medical School Finances 1993-1994" *Journal of the American Medical Assoication,* Vol. 268, 1992. pp.1149-1155.

[47]Jay Noren, "A National Physician Workforce Policy, " *Public Health Reports,* Vol. 112, No. 3, May/June 1997, pp. 219-221.

[48]Malcolm P. Cutchin, "Community And Self: Concepts for Rural Physician Integration and Retention," *Social Science and Medicine,* Vol. 44, No. 11, June 1997, p. 1661.

[49]George Herbert Mead, "Social Consciousness and the Consciousness of Meaning," *Psychological Bulletin,* Vol.7, 1910, pp.397-405. See also: G.H. Mead, *Mind, Self and Society,* Chicago, University of Chicago Press, 1934.

[50]Ferdinand Tönnies, *Community and Society, (Gemeinschaft und Gesellschaft)* Charles P. Loomis, Translator, New York, American Book Co., 1940.

[51]Cutchin, *op.cit.,* p. 1665.

[52]Beth B. Hess, Elizabeth W. Markson and Peter J. Stein, *Sociology,* Fourth Edition, New York, Macmillan Publishing Co. 1993. p. 75.

[53]Cutchin, o*p.cit.* p. 1664.

[54]Charles C. Nadelson, "Ethics, empathy and gender in health care." *American Journal of Psychiatry,* Vol 150, No. 9, 1993, p. 1309.

[55]Sara Carmel and Seymour M. Glick, "Compassionate-Empathic Physicians." *Social Science and Medicine,* Vol. 43, No. 8, October, 1996, pp. 1253-1261.

[56]Udo Schücklenk, "The Inferirority Complex of Primary Care Physicians," *Hastings Center Report,* Vol. 27, No. 6, November/December 1997, p. 51.

[57]Robert H. Coombs, *Mastering Medicine: Professional Socialization in Medical School,* New York, The Free Press, 1978, p.174.

[58]Liz Osborne, *Resolving Patient Complaints,* Gaithersburg, MD., Aspen Publishers, Inc., 1995, pp. 89-91.

[59]*Ibid.* pp. 92-94.

[60]*Ibid.* pp. 95-96.

[61]Susan Gilbert, "Forget About Bedside Manners, Some Doctors Have No Manners," *The New York Times,* December 23, 1997, p.F7.

[62]Maeve Ennis and J. Gredis Gudzinskas, "The effect of accidents and litigation on doctors," in: Charles Vincent, Maeve Ennis, Robert J. Audley, Eds., *Medical Accidents,* New York, Oxford University Press, 1993, p.167.

[63]Timothy Marjoribanks, Mary-Jo Delvecchio Good, Ann G. Lawthers and Lynn M. Peterson, "Physicians' Discourses on Malpractice and the Menaing of Medical Malpractice," *Journal of Health and Social Behavior,* Vol. 37, June 1996, pp. 163-178.

[64]*Ibid.* p. 166.

[65]American Medical Association/Specialty Society, *Medical Liability Project Fact Sheets.* Chicago, AMA/Specialty Society, 1992.

[66]L. Tancredi and J. Barondess, "The Problem of Defensive Medicine," *Science,* Vol.200, 1978, pp. 879-893.

[67]Harvard Medical Practice Study, *Patients, doctors and lawyers: medical injury, malpractice litigation and patient compensation in New York State,* Report of the HMPC, New York, 1990.

[68]Leonard Weinstein, "Malpractice-the syndrome of the '80's." *Obstetrics and Gynecology,* Vol. 72, 1988, pp. 130-135.

[69]Denise Grady, "Doctors Urged to Admit Mistakes," *The New York Times,,* December 9, 1997, p. F 9.

[70] Christine Maslach, *Burnout-The Cost of Carin.* Enblewood Cliffs, N.J., Prentice-Hall, 1982, pp. 30-31.

[71]Gernot Sonneck and Renate Wagner, "Suicide and Burnout of Physicians," *Omega,* Vol. 33, No. 3, December 1996, pp. 255-257.

[72]Avery D. Weisman, "The Physician in Retirement: Transition and Opportunity," *Psychiatry,*Vol. 59, No. 3, Fall 1996, p. 300.

[73]Ursula and Falk, *op.cit.*

[74]Weisman, *op.cit..* p.255.

Chapter V

Working by Hand- the World of the Surgeon

I

The history of surgery is as old as mankind. There is evidence that some ancient peoples conducted surgery as early as twelve thousand years ago. This was apparently the case is North Africa where trephination was used that early while Europeans adopted that practice 5,000 years ago. The word trephination suggests the three ends or prongs of the surgical instrument used to breach the skull. In America the practice of trephination began later. The oldest skulls showing evidence of a breach found in the New World are only 2,400 years old and were found mainly in Peru where trephination was used to relieve headaches or the consequences of head injury or other problems with a probable success rate of fifty percent.[1]

Many years elapsed from those pre-historic days to the developments of American surgery in the nineteenth and twentieth century. It is therefore not appropriate to recite that pre-American history here, not only because so many sources of that story are available, but also because we are chiefly concerned with American developments in this book.

Surely surgery in the U.S. gained immensely from the experiences of World War II which this country entered in 1941. During the ensuing four years, until the surrender of Japan in August of 1945, America's armed forces suffered 325,000 killed and 700,000 wounded. Thanks to the developments of penicillin and the sulfa drugs and the uses of blood plasma the proportion of fatalities among the wounded was far less in World War II than in the first World War. [2]

The developments in surgery since World War II during the twentieth century are of course dependent on all the earlier advances in surgery that came into use before and particularly during the nineteenth century. These advances concerned themselves very much with the use of various anesthetics (Greek=without feeling) such as ether, nitrous oxide and chloroform, first used by American dentists and later by physicians and surgeons. Injections of morphine, named after the Greek god of dreams, came into use to relieve local pain. Later, cocaine was also used to relieve pain and to increase the energy and "creativity" of surgeons, however, with devastating effects.

The nineteenth century also saw the rise of hospitalism, which we may define, as the move from home and the doctor's office into hospitals. Prior to the 1940's hospitals were places of extreme misery and frequent death due to infections, which could not be prevented or cured. At the end of the nineteenth century and the early part of the twentieth century hospitals came to be used more and more because of the great influx of immigrants into large American cities. These immigrants lived in hideous tenements under conditions of such overcrowding and poverty that neither treatment for disease nor surgery could be performed there. Hospitals, however, were feared as places of death and there were few of them. In fact, the mortality rate among hospital patients both in Europe and America stood around 74% in the 1870's. Furthermore, doctors too were at great danger when working in hospitals as even minor wounds incurred by a surgeon could lead to fatal infections.[3] Therefore there were only 173 hospitals in the entire United States in 1873. By 1913 there were 5,000 hospitals in this country a number which had increased to 6,291 by 1996.[4]

Much of the success of hospitals after the beginning of the 20th century was due to the work of Drs. Semmelweiss and Lister who initiated the antiseptic system into surgery at the end of the nineteenth century. Thereafter, "open surgery" became possible as gauze masks and rubber gloves were introduced into American hospitals in 1904. In addition, the skills and practices of surgeons also improved. Even at the beginning of the twentieth century surgeons used the same trephining as the ancient Egyptians and medieval barbers. In 1915, however, Dr. Harvey Cushing was able to report a fatality rate for brain tumors only 7.3% out of 149 operations.[5]

And so, as surgery has changed over the years various "truths" concerning its practice have also changed. For example, in 1929 it was "true" that cardiac surgery was impossible and that experimental procedures on the human heart were irresponsible. Therefore, Dr. Werner Forssmann was dismissed as a charlatan by the dictator of German surgery at the time, Ferdinand Sauerbruch. Sauerbruch claimed that Forssmann had conducted a "circus trick" when he inserted a ureteral catheter into his antecubital vein, directed it towards his heart, walked to the x-ray room, and had a radiograph taken. Forssmann felt no discomfort and reported that to Sauerbruch, his chief. That led Sauerbruch to prevent Forssmann from being appointed a surgeon at "a decent German clinic". Subsequently, Dr. Forssmann practiced urology until his retirement. Yet, in 1956 he was awarded the Nobel prize in medicine for his immense courage in experimenting on himself and making cardiac surgery possible. Sauerbruch had the good fortune of dying much earlier with all his prejudices in tact.[6] Another example of changing "truth" in surgery is that in 1952 it was "true" that prefrontal lobotomies were useful in various treatments of dying patients or emotionally ill patients and that the appearance of any ulcer was cause for an immediate operation. These and other practices are no longer "true" at the end of the century because medicine and surgery have changed so much that it can reasonably be said that clinical statements in the surgical literature are true for about 45 years. [7]

As the practice of surgery has changed it has become more and more successful. The earlier view that surgeons are next to barbers and butchers in reputation has given way to the exact opposite impression among the American public at the end of the twentieth century. This is best illustrated by the income of surgeons, as already mentioned earlier in this book. It may be recalled that general surgeons earned an average income of $223,388 in 1998 and that orthopedic surgeons earned even more, i.e., $310,475 a sum twice as large as that earned by the majority of physicians. These high earnings by surgeons have now come to an end. In view of the ascendancy of health insurers over the autonomy of physicians and surgeons, health plans have decreased the income of surgeons in particular. These reductions are severe and can consist of cuts in payments of nearly 50%. For example, California Blue Cross announced in June of 1998 that hip replacement surgery, which had previously been reimbursed at $4,602, would be reimbursed at only $2,380 a cut of 48%. Reimbursement for knee ligament replacement surgery was reduced from $2,460 to $1,364. Other reimbursement reductions were 44% for spinal fusion surgery; 32% for the setting of broken bones; 31% for rotator cuff surgery and 20% for lumbar surgery. Because the health care plans demand that a doctor who wishes to be affiliated with it must accept all patients in the plan and not just the higher paying ones, doctors feel severely deprived. Yet, "if doctors balk at any restrictions they can be blackballed from plans, losing access to thousands of patients."[8]

In order to fight back, doctors have now taken their case to the various State Medical Boards. These medical boards have the power to investigate complaints against doctors licensed in each state and can issue reprimands, fines, license suspensions and even license revocations for malpractice. Therefore, Mississippi passed a law in 1998 which permits the State Medical Board to hold HMO medical directors responsible for refusing the needs of a patient who then is harmed or even dies. A similar law was passed in Arizona in 1997 and both Ohio and California have such legislation pending.[9]

Pressure on surgeons and other doctors is of course not only derived from the intrusion of government and health maintenance bureaucrats upon the medical profession. Increasingly, patients backed by government are demanding more accountability from surgeons than ever before. This is particularly important because fear of HIV infection and the incurable consequences of AIDS have become a major health problem in the United States. This came to the attention of the newspaper reading public when David Acer, a dentist who died recently, infected at least three of his patients.[10]

Because AIDS is incurable, and because the fear of AIDS creates considerable emotional distress, the Maryland court of appeals has ruled that a surgeon infected with AIDS should have informed two patients of his condition before operating on them. State law in Maryland requires that surgeons explain procedures to patients and warn them of any material risk "inherent or attendant to the recommended treatment."[11]

Because surgery needs to be monitored by studying a surgeon's trend in performance, a British cardiac surgeon, Marc de Lavalle, has developed the "cumulative sum procedure" method of evaluating surgeon's techniques. This method seeks to prevent disaster by early recognition of unsatisfactory work by surgeons and/or trainees. It has been presented to the American Association for Thoracic Surgery. The principle idea of the "cumulative sum procedure" is to allow each surgeon to compare his performance with national averages in practice and risk. Without describing the details of this technique it is important to recognize that surgery, and particularly cardiac surgery, is always conducted in an atmosphere of high risk and exacting work conditions.[12]

Reports on the comparative performance of cardiac surgeons began in Pennsylvania in 1992 and have become increasingly common in all states since then. Since that year, (1992), Pennsylvania has published the Consumer Guide to Coronary Artery Bypass Surgery, which lists annual risk adjusted mortality rates for all hospitals and surgeons providing such services in that state. While such a "guide" may at first glance appear as a secure means by which candidates for coronary surgery can ascertain the competence of surgeons and the care given by hospitals, such a guide may in fact be both unreliable and harmful. This was found by Schneider and Epstein who investigated the influence of cardiac surgery performance reports on referral practices and access to care for cardiac surgery patients. They found that such reports tend to decrease the access to care for severely ill patients who need such surgery because their chances of survival are low and surgeons cannot afford to be blamed for their possible deaths. This is true despite the claim by state employed statisticians that they have developed a risk adjustment model to deal with high-risk patients. Surgeons believe that nevertheless they will receive a negative rating if their total caseload is too small to spread the risk adequately. Furthermore it should be considered that a cardiac surgeon, employed by a hospital must take direction from administrators who can destroy the career of any surgeon they dislike by giving him the most high risk patients available while rewarding their friends with an assignment of all low risk patients. In view of the competitiveness which abounds in the high-income surgery culture such political considerations are by no means uncommon.[13]

Insurers are of course greatly interested in information on outcomes and costs of cardiac operations since they will add or drop surgeons from their provider panels based on the "report cards" now in use in most states. Unfortunately the deficiencies of these reports are seldom given consideration by those who make such decisions.[14]

In an effort to discover the effect of performance reports for cardiac surgeons on the patients undergoing cardiac surgery Schneider and Epstein conducted a telephone survey of 474 patients who had undergone such surgery. They discovered that less than 1% of such patients knew the rating of their surgeon on these reports. Only 12% were aware that such reports exist and 56% said that they might be interested in seeing such a report *ex post facto*. Conclude Schneider and Epstein: "Efforts to aid patient decision making with performance reports are unlikely to succeed without a tailored and intensive program for dissemination and patient education."[15]

Even more significant than the ignorance of the public concerning the ratings of cardiac surgeons is a study by Hartz, Pulido and Kuhn which investigated the patient mortality rate for surgeons labeled "best" in the book, The Best Doctors in America. Included in that book are the names of doctors who were recommended as "best" by other doctors in their community and in their specialty. In addition, Hartz, Pulio and Kuhn used popular magazines and newspapers published in New York, Philadelphia, Pittsburgh, Milwaukee and Madison. The results of their study included more than 10,000 patients from 31 "best" surgeons and more than 74,000 patients from 243 cardiac surgeons not rated "best."

The outcome of this study indicates that there is hardly any difference in mortality rates among the so-called "best" surgeons or those who were not included in the "best" list. In fact, the small difference in mortality rates favors the category "other surgeons," whose mortality rate of 3.3 among their patients is less than that of the "best" surgeons whose mortality rate was 3.4. This then lead the authors of this study to the conclusion that "physicians chose the 'best' surgeons for political reasons, such as membership in the same health care organization". Ethnic and religious prejudices, misogyny or unpopularity for any reason were and are cause to be excluded from any list of "best" surgeons or doctors.[16]

It need not be elaborated here that "whistle blowers" risk a great deal and usually bring down upon them the wrath of the entire organization in which they work. One such example concerns a Nevada neurosurgeon who complained to the chairman of the neurosurgery department about the shoddy procedures and practice standards of a colleague. In the absence of any action by the chairman, the neurosurgeon also complained to the state board of medical examiners and the state governor. The outcome of these complaints was that the complaining neurosurgeon was deprived of his hospital privileges and fourteen cases were filed against this neurosurgeon by the hospital. When the neurosurgeon applied for a license in any other state the Nevada medical board "blackballed" him so that he could not practice anywhere. Eventually he had to declare bankruptcy and his Nevada license expired as well. Three years later, the Nevada medical board filed one patient's complaint against this neurosurgeon. The other thirteen complaints first mentioned by the board could not be substantiated and were dropped. The board of the hospital then refused to release to the surgeon the records of their investigation into that one complaint so that he would be hindered in his effort to defend himself at the subsequent hearing. Upon losing his case at that hearing the surgeon applied to the Nevada court of appeals known as the Supreme Court. That court dismissed all charges against that neurosurgeon because the board had evidently acted in bad faith and deliberately brought unwarranted charges against the neurosurgeon. The court ruled that the board had not acted to protect the public from an incompetent and negligent surgeon but had "wielded its power to ruin the career of an outspoken physician while simultaneously protecting a possibly negligent or incompetent practitioner who had questionable billing procedures."[17]

Another case, among many, of a similar nature occurred in New York. An excellent example of the manner in which a doctor can be deprived of his profession by the hostility of colleagues is the destruction of a surgeon's career by those within the profession. This concerns a surgeon who had graduated from a major Midwestern university and had also successfully completed his residency there.

Appointed to a surgical position in a specialty field, he soon found that the chief of his department was seldom present because he was simultaneously employed at another hospital. In short, the chief was a "no-show" employee who was nevertheless paid a large salary. Because the "chief" had no time to do any of the operations needed at that hospital, the new surgeon was forced to do the work of two. On salary, and receiving no private pay for each case, the newcomer worked far above capacity in order to "cover" the absentee surgeon. The hospital staff was aware that the medical director at the hospital had a son who was also a doctor. That son was given a free office by the absentee surgeon so that the medical director paid his debt for the free office by allowing the landlord to make money as a private surgeon in another hospital.

The newcomer, now already established, protested his immense surgery schedule but to no avail. He therefore resigned his position and took a surgical position at another hospital. Having resigned, he then notified a supervisory agency of the government of the absentee "no show" surgeon. Consequently, the inspector general came to look into the allegations and found them true. In addition they discovered that the chief received a "kick -back" for using medical and surgical supplies manufactured in his own factory and to the detriment of patients and the employer. Therefore, the "chief " and his followers were dismissed from their lucrative jobs.

To get even with the "whistle blower" his enemies and the friends of the erstwhile chief thereupon involved a TV station to "smear" the whistle blower. This was possible because a prominent surgeon in another city had a daughter who was the producer of a weekly TV "documentary." That producer sent two of her employees to visit the surgeon "whistle blower" in his office on the pretext of seeking advice concerning their "father in Florida". There they secretly taped an interview in which the surgeon assured them that he could safely operate on their "father in Florida" who, they said, they would bring to be seen by the surgeon. There was of course no "father in Florida." Instead of seeking consultation, the two visitors secretly taped the interview. In this interview, the surgeon assured them that he was as competent as any surgeon to conduct a bypass operation and that his record as a surgeon was average. The tape showing the interview was then shown on national TV with the assertion that the surgeon was evidently a liar since his record as a surgeon was not average but abysmal. Viewers of the television broadcast were told that the surgeon had a very high death rate, that his colleagues do not trust him and that he is the worst surgeon in his state.

The consequences of this "smear" on national television were immediate. Fearing that these allegations might be true, general practitioners no longer referred even one case to this surgeon. Suddenly, he had no income because he had no referrals. Indeed, many doctors recognized that this surgeon was indeed the victim of a political tactic. Yet, no one wanted "to get involved." Other surgeons feared for their own income and standing and said nothing in public that might have placed them into the "whistle blower's" camp. As the boycott of this surgeon continued his skill became less and less since frequent practice is of course the "life blood" of surgery.

Yet a third instance of political interference in the conduct of surgery in a public hospital deserves to be mentioned. This concerns a surgeon of Afro-American descent. Born in Louisiana he witnessed the activities of the Ku Klax Klan in his youth. Because his father was a dentist and an elected official in that state he had an early opportunity to recognize devastation of prejudice and discrimination. As a student he excelled at a prestigious, "Ivy League" college in the East and then graduated from the Harvard Medical School. Subsequently he held several positions until he was appointed as a surgeon and researcher at a large, urban, public hospital. The chief of his department, long married to paperwork and meetings and utterly incapable of surgery himself, assigned him his girlfriend as research assistant. That so-called research assistant was incapable of the work given her, but was nevertheless kept on the payroll because of her sexual connection to the chairman. The surgeon protested that his assistant could not carry out the work given her. But the chairman was adamant. Said he: "I'll bury that guy!" and with that sent him a notice of non-renewal or dismissal. His sole crime-he would not approve of the poor work of the chairman's girl friend. Furthermore, the outstanding record the surgeon had made for himself in previous appointments were too much for a chair whose jealousy was fueled by the competence of a younger colleague. No doubt competence can seldom compete with personal interests and who would deny that the personal interest of the chairman in his lady friend is far more important than the career of a surgeon or the safety of patients.

This and many other such cases abound in the surgery profession as the competition for profits and income is fierce and no method is evidently too bizarre to eliminate a competitor.

Political decisions based on private jealousies and personal prejudices are by no means uncommon in the profession of surgery and affect women even more than men. This is true because a good number of surgeons and other men suffer from "misogyny" which may be defined as the hatred of women. Despite that dictionary definition it is unlikely that the difficulty women surgeons face "on the job" are the product of a general hatred of all women by male surgeons. Instead it is evident that at the end of the twentieth century the position of professional women is still uncertain in areas which have traditionally always been male preserves. Undoubtedly a great "gender revolution" is now taking place in America. Nevertheless, innumerable professional opportunities still elude women because their presence in some work situations seems almost bizarre to men who have governed these areas of work for a lifetime. [18]

The masculine need to control the workplace and secure it against the intrusion of women is so particularly important to male surgeons because surgery is a body contact occupation. Surgery is by its nature intrusive and bloody. Hence, many men assume that women cannot do such work and react accordingly. In her study of "The woman in the surgeon's body," Cassell shows that male surgeons, suddenly confronted with female surgical residents, have difficulty living with the idea that women are found in a world in which "they do not belong." Women, found in the wrong place and possessing the wrong body are therefore seen by some male surgeons as not being real women, a view shared by men in other situations as well. The difficulty so many Americans have relative to the "gender revolution" is that they continue to resist the view that gender and sex are not the same thing. Thus, sex is biological and hence determined by genes. Gender is a social position. It is not fixed or "natural" but rather a category subject to change. Gender, however, is learned earlier than speech as we are confronted with the distinction between mother and father at birth. Hence, nothing is harder to learn than gender changes related to the sexual division of labor. Therefore, the behavior of women surgeons is expected to be different from that of male surgeons even as this female behavior is criticized. For example, female surgeons are not allowed to indulge in "doctor fits." These "doctor fits" are temper tantrums displayed by some surgeons in the operating room. Female nurses may complain about such conduct to others but submit to such ugly behavior on the part of male surgeons by acting as if they were working on top of a pile of dynamite that could explode any minute. Here is an example of such conduct as described by an operating room nurse. "One of our surgeons is acting deranged. He's always been verbally abusive to everyone on the staff. But now he goes into tirades and shakes all over at the slightest provocation-even a simple question about a patient's diagnosis. ...Lately he has been throwing sharps including scissors and saws. He slams down instruments on the patient's chest or leg to make a point. Once he stormed out of the OR.............. because he did not like the scrub nurse." [19]

Another example of similar conduct by a surgeon concerns the suspension of Dr. John Bell-Thomson, a heart surgeon, by the New York Board of Medical Conduct. Thomson was suspended for one year because he allegedly pushed a nurse, spilled blood on another nurse and threw a towel at a third nurse. He was also accused of setting fire to a patient's hair; subjecting a patient to an anesthesia although she was not given an operation; neglecting to arrive at a hospital for an emergency; throwing a clamp at a nurse and spilling blood on her; engaging in dangerous experimental surgery leading to the patient's death; hitting a nurse in the stomach and throwing a towel into the face of another nurse. [20]

There is of course no doubt that surgery is an occupation involving frequent and enduring stress. Therefore it may be well to introduce music into the operating theater as suggested by a study conducted by Allen and Blascovich. They found that music improved the task performance of surgeons and report that all surgeon/participants in their study endorsed the view in the beneficial effects of music. This was particularly true when the music was self selected. Such music reputedly is related to improved autonomic response.[21]

Yet, even those who believe that music in the operating room can reduce tension and prevent the kind of outburst just discussed they cannot overlook that violent conduct by a woman surgeon is at once condemned and labeled the behavior of a "bitch". Cassel reports that every woman surgeon she asked agreed that a woman surgeon who "throws a tantrum" is met by nurses who act "slow and sulky" even when it is well known to OR nurses that a slow operation is more dangerous to the patient than a fast operation because the patient must, in that case, remain under anesthesia longer. [22]

The issue, which must be resolved as women enter into the heretofore male bastion of the operating room as surgeons, is the issue of dealing with the incarnate social order, which previously prevailed. Here incarnate refers to the centuries old belief that the superior position of men and the inferior position of women is literally the product of physical differences between the sexes and therefore cannot be changed. Those who believe this are of course shocked to see a woman surgeon or woman general or woman business executive deny the most basic assumption by which they have lived since their birth.

Therefore it is a reasonable suggestion that surgeons, and scientists elsewhere, be trained in ethics and sociology. This would make it possible for them to recognize the need for gender equality in end-of-the-century America and also to deal with patients in a more compassionate manner than was heretofore the case. Comparison between the interest of physicians and surgeons concerning bioethics reveals that surgeons are significantly less interested in attending educational programs concerning ethics and that surgeons are also less interested than internists of availing themselves of clinical ethics consultation services than is true of other doctors. This finding has been observed in various parts of the United States and is not limited to Chicago and New York, where special studies were made concerning the differences between surgeons and physicians in this respect. In fact, a study by Simpson shows that at a Chicago community hospital 53 out of 59 requests for ethics consultation came from internists and only five, or nine percent, from surgeons.[23]

Paola and Barton surveyed medical and surgical literature and found a statistically significant difference between medical and surgical literature in terms of the amount of space devoted to bioethics. All these indications reveal that surgeons are less interested in the bioethics debate than internists. It may well be that at least one reason for this discrepancy is that the high-tech world of the surgeon leaves less time for dealing with anything other than technology.

The ethical issues confronting surgeons can surely not be less important than the ethical issues confronting physicians. Such issues may well be to decide whether or not surgery is futile in a patient or whether the patient has the capacity to consent to the surgery. Another ethical question that arises again and again is whether the risk of surgery outweighs the advantages surgery could produce. There are many other ethical questions involving surgery which could be discussed in the literature. Surgeons, it has been found, are much more interested in independent decision making than is true of other doctors. Therefore, surgeons do not like to deal with the ethics issue because they generally resent having an outsider tell them anything. Surgeons prefer to make decisions themselves and are less tolerant than internists of subordinate decisions. In short, the tradition of surgery is more authoritarian than is true of internal medicine so that surgeons are more likely to consider the ethics debate now under way in the profession a threat to their autonomy.[24]

II

Surgeons, like other professionals, have always claimed a right to autonomy of action on the grounds that their primary concern is the well-being of their patients. The health and safety of their patients, say surgeons, are more important to them than anything else. Nevertheless, many surgeons have been unable to recognize the needs of their patients and the needs of the patient's families. Precisely because of these needs the autonomy of surgeons is restricted even if these needs often go unanswered. Families of those about to undergo surgery are usually frightened and experience a death threat. This death threat is particularly strong among those family members who have not been hospitalized themselves. Such frightened families often communicate their anxiety to the patients and thereby hinder recovery.[25] Therefore communication between the surgeon and his patient and his patient's family is very important to them. Patients want to be treated as people and not as objects, an attitude which surgeons, if hospitalized, would want for themselves.

An unusual report concerning the patient's perspective in surgery comes from a surgeon who herself underwent surgery in a Pittsburgh, Pa. hospital. She reports how she felt as the oxygen mask was placed over her face by a surgeon with whom she was working. Because she knew her surgeon so well she did indeed have a comforting and secure feeling about her surgery. She comments: "I realized during my convalescence that this is how every patient should be treated by his or her physician (surgeon)." [26]

Meredith has published a study of patient satisfaction with communication in general surgery and reports that "for the majority of patients the ….meeting they have with the surgeon will have an important influence on their feelings about communication, and the use they make of information sources on the ward and beyond." [27]

The need to communicate adequately with patients and their families does of course limit the autonomy of surgeons. Furthermore, surgeons, like all doctors, must accept the limits upon action imposed by the hospital in which they work. This means that surgeons are subject to the controls of hospital management and the resources the institution can allocate. Surgeons who make a mistake are also much more subject to the scrutiny of others than are physicians. This is true because surgery is a hospital enterprise and its results can be evaluated much sooner and better than medical results, particularly if conducted in the doctor's office. If surgeons make a mistake, the hospital in which the surgeon works can be fined by state health departments. In cases of fraud or unethical conduct by a surgeon the hospital can also lose its right to conduct some operations. This was the case at the prestigious teaching hospital Presbyterian Hospital of Manhattan in New York. Here two doctors were discovered to have run a "cash-only" plastic surgery business by seeing patients privately when there was no supervision. Similarly, at Bridgeport Hospital in Connecticut, the then chief of neurosurgery, a very competent surgeon, mistakenly operated on the wrong side of a patient's brain. Although he recognized his error himself, minimized the damage and completed the right operation successfully, an outside reviewer was nevertheless called in to evaluate the possible damage done by that chief of neurosurgery at that hospital.[28] In a similar case in Switzerland, the director of chest surgery at a Geneva hospital was forced to resign his position and pay a large fine because he caused the death of one patient by perforating her lung and the death of another by causing a hemorrhage when he "ligatured the upper pulmonary vein in error."[29]

Surgeons are certainly not alone in creating a "mishap in the operating theater." Hospital management have done so as well as illustrated by the accusations against the giant for-profit hospital chain, Columbia /HCA Healthcare. The chain has been accused of overcharging extensively, billing Medicare for blood tests never undertaken, pretending that patients had "complications" which did not exist but which the hospital could use to gain illegal payments. Such practices by hospital administrators reflect on their surgeons as well, even as hospitals are held responsible for everything that occurs within their walls.[30] Hence, restraints placed systematically on surgeons are the most obvious reasons why surgeons do not really have the autonomy they claim.[31]

Events at a Long Island, N.Y. hospital demonstrate how the interest of hospital administrators to save money can risk the lives of patients and the reputation of surgeons who have no control over such administrative decisions. At the hospital on Long Island, as in hospitals all across the country, private anesthesiologists are being replaced by salaried anesthesiologists, a circumstance which some surgeons blame for the increased number of deaths which have occurred in some operating rooms since these changes were made. If that is the case, then surgeons are working under restraints created by people outside the operating rooms in which surgeons must perform for the sake of their patients' lives.[32]

In addition to these restraints, surgeons also depend on referrals from primary care physicians and on the willingness of insurers to pay for surgical and hospital services. Finally, surgeons also depend on the willingness of patients to submit to surgery and to keep their appointments. Therefore, there is an inherent contradiction built into the profession of surgery. Even as their autonomy is highly prized, surgeons must in fact work under all the constraints just listed.

There are also additional daily problems confronting surgeons. Fox describes these daily interruptions, delays, over-running of lists and other inefficiencies that appear to contradict the values embodied in the surgical enterprise.

For example, on some days some patients arrive late or not at all, while other patients are suddenly removed from the lists while others with quite different procedures are substituted. At other times, too many patients are scheduled so that the work of the surgeons lasts into the evening. There are occasions when instruments are not available or not ready at the same time as the patient. All of these problems cause constant delays in surgical procedure and, according to Fox, are the norm, and can be expected.[33]

Even more chaotic than the conditions facing surgeons dealing with scheduled surgery are the conditions found in trauma surgery. Trauma means wound and is generally produced by accidents or violence. Uniform Crime Reports and the National Crime Victimization Survey published each year by the Justice Department indicate that Americans suffer approximately 23,000 homicides and two and a half million aggravated assaults each year. If the six and a half million "simple assaults" and 433,000 forcible rapes are added to these figures then there are approximately 9.5 million reported acts of violence in the United States each year. The street crime and violence problem in the United States is however much worse than the numbers reported to agencies which keep such statistics. Criminologists agree that there is a "dark figure" of crime in America and that there are many more "hidden" crimes than those known to the police or the courts. Because the American population stands at around 263 million in 1999 the chances of a person becoming a victim of violent crime are around five percent. It may seem to some that 5% is a low figure, which guarantees that the safety of 95% of Americans is not compromised. It needs to be considered, however, that such violence has been the most common cause of death of young Afro-American men for a score of years. Unfortunately, this is not abating at the end of this century despite the downturn of violent crime in America during the five years ending in 1999.[34]

For the Afro-American ethnic group this means that entire families, neighborhoods and communities have been decimated by violence. There are many Americans who live in constant fear of homicide or other violent means of conflict resolution. This fear of violence overshadows the lives of those most affected and can be understood by noting that 44% of the victims of violent assaults in trauma centers are re-hospitalized with further wounds during the five years ensuing after their previous hospitalization. Few of the victims of these assaults with deadly weapons are insured so that American hospitals are financially threatened by the use of large resources required to care for these patients. It has been estimated that for each firearm fatality in the United States, 2 persons sustain non-fatal injuries that lead to hospitalization and 5 persons sustain injuries requiring outpatient treatment at a cost of $4 billion. Handguns are used in 71% of assaults leading to hospitalization and shotguns are used in 23% of such cases. Because most of the victims of these shootings are poorly insured or not insured at all, losses associated with providing care to the uninsured is a major concern for trauma centers. This can mean that neither the hospital nor trauma surgeons will be paid adequately for their services to gun-injured patients.[35]

Surgeons are of course most responsible for saving these critically injured victims of violence as surgeons in American hospitals respond to this problem every day. As the trauma surgeons Cornwell, *et al* say: "...there are few emotions to match the exhilaration of saving a critically injured victim of violence." [36]

Violence inflicted on the young by each other is not confined to criminal activity. It also includes violent sports. For that reason there are surgeons who have specialized in sports medicine and who have formed a society of their own called American Orthopaedic Society for Sports Medicine. These surgeons are frequently team physicians for football teams and other sports teams whose activities can involve various injuries. Orthopaedic surgeons comprise only 3% of all American physicians so that some teams use primary care physicians as team doctors. However, almost all sports injuries are musculoskeletal in nature and are therefore best treated by orthopaedic specialists.[37]

Trauma is not limited to violence mostly inflicted on the young because it also includes accidents mainly suffered by the old. Injuries of all kinds occur much more in the evening and on weekends than during working hours. In fact, three quarters of trauma cases are seen after business hours. The needs of such patients are of course immediate and time sensitive. Therefore, trauma surgeons refer to their work as "primary care in the pit" as they have to be "on line" waiting for these patients. Such patients may have been involved in auto accidents, fires, street violence or other injury and domestic violence. The American Academy of Facial Plastic and Reconstructive Surgery has therefore offered reconstructive surgery to the victims of domestic abuse at no cost to the domestic violence survivor. This program is called "Face to Face" The patients of such plastic surgery are women. Dr. Wayne Larrabee, president of the academy says that 75% of women who have been abused receive injuries to the face and head. The "face to face" program works by listing a national 24 hour toll-free telephone number which links women with a participating surgeon in their community. The importance of this service cannot be overestimated since the victims of domestic violence are often unable to seek a job or return to work until their face has been reconstructed. Dr. Lori E.

Hansen who runs a private surgical practice in Oklahoma City reports that those who are about to go to work after having been victimized in a domestic attack will invariably say: "Every time I look in the mirror I see this cigarette burn, these baggy eyes, or my broken nose and it reminds me of the abuse." Therefore, says Hansen, the patients see plastic surgery "as a whole new lease on life." [38]

That "new lease on life" should be available to all who need it. Insurance companies, however, view all plastic surgery as pure cosmetics and generally refuse payment for such procedures. Dr. Deborah Sarnoff reports the case of a little girl who had a "hemangioma (a birthmark) the size of a golf ball on her forehead whose insurance company denied coverage for laser treatments." [39]

In Long Island Children's Museum there was an exhibit called Art and Emotion. Dr. Frederick N. Lukash, a plastic surgeon, collected the pictures in that exhibit. Dr. Lukash has changed the lives of children and adults because he has been able to correct physical defects, which occur at birth. Scott Caldwell is one of the children whom Dr. Lukash helped. Born without the normal cartilage crease in his ears, he was the butt of endless teasing in school and on the playground because his ears protruded so much. Then, after his operation he was no longer called "Dumbo", "Big Ears" and "Mickey Mouse" by other children. [40] Obviously plastic surgery would have been helpful to Dr. Sarnoff's little patient and was helpful to Scott Caldwell and many others who have been injured.

Now it turns out that plastic surgery is most helpful to the surgeons who have been deprived of their erstwhile income by the health maintenance organizations. Dr. Phillip Haeck, a Seattle plastic surgeon is an excellent example of the manner in which such surgeons have been forced to enter into procedures not covered by insurance companies. After managed care companies cut his income by 60% to $1,980 for reconstructive breast surgery for cancer patients, Dr. Haeck switched to cosmetic surgery, which is not covered by insurance companies. He is now earning $3,800 in less than two hours for one breast enlargement. Thousands of other surgeons, disgusted and frustrated by the intrusion of managed care into their private practices, have been building lucrative practices in cosmetic surgery, correcting myopias with lasers, removal of wrinkles, face lifts, nose jobs, hair transplants for men, vein surgery, chemical peels of unsightly skin and liposuction to remove fatty tissue. The fees for such procedures can range up to $20,000. As a result of managed care it has now become easier for surgeons to earn more money from patients without insurance than with insurance. For those who cannot afford these fee-for-service arrangements and must therefore remain with their insurance companies it means that the best surgeons are no longer available to them, the managed care patients. The evidence is that those surgeons who can will withdraw from the mindless bureaucracy of the insurers and the health maintenance organizations. Not only plastic surgeons, but eye surgeons have shifted from receiving less than $1,000 for a lens implant for a cataract patient to the use of lasers to correct nearsightedness for which patients will pay $1,500 to $2,000 per eye. Penis enlargement surgery is now practiced by urologist- surgeons for which they can charge from $4,800-$7,000 privately instead of accepting $600.- from an insurer for treating enlarged prostate glands. Urologists have also entered the field of infertility treatments.

The reason surgeons can earn such large fees is found in the increase in family income prevalent in the U.S. since 1994. That increase has been remarkable as the top 20% of Americans are earning more than $105,000 each year. Consequently the health maintenance organizations have driven some skilled surgeons out of the treatment of disease and into elective surgery to the detriment of the poor and the advantage of the rich.[41]

III

Because costs are such a vital issue in the treatment of American patients it has been suggested that money and lives could be saved if high-risk operations were performed at large regional hospitals. There surgeons can perform many operations each year while at smaller hospitals surgeons have only occasional patients with high risk conditions.

A study by Dr. Toby Gordon and Dr. John L. Cameron, chief of surgery at Johns Hopkins Hospital, revealed that of the 271 so –called "Whipple" operations for pancreatic cancer there were six deaths, resulting in a 2.2% mortality rate. This is far less than is true in hospitals whose surgeons have fewer opportunities to conduct such operations.[42]

In any event, autonomy of action has almost disappeared from the profession of surgery even as more and more treatments can be performed while fewer and fewer patients have access to these new developments.

That these developments in surgery have reached truly amazing proportions is visible by inspecting an entire body catalogue of parts that are now replaceable. These replaceable body parts include brain shunts and electrodes implanted in the brain to control body seizures; phrenic nerve stimulators to control breathing disorders; electronic stimulators to restore hand movements; artificial corneas, lens replacements and ocular replacements of an eye; cochlear implants replacing the inner ear and artificial outer ears; silicone or plastic implants to replace bony structures of the face; dental implants to repair or replace the jaw; replacements for arteries and veins; pacemakers, ventricular bypass devices, defribillators and artificial hearts; artificial bones and joints and numerous urological devices to deal with prostate, penile, testicular and intrauterine problems. Research is now underway to create artificial lungs, livers, and other organs. In short, almost everything is or will be replaceable through the art and skill of surgery, including artificial hearts.[43]

In March of 1983, Barney Clark died at the University of Utah Medical Center after surviving 112 days with an artificial heart. He was not the first to receive an artificial heart for it was Christian Barnard, a South African surgeon who performed the first human heart transplant in 1967. It was on October 26, 1984 that Dr. Leonard Bailey replaced the heart of a 12-day old girl with the heart of a baboon at Loma Linda Medical Center in California. Although the child died twenty days after that implantation, the use of an artificial heart was indeed an astonishing achievement. Then, on November 15 of that same year, Dr. William DeVries in Louisville, Kentucky implanted a plastic and aluminum artificial heart into the chest of William Schroeder, whose heart was failing rapidly. Schroeder died on August 6, 1986. Since then, this procedure, erstwhile considered impossible has been repeated on numerous other patients.[44]

Surgery depends of course on surgeons and the advances here mentioned are the products of the ingenuity of that minority of scientists who, in any science, advance the state of human knowledge out of proportion to their numbers. One such surgeon is Dr. Samuel Pallin of Arizona. An ophthalmic surgeon, he invented and holds a patent on a procedure for stitchless cataract surgery. He therefore demands that other surgeons using his patented techniques pay him royalties each time they use it. Dr. Pallin is not alone in this effort to earn money by patenting techniques they may or may not have invented.[45]

It is entirely possible that the patent on a surgical technique could be held by someone who was first to think of patenting it, even if he was not the first to develop it. This trend to patent surgical techniques is undoubtedly motivated by the decrease in income now facing surgeons. It is, however, regarded as unethical by many members of the profession. In fact, the American Medical Association's Council on Ethics and Judicial Affairs has decided that patenting medical methods violates the Hippocratic oath as well as A.M.A. ethics guidelines. Yet, others argue that device patents have existed for years and that the

A.M.A. has never objected to such patents. In fact, there are numerous patents on various surgical procedures now held by doctors. These include implanting a knee prosthesis, closing an incision in muscle tissue, calculating risk of coronary heart disease, treating chronic ear infection, treating rheumatic arthritis, performing laser surgery without damaging nearby tissue, treating bone disorders, treating aneurysms, treating shingles, doing radiosurgery of the eye, scanning an internal organ and treatments concerning HIV infections and AIDS. It may take drawn-out court battles to decide whether doctors may hold patents on these and other procedures. Meanwhile, Congress has passed a law prohibiting the issue of a patent for medical research. This then raises the question of whether such a law will inhibit research that would otherwise be of benefit to all patients.[46]

A far different innovator than Dr. Pallin is the Brazilian surgeon Dr. Randas Jose Vilela Batista who invented the procedure of cutting a piece from the enlarged hearts of patients suffering from congestive heart failure. This heart reduction surgery has permitted 60% of patients with no other hope of survival to live at least another two years. This operation would replace heart transplants that in any event are only available to one percent of the world's population.[47]

Research is the life - blood of any science and the foundation of surgery as well. It is therefore not surprising that procedures which were nothing more than science fiction thirty years ago are reality today. Among these is the development of robot surgery. Robota is a Czech word referring to drudgery or the work of an automaton. As such, robots have become common tools in the automobile industry and other factories. The drug industry has used robots for some time to screen and analyze its programs. Now the Institute of Urology in London, England is using a robot for prostate removal. This procedure was developed by Dr. Brian Davies who also designed a robot to help fit prosthetic knee implants. In the United States the Jet Propulsion Laboratory at the California Institute of Technology in Burbank is developing methods of using robots for brain, eye, ear, nose, throat, face and head surgery. It is claimed by developers of robots that these devices have several advantages over human beings, including greater accuracy, precision and reliability. Robots are programmed to allow a surgeon to take over at any time. With that and other safety devices included, it is certain that robot technology will replace most human surgery in a few years. Together with virtual reality and telesurgery these methods will make human surgery obsolete very soon. Telesurgery allows distant surgeons, even in foreign countries, to supervise operations at remote locations. This is reported in the Japanese publication, Journal of Computer Aided Surgery. It is also in

Japan that engineers have produced a simulator for abdominal surgery, an endoscope with a laser scalpel and a new generation of robots with tiny motors.[48]

Virtual reality is provided by a device developed in the United States which supplies three dimensional maps as well as continuous magnetic resonance imaging. The development of virtual colonoscopy and virtual bronchoscopy is also under way as is a procedure creating a detailed replica of a patient's tissues. All are indications that science-fiction of yesterday is today's reality. [49]

Summary

Surgery has a different history than medicine. While surgery was at one time viewed as the work of charlatans, surgery is today a most prestigious and high income profession. Because of the intrusion of the business world into medicine and surgery through the H.M.O.'s surgeons are losing much of their erstwhile autonomy. Political considerations affecting minorities and women are preventing these groups from fully participating in the profession. Ethical issues are an important aspect of surgery as is communication with patients. Surgeons are constantly confronted with the consequences of violence but have been of great help to many patients through the use of plastic surgery and the developments in transplant surgery. Most recently, developments in robot technology have been used to conduct surgery with some success. Because doctors are not alone in providing health services to the American public we will now examine the contributions of non-physicians and surgeons to the health delivery system in this country. We begin by discussing the nursing profession in the next chapter.

NOTES

[1] No author, "Skullduggery," *Scientific American*, Vol. 262, No. 6, June 1990, p. 34.

[2] James H. Cassedy, *Medicine in America: A Short History*, Baltimore, The Johns Hopkins Press, 1991, p. 126.

[3] Ronald L. Numbers, *Almost Persuaded*, Baltimore, The Johns Hopkins University Press, 1978, p. 1.

[4] John W. Wright, Editor, *The New York Times Almanac*, New York, Penguin Putnam, Inc., 1997, p. 382.

[5] Sean I. Savitz, "The Pivotal Role of Harvey Cushing in the Birth of Modern Neurosurgery," JAMA, Vol.278, No. 13, October 1, 1997, p. 1119.

[6] Werner Forssmann, *Experiments on Myself: Memoirs of a Surgeon in Germany*, New York, St. Martin's Press, 1974.

[7] John C. Hall and Cameron Platell, "Half-life of truth in surgical literature," *The Lancet*, Vol.350, December 13, 1997, p. 1752.

[8] Milt Freudenheim, "Insurers Tighten Rules and Reduce Fees for Doctors," *The New York Times*, June 28, 1998, p. 1.

[9] Nancy Ann Jeffrey, "New Threat for HMO's: Doctor Discipline Boards," *The Wall Street Journal*, July 13, 1998, p. B1.

[10] Phyllida Brown, "Dentists and surgeons in the U.S. face compulsory HIV testing. *The New Scientist*, Vol. 129, No. 1753, January 26, 1998, p.21.

[11] No Author, "Court Says Surgeon Should Have Disclosed HIV Status," *JAMA*, Vol.124, May 1993, p. 165.

[12] Tom Treasure, "Where did I go wrong?" The Lancet, Vol. 344, August 13, 1994, pp. 419-420.

[13] Eric C. Schneider and Arnold M. Epstein, "Influence of cardiac surgery performance reports on referral practices and access to care." *The New England Journal of Medicine*, Vol. 335, No. 4. July 25, 1996, pp. 251-256.

[14] Lloyd M. Kreiger, "Cardiac Surgery Performance Reports," *The New England Journal of Medicine*, Vol. 336, No. 6, February 6, 1997, p. 442.

[15] Eric C. Schneider and Arnold M. Epstein, "Use of Public Performance Reports: A Survey of Patients Undergoing Cardiac Surgery," JAMA , May 27, 1998, p. 1638.

[16] Arthur J. Hartz, Jose S . Pulido and Evelyn M. Kuhn, "Are the Best Coronary Artery Bypass Surgeons Identified by Physician Surveys?" *American Journal of Public Health*, Vol. 87, No. 10, October 1997, p. 1645.
[17] No author, "Nevada Supreme Court Overturns Discipline of Neurosurgeon," *JADA*, Vol.124, June 1993, pp. 116-117. See also: Alan J. Mishler vs. The State of Nevada Board of Medical Examiners, #22397. 849 P.2d P. 291.
[18] Gerhard Falk, *Sex, Gender and Social Change, The Great Revolution*, Lanham, New York, Oxford, The University Press of America, 1998.
[19] No author, "Clear and Present Danger," *Nursing*, Vol. 25, No. 9, September, 1995, p. 9.
[20] Henry L. Davis, "State suspends top Buffalo heart surgeon over conduct," *The Buffalo News*, August 19, 1998, p. A 1.
[21] Karen Allen and Jim Blascovich, "Effects of Music on Cardiovascular Reactivity Among Surgeons," *JAMA*, September 21, 1994, p. 882.
[22] Joan Cassell, "The Woman in the Surgeon's Body: Understanding Difference," *American Anthropologist*, Vol. 98, No.1, pp. 41-53.
[23] K.H. Simpson, "The development of a clinical ethics consultation service in a community hospital," *Journal of Clinical Ethics*, Vol.3, No.2, 1992, pp. 124-130.
[24] Frederick Paola and Sharon S. Barton, "An 'ethics gap' in writing about bioethics: a quantitative comparison of the medical and the surgical literature," *Journal of Medical Ethics*, Vol21, No. 2, April 1995, pp. 84-88.
[25] Larry Vendecreek, Deborah Frankowski and Susan Ayres, "Use of the Threat Index with Family Members Waiting during Surgery," *Death Studies*, Vol.18, No.6, 1994, pp. 641-647.
[26] Jennifer L. Garfein, "The Patient's Perspective," *JAMA*, Vol.275, No. 17, May 1, 1996, p. 1371.
[27] Philip Meredith, "Patient Satisfaction With Communication in General Surgery: Problems of Measurement and Improvement." *Social Science and Medicine*, Vol.37, No. 5, September, 1993, p. 591.
[28] No author, "Brain Surgeon Who Made a Mistake Is Reinstated," *The New York Times*, October 4, 1995, p. C 4.
[29] Alan McGregor, "Sentenced for homicide," *The Lancet*, Vol.342, No. 8871, September 4, 1993, p.610.
[30] No author, "Mishap in the Operating Room," *The Economist*, Vol. 344, No. 8028, August 2, 1997, p.48.

[31] Jan Fisher, " Plastic Surgery, Unsupervised, Leads to a Fine for a Hospital, " *The New York Times,* December 19, 1997, p. B1.

[32] Elisabeth Rosenthal, "Post-Surgery Deaths Prompt Inquiry at a Queens Hospital," *The New York Times,* August 1, 1995, p. A 1.

[33] Nicholas J. Fox, "Postmodernism, rationality and the evaluation of health care," *The Sociological Review,* Vol. 39, No. 4, November 1991, p.725.

[34] Steven E. Barkan, *Criminology: A Sociological Understanding,* Upper Saddle River, N.J., Prentice Hall, 1997, p. 60.

[35] Mary J. Vassar and Kenneth W. Kizer, "Hospitalizations for Firearm-Related Injuries," *JAMA,* Vol.275, No. 22, June 12, 1996, pp. 1734-1739.

[36] Edward E. Cornwell III, David Jacobs, Mark Walker, Lenworth Jacobs, John Porter and Arthur Fleming, "National Medical Association Surgical Position Paper on Violence Prevention," *JAMA,* Vol.273, No. 22, June 14, 1995, pp. 1788-1789.

[37] Arthur L. Boland, "Our Qualifications as Orthopaedic Surgeons to be Team Physicians," *The American Journal of Sports Medicine,* Vol. 24, No.6, November/December 1996, p. 712.

[38] Rebecca Voelker, "Surgeons Offer 'New Lease' After Domestic Abuse," *JAMA,* Vol.274, No. 20, November 22/29, 1995, p. 1573.

[39] Linda Saslow, "When Insurers Deem That Surgery Is Purely Cosmetic," *The New York Times,* November 23, 1997, p. 14.

[40] Bruce Lambert, "Picture This: Big Smiles After Surgery," *The New York Times,* October 18, 1997, p. B1.

[41] Milt Freudenheim, "As Insurers Cut Fees, Doctors Shift to Elective Procedures, " *The New York Times,* November 17, 1996, p. 24.

[42] No Author, "Centers Suggested for High –Risk Surgery," *The New York Times,* January 19,1995, p. 13A

[43] Warren E. Leary, "The Whole Body Catalogue," *The New York Times,* July 8, 1997, Sec.C, pp. 1-6

[44] Dennis L. Breo, "Two surgeons who dared are still chasing their dreams," *JAMA,* Vol. 262, No. 20, November 24, 1989, 2904.

[45] Sabra Chartrand, "Why is this Surgeon Suing?" *The New York Times,* June 8, 1995, pp. D1-5.

[46] Teresa Riordan, "Patents: New legislation seeks to exclude surgical procedures from patent protection," *The New York Times,* March 6, 1995, p. D2.

[47] Daniel Hart and Alice Park, "Too Big a Heart," *Time, Special Issue,* Vol. 150, No. 19, Fall 1997, pp. 35-37.

[48] David B. Jack, "Robot surgeons: never mind the cost, feel the quality," *The Lancet,* Vol.348, No. 9035, October 26, 1996, p. 1160.
[49] Elizabeth Finkel, "Surgery moves into the third dimension," *The Lancet,* Vol.348, No. 9043, December 21/28, 1996, p. 1726.

Chapter VI

The Caring Profession-Nursing the Sick

I

On March 12, 1998 the U.S. Bureau of Labor Statistics reported that there were then 1,908,470 registered nurses in the United States.[1] A registered nurse is one who has passed the national licensing examination known as the State Board Test Pool. This examination became nation-wide in 1950 when all U.S. states and some Canadian provinces adopted the same examination as a means of obtaining nursing licensure and registration.[2]

The income of nurses varies widely because the responsibilities of nurses range over such a large area of work. Anesthesiology nurses earned an average salary of $73,756 in 1997 but a "head nurse" and all others earned a good deal less than that. "Head nurses" received an average of $47,270 in 1997, "charge nurses" earned an average salary of $42,480, "staff nurses" earned $41,704, "operating room nurses" $41,412, intensive care nurses" $40,435, "medical-surgical nurses," $39,499 and "emergency room" nurses $39, 062. It is evident from this list that the median annual earnings of registered nurses, $36,244 is less than half of the average salary earned by anesthesiology nurses. It is also noteworthy that male nurses earn 5% more than women, who constituted 94% of the membership in that profession in 1997.[3]

The earnings of Licensed Practical Nurses are a good deal less. Typical of the education of L.P.N.s is the law in the State of Washington requiring 450 hours of special preparation and 5 months on-the-job training to attain a practical nurse license.[4] The earnings of licensed practical nurses reflect this difference in training. The median income of the 640,000 American L.P.N's was $25,000 a year or 69% of the median earnings of registered nurses in 1997.[5]

The licensing of registered and practical nurses is now only a half a century old. Its original purpose was not only to protect the public but also to give nurses and other licensed professions the independence a license implies. Yet, now, at the end of five decades of government regulated licensure, a number of states have proposed the disbanding of regulatory boards to allow unlicensed workers to provide at least some home and community services. The consequence of that procedure must be that without government controls, oversight falls to the employer, making that method a *de facto* institutional licensure. Such a trend would return the nursing professions to the time before 1950 when nurses were viewed has having primary responsibility to the employer and not the patient. The license reversed that approach and allowed nurses to be more responsive to the needs of the patient than the financial interests of institutions. In view of the tremendous drive to lower costs of medical care underway at the end of this century it is almost certain that institutional licensure will sacrifice the interests of the patient to the financial advantages of hospital administrators. Obviously, nurses would not be free to speak out in favor of patients if their employer is also the regulator. This demonstrates that financial interests so dominate the American health delivery system that Hippocrates has indeed been assailed if not betrayed and that every level of health care is about to be "dumbed down" to save money. [6]

Even as nurses are concerned about the gradual encroachment of unlicensed and untrained personnel into their area of expertise, nurses themselves are entering the practice of medicine on the grounds that they know as much about the treatment of patients as any graduate of a medical school. Convinced that this is so, 52% of patients surveyed in 1998 were "very willing" to see a registered nurse rather than a physician. If it is true that nurse-practitioners can function like doctors of medicine with only five years of schooling past high school, then it becomes legitimate to ask: "Why should the medical education of primary care physicians take in excess of ten years?" There are those who would deny the need for a medical education. However, Kassirer argues that nurses cannot perform as well as physicians because nurses are not sufficiently trained to recognize a complex medical problem that "requires reasoning from first principles." We would wonder how it is possible that medical care of patients requires less training in 2000 than it did in 1980. [7]

It is therefore most likely that the effort to give nurses the responsibilities heretofore allocated to physicians is driven, once more, by financial considerations. These financial considerations are the chief concern of health maintenance organizations that have lobbied the government successfully in gaining the right of nurse-practitioners to receive reimbursement from Medicare. Medicare is only one of five basic programs under which the federal government buys health care. The others are: the Department of Defense Civilian Health and Medical Program of the Uniformed Services, the Federal Employees' Health Benefit Program, the income tax provisions subsidizing health care expenditures and Medicaid. The inclusion of nurse-practitioners among those receiving payments from Medicare was contained in the Balanced Budget Act of 1997 which Congress passed and which was signed into law in August of that year. This law extended the Community Nursing Organization pilot project until the end of 1999. Community nursing organizations are managed care programs operated by nurses. These programs offer Medicare benefits to the old in non-institutional settings, i.e. in nurses' offices. The programs are run by nurse practitioners.[8] Such nurse practitioners are also known as advanced practice registered nurses and clinical nurse specialists. Heretofore, such nurses had to either work in nursing homes or in narrowly defined rural areas. In nursing homes registered nurses have achieved dominance in decision making because doctors visit nursing homes only temporarily and because many nursing home managers have no medical or nursing training themselves. Therefore, such managers must rely on nurses for advice both on the strategic decision making level and in regard to the day-to-day, tactical type decisions.[9]

Prior to the Balanced Budget Act of 1997 those nurses who practiced outside defined rural areas had to be supervised by a physician and to be in the physical presence of a physician while administering services. Under these circumstances the supervising physicians and not the nurses billed Medicare. Therefore, the right of nurses to bill Medicare themselves will reveal the volume and the kind of services performed by nurses. Although the new Medicare law intends that nurses work in collaboration with a physician, several states, under pressure from the American Nurses Association have avoided the issue of physician collaboration. This then indicates that the emerging health delivery system in America is about to become stratified beginning with unlicensed practical nurses and ranging all the way to highly trained medical specialists whom the patient will only see after visiting the entire array of providers leading to the final diagnosis. This system is undoubtedly far more efficient than the chaos prevailing before 1995. Nevertheless, this stratified system involves the inherent danger that a patient will be permanently injured or die before a "provider" sees him who can recognize the patient's problem and deal with it.[10]

The tendency of hospitals to substitute licensed practical nurses and unlicensed assisting personnel for registered nurses, together with the introduction of nurse practitioners, has altered the future of the nurse labor market considerably. Traditionally, two thirds of all registered nurses had been employed in hospitals. However, the effort to reduce costs at any price has recently led to the substitution of licensed practical nurses for registered nurses. Likewise, changes in other areas of employment have also affected nurses in recent years. This means that there has been a shift in nursing personnel out of hospitals and into health care organizations. As hospitals have "downsized," nurses have lost their jobs. This has been most frequent in Southern California, New York and Connecticut. In those states intense competition between managed care organizations has led to hospital downsizing and a decrease in nurse employment. This decrease includes licensed practical nurses who are being replaced by aides who are now being trained, more or less, as so-called "multi-skilled workers" to reduce costs.

It remains to be seen whether these measures will really reduce costs. Because hospitals are discharging patients earlier the need for home health care is now greater than ever before. Therefore, the use of registered and licensed nurses in home health care has risen substantially as RN's particularly use a "high-tech" approach in caring for their patients. This trend has increased the pay of nurses so that it may well be that the costs associated with the early discharge policies of hospitals will be absorbed by the home health care costs these discharges must entail. In addition, the ever growing pressure to impose a mechanistic medical model on nursing can and will result in undermining the basic values of the nursing profession. This failure to recognize the need for humanitarian caring for the sick and disabled must result in job dissatisfaction, stress and frustration and confrontations between patients, nurses and administrators. The great German sociologist Max Weber foresaw this development when he said in The Protestant Ethic and the Spirit of Capitalism: "....for the last stage of this cultural development it might well be truly said: specialists without spirit, sensualists without a heart, this nullity imagines that it has attained a level of civilization never before achieved." [11]

That word from Weber surely applies to nursing homes which have increased so much during the ten years ending in 2000. Therefore, a good number of registered nurses have indeed been absorbed into nursing homes in recent years. However, here too aides have been hired in record number to keep expenses as low as possible. The sum of all this stress on finances is of course that patients are treated mainly by untrained or under-trained health delivery workers, a situation over which the patients who need help the most have the least control. [12]

Registered nurses have traditionally been trained to work in hospitals and not in nursing homes or home health care situations. Therefore, the basic educational curriculum in nursing schools is now being changed so that future nurses will be able to practice alone. Responding to that need, the American Association of Colleges of Nursing has developed new standards for baccalaureate nursing education.[13]

II

The primary purpose of state legislatures in requiring a professional practitioner to hold a license is reputedly the need to protect the public. Indeed, if anyone could practice nursing without training of any kind then such a license would hardly serve a legitimate purpose. Of course, relatives and friends continue to nurse those near and dear to them at home and even in part in hospitals and nursing homes solely on grounds of love and duty. Similarly, almost everyone has given medical advice to members of his family or "practiced law" on anyone willing to listen.

Licensing is therefore an effort to protect those who pay for the services of someone who, they believe, can be trusted to know how to best meet their needs. The public, as well as legislators have evidently decided that nursing has developed sufficient clinical skills to trust its practitioners to practice on their own, i.e., to be autonomous. Additionally, universities and the profession itself have developed enough internal agreement to be able to supervise their own members and to set limits as to their competence. Practically, state legislatures become willing to enact licensing requirements when a profession has achieved enough "grass roots" support to make licensing politically feasible.[14]

This "grass roots" support was engendered by home health care nurses, who, as we have seen, have increased their importance during the past several years as admissions to hospitals have decreased and accelerated discharges have become the rule. Many patients who would have been cared for in a hospital are now receiving home health care. Therefore, nurses who were discharged from hospital jobs are now performing in home health care, although doctors do not always recognize contributions from the nursing profession. The type of knowledge and skills learned by nursing students at the baccalaureate level is of course such that it can be applied to home health care as well. Yet, there is concern that these skills and that knowledge will gradually be lost by nurses who do not see patients in the context of the hospital. Home health care places almost all of the responsibility for the patient on the shoulders of the nurse. That responsibility includes extensive documentation, i.e. "paper work". Because patients who are discharged early from hospitals after an operation need the skills of medical-surgical nurses, such nurses are sought out by home health clinics. Executives of such clinics say that it takes at least six months, if not eighteen, for an erstwhile hospital nurse to become efficient in home health care. Therefore, a program is needed which can be used to prepare acute care nurses for home health nursing demands. One such program has been developed in the State of Washington. There, nurses have listed case finding, screening, assessment, case management, a number of administrative and legal issues and a caregiver value orientation as the most important needs which should be taught to all home health nurses. [15] Numerous other proposals by a variety of administrators, writers and nurse-practitioners all agree that home health nurses should be competent in physical assessment and diagnosis and have a good knowledge of nutrition and family counseling.

In Massachusetts the American Nurses Association has developed a curriculum yielding twelve college credits towards the RN-BSN degree. Upon completion of that degree and the gaining of some experience a master's program in community health nursing is now available in many American universities and colleges. Local home health agencies, however, increasingly hire nurses with an Associates degree, i.e. a degree granted by a two year community college. Therefore, advanced degrees are usually earned by those who are already working with two years of training and who must therefore be accommodated by coming to class in the evening. Many such students have been out of school for years and need special orientation to libraries, computers and other methods not in vogue at the time of their graduation.

In Omaha, Neb. a four-fold curriculum is taught to home health care nursing students and to working nurses. This includes environment, psychosocial behavior, physiological behavior and health related behavior. The curriculum includes the study of 44 problems that are designed to "stimulate the student's awareness of the breadth of home health practice." [16]

Home health care nurses are also expected to be able to work for insurance companies and in managed care organizations. These organizations have created an "upswing" for nurses with graduate degrees. This development confirms the view that the future in the nursing profession will increasingly belong to the "advanced practice nurses" who are in fact practicing medicine. These nurses diagnose and order medicine and decide when a patient is ready to go home. Such nurses are supplanting physicians. Because this opportunity to practice medicine without having to undergo the rigors of a medical school education is so attractive, enrollment in master's degree programs at nursing schools has risen by nearly 2 percent each year since 1996. Enrollment at bachelor's level programs fell by nearly 7 percent during the same years. Consequently, the number of universities offering programs for nurse practitioners have also increased. In 1992 there were 119 such programs. At the end of 1997 there were 202 with more in preparation. Acute care specialization has also increased so that 26 schools offered training in that specialty at the end of 1997 while only one such program existed in 1992 at the University of Pennsylvania. Here students are taught how to make decisions concerning treatment, drug therapy and the use of appropriate technology. Students in such programs are generally registered nurses with eight to nine years experience. Because the kinds of programs offered by different universities vary so much in requirements and in faculty preparation the Commission on Collegiate Nursing Education has published criteria designed to standardize such programs.[17]

One such program was instituted at Syracuse University's school of nursing. It is one of the schools offering a master's degree for a nurse practitioner. This costs $20,000 while a graduate certificate program in the same specialty costs the student $8,000.- Because of these high costs and because of the intense and difficult course work needed to attain such a degree, students who had already spent a year in the program were shocked to learn in August of 1998 that Syracuse University had never received New York State certification to operate such a program. Twenty two students were affected by the failure of the dean of nursing to tell them that the state had three times turned down the Syracuse University proposal to certify the family nurse-practitioner program. The state Education Department refused to do so because of a lack of faculty qualifications as family nurse-practitioners. Evidently, the administration of the university concealed this information from the students because they did not want to lose thousands of dollars of federal funding that came with those students.[18]

State certification seeks to assure that advanced practice nurses are trained to conduct physical examinations, diagnose and treat minor illnesses and injuries, order lab tests and X rays and interpret results, and counsel patients. Advanced practice nurses are now also preferred by women who need "colposcopy", which is a visual examination of the cervix to discover the possibility of cancer. In view of the many tasks nurses have now undertaken it is significant that a recent review of 210 studies comparing the care given by doctors and nurses found that nurses perform as well as physicians. Nevertheless, it must be remembered that nurses do not possess a medical education and may have difficulty diagnosing ambiguous symptoms.[19]

Community health nurses may be private practitioners. Others have entered the field of public health nurse. In that capacity nurses seek to compete with social workers and with doctors, particularly in rural communities. In such communities patients are often more sick and in need of more services than is true in cities. This is so because of early patient discharge, short hospital stays, increased "ambulatory" care and home health care.[20]

Technology has also given community health nurses an opportunity to enter into areas of care once reserved for the hands of physicians. Intravenous therapy, wound irrigation, respirators used at home by patients and other devices are now the province of nurses. Nurses also counsel family caregivers, particularly in hospices and in other settings among the terminally ill. This situation is particularly acute with the growing number of AIDS patients as AIDS has reached epidemic proportions in this country.

Because acquired immune deficiency syndrome is a transmissible and frequently fatal disease, nurses rightly perceive a personal vulnerability in caring for such AIDS patients. This means that nurses who work with AIDS patients are likely to suffer an increase in death anxiety leading to avoidance, extreme precautions and a lack of regard for those suffering from the disease. It is therefore in the interest of dying patients and the nursing profession if means could be found that can overcome death anxiety. Such means can be a greater awareness of ourselves as members of a group of family and friends. That kind of awareness has the merit of calling attention to the endless continuity of life and therefore reduces death anxiety. Furthermore, those who hold some fundamental values, be they of a religious or philosophical nature, are also less anxious about death or non-being. Death can be given meaning by such a set of values, particularly if we have some important life goals that we are working to fulfill. Surely, the care of the sick and the dying can be such a life goal. Hence, nurses who care for AIDS patients can be induced to recognize the importance of their work and the meaning their work gives their lives. There are of course those who interpret death as punishment and who fear going "to hell" and suffering unpleasant cruelties after death. Such notions certainly heighten death anxiety. There are innumerable explanations for death anxiety, ranging from Freud's view that death anxiety is really a fear of castration and separation anxiety. There are others who seek the cause of death anxiety in deprivation in the mother-child relationship; as loss of control and fear of pain. There are many other "explanations." It has been proposed that those who view themselves as more than a physical body can accept death without fear because they see death as part of life. Such an attitude can view death as another form of being outside the body and without bodily constraints in which the self does not cease to exist. Because Americans principally interpret the world in purely physical terms, death anxiety can be high among the religious as well as the non religious segment of the American population. Religious conduct consists of participation in ritual and therefore has visible and physical aspects. It is however awareness of our connection to the universe that permits us to recognize our co-existence with other living things which reduces death anxiety and confronts the view that death is final or even absolute. In fact, in the Buddhist and Hindu tradition death is viewed as liberation and hence can be confronted without fear. This view is of course open to anyone and is not confined to the Hindu-Buddhist tradition.[21]

Finally, a high exposure to death also reduces death-anxiety although Americans are seldom present at someone's death as are nurses.[22]

Nurses are far more likely to be caring for dying patients than is true of doctors. Therefore nursing educators have been interested in teaching nursing students how to provide physical, emotional and spiritual support to the dying patient and his family. Beck reports on the feelings of nursing students as they came to deal with the imminent death of their patients. According to that report, nursing students generally experienced one or more of six reactions as a consequence of dealing with dying patients. Initially students experienced fear. Later they became more comfortable with their feelings towards the dying although many sought to emotionally distance themselves from the dying patient and his family. Many nursing students, as well as many people everywhere, believe that they lack the right words to use in face of death and therefore feel uncomfortable discussing death. Many nursing students, as well as others, also feel anger at physicians for not doing more for the dying patients. A second reaction of nursing students to their dying patients was contemplation of the dying patient's life and the kind of life that patient had led. Thirdly, nursing students realized that the dying patient's family became part of their responsibility as well. The grieving family is evidently very much in need of support so that a nurse will have to decide how to divide her time between the dying patient and the family. Nurses and nursing students also feel helpless in giving the dying patient more pain medication and in carrying out the dying patient's last wishes. Often nurses know these wishes better than family who may not be present when such wishes are made. Nursing students and others also learn that holding a dying person's hand and speaking or praying with the dying patient is most useful in providing comfort to the dying. Discussing the patient's imminent death is essential in such a situation as the fear of dying ebbs and flows in such patients. The sixth and most important lesson nursing students learned was that unconditional and non-judgmental caring helps not only those who eventually get well but also helps those who die. This illustrates that the help anyone can give the dying is not wasted but of great importance. [23]

It is of course on that principle that the hospice movement was founded by Cicely Saunders in London, England. The first hospice in the United States was established in Branford, Connecticut in 1974. Today there are 3,000 hospice programs in this country serving 450,000 patients at any one time. Currently these programs are growing at the rate of 17 percent annually. [24]

No conclusive research concerning these hospices exists now. The National Hospice Organization does have a survey asking families to report their satisfaction with the outcome of hospice care and that appears to be positive. However, the health maintenance organizations, in their anxiety to make money, have minimized the emotional and spiritual care which was the basis for the hospice movement at the outset. That beginning occurred in London, England in 1967 when the first residential hospice was opened in that city. Initially, hospices were supported by religious groups who did not charge their patients. These constitute about 20% of American hospice today (1999). Thereafter, secular community based organizations initiated about 28 percent of American hospices while hospitals support another 28 percent. Nineteen percent of hospices are divisions of home health care agencies, 6 percent are hospice corporations and one percent are divisions of nursing homes. Another eighteen percent of hospices are privately owned. Michael Sorrow, director of Southwest Christian Hospice, has said that "Once Medicare and Medicaid came out with the benefit, every Tom, Dick and Harry jumped into the hospice business to make money on it." Likewise, Jack Gordon, president of the Hospice Foundation of America accuses the HMO's of refusing to pay for bereavement care "because after the patient is dead they don't want to spend any money." No doubt, the "Business First" attitude of the H.M.O.s has deprived the hospice movement of much of its reason for existence in limiting the care given patients and survivors. The H.M.O.s want the clergy to deal with the dying for free because they don't want to pay social workers and nurses. They seek to cut the cost of care below the Medicare and Medicaid reimbursement rate in order to profit from the difference between costs and income. This was possible because heretofore Medicaid and Medicare paid a flat daily rate no matter how much or how little service was rendered the patient. Evidently, this system leads to minimizing the amount of service given the dying although Medicaid and Medicare have also enlarged the number of dying patients to whom hospice care can be made available.

In November of 1997, Oregon became the first state to permit physician-assisted suicide. Thereupon the health maintenance organizations began to lobby for such laws in all other states because their profits increase as patients die sooner. Because assisted suicide is cheaper HMOs and insurance companies favor hospices which allow assisted suicide.

There are now 2,154 hospices in the United States. In 1997 Medicaid paid $94 a day for home care and $419 for general inpatient care to the eighty percent of hospices now Medicare certified. More than 90% of hospice care occurs in patients' homes and is generally administered by nurses.[25]

III

The care of the old living in the community is another function assigned to public health nurses. This interest has became most important in recent years as the American population has lived to a greater age and as the emphasis in nursing has shifted from acute care to prevention. Nurses dealing with the old must of course be well informed about chronic illness with particular reference to cardiovascular and pulmonary conditions.

Such nurses may be called "geriatric nurse practitioners." These specialists can help the old maintain their independence and lower the chance that they will have to go to a nursing home. This view is supported by a three year controlled study of more than 400 senior citizens with an average age of 81 and living at home when the study began. This study concluded that at the end of 3 years the study subjects were 60% less likely than the control group to need assistance with the most basic activities of daily living such as bathing, dressing and moving about the house. As a consequence there was also a 60% decline in the chance of the study subjects moving into a nursing home during the three years involved.[26]

Community nurses are of course concerned with patients "from the cradle to the grave." Therefore, such nurses are also engaged in baby and child care, particularly because there are numerous rural counties in America which have no medical resources other than a public health nurse. For example, in Alabama 26 out of 67 counties have no obstetrical services other than a public health nurse. These nurses live in generally inaccessible areas and therefore find it difficult to participate in continuing education available only at colleges and universities in larger communities.

In a national survey, Stevens and Silverman found that 76% of their respondents said that no continuing education was available in their area for non-BSN community health nurses. In view of the foregoing discussion of the numerous responsibilities of such nurses it is evident that telecommunications classes wold be the only means of reaching such nurses. Unfortunately, such classes are now available in only 50% of the states. [27]

Because nurses have become heavily involved in the delivery of babies, known as midwifery, education for this profession is provided at various universities at the graduate level for those nursing students who have passed a certification examination. Today, in 1999, certified nurse midwives are autonomous patient care providers. They provide prenatal care, labor and delivery management, well-woman gynecology, normal newborn care, and family planning. Certified nurse midwives now also have prescription authority. There are about 5,200 certified nurse midwives in the U.S. In addition to private practice they are found in community clinics and sponsored health care programs. In recent years they have accounted for 196,225 American births or about 5% of all U.S. deliveries.[28]

Brown and Grimes report that in more than 50 studies nurse midwives have shown themselves to be the equals of doctors in the delivery of pre-natal and natal care. According to these 50 studies, C-section, fetal distress and neo-natal mortality rates were the same whether treated by a physician or a nurse. [29]

Another area of child nursing which has traditionally been the exclusive domain of registered nurses is school nursing. This is an aspect of independent nursing which has long been accepted by the public. [30]

In 1998, the Health Resources and Services Administration of the U.S. Public Health Service contracted with the American Association of Colleges of Nursing to determine how nurse practitioners, certified nurse midwives and physician assistants can be used to meet health care needs in underserved areas in the United States. Such a contractual arrangement is important to Americans living in rural areas because the National Health Services Corps is the only source of health care for many Americans. Under the four- month contract the American Association of Colleges of Nursing will evaluate the availability of health care in rural locations and will also report the specialties of health care providers in such areas. The purpose is evidently to determine which clinics are eligible for Federal funding and to provide scholarships and educational loan programs to attract nursing and other health professions students to the National Health Services Corps.[31]

The need for new methods and new curricula in training nurses is determined by the evolution of nursing into a technologically sophisticated practice discipline. This may not be the choice of nurses themselves. Yet, advances in electrophysiological monitoring systems, computerized surgical techniques and integrated hospital information systems force nurses to become proficient in the use of computer technology as well as the traditional practice of nursing. The development of nursing technology is called "informatics" and has become the newest field of nursing specialization. Nursing "informatics" combines computer information and nursing sciences. Most Americans, whether in nursing or not, are of course at least somewhat acquainted with the use of computers which are already installed in almost all grade schools in America. Nevertheless, about 30% of nurses report that they are uncomfortable with computers, are intimidated by computers or have had no experience with them.[32]

The outcome of the ever-increasing use of technology in nursing is, hopefully, greater productivity and efficiency on behalf of the patient without losing sight of the patient's emotional, social and spiritual needs. Therefore, it is recommended that nurses investigate more carefully the stories patients tell about their hospital experiences. Such investigation will reveal that many patients have had negative experiences in hospitals and other treatment centers but are given no opportunity to discuss these feelings with nurses. [33]

The reason for failure to give patients experiences much credence is that researchers have limited their information to those areas of knowledge which concern them. They view themselves as "experts" and seek to determine what is or is not information. Yet, patients are in fact the real "experts" concerning their treatment so that research methodology must include the patient if it is to be valid.[34]

Another consequence of the many changes in the nursing profession at the end of the 20th century is the need to delegate many erstwhile nursing responsibilities to nonprofessional personnel who deliver patient care. There are a number of reasons for this need to delegate. First among these reasons is the unwillingness of hospitals to employ a sufficient number of registered nurses despite the availability of such nurses. Evidently, the few registered nurses who are employed cannot do everything themselves, not only because of time limitations but also because "short cuts" and haste can put patients at risk. The early discharge programs mandated by health maintenance organizations; advanced technology and the ever - increasing demand for patient's rights are additional reasons for the need to delegate nurses' tasks to others. Such delegation can involve a risk to the patient and can also lead to legal liability to the hospital and the nurse if the patient is injured or maltreated because a nonprofessional was empowered to treat a patient. Not only is it possible for a non-professional to perform a task incorrectly, but non-professionals are less likely to recognize a change in a patient's status than is true of professionals.[35]

Despite these threats to the well-being of hospitalized patients, some health-care facilities are "cross training" janitors, housekeepers, security guards and aides and "multi-skilled" workers who are assigned to nursing duties. This "cross-training" may range from a few hours to six weeks. Few hospitals require a high school diploma from those now involved in such "cross-training" and hence responsible for the well being of patients. Patients are of course not only concerned with pills and instruments but with their survival and the administration of life support.

The phrase "life support" is readily identified as a series of technological inventions such as mechanical ventilators, dialysis machines, intravenous pumps, biomedical research, surgery and medication. These physical methods are undoubtedly important in permitting the survival of many patients who would have died if these contrivances were not available. There is however one more life support available in our health delivery system. That life support is the 2.2 million nurses who are the second largest profession, after teaching, in the United States. Staffed almost, but not entirely, by women "these women and men weave a tapestry of care, knowledge and trust that is critical to patients' survival." [36]

Because cost-cutting is the most important motive driving hospital and insurance administrators, American hospitals are already using 20% fewer nurses than is the case in other industrialized nations. Despite the fact that nurses cost only 16% of hospital expenditures, many hospitals are planning to reduce their nursing staff up to 50 percent.

As the cost-cutting epidemic has reduced the number of competent nurses greatly, those who are still employed are now forced to spend almost all their time writing reports and "documenting" each patient endlessly. As a result, patients can hardly expect to be seen by the limited number of registered nurses still available as their economic security and professional career depends on what they write and not whom they nurse.

We have already seen that the median salary of nurses in 1998 was approximately $36,000.-. Physicians earn about four times more. The highest earnings among those working in hospitals or anywhere in the health delivery system does not go to physicians but to the so-called "bean counters," i.e. executives interested in the business aspects of health care. A recent survey of executive salaries in health care revealed that the average total cash compensation of hospital executives is $188,500 and that large hospitals pay as much as $281,000 annual salary. For-profit health maintenance organizations pay yet more. Richard Scott, chief executive officer of Columbia Health Care Corporation received more than $2 million in 1996. The seven largest for-profit health maintenance organizations paid their CEOs an average of $7 million.

The immense salary discrepancy between the compensation given nurses and the compensation given doctors and business managers in health care represent the value placed on the work of each profession in the eyes of the American public. Income reflects status in America. Men constituted only 7% of all American nurses at the end of this century. Hence nursing is mainly a female profession and is therefore devalued so that nursing pays less than do other aspects of the health related professions dominated by men. This discrepancy is gradually lessening but is nevertheless very much in force in 1999.[37]

There is an additional reason for the devaluation of nursing in comparison to the practice of medicine and the practice of accounting in the health delivery system. That reason is the devaluation of the work that nurses do. In part, that devaluation is contingent on the belief that anyone can nurse because everyone has on numerous occasions nursed children and relatives at home. Furthermore, nurses work frequently goes unrecognized because they remind us of our failure to be in control. Nursing reminds us of our pain, of our fears, of our worst moments. Indeed, nurses are now more than ever competent to use the most sophisticated technology. Yet, we attribute sophistication and knowledge to doctors and minimize the help derived from our nurses who may clean our most intimate areas one minute and administer our medicine the next. All this is viewed in the nursing profession as evidence that caring for the patient is still the most important task of the nurse.[38]

Because the nursing profession has always maintained that caring is their most important task emphasis on caring has evolved into the profession's subculture. Every occupation is a sub-culture. This means that every occupation includes fundamental attitudes, values and beliefs which define the work the occupation demands of its practitioners. This is true of nursing as well as it is true of other occupations and professions. We have seen that nursing has changed a great deal in recent years and that therefore cost containment, technology and its attendant bureaucracy have all militated against caring for patients as people.

Nursing surely seeks to strive for independence from the medical profession and to create a unique place for itself in the conglomerate of health delivery systems. Therefore it is of the utmost importance that nursing continue in the tradition of caring for the patient even as more and more radical changes are occurring in the intellectual development, training and education of the profession.

These changes are visible if we examine the trends in nursing education which have occurred during the past thirty years. Thus, in 1965 eighty percent of all new nurse graduates were trained in hospital diploma programs. After 1988, less than 12 percent of new graduates came from hospital diploma programs while the vast majority graduated from college and university four-year programs. Included in any form of education for nursing is clinical practice that is generally undertaken by clinical teachers on the staff of the university. Such practice must of necessity occur in a hospital so that a division develops between the classroom education and the "hands-on" education provided by clinical teachers in the territory of the hospital nurses. Paterson has described the experiences of clinical nursing teachers in such a hospital setting. She shows that success in providing a clinical education to students depends largely on an understanding of the relationship of temporary systems to permanent systems in the negotiated order of the hospital.[39]

A temporary system in a work situation can be auditors, researchers involved in a temporary research project or politically appointed task forces. Likewise, clinical teachers and their students are a temporary system intruding on the routine of the permanent system. According to Paterson, the language used by permanent staff concerning clinical teachers and their students reveals a real division of territory between the temporary outsiders and the regular nursing staff. Even the language used by regular staff concerning students differs from the language used by students and their clinical teachers. Staff refer to "your students" when addressing clinical teachers. They talk about "our conference room" and "our medication room" and view the presence of students not as an opportunity to teach but as help with their workload. These attitudes result in an "us against them" situation for both clinical teachers and staff nurses and has as a consequence that many clinical teachers cannot carry out their ideas of how to train nursing students in hospitals. Defensiveness, territoriality and separateness all militate against the nurse student and finally against the patient.[40]

It has become customary now to train medical students, nurse students, pharmacy students and physical therapy students together. The purpose of such "togetherness" is to introduce students to the fact that after graduation they will be faced with the team approach in their professional life. This team approach is particularly difficult for physicians who have traditionally given orders which others followed. In these situations a number of questions arise such as: "Whose diagnostic acumen is most respected?" or "Who initiates treatment?"

"Who prescribes medication?" These issues are of course the outcome of the new role of nurse-practitioners. [41]

In addition to using the team approach to cut costs hospitals, and particularly those owned and operated by health maintenance organizations, rush patients through so-called "accelerated care." The purpose of this approach is to increase the profits of HMOs to the maximum even as patients are moved from suture to discharge in less than 48 hours. This high speed "treatment" is achieved by having nurses draw blood, do an EKG or electrocardiograph and also teach patients about medication. All of these tasks were at one time done by specialists. In the mad rush to move patients in and out of the hospitals, baths, backrubs and any kind of personal attention to the patients is gone. Some have called this "hit and run" nursing. In California, 7,500 members of the California Nurses Association went on strike against Kaiser Permanente hospitals in 1997 until that H.M.O. agreed to let the union select an 18 member nurse quality committee. This was prompted by deaths in Kaiser hospitals caused by inattention and the use of low-skilled workers as well as the stress put on nurses whose ranks had been sharply reduced in layoffs. [42]

IV

The future of nursing in America has already been determined. That future is the permanent addition of the nurse-practitioner to the health delivery system in the United States. Indeed, the profit motive on the part of health maintenance organizations has led to the substitution of nurses for physicians as the primary care "doctors" in many communities. In part, this development was the result of the great anxiety of physicians to specialize and earn larger and larger fees. As the costs of health care increased, employers kept pressuring health maintenance organizations to keep the premiums down. This in turn led to the present state of health care in America in which a glut of specialists and a dearth of primary care physicians unintentionally "invited" the up-grading of nurses to the nurse-practitioner role. Nurse practitioners seldom earn more than $65,000 a year in sharp contrast to primary care physicians who average $135 thousand per year. [43]

It can be assumed that nursing will continue to be professionalized. The best indication for this assumption is the establishment of the National Center for Nursing Research. This indicates that the profession has recognized that research is the basis for professional progress in any field of human endeavor because that which does not progress, dies. The National Center for Nursing Research focuses on both acute and potential health problems. This is done by attempting to prevent disease and by promoting health. For example, the profession has been active in trying to reduce smoking, particularly among children even as the profession has encouraged numerous preventive measures such as exercise, nutrition and public health measures.

One of the consequences of the increased status nurses have attained for themselves by usurping the doctor's "turf" is that the same shift in professional responsibility which has benefited the nursing profession now threatens to undermine their authority. Financial considerations have led to the introduction of so called "ancillary" personnel into hospitals and doctor's offices. These ancillaries label their tasks "nursing" and thereby threaten to take away at one end what has been gained by the profession at the other end.[44]

Nurses, like all American professionals, will be faced with two major changes in their ranks. These changes concern gender equality and racial and cultural diversity. At present, only 4% of American nurses are black. Those blacks who are in nursing blame this situation on racism while white nurses usually claim that blacks have poorer preparation and lower grades in high school and college than whites. They believe that blacks are generally not educationally motivated to gain jobs in areas depending on a high degree of education and skill. Whatever the reason for the underrepresentation of blacks in the nursing profession, black nurses founded the National Black Nurses Association in 1971 "for the professional development of the professional black nurse."[45]

Because more black nursing students are enrolled in associate degree programs than in any other type, the NBNA claims that this enrollment is the product of racism. Because black nursing students seldom engage in study leading to the B.N.S. degree it is certain that leading positions in the profession will seldom be allocated to a black. Racism, combined with this apparent lack of education, will continue to lead to a dearth of blacks in administrative and teaching positions in nursing.[46]

Men are also grossly underrepresented in nursing. The reasons for this imbalance lie mainly in popular conceptions of the male role in American life. Thus, many Americans believe that men who enter nursing must be homosexuals. Further, it is commonly believed that men who enter "female" occupations do not make good role models for their children. In addition it is believed that men who enter nursing must have failed at more masculine professions such as medicine, dentistry or pharmacy. These beliefs are contradicted by male nursing students and male nurses. Thus, Anders reports that his own survey showed that men who enter nursing are primarily motivated to enter nursing because they "liked people and enjoyed helping others." Job availability and job security were also cited by male nurses as reasons for entering the profession. Others said that they had a great deal of interest in the biological sciences. Most male nurses seek to enter traditional male settings such as emergency rooms, intensive care units and anesthesia units in their nursing career.[47]

Male nursing students are generally older than female nursing students because many of them had failed at another occupation before entering nursing school. This fact may bear out one of the popular beliefs about male nurses. Men in the nursing profession must also be re-socialized. This means that men in the profession must at least understand the female point of view or act in a manner reflecting female attitudes and roles. Since men are not usually attuned to occupations involving the care of other people, men must first learn the care-giver role, a role women have already accepted at a younger age. Male nurses also have to learn to examine women, an activity few men have ever learned and one that their patients seldom expect. A male nurse must also learn how to get along with a mainly female nursing staff.

Teamwork is very important in nursing. Therefore male nurses have to learn to work on a team with large numbers of women. Since the experiences of men and women differ, men have a different attitude than women have. Men in all walks of life have been taught that team work is very important. It is also probable that men have worked in situations other than nursing which require team work because team work is part of the American culture.[48]

Men who enter nursing must also learn to live with a great deal of criticism and discrimination. This criticism is related to the general American belief that male nurses are playing a female role and that nursing is a low prestige occupation. The fact is that nursing has held a middle range position in the prestige ratings of occupations in the Untied States for many years. Physicians have held the first rank among occupations in the opinion of Americans as long as such public opinion polls have been taken. Yet, pharmacists, veterinarians, teachers other than professors, accountants and librarians all rank lower than registered nurses in such prestige scales.[49]

Men in nursing reflect the same anxieties associated with any minority status. Gender role conflict is only one reason for such anxieties. Since sex role socialization begins at birth men in nursing will undoubtedly have to make some major adjustments when facing an overwhelmingly female world each day. It is of course true that the gender revolution which has permitted women to enter into many traditional male occupations has also furnished men with cause to enter nursing. Theoretically, then, men should have social permission to play a compassionate or caring role just as women now insist that they have the right to be assertive. Nevertheless, sexism is still a strong force in American culture so that men in nursing must continue to live with the rejection their career choice inevitably produces. It is of course possible that men in nursing are already more tender minded than other men. It is also possible that men who chose nursing because they could not meet the demands of the male economic world acquired some learned female characteristics in order to carry out the demands of the profession. For example, a comparison between male engineers and male nurses found that relationship factors are much more important to male nurses than to male engineers. [50]

In any event, male nurses encounter negative attitudes not only from their friends, relatives and acquaintances but also from the health care environment. Nowhere is that more in evidence than in the obstetrical or midwife area. Male nurses are a visible minority in that situation although most physicians who practice in that field are men. Nevertheless, even nurse educators have perpetuated stereotypes which are detrimental to men entering the field of obstetrical nursing. These attitudes lead to a great deal of discouragement for men seeking to enter obstetrical nursing. In fact, the anxiety produced by nurse educators concerning men in obstetrical nursing will suffice to discourage most male nurses to enter that field. This anxiety is produced by the beliefs of many obstetrical patients that men are unacceptable as obstetrical nurses. In addition, participation of male nurses in such deliveries is usually deemed unacceptable to female nursing students and others. Yet, male doctors find no such opposition to their participation in the birthing process. [51]

A study of 506 boys in a Rhode Island High School concluded that High School seniors view nursing as the least acceptable occupation for men. These students thought that the nursing occupation violates sex roles in vocational choice. Male high school seniors in that Rhode Island study agreed that male nurses are lazy and of low intelligence. There is, of course, no evidence that men in nursing are less intelligent than other men. It suffices that this is commonly believed in order to discourage men who are considering nursing as a career.

Despite all of these obstacles the number of men who have entered the profession of nursing at the end of the 20th century has grown. Therefore, a larger and larger number of male role models will permit other men to make the same choice. A gradual decline in cultural prejudice against male nurses will develop in the next few years. This will improve the prestige of the occupation, increase the income of those serving in that capacity and contribute to gender equality for all those who must earn their livelihood. [52]

The essential issue relative to the earning of one's livelihood under optimum conditions is the need for power. The entire history of nursing so far has been the history of a powerless community dependent on the good will of doctors. Most recently, however, nurse have demanded and gotten some power to make their own decisions. In addition it is to be hoped that nursing education will cease to socialize nurses into subordination. Nurses have recently succeeded in forming their own political action committee. Called Nurses Coalition for Action in Politics. This group seeks to resocialize women to gain equality with physicians and to conduct themselves as equals in the presence of physicians. It is of course argued by some that women in power create a good deal of hostility from men with less power and that therefore nurse executives are fired at increasing rates. Much of the hostility to nurses is derived from the fear of physicians who suspect that nurses are an economic threat to them. Hence, it is risky for nurses or women anywhere to be assertive. Nurses are therefore now attempting to reorganize hospitals from the present patriarchal structure to one in which equality of gender is taken for granted. Nurses believe that physicians now take credit for work and expertise delivered by nurses. Nurses also say that hospital administrators want nurses to do more and more without having authority to make their own decisions. Nurses hope to achieve professional equality by the use of political activism. Nurses strikes and demands for better pay and better working conditions in many American towns and cities have underscored these demands.[53]

Summary

There are nearly two million registered nurses in the United States earning an average salary of $36,000 per year. There are also 600,000 licensed practical nurses earning about $25,000.- per year. Presently the drive to save money is leading some legislatures to consider revoking state licensures. The same motive has led Medicare to reimburse nurse-practitioners instead of doctors. The federal government now has five programs subsidizing health care. All this had led to a stratified health delivery system ranging from utterly untrained to highly specialized physicians. As hospitals have "downsized" and laid off registered nurses home-health care nursing has increased as has an interest in attaining nurse-practitioners licenses through further university based education.

Nurses are now functioning on their own and outside of institutions. They are responsible for the dying, for the old and for the very young even as so called "multi-skilled" are used to cut costs in hospitals.

Nursing is even now mainly the work of white women as a number of factors tend to limit the participation of minorities and men in the profession. Nurses say that their next objective must be the attainment of political power so that they can achieve equality with doctors. Doctors and nurses are of course not the only health care deliverers in the United States because mental health is as important to all of us as is our physical well being. Therefore, psychotherapy in all its facets shall be the content of our next chapter.

NOTES

[1] Bureau of Labor Statistics, *Occupational Employment Statistics,* March 12, 1998, Table # 32502..

[2] Philip A. Kalisch and Beatrice Kalisch, *The Advance of American Nursing,* 3rd Edition, Philadelphia J.B. Lippincott Co., 1995, p. 375.

[3] John Manuel Andriote, "The 1998 Survery," *Working Woman,* February 1998, p.45.

[4] Kalish, *op.cit.,* p. 371.

[5] Bureau of Labor Statistics, *op.cit.* ,March12, 1998 table #32505

[6] Lucille A. Joel, "Your License to Practice," American Journal of Nursing, Vol.95, No. 11, November 1995, p. 7.

[7] Ivan Oransky and Jay Varma, "Nonphysicians Clinicians and the Future of Medicine," *JAMA,* Vol.277, No. 13, April 2, 1007, p. 1090.

[8] Connie Helmlinger, "ANA Hails Landmark Law as Nursing Victory," *AJN* Vol. 97, No. 10, October 1997, p. 16.

[9] Ruth R. Anderson and Reuben A. McDaniel, Jr., "Intensity of Registered Nurse Participation in Nursing Home Decision Making," *The Gerontologist,* Vol.38, No.1, February 1998, pp. 90-100.

[10] David Keepnews, "New Opportunities and Challenges for APRNs." *AJN* Vol. 98, No.1, January 1998, pp. 46-52.

[11] Max Weber, *The Protestant Ethic and the Spirit of Capitalism,* Talcott Parsons, Trans., New York, Scribner, 1956, p.24.

[12] Peter I. Buerhaus and Douglas O. Staiger, "Future of the Nurse Labor Market According to Executives in High-Managed Care Areas of the United States," *Image: Journal of Nursing Scholarship,* Vol. 29, No. 4, Fourth Quarter, 1997, pp. 313-318.

[13] American Association of Colleges of Nursing, "Baccalaureate nursing education for the future: Defining the essential elements," Washington, D.C., 1997.

[14] Patrick H. DeLeon, Diane K. Kjervik, Alan G. Kraut and Gary R. Vanden Bos, "Psychology and Nursing: A Natural Alliance, *American Psychologist,* Vol.40, No. 11, November 1985, p. 1153.

[15] Virginia Kenyon, *et al,* "Clinical competencies for community health nurses," *Public Health Nursing,* Vol. 7, No. 1, 1990, pp. 33-39.

[16] Katherine A. Meyer, "An Educational Program to Prepare Acute Care Nurses for a Transition to Home Health Care Nursing," *The Journal of Continuing Education in Nursing,* Vol.28, No. 3, May/June 1987, pp,124-129.

[17] Nancy Shute, "A surge in graduate programs for nurses," *U.S. News and World Report,* March 2, 1998, p. 89.

[18] Associated Press, "Syracuse nursing students seek lawyer in administrative mix-up," The Buffalo News, August 11, 1998, p. A-4.

[19] Janet Cromley, "When Your Doctor is a Nurse," *Good Housekeeping,* " Vol. 225, No.2, August 1997, pp. 145-146.

[20] Lorraine Aiken, "Transformation of the nursing workforce," *Nursing Outlook,* Vol.43, No.5, 1995, pp. 201-209.

[21] Larry Dossey, *Space, Time & Medicine,* New Science Library, Boston, 1982.

[22] Deborah Witt Sherman, "Correlates of Death Anxiety in Nurses Who Provide AIDS Care," *Omega,* Vol. 34, No.2, 1996-1997, pp. 117-136.

[23] Cheryl Tatano Beck, "Nursing Students' Experiences Caring for Dying Patients," *Journal of Nursing Education,* Vol. 36, No.9, November 1997, pp. 408-415.

[24] Art Moore, "Hospice Care Hijacked," *Christianity Today,* Vol.42, No.3, March 2, 1998, pp. 38-41. .

[25] *Ibid.* p. 39.

[26] H.E.Stuck and H,U. Aronow, "A trial of annual in-home comprehensive geriatric assessments for elderly people living in the community," *New England Journal of Medicine,* Vol. 333, No. 18, 1995, p. 1184.

[27] Carole Kelly, "Surveyeing Public Health Nurses' Continuing Education Needs: Collaboration of Practice and Academia," *The Journal of Continuing Education in Nursing,* Vol. 25, No3, May-June 1997, pp. 115-123.

[28] Lauren Hunter and Vanda Lops, "Certified Nurse Midwives," JAMA, Vol. 277, No.13, April 2, 1997, p. 1095.

[29] Susan Brown and Dorothy Grimes, "Who's number one in primary care, RNs or MDs ?" *RN,* Vol.59, No. 4, April, 1996, p. 16

[30] Elaine Brainerd, "School Health Nursing Services Profess Review: Report of 1996 National Meeting," *Journal of School Health,* Vol. 68, No.1, January 1998, p.12.

[31] Carole A. Anderson, "Nurses to Recommend Provider Mix in Shortage Areas," *Public Health Reports,* Vol. 113, No. 1, January/February 1998, p. 113.

[32] Jean Nagelkerk, Patricia M. Ritola and Patty J. Vandort, "Nursing Informatics: The Trend of the Future,"
The Journal of Continuing Education in Nursing, Vol.29, No. 1, January/February 1998, p. 17.

[33] Lynette Leeseberg Stamler and Barbara Thomas, "Patient Stories: A Way to Enhance Continuing Education," *Journal of Continuing Education in Nursing*, Vol. 28, No. 2, March/April 1997, pp. 64-68.
[34] Stanley J. Heymann, "Patients in Research: Not just subjects, but partners." *Science*, Vol. 269, pp. 797-798.
[35] Sally Thomas and Gale Hume, "Delegation Competencies: Beginning Practitioners' Reflections," *Nurse Educator*, Vol. 23, No. 1, January-February 1998, p. 38.
[36] Suzanne Gordon, "The Quality of Mercy," *The Atlantic Monthly*, Vol. 279, No. 2, February,1979 p.81.
[37] Gerhard Falk, *Sex, Gender and Social Change; The Great Revolution*, Lanham, MD., The University Press of America, 1998.
[38] Gordon, *op.cit.* p. 87.
[39] Barbara L. Paterson, "The Negotiated Order of Clinical Teaching," *Journal of Nursing Education*, Vol.36, No. 5, May 1997, pp. 197-205.
[40] *Ibid.* p. 205.
[41] Circe Cook, " Reflections on the Health Care Team: My Experiences in an Interdisciplinary Program."
JAMA, Vol.277, No. 13, April 2, 1997, p. 1091.
[42] Peter T. Kilborn, "Nurses Get New Role in Patient Protection," *The New York Times*, March 26, 1998, p. A 14.
[43] Milt Freudenheim, "Nurses Treading on Doctor's Turf," *The New York Times*, Nov. 2, 1997, Sec. 4, p. 5.
[44] Janice B. Lindberg, Mary Love Hunter and Ann Z. Kruszewski, *Introduction to Nursing*, Philadelphia, Lipppincott-Raven Publishers, 1998, pp. 428-429.
[45] Jeanette Vaughan, "Is There Really Racism in Nursing?" Journal of Nursing Education, Vol. 36, No. 3, March 1997, pp. 135-139.
[46] Ibid. p. 137.
[47] Robert L. Anders, "Targeting Male Students," *Nurse Educator*, Vol. 18, No.2, March/April, 1993, p. 4.
[48] Helen J. Steubert, "Male Nursing Students' Perception of Clinical Experience," *Nurse Educator*, Vol. 19, No.5, September-October 1994, pp. 28-32.
[49] Beth B. Hess, Elizabeth W. Markson and Peter J. Stein, *Sociology*, New York, Macmillan Publishing Co., 1991, p. 179.
[50] Michael Galbraith, "Attracting Men to Nursing: What Will They Find Important in Their Career?" *Journal of Nursing Education*, Vol. 30, No.4, April 1991, pp. 182-186.
[51] Roy A. Sherrod, "The Role of the Nurse Educator: When the Obstetrical Nursing Student is Male," *Journal of Nursing Education*, Vol.28, No.8, October 1989, pp. 377-379.

[52] Shirley Davis-Martin, "Research on Males in Nursing," *Journal of Nursing Education*, Vol. 23, No. 4, April 1984, pp. 162-164.
[53] Joan J. Roberts and Thetis M. Group, *Feminism in Nursing*, Westport, Con. Praeger, 1995, pp. 330-331.

Chapter VII

Healing the Soul: Psychotherapy Now

I

Knowledge of human emotions remains in its infancy even today, at the end of the 20th century. This should not be surprising because an effort at the scientific study of so-called "mental illness" is only slightly more than one hundred years old. If we are willing to credit Jean Charcot (1825-1893) with making the first effort to apply the methods of scientific observation to the study of severe neurotics and the treatment of neurologically damaged patients then credit for the development of psychotherapy into a healing profession belongs to him. Charcot was a French neurologist who discovered that many bodily symptoms make no anatomical sense. He therefore called these symptoms "psychogenic." This is not to say that hysteria was unknown before Charcot. However, we can safely say that Charcot was the first neurologist to take such symptoms seriously, to regard them as real and to seek to treat them by means of hypnosis.[1]

Hypnosis, so named after the Greek god of sleep Hypnos, did not always remove the symptoms so treated. However, even when the symptoms such as blindness or lameness disappeared, they often returned in another form so that an erstwhile "blind" person could now no longer walk. It was therefore Sigmund Freud (1856-1939) and his associate Joseph Breuer (1842-1925) who recognized that the symptoms then treated by hypnosis had an underlying cause which was suppressed in the memory of the patient and would therefore reappear again and again. Freud and Breuer thereupon treated one of Breuer's patients whom they called "Anna O." with a new method Freud called psychoanalysis. This method permitted Freud and Breuer to release the repressed memories of the patient, allow her to recall events she had suppressed and thereby remove her hysterical symptoms permanently.[2]

An enormous literature has developed around Freud, psychoanalysis and his numerous followers and detractors since then. This vast literature began with the numerous writings of Freud after Joseph Breuer disassociated himself from Freud's further research. Much of what Freud wrote did not meet the test of scientific inquiry and is generally discarded by present psychologists. This is in part due to the inability of present day psychologists to find means of proving many of Freud's theories. Another reason for the rejection of Freud by present day psychologists is that "knocking" Freud is fashionable. Supporters of Freud can hardly expect to be granted an advanced degree in psychology from an American university since differences of opinion are seldom appreciated in the academic environment. There, conformity is highly prized and deviation from current lines of thinking are not often rewarded.

Nevertheless, Freud contributed at least this: that there is internal conflict in each of us and that we are not aware of this conflict and that therefore we do not know ourselves and are not "masters of our own soul." Furthermore, Freud demanded that psychology deal with the whole of humanity. Hence he applied his theories not only to neurotic symptoms, but also to personality patterns, to social groups, to families, humor and "slips of the tongue," and dreams. Freud also investigated artistic productions, religious thought and a host of other issues. Hence, Freud outlined human needs and laid the foundation of modern psychology, which remains in a state of marginality between science and art, between proved certainty and marginal interpretations.

During the many years which have elapsed since the days of Freud a number of professions have contended for the right to treat patients with emotional difficulties. These professions are psychoanalysis, social work, psychiatry and clinical psychology. There are also pastoral counselors whose approach stems mainly from religion. In addition, some nurses now also claim expertise in psychotherapy as do such groups as faith healers, bartenders and hairdressers.

Those professionals who today (1999) claim to have the competence to deal with an entire array of emotional shortcomings are all intellectual descendants of Freud. Prior to Freud's work so called "insanity" was considered incurable. Therefore, the "insane" were incarcerated and given no attention by the medical profession. Instead a variety of gross methods were used to deal with "insanity." The "insane" were bled. Others were placed into restraints of all kinds because it was believed that "insanity" was caused by too much blood "rushing" too fast to the brain. Freud, then, had one more merit. He "legitimized the concept of basing treatment entirely upon talk." This permitted the growth of psychotherapy from sources other than the medical profession and hence legitimized the role of the psychotherapist."[3]

Today, psychological treatment is familiar to most Americans and is regarded as an acceptable means of dealing with personal problems. Psychiatrists are viewed as practicing a medical specialty. They are graduates of medical schools and hence hold the M.D. degree. The income of psychiatrists in 1998 averaged $136,000 per year. This is slightly more than is earned by family practitioners and pediatricians but constitutes the lowest income among medical specialists.[4]

Like other medical specialists, psychiatrists spend four years in a residency program and are then certified by a board by means of an examination. Of the more than 36,000 psychiatrists now practicing in the United States, about 60% are engaged in private practice. Psychiatrists, unlike other physicians, must deliver one hour's work for one hour's pay. Traditionally, the patients of psychiatrists came each week for some time, occasionally, years. Capitation has of course reduced the opportunity to treat patients on a long term basis. While other physicians draw their income from a large pool of patients who come only once or twice a year, the loss of even one patient can make a difference in the psychiatrists income. The American Medical Association also reports that psychiatrists spend less time per week in patient care than any other medical specialist.[5]

It is therefore incumbent upon psychiatrists to redefine their profession. This is necessary because new knowledge and new procedures in the treatment of emotional illness demand this. Obviously, social and economic forces also call for such changes. Therefore, psychiatry can rescue itself by placing greater emphasis on major mental disorders, neurobehavioral disorders, substance abuse and psychopathological conditions which complicate other medical conditions. The relationship of psychiatry to neurology needs to be given more attention in medical schools so that psychiatry will be distinguishable from non-medical therapy and its practitioners. If this is not done, then psychiatry will become a dying profession as classical psychoanalysis is already. One reason for this is that the mental health community regards psychoanalysis as an unproven and antiquated method of treatment. More important is the length of time and the immense cost it takes to become a psychoanalyst. Those who wish to graduate into that profession must undergo personal analysis. This takes as long as the psychoanalyst thinks it should take so that there is no certain graduation for someone in that program. Because psychoanalysis is so expensive for the patient analysts cannot have more than a handful of patients at any time. In fact, a study in Boston, MA, found that the average psychoanalyst had only three analytic patients whom he treated for about eleven hours each week. [6]

Social work grew originally from a wish to render direct aid and relief to those needing public assistance. Therefore, social work was practiced in the courts, in welfare agencies and in schools as well as community organizations. Social work has always maintained a more direct and pragmatic approach to helping those in need. Nevertheless, psychoanalytic information was included in the curricula of some social work schools in the first half of the twentieth century.

Private practice for social workers was almost unknown before 1940. In that year there were only four full time social workers in private practice and there were 36 part time social workers practicing privately. Thirty five years later there were an estimated 2,189 social workers in private practice, the majority full time. In 1982 17,800 members of the National Association of Social Workers were practicing privately. These social workers charged $50.- to $60.- per session for a fifty minute "hour." [7]

In 1996 there were 246,000 medical and psychiatric social workers in the United States. Their average income was $33,000 a year. This includes psychiatric social workers in private practice and those working for various agencies.[8]

All of the professionals just discussed may be called psychotherapists. Henry, Sims and Spray have shown that all of these professions are linked by common types of practices, similar patients, and a common view of the world. This is confirmed by another study showing that the majority of psychotherapists were largely upward mobile urban Jews as was true of Sigmund Freud. Fifty two percent of psychiatrists and 62 percent of psychoanalysts are Jewish although Jews were only 3% of the American population at the time of the Henry et al. study. These therapists had rejected their Eastern European Jewish ancestry together with the political and religious views of their parents and grandparents. Catholics, who are 25% of the American population, are very much under represented among psychiatrists and are over represented among social workers.

The most important and most significant finding of the Henry *et al* study was that: .....it is important to query the social utility of having four highly organized, well-equipped, self-sufficient training pathways, each of which produces psychotherapists. The end product is startlingly similar. Only the intervening years of expensive, highly complex training are different. These differences appear to have questionable relevance to the practice of psychotherapy, at least as seen by the psychotherapists themselves. Further, these differences do not appear in the work activities of their subsequent professional lives."[9]

In view of the effort of health maintenance organizations to limit costs, social workers and master's level "family counselors," are now underbidding doctors of psychology just as these Ph.D.'s have underbid psychiatrists. This seems very reasonable to the payers, i.e., insurance companies and health maintenance organizations who see no difference in the kind of treatment provided by each profession and who are, as always, concerned with costs and not with outcomes. In this case, however, the outcome is generally the same for the patient so that a social worker, while unable to prescribe medicine, can nevertheless achieve as much by talking as can a high priced psychiatrist. Clinical psychology, which has a different history than medical psychiatry, represents an American development. Clinical psychology was founded by Lightner Witmer in 1896 when he opened the first such clinic for the purpose of helping children who had learning disabilities. From the first, Witmer cooperated with social workers in an effort to deal with social conditions of a harmful nature which he believed needed to be addressed by psychologists as well as social workers. The profession of clinical psychology grew as other practitioners made advances in the assessment and diagnosis of developmental disabilities. [10]

Around 1939, a small number of clinical psychologists began to conduct therapy under the supervision of psychiatrists. These psychologists were thought of as "psychiatric aides." Then, after World War II the Veterans Administration established psychological internships. That program had 200 trainees in 1946. Fifty years later, in 1996, the profession employed 92,630 members. At first, the psychologists trained under that program were oriented toward psychometrics and research. Because the psychologists were employed in hospitals, the VA established doctor's degrees as the entry degree and that degree included training in psychotherapy, again under the supervision of psychiatrists. In the long run, however, psychologists succeeded in escaping that supervision despite the strenuous efforts of psychiatrists to depict clinical psychologists as dangerous to the public.[11]

Now, at the end of the century psychiatrists and psychologists face the fact that psychotherapy had been opened to other professions and in particular to over 246,000 medical and psychiatric social workers whose average income is about $36,000 a year. The same arguments once used by psychiatrists to prevent the entrance of psychologists into their area of expertise are now used by both to defeat the efforts of psychiatric social workers to establish themselves in private practice. Social workers now have a powerful ally in their quest for independence. Just as the Veteran's Administration found it convenient to support clinical psychologists after World War II, so the health maintenance organizations support social workers as therapists because they cost less and have had the same results and outcomes as psychiatrists and psychologists. In fact, the HMOs are now (1999) using psychiatrists only for brief diagnostic assessment and for the prescription of medicine, two functions only they can do. [12]

To sum up the situation of clinical psychologists and psychiatrists at the end of the twentieth century, "an army of new master's level mental health professionals has now joined clinical psychologists (and psychiatrists) in the consulting room." Master's-level psychologists are now being produced at the rate of 6,000 per year. Like psychologists at an earlier time, they too demand autonomy and will undoubtedly succeed. Meanwhile the Veteran's Administration is reducing the number of psychologists employed by them as Veteran's Hospitals are closing in face of the ever declining number of veterans still remaining from the Second World War, the Korean War and the war in Viet Nam.

Added to this declining need for Ph.D. psychologists and psychiatrists is the anxiety of the health maintenance organizations to use cheaper help who have only the master's degrees but appear to be able to gain the same results as expensive doctors.[13]

II

Unlike other helping professions, such as medicine and nursing, almost all psychotherapy does not have physical substance but depends on talking. There are of course also pills and medicines and the now-abandoned frontal lobotomy techniques which have physical substance and, in some cases, salutary effects. Nevertheless, psychotherapy, however administered consists first and foremost of the ability of the therapist to form a relationship of trust with the client.

This was well understood by the philosopher Martin Buber (1878-1965) whose most significant work is *I and Thou*. That work distinguishes between the relationship that is direct, mutual, present and open and the "I-It", or subject-object relationship in which one relates only indirectly and non-mutually for the purpose of using the other. Buber calls the knowledge that we are "made present" by the other person, "confirmation." By this term Buber means the emotional invasion of one person by another person so that one can actually experience "the other" and "imagine what the "other" is feeling, thinking and knowing." [14]

Buber's dialogical psychotherapy is of course well known and has been used by almost all "schools of psychology." Friedman shows that numerous psychotherapists have been directly or indirectly influenced by Buber. He cites examples from Freudian, Jungian, Rogerian, Gestalt and existentialist therapies which plainly indicate their debt to Buber's works. In particular, Friedman cites the work of Boszormenyi-Nagy and Krasner who wrote in 1986: "Martin Buber contributed more to building the foundations of accountable human relating than any other thinker of our time."[15]

This foundation, applied to the practice of psychotherapy, consists of the insight that in the practice of psychotherapy the relationship between patient and therapist is the primary tool used to bring about change. Inspection of the professional literature reveals, however, that in all areas of psychotherapy, writers are far more devoted to examining the patient half of this relationship than it is to understanding the therapist's part.

It is nevertheless safe to say that the knowledge therapists have accumulated can only be helpful to the patient if the therapist also knows who she is and how her own personality influences therapy.[16]

Therefore the outcome of therapy depends more on what is meant and understood than on what is said and done. Many years ago Hans Strupp wrote this: "The person of the therapist is far more important than his theoretical orientation. In the end each therapist develops his or her own style and the theoretical orientation fades into the background." [17]

Therefore, the theoretical orientation of a therapist, whether Freudian or Rankian or whatever, is more often related to the needs of the therapist than to the outcomes that a theory can produce. Not the theory but the therapist determines the patient's success in dealing with his difficulties so that it is legitimate to say that the theory followed or applied is probably a matter of indifference to the patient.

A recent study of clinicians' attitudes, which they themselves believe help clients, yielded general agreement among respondents to the question: "what do you think is helpful to patients?" Four behaviors were generally agreed upon. These are: being authentic and honest, personally identifying with client issues, attending to impact of self, and using self disclosure. [18]

There was a time when it was believed that therapists must be "blank screens" whose personalities must not be revealed to the clients in any fashion. That time is over. Today, (1999) mutuality is the key to therapy within a two-person psychology. This mutuality includes self-disclosure because it is impossible for a therapist not to self-disclose. This means that therapists must learn to benefit from orientations which satisfy their internal needs. These internal needs include the need to gain at least some appreciation from their clients. That, however, is seldom forthcoming and leads some therapists to experience a condition which has sometimes been called "burn out". This term was first used by the New York psychoanalyst Herbert Freudenberger in an attempt to describe the occupational exhaustion suffered by some in the helping professions. He described "burn-out" as exhaustion, fatigue, and the loss of commitment by the therapist to the clients welfare. Therefore, "burnout" is not the same as overwork which can be cured by taking a vacation. The "burnt-out" therapist has lost faith in his ability to heal. The "burnt-out" therapist becomes a "case" himself. Depression, a negative attitude towards work, self-blame for not achieving more for the clients and a cynical attitude towards clients are additional symptoms of this condition. A cynical attitude includes blaming the clients for their own problems.

Those who have dealt with the problem of "burn-out" are generally agreed that the most enthusiastic professionals are most at risk of suffering "burn-out." These are therapists who have overextended themselves, who expect too much from themselves and who sometimes substitute their work for their social life. Such therapists are often perfectionists who are compulsive and whose over-achievement orientation leads them to work endless hours.

"Burn-out' is also related to personal stresses in the life of the therapist. A good example is the so-called "mid-life crisis" which affects some people most severely because it is a time in the lives of many Americans when they feel they have achieved less than they had hoped. This sense of impotence is further aggravated by the kind of clientele most therapists must deal with most of the time. It is rare for a therapist to have a client who is reasonable, educated and non-demanding. Much more often therapists must deal with people who threaten suicide, or who are in trouble with the law or who want disability. Such clients certainly leave therapists wondering why they spend so much energy on so little success and believing that they are powerless.

The feeling that one is powerless is particularly aggravated in not-for-profit "agencies" in which a host of supervisors and other bureaucrats interfere incessantly in the client-therapist relationship. In addition, such agencies destroy the morale of their therapists by instituting periodic pay freezes and staff cutbacks. This in turn means that those still employed have a larger case load than before even as it has been demonstrated to them that they have no security but work at the whim of "administrators." This in turn leads to the most vile of office politics which beset almost all not-for-profit agencies, particularly because the pay is low and better salaries and at least some occupational prestige is to be had only by manipulating oneself into a supervisory/administrative position and not by servicing clients. Added to all these burdens are the problems presented to all therapists by the innovations of the health maintenance organizations.[19]

Health maintenance organizations like to call their invasion of the client-therapist relationship "managed care." This term implies that the HMOs are indeed interested in caring for the patient. To do so efficiently, they say, they seek to manage his care so as to save money by avoiding the unnecessary use of expensive psychiatrists and by preventing clients and therapists to define the limits of treatment as the end of the clients insurance coverage.[20]

Most important for the therapist-practitioner is that managed care has moved control of treatment from the clinician to the entrepreneur whose sole interest is profit. To maintain that control and insure the largest profit possible, HMOs have instituted an immense "wall of paper" which the practitioner must penetrate if he wishes to be paid for his services. Innumerable "forms" must be filled out in detail and must describe conditions which suit the opinions of insurance clerks even if they are not at all what ails the patient. Managed care also demands that the practitioner gain advance approval from the clients insurance company before treatment may begin. That approval is usually limited to three sessions. Practitioners are told that they can ask for more sessions if they prove that this is necessary. However, practitioners also know that if they ask for too many sessions they will be dropped from the insurance companies roster of approved therapists and will therefore be put out of business. Meanwhile, patients are told that they are entitled to twenty or more sessions of psychotherapy. Therapists in turn must pretend to the patient that brief therapy is all he needs since insurance companies have been known to remove from their panel any therapist who tells a patient he needs more sessions.

Insurers also use paper work as a means of cheating therapists of their pay. Thus, health maintenance organizations will refer a patient to a therapist but claim later that they know nothing about such a referral and therefore refuse to pay. Another method of using paper work to avoid payment is for insurers to fail to send the therapist "billing forms" or "closing forms." The therapist is then told that he will not be paid because he did not send in the needed forms which the insurance company will not send. Innumerable telephone calls are also used by insurers to avoid payment. Insurance clerks will tell a therapist that they will call him back concerning approval to treat a patient. They never call and thereby avoid payment for treatments already administered. Because insurers are often located in time zones quite far from the place of treatment, the demand that all calls must be made during "business hours" becomes a burden upon the provider. Surely, East Coast and West Coast business hours are not the same. Therefore, it is in itself an imposition on the provider to make such a demand which serves again as a means to avoid payment. There are also instances in which insurance companies arbitrarily refuse to pay and give no reason for this refusal. Added to all these subterfuges and evasions by insurers are a confusion of "forms" which employee assistance programs send to providers. Each EAP uses a different form so that it becomes an art in itself to know how to deal with the welter of bureaucratic obstruction these "forms" are intended to provide.

Because managed care seeks to avoid any expensive procedure a considerable "second opinion" business has now developed. Reliance on a "second opinion" not only questions the practitioner's clinical judgment and integrity but it also adds to the cost of treatment. It is wasteful. Therefore, insurers seek to save the extra cost by preventing other clients from having access to a therapist.

In the past, length of treatment and the use of one clinician or another was determined by the client and was private. Now, managed care organizations have substituted the judgment of their employees over the judgments of the client and the professional clinicians. Managed care organizations now decide whether a potential client's problem is severe enough to warrant treatment, how long that treatment can last and what the outcome of that treatment must be.

All of this interference in the client/therapist relationship results in resentment by the therapist and the client and thereby affect treatment adversely. It also results in many misguided decisions. [21]

Further, resentment is caused by the demand by some insurers that providers accept mandatory supervision by other mental health professionals who are committed to the insurer who employs them.

There are even insurers who demand that clinicians say nothing unfavorable about the managed care organization on pain of being dropped from its panel of approved providers. This directly limits the free speech rights of such providers. In sum, managed care is interested in lower costs for its client/employers even as more and more Americans are left without treatment of serious problems. It is doubtful whether there really is a cost reduction in all of this. Instead it appears that the costs of mental health treatment are still the same but that the income from these treatments has shifted from the providers to the managed care industry.

There is yet another cost associated with the current assault on mental health of the American people by the business community. That cost can be seen in our suicide rate. This has been about eleven per 100,000 Americans during the 1990's. Of the 31 thousand Americans who kill themselves each year many are teenagers. In fact, suicide is the third leading cause of death among the young, i.e. among those aged 15 to

25. Evidently, many of these suicides could be prevented if adequate access to mental health therapy were available. [22]

Another example of our inability to deal adequately with our emotional lives is the rate of unmarried motherhood. In 1995 thirty percent of all births in the United States were to unmarried mothers, an increase from only 5% in 1950. [23]

Alcoholism, drug addiction, divorce, juvenile delinquency and a host of other social and emotional problems plague Americans at the end of the century. Many need help and deserve it alone because all of American society suffers from the consequences of emotional problems of those affected and those who live with them. Yet, the reduction of mental health services by the HMO industry comes at a time when America is barely out of the psycho-social Dark Ages. [24]

Group psychotherapy is an area of therapy which has been developed over the past fifty years because it was a direct outgrowth of World War II experience. At that time, some therapeutically derived principles were developed which include at least confidentiality, an aspect of therapy which is essential in any setting. Yet, in the managed care system the payer demands a great deal of information from the therapist in order to determine the need, duration and form of psychotherapy. This is a violation of trust in the first place but becomes even more aggravating in the group setting which is almost unknown to the managed care industry. To that industry, group treatment appears cheaper than individual treatment but its meaning is unknown or not understood. Yet, advanced social work theory contends that "the whole, the community or group, comes first; that the universe is not invented or created by individuals but is, in fact, irreducibly whole" and that, "the irreducible state of human life is membership." If that is so, then group therapy may indeed be the manner in which therapists and their patients can accommodate the demands of the health maintenance industry even if that industry understands only the bottom line. [25]

Falck has shown that the principal difficulty American therapists and their clients have regarding group therapy is the extreme individualism practiced here. Hence, two obstacles prevent an early move into that direction. The first is the interest of the therapist who needs to maintain his income by holding on to as many individual patients as possible. The second is the failure of the profession to recognize that "the member is universal, that all human life, in some way and in some form, is the life of the member." [26]

If it is the common goal of HMOs and therapists to provide cost-efficient and yet good and sufficient help for psychiatric patients, the group therapy may find support from both sides of the argument.

At this time, however, such agreement has not been achieved. Instead, health maintenance organizations are leveling tremendous pressure upon all practitioners of psychotherapy. This can be seen in the fact that 47 percent of clinicians say that managed care has reduced their caseload. Fifty three percent of providers say that they changed their treatment approach because of managed care. Sixty three percent of clinicians have shortened their treatment of patients because of managed care and over 55 percent of clinicians say that they have had trouble collecting their fees from insurance companies.[27] The consequences of that pressure include rage, despair, powerlessness and fear and the possibility that these emotions will be displaced upon the patients.[28]

These feelings were well expressed by Dr. Alan Goldman in The Los Angeles Times when he wrote: "I am a physician, and each day I sense that I am slowly dying. Mine is not the sudden, unexpected death of a heart attack or a brain hemorrhage. It is an illness of the spirit." [29]

The ultimate goal of the HMO's/insurance companies is to avoid paying the therapists fees. The following authentic examples will illustrate the procedures utilized to effect these goals: Patient X telephones for an appointment at a therapists office. He is told to call the HMO for authorization. He does so, telling the insurance company that he has been seen twice previously through an employee assistance program by the therapist. The HMO turns him away stating that now the therapist must call for a review. The therapist calls, explains the situation and is informed that under those circumstances the patient must call and that "they (namely the patient) must have misunderstood." The therapist calls the patient again but is now handled by a different representative of that HMO. This time he is advised that the computer "is down" and the patient should call the next day. By that time the patient is so discouraged that he does not telephone at all. He keeps an appointment with the therapist which had been tentatively arranged. When the therapist calls the HMO after the first session the clerk at the HMO informs her that the session cannot be reimbursed since there is no authorization for it.

Another scenario: the patient has been seen by the therapist for the allotted three sessions. She telephones the HMO. An automatic voice machine tells the therapist (after she has pushed five buttons on her telephone as directed by the voice) that she should leave her name and telephone number at least three working days in advance. Also they want the patients name. In addition they want the exact time when the therapist can be reached by telephone for a review. Now the problem is that she must interrupt her work day to conduct this review and justify why patient X needs three more appointments. If she gives a diagnosis which the insurance company decides is not reimbursable, the authorization is not given. Thus again there is no reimbursement. Therefore the therapist must suppress her integrity and give a false diagnosis acceptable to the insurance company.

The HMO /insurance company has a voice machine which vocalizes that the therapists request will be taped in order to reassure "quality assurance". This is a mere statement to create fear in therapists so that they must be careful in their utterances and also to protect the insurance companies from becoming involved in lawsuits. This is justified by claiming that the insurance companies are the enforcers of quality of service.

If a therapist asks the HMO for more than the average allotted sessions for a very seriously emotionally ill client the therapist jeopardizes her standing and is in danger of being excluded from that insurance company. The number of sessions paid by an insurance company are closely monitored and reviewed. This creates a hazard for the very conscientious therapist because she will be removed from the insurance company's panel if she uses more sessions than it is willing to pay, regardless of the patient's need. Should, however, a client commit suicide because his therapist could not help him during the limited number of sessions allotted by the insurance company, the responsibility will be the therapist's. The therapist will then be fired from the providership and also be sued by the suicide's next- of - kin for malpractice. The therapist is therefore in the proverbial "catch twenty two mode."

Another very time consuming and problematic situation is the volume of paper work that must be completed for each client. There are long lists of possibilities that must be considered and included in these sheaves. These directives from HMOs are unrealistic statements requiring that estimated numbers of visits must be given based on the estimated seriousness of the emotional condition of the patient. Of course the reality is that this is nothing but guess work. For the most part these endless questionnaires must be filled out during the first session and mailed promptly to the insurance company. In addition a billing form is also required. If so much as a minor blank is omitted by the provider there is no reimbursement. Then forms are returned and the therapist must try again. If the patient does not return after that initial session, then the therapist has spent enormous amounts of time for very little money. These exercises in filling out unrealistic forms are also seen to demonstrate a lack of caring to the patient who wants to free himself of his emotional problem by having the therapist listen to him without the distraction of pencil pushing.

These practices during the initial session with the therapist are very disturbing for a distressed human being who has come to get relief from his psychic pain. For the therapist these practices too cause emotional pain. She feels with her client because she cannot devote her full attention to the person and to the skills she has studied for so many years. She feels that her integrity is challenged and that she is in a business rather than in her chosen profession.

Many a troubled individual does not return after an initial paper and pen session. Thus the patient is left with his troubled psyche and one must wonder how many of these discouraged persons can be counted among the attempted or completed suicide statistics.[30]

III

Trust in the integrity of the psychotherapist is of the greatest importance to the profession. Therefore it can be said with certainty that unless the client gives informed consent, psychotherapists are under a legal and ethical obligation to neither confirm nor deny even whether there has been any contact with a client. Because HMOs demand a great deal of information about the course of therapy before agreeing to pay the therapist's fee that confidentiality is violated.

There are yet other situations in which pressure is brought on psychotherapists to disclose the confidences imparted to them in therapy sessions. One such situation concerns college students who talk to therapists on or off the campus. Both parents and faculty members, who sometimes regard themselves in loco parentis, have been known to seek information from therapists concerning students' activities. Faculty will sometimes refer students to a psychotherapist and then expect to be kept informed concerning the student's "progress." No doubt, such requests come from involved and caring persons. Nevertheless, they cannot be answered without the student's consent. Yet, a 1991 study revealed that 35% of psychotherapists working within a university have answered such requests without the consent of their student/patient.[31]

Because the communication between a therapist and his patient/client are the very foundation upon which trust between them is built, the Supreme Court of the United States ruled on June 13, 1996 in Jaffee vs. Redmond that these communications are privileged and need not be disclosed in cases heard in a federal court. This decision referred to a social worker as a therapist or psychotherapist, called the client a patient and labeled the sessions between them either counseling or psychotherapy, interchangeably. Because the decision dealt specifically with a licensed social worker it is unknown whether it would also cover licensed counselors.

It is important to understand that the Supreme Court in Jaffee created a privilege for the patient of a licensed therapist. This decision differs therefore from a number of state statutes which already extended such a privilege to mental health professionals. Such professionals are psychiatrists, social workers, psychologists but not "psychotherapists." The importance of the Jaffee ruling gives legal protection to master's level social workers and others because their client has the privilege.[32]

It is evident that genuine therapeutic work depends on the client feeling safe in disclosing intimate and personal aspects of his life. Clients would hardly share such information unless they could be certain that their trust will not be violated. Because some legal requirements have demanded disclosure in the past, confidentiality has not been absolute. No doubt many a client was shocked to discover that the law could be used to force his therapist to disclose matters the client believed could never, under any circumstances be told to anyone. The difficulty here lies in the difference between confidentiality which is an ethical standard and privileged communication which is a legal concept. Accordingly, privileged communication must meet these legal requirements. 1. The communications must originate in the confidence that they will not be disclosed. 2. Confidentiality must be essential to maintaining the relationship 3. The relationship, in the opinion of the community and society is important and should be sedulously fostered. 4. The injury that disclosure would cause to the relationship is greater than the benefit to litigation that would be gained.[33]

For many years the concept of privileged communication was extended only to the attorney-client relationship. More recently, other professions have also been given this privilege but no uniformity has developed. This means that some states will allow some professions to have this privilege while in other states the same profession is not "covered" by the law.

Despite this confusion it can safely be assumed that state courts too will follow the example of the federal courts in this matter. This is most likely as the Supreme Court made these observations in Jaffe: "The key to successful psychotherapeutic treatment is communications without fear of public disclosure" and, "reason and experience lead to the conclusion that protecting confidential communications between psychotherapists and patients promote societal interests that outweigh the need for evidence in courts of law."[34]

Now it must be evident from the foregoing that if trust in the integrity of the psychotherapist can be held to be the very cornerstone of such a relationship, then the exploitation of a patient by a therapist can never be condoned. Nevertheless, the word "exploitation" is subject to numerous interpretations. Can everyone agree that "when you touch the patient the therapy is over." Does this mean one cannot shake hands? Can a therapist hug a child? Is a touch on the arm at a time of major grief allowed? In view of our litigious society it appears that any form of touching can be interpreted as illegal and as a betrayal of trust. [35]

Two views concerning trust in psychotherapy have now developed in the profession. There are those who appear to be dogmatic, rigid, confining and narrow. In that view even the expression of some friendship for a patient leads to the accusation of "non-sexual" exploitation of the patient. Others, who view themselves as "liberal" on this issue say that such prohibitions make therapists into "non-human entities" without warmth or caring.[36]

Three forms of possible patient exploitation are listed by Twemlow in his excellent discussion of this issue. First, there is "boundary inattention", a phrase used to indicate the entrance of a patient into the dreams and personal time of a therapist. This condition may involve sexual fantasies about a patient and is therefore very close to "boundary crossing." "Boundary crossing," does not include sexual conduct but will include accepting gifts from a patient; reducing a patient's fee or even giving free therapy; eating a free meal at a restaurant owned by a patient; attending an important social function for a patient including a wedding; participating in a book discussion group with a patient; giving a patient a ride; visiting a patient at home.

Finally, says Twemlow, there are "boundary violations". Such violations are not acceptable to either "liberal" or " conservative" therapists. These violations include physical exploitation, failure to properly diagnose and evaluate; failure to keep one's knowledge up to date; failure to set limits; retaining a patient longer than necessary, and failure to seek consultation if not supervision and sexual exploitation.[37]

There is one fundamental prohibition in the practice of therapy. This prohibition is best expressed in this sentence: "Under no circumstances should a therapist ever engage in sexual intimacy with a patient." Therapist – patient sexual intimacies are in all instances wrong and must be avoided. Pope *et al* refer to behavior that could lead to sexual intimacy as "the slippery slope." They therefore advise that "each therapist must carefully consider actions that may lead, by small, seemingly insignificant-in-themselves increments, toward sexual intimacy."[38]

Additionally, under no circumstances should the therapist ever communicate, explicitly or implicitly, that sexual intimacy is a possibility. This includes the use of a hug at the end of a session, even if a patient asks for it or seems to need it. The decision whether or not to deliver a hug depends on the most important consideration, i.e., whether or not the behavior of the therapist is consistent with the patient's welfare. This is important if it accommodates the therapist's enjoyment since "nothing can justify a therapist's choice to violate the most fundamental ethical responsibility and to place the patient at risk of lasting harm."[39]

The Hippocratic oath, now over two thousand years old, specifies that the medical practitioner must refrain from the seduction of males and females. The professional codes of psychologists, social workers and all who call themselves therapists consider sexual contact with patients unethical. Nevertheless, Len and Fischer report that 30% of therapists engage in such practices. Whether the number is that high everywhere may be subject to debate. It is however not a matter of debate as to the public's view of such conduct in the American context. Therefore, Wisconsin became the first state in the union to criminalize sexual exploitation of patients and fourteen other states have already enacted similar laws. In some states which have such laws, that offense is now a felony. A felony is an offense which is usually punishable by imprisonment for more than one year. Felony statutes concerning therapist-client sexual relations are now in effect in Arizona, California, Colorado, Connecticut, Florida, Georgia, Iowa, Maine, Minnesota, New Hampshire, New Mexico, North Dakota, South Dakota, Texas and Wisconsin. The statutes in these fifteen states use a variety of definitions of psychotherapy, patient, therapist, and sexual contact. These laws seek to punish the perpetrator. They therefore differ from civil remedies that seek only to compensate the victim. These laws hold the therapist responsible even when there is consent on the part of the patient. The reasoning here is that unlike rape, the therapist is paid to be of help and to do no harm. These felony statutes also include mandatory report requirements on the part of anyone who may know about such conduct. Anonymous reporting is also allowed in some states.[40]

The consequences of these laws are a two-sided sword. No doubt these laws protect some patients from the sexual abuse of predatory therapists. These laws also build a wall of distrust between the therapist and the patient. These laws also pit one therapist against another, in that a therapist can eliminate his competition by anonymously reporting sexual misconduct by another therapist, true or not. Surely, any male therapist must be aware that his reputation, his livelihood and his freedom can be forfeited by any female patient he may treat. Therefore, it has become dangerous for male therapists to treat female patients so that henceforth therapy by men will have to be conducted on a same sex basis.

IV

The majority of psychotherapists today (1999) are women. This came about because after 1989 56 percent of doctorates in psychology were awarded to women. For some time prior to this, women have been the majority in the field of social work. Therefore, female psychotherapists are *ipso facto* treating men.

When the therapist is a woman and the patient a man the risk of crossing the appropriate sexual boundary is of course a good deal less than when the opposite is the case. For men, as we have seen, a cross sexual therapy situation must remain no more than a business proposition devoid of any hint of intimacy or even friendship. In part, this is necessary because men have been socialized to view women as sex objects, first and foremost, while women have been socialized to hide such feelings if they have them at all. As a consequence, female therapists are much more at risk of experiencing sexual harassment from male patients than male patients are at risk of sexual harassment from female therapists. A study by de Mayo indicates that more than half of all female therapists have experienced sexual harassment by patients. de Mayo also found that the same patients persisted in sexualizing their therapy sessions with a female therapist; that occasionally therapists felt a sense of danger in that the patient behaved in a manner that threatened the personal safety of the therapist and that some patients who engaged in sexual harassment were psychotic so that their harassing conduct was viewed as manifestations of psychopathology.[41]

In view of the sexual aggression by male patients which some female therapists experience in their practice, it is worthwhile to consult the work of Beth Erickson. She has discussed the relationship of female therapists to male clients in her 1993 book Helping Men Change. She recommends two strategies female therapists need to use in treating men. These are: first, that women continue to exhibit warmth and nurturing because those are the "elements that make us women," and "women must learn to do what traditionally has been considered the man's prerogative and responsibility." [42]

Erickson lists these characteristics she thinks women must be if they wish to work effectively with men. These characteristics are: create a "holding" environment. She means a place that is safe and where the patient can experience healing through the therapist-client relationship. Another characteristic of a female therapist, says Erickson, should be response. This means that the therapist needs to hear what the client has to say about himself, not about the therapist. Third, Erickson demands that the female therapists not be apologetic or regretful about being a woman. Fourth, she believes that female therapists should be comfortable around men. Fifth, female therapists, according to Erickson, need to be comfortable discussing uncomfortable topics including sex, and the most uncomfortable topic of all, money. Sixth, Erickson thinks that men need to learn that they are not separate but connected. She holds that women have precisely the opposite problem. Seventh, Erickson wants female therapists to establish authority so that "he can respect her enough to follow her lead." Finally, Erickson says that the female therapist must be capable of firm benevolence, meaning she must be able to confront and yet comfort.[43]

Men and women are of course not only biologically distinct. Sociologists have used the word "gender" to distinguish the social, cultural and learned differences between women and men so that it is indeed true that women and men belong to different sub-cultures. Therefore, women who treat male patients and vice versa need to understand some aspects of the culture in which the sexes are immersed and which influence their thinking in so divergent ways.[44]

This is also true of therapists who deal with people whose world is influenced by religious beliefs at variance with that of the majority. Orthodox believers and fundamentalists serve to illustrate the need for therapists to be attuned to the cultural environs in which their clients live.

Because those who adhere to fundamentalist or orthodox religious views generally define themselves as a community, the number of patients included in such a community is small. The evidence shows that religious commitment has a more positive association with mental health than is true of either neutral or negative attitudes toward religion. This is so because religious ceremony, social support, prayer and a relationship with the respective deities are in the first place methods of bolstering the ego strength of the followers of any religion and because religion defends in large measure against the most frequent afflictions of everyday life.

Orthodox Jews seldom resort to psychotherapy. Those who do so, however, can be treated by all those means used to treat anyone else. Such treatment will involve more patience than is normally necessary. This is so because orthodox believers need a good deal of time to discover whether a non-orthodox therapist can be trusted. The orthodox may also require conduct not normally used with other patients. For example, leaving the door open or at least slightly ajar during a therapy session; consulting with the rabbi of an orthodox Jew as to the treatment to be given or even allowing a chaperone to be present.

Evidently, only a therapist capable of considerable flexibility can undertake to treat such a patient.[45]

Such flexibility is also required of a therapist treating an evangelical Christian. Traditionally, evangelicals have viewed psychotherapy with suspicion because Sigmund Freud was viewed as an atheist and because Freud and his followers ridiculed all religion as antiquated nonsense. For decades no effort was made by either group to recognize the other or to be in touch with those seen as utterly foreign to the efforts of the in-group. In the 1960's liberal Christians did begin to acknowledge psychotherapy particularly because their young people were increasingly attending college where they learned a great deal about psychology, sociology and other helping social sciences. In addition, many evangelicals became disillusioned with the spiritual approach to emotional problems. This then led to the entrance of evangelicals into the profession of therapist and into the position of patient.

Of course, evangelicals, like orthodox Jews have the support of an "in-group" of believers and the further support of ritual, prayer and belief. Among these strongly held beliefs is the belief in sin and in the denial of emotional pain. These attitudes evidently prevent effective therapy unless, once more, the therapist understands this sub-culture and has the patience to deal with it.[46]

We have seen that gender and religion influence the therapist/client relationship. That is also true of ethnicity and national origin. Therefore, therapists who practice in areas which have a large immigrant population will be confronted with people who may have a totally different world view than is normally known in the United States. Consider that a Japanese couple appeared in the office of a therapist in the company of the husbands mother. This seems so outlandish to Americans that it resembles bringing ones mother on a honeymoon. Yet, in Japanese culture the relationship between a son and his mother is considered more important that the relationship between spouses.[47]

Other ethnic groups in America have different views and attitudes concerning psychotherapy. Protestant Anglo-Saxons are less likely to exhibit emotions than are Jews. Middle Easterners, Asian Indians, Europeans and Native Americans all have a different attitude towards therapy. The husband-wife, parent-child and work attitudes differ among each other as do beliefs about oneself and ones' meaning in the universe. This is very much true of the dominance issue in all families. "Who's the boss?" is an issue decided in every family in accordance with its view of the world. Similarly the therapist must be aware that every family has a history which only insiders understand. That history is closely tied to the ethnic background of the client/patient.[48]

V

The personal problems of psychotherapists must not be underestimated if we are to understand this profession. These problems include psychological distress which may be defined as emotional exhaustion. This difficulty is the most often encountered by psychotherapists, followed closely by episodes of anxiety and depression. Alcohol consumption is yet another personal problem that haunts some psychotherapists, mostly men. Finally, drug use is reported by some, but not very many, psychotherapists.

Because these problems are quite acute among psychotherapists, they themselves have often been in therapy. That in turn requires a great deal of emotional and financial investment by the therapist. Personal therapy is not the only means used by psychotherapists to sustain themselves. Prayer and meditation are used by many and an unusually higher number, i.e., fully one third engage in physical exercise. Most psychotherapists also enjoy friends, family and children.[49]

These children of psychotherapists, like the proverbial "preacher's kid" have been the object of myths and stereotypes for years. These myths include that therapist-parents are unemotional, cold, humorless, distant, narcissistic and endlessly analytical or interpretative. From this stereotype it is then abstracted that the children of therapists must be abnormal, psychologically impaired and that these childhood problems are directly traceable to the behavior of the parent-therapist.[50]

Golden and Farber asked a number of children of psychotherapists what they knew about their parent's profession. From this study Golden and Farber discovered that almost all children of psychotherapists knew that "sessions" last from 45 minutes to an hour. They also knew that the process involves talking and problem solving; that most problems patients bring to therapists involve relationships and that it takes a good listener to be a good therapist. Children of therapists thought that the greatest advantage deriving from their parent's profession for them was that their therapist parent knew how to handle all kinds of childhood crises and emotionally painful situations. They thought that the greatest disadvantage of having a parent/psychotherapist was the tendency of the parent to question intrusively, their know-it-all attitude and their constant focus on everybody's feelings.

With reference to other peoples reactions to the knowledge that their parent is a psychotherapist, most children experienced no reaction from others concerning their parent's profession. However, those who did patients bring to therapists involve relationships and that it takes a good listener to be a good therapist. Children of therapists thought that the greatest advantage deriving from their parent's profession for them was that their therapist parent knew how to handle all kinds of childhood crises and emotionally painful situations. They thought that the greatest disadvantage of having a parent/psychotherapist was the tendency of the parent to question intrusively, their know-it-all attitude and their constant focus on everybody's feelings.

With reference to other peoples reactions to the knowledge that their parent is a psychotherapist, most children experienced no reaction from others concerning their parent's profession. However, those who did collect some reaction to the news that they have a psychotherapist mother or father reported the negative stereotypes already reviewed. [51]

Such negative stereotypes will of course affect the therapeutic experience of the patient because perceptions of psychotherapists and psychotherapy are related to treatment expectations. Such expectations, in turn, have "significant implications for persistence in therapy and treatment outcomes."

These expectations include the request by some patients that their therapist should give them, or refer them to a physician who will give them, a so-called SSRI. That abbreviation means "selective serotonin reuptake inhibitor." Serotonin raises blood pressure and is believed to block depression.

Most common among these SSRI drugs are Prozac, Paxil, Zoloft and Serzone. These medications maintain high levels of serotonin circulating in the brain. High levels of serotonin are associated with a "euthymic" or good spirit mood, sound sleep, a good appetite and pain relief. HMOs like these medications because they can be prescribed by primary care physicians, thus reducing the cost of sending a patient to a psychotherapist. Prozac costs only $500.- a year which is a good deal less than the cost of psychotherapy. There are also ambitious business people who seek to use Prozac for the same reason that athletes use steroids.

Essentially, the wide use of such drugs indicates that many Americans are unwilling to live in reality. Reality means that life includes happiness and sadness, good health and illness, success and disappointment, contentment and anxiety. But because of the widely advertised use of SSRIs there are now those Americans who imagine that they need not suffer any pain or sorrow but should live in a world created by drugs. This then raises the question of what it means to be human. Is a life dictated by drugs really a human existence? For psychotherapists the use of these pills means that the personal functions they provide are now provided by a pill and not a person. In addition to the fear that drugs will make psychotherapy unnecessary is the fact that many Americans now believe that anyone can live a hedonistic life by swallowing drugs. It can of course also be argued that the states usually called "the human condition" are nothing more than biochemical deficiencies. Surely it cannot be denied that many diseases and afflictions of mankind which were at one time considered the inevitable fate of all men have been eliminated or at least alleviated by drugs. Therefore, the use of pharmaceuticals as a means of delivering health care is of the greatest importance.

Summary

The first efforts to treat mental or emotional problems were made by Charcot, Freud and Breuer at the end of the 19th century. These early researchers recognized the hidden part of the human personality and thereby laid the foundations for psychotherapy. Freud invented psychoanalysis which is based on talking and not on physical intervention. Therefore, not only psychiatrists with a medical background, but also social workers, psychologists and religious counselors gained access to psychotherapy.

That therapy is based on the relationship of the therapist to the client/patient and rests on trust and the identity of the therapist more than on any theory. Because so much depends on the therapist herself, some suffer "burn out" and all need a good deal of support in order to deal with the vagaries of their patients, the bureaucracies of "agencies" and the interference of the HMOs. The need for "boundaries" is of great importance in treating psychotherapy patients some of whom have now substituted the use of drugs for such treatment. It is the use of drugs in the American health delivery system that is the subject of our next chapter.

NOTES

[1] Henry Gleitman, *Psychology,* Second Edition, New York, W.W. Norton & Co., 1986, p. 414.

[2] Sigmund Freud and Joseph Breuer, "Studies in Hysteria," in James Strachey, Editor and Translator, Sigmund Freud, *The Complete Psychological Works,* Vol. 2, New York, Norton, 1976.

[3] Thomas Maeder, *Children of Psychiatrists and other Psychotherapists,* New York, Harper & Row, 1989, p. 26.

[4] Lisa Kalis, "Salary Report," *Working Woman,* Vol. 23, No. 2, February 1998, p. 41.

[5] American Medical Association, *Socioeconomic Characteristics of Medical Practice,* Chicago, American Medical Association, 1993, p. 66.

[6] Maeder, *op.cit.* p. 35.

[7] Marquis Earl Wallace, "Private Practice, A Nationwide Study," *Social Work,* Vol. 27, 1982, pp. 262-267.

[8] Bureau of Labor Statistics, "1996 National Occupational and Wage Data," Washington, D.C. *Occupational Employment Statistics,* August 24, 1998, p.1.

[9] William J. Henry, John H. Sims, and S. Lee Spray, *The Fifth Profession: Becoming a Psychiatrist,* San Francisco, Jossey- Bass, 1971.

[10] Keith Humphreys, "Clinical Psychologists and Psychotherapists," *American Psychologist,* Vol. 51, No.3, March 1996, p. 190.

[11] *Ibid.* p. 191.

[12] Morris Greenblatt and Paul Rodenhauser, "Mental health administration: Changes and challenges." *Administration and Policy in Mental Health,* Vol. 31, 1993, pp. 97-100.

[13] D.I. Cheifitz and J.C. Salloway, "Patterns of Mental Health Services Provided by HMOs." *American Psychologist,* Vol. 39,1984, pp. 495-502.

[14] Maurice Friedman, "Buber's Philosophy As the Basis for Dialogical Psychotherapy and Contextual Therapy," *Journal of Humanistic Psychology,* Vol. 38, No. 1, Winter 1998, pp. 25-40.

[15] *Ibid,* p.31.

[16] Jana K. Edwards and Jenniger M. Bess, "Developing Effectiveness in the Therapeutic Use of Self," *Clinical Social Work Journal,* Vol.26, No.1, Spring 1998, p. 90.

[17] Hans Strupp, "The therapist's theoretical orientation: an overrated variable," *Pschotherapy: Theory, Research and Practice,* Vol. 15, No. 4, April 1978, pp. 314-317.

[18] N.F. Coady and C. S. Wolgien, "Good therapists' views of how they are helpful," *Clinical Social Work Journal,* Vol.24, No. 3, 1996, pp. 311-322.

[19] William N. Grosch and David C. Olson, *When Helping Starts to Hurt,* New York, W.W. Norton & Co., 1994, Chapter 1.

[20] Kevin Corcoran and Vikki Vandiver, *Maneuvering the Maze of Managed Care,* The Free Press, New York, 1996, pp.25-27.

[21] *Ibid.* p. 29.

[22] Center for Disease Control, The National Institute of Mental Health, "Suicide Rates in the United States," 1995.

[23] Allan Guttmacher Institute, *Sex and America's Teenagers,* New York, The Institute, 1994.

[24] Dana C. Ackley, *Breaking Free of Managed Care,* New York, The Guilford Press, 1997, p. 29.

[25] Hans S. Falck, *Social Work: The Membership Perspective,* New York, Springer Publishing Co., 1988, p.188.

[26] *Ibid,* p.188.

[27] Corcoran and Vandiver, *op.cit.,* p.33.

[28] Henry I. Spitz, "The Effect of Mental Health Care on Group Psychotherapy: Treatment, Training, and Therapist-Morale Issues, *International Journal of Group Psychotherapy,* Vol. 47, No.1, Summer 1997, p. 28.

[29] Alan J. Goldman, "Commentary," *The Los Angeles Times,* January 21, 1996, p. B5.

[30] Len Sperry and Harry Prosen, "Contemporary Ethical Dilemmas in Psychotherapy," *American Journal of Psychotherapy,* Vol. 52, No.1, Winter1998, pp. 54-65.

[31] Paul Sherrry, Robert Teschendorf, Silas Anderson and Frank Guzman, "Ethical beliefs and behaviors of college counseling center professionals," *Journal of College Student Development,* Vol.32, 1991, pp. 350-359.

[32] Theodore P. Remley Jr., Barbara Herlihy, and Scott B. Herlihy, "The U.S. Supreme Court Decision in *Jaffe v. Redmond*: Implications for Counselors." *Journal of Counseling and Development,* January/February 1997, Vol. 75, pp. 213.

[33] J.H. Wigmore, *Evidence,* 3rd Ed., Boston, Little, Brown, 1961.

[34] *Jaffe v. Redmond* et.al. 1996, WL 315841 (U.S. June 13, 1996).

[35] Stuart W. Twemlow, "Exploitation of Patients: Themes in the Psychopathology of their Therapist" *American Journal of Psychotherapy*, Vol.51, No.3, Summer 1997, p. 359.
[36] Judd Marmor, "Letter to the Editor," *Psychiatric News*, March 18, 1994, pp.22-23.
[37] Twemlow, *op.cit.* p.363.
[38] Kenneth S. Pope, Janet L. Sonne and Jean Holroyd, *Sexual Feelings in Psychotherapy*, Washington, D.C., American Psychological Association, 1993, Chapter 10.
[39] *Ibid.* p. 185.
[40] Katherine S. Haspel and Linda M. Jorgenson, *"Legislative Action Regarding Therapist Sexual Misconduct: An Overview*, Professional Psychology, Research and Practice, Vol.28, No.1, February 1997, pp.63-72
[41] Robert A . deMayo, "Patient Sexual Behavior and Sexual Harassment: A National Survey of Female Psyhologists," *Professional Psychology: Research and Practice*, Vol.28, No. 1, February 1997, pp. 58-62.
[42] Beth M. Erickson, *Helping Men Change; The Role of the Female Therapist*, Newbury Park, Cal., Sage Pulicatons, 1993, pp. 24-25.
[43] *Ibid.*, pp. 37-43.
[44] Gerhard Falk, *Sex, Gender and Social Change:The Great Revolution*, Lanham, MD., University Press of America, 1998, pp. 342-343.
[45] Howard C. Margolese, "Engaging in Psychotherapy with the Orthodox Jew," *American Journal of Psychotherapy*, Vol. 52, No. 1, Winter 1998, pp. 37-53.
[46] Truman G. Esau, "The Evangelical Christian in Psychotherapy," *American Journal of Psychotherapy*, Vol.52, No.1, Winter 1988,pp. 28-36.
[47] Evan Imber-Black, "Developing Cultural Competence: Contributions from Recent Family Literature," *American Journal of Psychotherapy*, Vol.51, No. 4, Fall 1997, pp. 607-610.
[48] *Ibid., p. 609.*
[49] Michael J. Mahoney, "Psychotherapists Personal Problems and Self-Care Patterns," *Professional Psychology: Research and Practice,*Vol.28, No.1, February 1997, pp. 14-16.
[50] Valerie Golden and Barry A. Farber, "Therapists as Parents: Is It Good for the Children?" *Professional Psychology: Research and Practice*, Vol.29, No.2, March 1998, pp. 135-139.
[51] *Ibid.,*p. 138.

Chapter VIII

Magic Potions: Pharmacy for Everyone
I

When the American Pharmaceutical Association was organized in 1852 pharmacy was as old as religion. Whether in China or India, in Peru or Greece, primitive men understood that "nature cures the disease while the remedy amuses the patient."[1]

Ancient and medieval accounts of pharmaceutical treatments show that healing was based on the belief that disease was caused by the presence of spirits in the body. It was further assumed that purification from sin would have an effect on the four humors which the 2nd century Greco-Roman physician Galen (130-200) classified as blood, phlegm, yellow bile and black bile.[2]

It was therefore not until the nineteenth century when science had advanced far enough in Europe and the United States that these notions were laid to rest in the Western world. Today, the pharmaceutical industry discovers, develops, produces and sells drug products. Such products reputedly prevent and cure some diseases and relieve the symptoms of others. As a consequence new drugs have been found in ever increasing numbers since the 1940's. This has led to the cure of numerous previously incurable diseases, prevented epidemics, reduced the length of hospital stays and increased life expectancy. For example, a white female born in the United States at the end of the century can expect to live 79 years. Men and blacks included, the average life expectancy in the United States was 76 years in 1997. By contrast, the a white female born in the United States at the end of the century can expect to live 79 years. Men and blacks included, the average life expectancy in the United States was 76 years in 1997. By contrast, the life expectancy of the entire world population was only 64 years in that year.[3]

This immense advance in life expectancy over earlier years in the history of man is surely the product of research and development by the drug industry. That industry is heavily regulated in the United States primarily through the Food and Drug Administration which must approve of every new drug sold in the market. Today (1999) the science of pharmacology, or the study of drug effects, has given rise to the professions of pharmacologist and pharmacist. The former profession is responsible for research into the further development of the pharmacological sciences while pharmacists are responsible for the distribution of drugs to patients and the education of patients concerning the drugs they take. Therefore pharmacists are expected to adhere to a code of ethics imposed by the American Pharmaceutical Association. These ethics include the confidentiality of records and the accuracy of drug delivery to the patient.[4]

Ethical dispensation of drugs also place the pharmacist into a dilemma. Can a pharmacist question the doctor who wrote the prescription if the pharmacist believes that the patient may be visiting several pharmacies and that the medication will therefore do him harm? This question then goes to the issue of protecting the patient from harm. Ethics, of course, includes more than the protection of patients. It also involves such virtues as truthfulness, charitableness, temperance and friendship. Such characteristics, no doubt of importance to everyone, bear directly on the covenant pharmacists reputedly conclude with each patient. This "covenant" consists of a mutually beneficial exchange. Unlike a secular contract, a covenant is expected to have a moral dimension beyond that which is demanded by law. The idea of a covenant between the pharmacist and the patients is related to the recently developed view of the profession which calls for "pharmaceutical care" and abandons the earlier view that pharmacists merely count and deliver without knowing the patient or having any relationship to him. These ethics in pharmaceutical care have accompanied the great changes in the education of pharmacists during the twentieth century. Hence it is evident that new developments in ethics and in education are two of the principal changes that have come to the profession in the last decade of the twentieth century. In part the demand for more education for pharmacists was a reflection of developments in medical education.[5]

At the beginning of the twentieth century physicians strengthened their profession by reforming and standardizing medical education. As we have seen, the so-called "Flexner Report" led to a level of medical education and practice which gave physicians the full responsibility for the treatment of patients including medicines ordered. The author of the report, Abraham Flexner, argued in 1915 that pharmacy was not a profession because the education of pharmacists was so minimal. To answer this critique the American Association of Colleges of Pharmacy required a three year college course in 1925 and Ohio State University began that year to offer the four year bachelor's degree in pharmacy. In 1928 the AACP began to require the four year degree effective in 1932. This then led to an increase in the number of pharmacists in the United States so that by 1940 the country had 115,000 pharmacists working in 58,000 stores. In 1946 a Pharmaceutical Survey was inaugurated by all major pharmaceutical organizations. Although this survey recommended that a doctoral program consisting of six years of study be adopted by colleges of pharmacy this seemed too radical then. Therefore a five year program was followed by most colleges of pharmacy.[6]

In view of the ever increasing demands on pharmacists and the immense growth of pharmaceutical knowledge, sixty of America's 75 colleges of pharmacy have announced plans to expand their four year degree program to a six year program. The State University of New York at Buffalo School of Pharmacy is the institution to make that change most recently (1998).

This increase in the requirements for a degree in pharmacy was mandated by the American Council on Pharmaceutical Education which demands that in 2000 all American schools of pharmacy must expand their curriculum to six years. The degree to be awarded to the six year graduates will be the Doctor of Pharmacy (Pharm. D.). It is expected that pharmacists will then demand the right to prescribe drugs while physicians will continue to diagnose patients. This means that a division of labor will result so that physicians whose prime competence lies in diagnosis will do just that, even as doctors of pharmacy will prescribe for the patient that product which the pharmacist deems best. Pharmacists have now proclaimed "clinical pharmacy," or "pharmaceutical care" as their professional goal, because pharmacists believe they can successfully perform clinical functions in addition to dispensing.

In view of this development the American Medical Association has announced its fierce opposition to this trend. Drug store owners are also opposed because they fear the increase in the length of education for pharmacists will increase their salary costs even as fewer people will be

willing to undertake so long a curriculum. Yet, it is fair to predict that
the doctorate will become commonplace in the pharmacy profession in
the next few years and that the number of prescriptions filled by
pharmacists will increase even more from the current (1998) 2.5 billion
to more than 2.6 billion early in the next century. [7]

Likewise costs for pharmaceutical products will also increase. In
1996 Americans spent $78 billion on pharmaceuticals. That is expected
to increase to $171.1 billion by 2007 in part because of the increased
use of such products by an aging population but also because of the
ever lengthening training and education needed to perform as a
pharmacist. In 1998 the Bureau of Labor Statistics reported that the
179,140 pharmacists then practicing in the United States were earning a
mean wage of $26.60 an hour or $55,328 a year. In fact, the BLS
showed that in 1997 more than 65% of pharmacists were earning
between $50,000 and $90,000 a year. All pharmacists do not work in
community pharmacies. There are also 25,000 pharmacists employed
by hospitals and other institutions. In addition, over 53,000 pharmacy
assistants and 85,000 pharmacy technicians are now employed in
pharmacies around the country. [8]

It is therefore axiomatic that pharmacy has become an ever more
important part of the health care delivery system. As a profession
pharmacy has the mission of assuring the safe and effective use of
drugs in patients. That mission is explained to pharmacy students at the
outset and is reinforced by the honor code used by most pharmacy
schools as a lesson in the support of a code of ethics all pharmacists
must follow. [9]

Pharmacists are also required to sit for the board of pharmacy
examination. In 1996 the Executive Committee of the National
Association of Boards of Pharmacy instituted the new North American
Pharmacy Licensing Examination which has been administered to
pharmacy graduates in both the United States and Canada since March
1997. Drug therapy occupies one half of that examination with an
emphasis on patient outcomes. Twenty-five percent of the test involves
the accurate dispensing of medications and the other quarter of the
examination deals with the promotion of public health. [10]

Passage of that examination assures the pharmacy graduate of a
license to practice. Licensure, of course, makes pharmacists dependent
on the power and control of an unseen board who can remove the
license of the pharmacist at any time. There are some who say that the
consequences of this kind of control are that any member of the
profession not liked by powerful politicians within the profession can
lose his license to earn a livelihood. Therefore it is possible that
pharmacy, like all licensed professions, is practiced only by those

found to be "politically correct" and not offensive to political manipulators within the profession.

This then leads to an inherent conflict within each licensed profession. Even as licensure is used to insure political conformity it is also a means by which the state protects everyone from incompetent or even criminal practitioners. The benefits of professional licensure are not to be underestimated. Included is the power to decide who may be admitted to the profession; authority to give or withhold a service or a substance in accord with the judgment of the practitioner. In addition, professional licensure allows the practitioner control and autonomy which, prior to the arrival of the health maintenance organizations, was a central feature of pharmaceutical practice. The respect of the community is one more feature of professional autonomy as evidenced by the position of pharmacy within the prestige ratings of occupations in the United States.[11]

A telephone poll conducted by the Columbia Journalism Review revealed that admiration for the ethical rectitude of pharmacists exceeds that of any other occupation mentioned by the interviewers. 81 percent of those interviewed rated the honesty and ethical standards of pharmacists as very high or high. Clergy received a rating of 76% in this survey, doctors 59%, journalists 57%, academics 54% and police 25%. The lowest ratings were attributed to car salesmen, labor union leaders, public relations people and lawyers.[12]

The daily work of most pharmacists consists primarily of filling prescriptions, literally, "a writing in front" and used by physicians to order medication for a patient. Beginning in 1995 the Department of Health, Education and Welfare of the U.S. has proposed that pharmacists include written information concerning the side effects and dangers of drugs received by a consumer. Thereafter, the Food and Drug Administration enforced the inclusion of such information in the 3,300 drugs now available to patients in the United States. Then, in January of 1997 the so-called MedGuide plan was adopted by American pharmacists. This is a computerized method of alerting patients to drug risks by means of including comprehensive literature in every prescription. It is hoped that this plan will sharply reduce the accidental misuse of drugs which hospitalizes two million Americans every year.[13]

The inclusion of literature in the medications issued by pharmacists is not accepted by everyone. Some physicians believe that such literature is objectionable because it frightens patients into non-compliance with their prescriptions. An example of such a view is a letter to the editor of the American Journal of Psychiatry which reads in part: " I have concluded that a major reason for non-compliance with psychotropic drug prescriptions is the "advice" proffered by dispensing pharmacists-advice which may be contradictory to that intended or provided by the prescribing psychiatrist. .....Well-intended help of the dispensing pharmacist can result in fearfulness of the patient about taking the prescribed medicine."[14]

In addition to these changes in education and responsibility of the pharmacy profession, the entrance of women into the profession constitutes yet another change in the practice of pharmacy during the last quarter of the twentieth century. This has led to a true feminization of the profession. Statistics underscore this contention. For while women were 24% of American pharmacists in 1996, they constituted only 10% of pharmacists in 1983.[15]

In view of the large female pharmacy student enrollment now under way, that proportion will increase and no doubt reach 50% in the next few years. Now, traditionally, professional women tended to work full time only until they were married and had children if they worked at all. After 1980, however, over 90 percent of female pharmacy graduates worked full time even as there was a delay in marriage and child bearing in the younger cohorts in that and subsequent decades. [16]

The ever increasing corporatization of American pharmacies and the increase in female participation in the profession appears to suit female proclivities as visible in all professions. In the past only 10% of female pharmacists as compared to 50% of male pharmacists owned stores. The explanations for this phenomenon are first that the number of independent settings for pharmacists has declined rapidly as the "chain" stores increased and second that young women graduates are not interested in private ownership because they are also responsible for the preservation of husbands and the raising of children. This is best understood in light of the need for store owners to work 70 hours or more each week. It is also noteworthy that the decline in independent pharmacies has led to a greater equalization of income for both sexes. In 1996 female pharmacists earned 89% of the earnings of male pharmacists in hospital settings, ninety-two percent of male earnings in independent pharmacies and 95% of male earnings in chain pharmacies. Because women entered the profession mainly during the five years ending in 1997, part of the reason for the lesser earnings of women lies in the lesser number of years of experience most women have accumulated in the profession.[17]

A study by Roberts indicates that more women than men would choose pharmacy again if they could make another career choice even as the opportunities for running an independent pharmacy declined. This is in accord with the additional finding that women, more than men, believe that the satisfaction they gain from the pharmacist profession lies in the security their profession affords them. In fact, women chose "security" as more important than eight other characteristics of the occupation available to them. Male pharmacists chose "autonomy" as first among such choices as: ability to use knowledge; challenge and variety and salary.[18]

II

Pharmacists are expected to follow a code of ethics which lists seven statements developed by the American Association of Colleges of Pharmacy including the promise to "consider the welfare of humanity and relief of human suffering my primary concerns."

These concerns are of course also demanded of the medical profession. There are those who argue that doctors are losing control over which prescription drugs patients will get and that therefore pharmacists ought to supplant doctors in insuring that patients are not at risk from this development. This development would seem the most reasonable. Health maintenance organizations and big drug companies, however, seek to install so-called pharmacy benefit managers into this gap because consumers and their insurers spent $78 billion on 2.5 billion prescriptions in 1996.

Financial considerations are of course more important to insurers in deciding which medication a patient will receive than the outcome for the patient. Large insurers get rebates from drug companies if the insurer places them on their list of approved drug companies. This can have serious consequences for patients. For example, a patient using a pill to control high blood pressure may find that his insurer will not pay for the pill because it is manufactured by a drug company not on their list. Undoubtedly there are many patients who can just as well use a pill manufactured by a drug company which is on that list. However, there are patients who cannot control their blood pressure unless they use a pill not covered. Such patients must either pay the cost of such medication themselves or risk the consequences of receiving no treatment or the wrong treatment for their condition. This means that anyone who signs on to a health maintenance plan will be restricted to using only those medications manufactured by a drug company with whom the insurer has a contract.

In addition to living with the restrictions placed on them by "managed care", patients are also faced with the consequences derived from the rebates received by pharmacists from drug manufacturers. This gives pharmacists an incentive to switch patients to medication which may not be in the patients interest. Doctors frequently allow this because they truly believe that the patient is not adversely affected;

they cannot afford the administrative costs of fighting the huge insurance companies and they fear being dropped from the health maintenance networks if they don't prescribe the preferred drug.[19]

In sum, drug makers seek to increase their profits by several means. First, drug manufacturers offer rebates to managed care companies who decide to pay only for those drugs made by the manufacturer offering them the largest rebate. Second, drug companies exert pressure on doctors and pharmacists to change a patient's prescription. This is done by letters, faxes and calls which reach some doctors ten to twelve times a day. Third, pharmacy benefit managers have now been bought by drug manufacturers so that these PBMs no longer succeed in lowering the costs of drugs. Thus, Merck now owns Medco Containment Services, Smith Kline Beecham owns Diversified Pharmaceutical Services and Eli Lilly own PCS Health Systems. Other drug companies have paid huge amounts to pharmacy benefit managers to assure that only their products are given to patients these "managers" control. Fourth, health maintenance organizations are limiting the number of drugs available to patients to as little as 48% of what is available even if this means that some patients cannot get what they need to survive.

The outcome of all this is that patients can no longer rely on doctors and pharmacists to protect them. This is true because the amount of paper work and argument needed to switch a patient from a medication that does not work to one that does work is so great that few doctors or pharmacists are in a position to undergo the ordeals the insurers impose on them in order to protect the patient from harmful or ineffective medication. [20]

The old are even more at risk with respect to drugs given them. For example, one fourth of all old hospital patients receive six or more prescription drugs. In addition, many old people also take three "over-the-counter" drugs at the same time. Therefore, nearly 25% of hospital admissions of the old are the result of taking such drugs incorrectly. A recent study reveals that this problem is particularly visible among those retired citizens who live in board and care facilities. Such facilities should not be confused with nursing homes because board and care facilities do not provide nursing care. That group of patients who had inappropriate prescriptions generally suffered side-effects which overrode the intended benefits of their prescriptions.[21]

In 1990 federal law began to require that all pharmacists must offer counseling and written information to Medicaid customers. Consequently, most pharmacists now keep records for their customers so that they look for potential dangers involved in medicines sold to such customers. It has therefore become important that patients shop at the same pharmacy at all times.[22]

Despite all of these precautions there are some dangers in drug use which cannot be avoided. A pharmacist can misinterpret a doctor's handwriting or a patient sees several doctors and fails to inform all of them that he is taking a medication prescribed by another doctor. All of these possibilities militate in favor of giving pharmacists the sole responsibility of prescribing and filling a prescription based on the doctor's diagnosis.[23]

We have already seen that pharmacy is a profession in transition from a supporting role supervised by physicians to a more mature patient-oriented, self directed clinical role.

Adamcik *et al* have made a detailed study of the role expansion now facing the pharmacy profession. They report that the eventual success of the profession in assuming independence from the medical profession lies first in reaching a consensus among its practitioners to the effect that such independence should and can now be achieved.[24]

Historically, pharmacists were seen as "physician's cooks." Nevertheless, before the large scale expansion of drug manufacturers, pharmacists consulted with patients, acted as community health care advisors and mixed and manufactured medicine themselves. After the growth of the industry and now (1999), pharmacists became pill counters who also labeled, poured and recorded. This led to a decline in the professional standing of pharmacists and the current effort to "re-professionalize" pharmacy towards a more clinical role.

That clinical role is envisaged to include the monitoring of patient's drug therapy responses, the selection of the appropriate drug or dosage once a diagnosis is made by a physician and fulfilling the role of drug expert on a health care team. This means that the ambiguous role of the pharmacist in the health delivery system is about to come to an end as pharmacy enters into a truly professional role. A "profession" is here defined as an occupation which has a high degree of systematized knowledge. Such systematized knowledge leads to autonomy because outsiders cannot evaluate the members of the profession. In the second place, a profession is mainly interested in serving the community unlike salesmen whose sole interest is their own income. A high degree of internalized ethics and a system of social rewards such as prestige, honor, and high income are also criteria of a profession.

This functional analysis needs to be augmented by an understanding of the conflict model of understanding professions. This refers to the ability of a profession to create boundaries around themselves. Every profession needs to maintain a boundary defense so that the profession can control enough resources to protect itself. That being the case, it is not surprising that physicians are quite antagonistic to the role expansion of pharmacists now under way. Adamcik *et al* found that physicians are most antagonistic towards the increasing independence of pharmacists in the community because physicians cannot control or supervise community pharmacists very well. In the hospital setting the antagonism of physicians for the expansion of the pharmacist's role is less severe because hospital pharmacy is very public and easily supervised by doctors.

It appears that nurses are somewhat less antagonistic towards the role expansion of pharmacists because nurses are less likely to monitor patients' drug responses or order laboratory tests than doctors or pharmacists. However, nurses are not wholeheartedly in support of pharmacists efforts to escape physicians' supervision because nurse practitioners now believe that they can do what pharmacists have traditionally done and more.

It should be added that physicians are also worried about the possibility and even the certainty that patients can walk into a pharmacy and have their blood pressure checked, their medicine adjusted and buy an over-the-counter medicine without consulting a doctor at all. This pattern of change threatens to reduce physicians to dealing only with the sick and wounded thus losing all access to ambulatory patients. [25]

Even now, in 1999, pharmacists do more than dole out drugs on doctor's orders. Indeed, pharmacists no longer spend time mixing chemicals in their apothecaries. Pharmacists do, however, provide important services to their customers. Most important is that pharmacists provide patients with high quality information at no cost. Pharmacists are also accessible at any time. This is surely not true of doctors. Pharmacists also keep "drug profiles" for their customer/patients. This is a record of all past prescriptions the customer has used along with relevant health conditions. Such a list includes allergies, infections and disorders that could be aggravated by drugs the customer/patient is taking. These profiles permit the patient to visit a drug store anywhere in the country and have a pharmacist call back to get the information from the home pharmacy. Drug profiles also help pharmacists catch mistakes which could be serious and even lethal. In the event a pharmacist believes that a doctor has made a mistake or that the patient has used drugs prescribed by another doctor which could cause a problem, the pharmacist can refuse to fill the prescription, call the doctor, discuss the problem and make every effort to protect the patient/customer. [26]

Such protection is particularly important for patients over the age of fifty when the body absorbs, metabolizes and eliminates drugs more slowly. Furthermore, as people age they take more medicines which increases the risk ipso facto. Old people are also advised to take reduced doses of drugs, a precaution doctors and pharmacists often forget in the rush of their daily responsibilities. In 1995, New Choice journal published an entire list of medications that may cause unwanted side effects in older patients.[27]

We have seen what pharmacists can do to prevent these hazards. However, what can be done is not necessarily done. Dr. Marcus Reidenberg, a pharmacologist at New York Hospital-Cornell Medical Center says that :"...systems to correct prescription errors in this country are of very limited reliability." A 1996 study of 245 pharmacies across the country revealed at that time that well over one half of all pharmacies in that study failed to warn consumers that some prescriptions for drugs can be risky if not deadly when taken.

It can be expected that as more and more pharmacists enter clinical practice the stereotypes concerning them will gradually disappear. Physicians will eventually accept the view that pharmacists are drug experts who can and should prescribe and deliver prescriptions based on physicians' diagnosis. This is important because physicians can hardly master the field of pharmacology in addition to their own. Hence, the division of labor in this area of vital concern will inevitably succeed as it has always succeeded in complex societies. [28]

In addition to the burden which the ever increasing number of drugs present to the physician, doctors and pharmacists are also confronted with the politics involved in the so-called "war on drugs" conducted by government. If doctors of pharmacy and not doctors of medicine were in charge of prescribing pain killing drugs the consequences of the present policies would not occur because pharmacists have a far more believable reputation in dealing with drugs and their consequences than physicians.

Law enforcers need to prove that they get results. Now it is of course far easier for drug law enforcers to investigate and destroy the livelihood of physicians than to deal with the truly dangerous terrorists who import and sell illegal drugs all over this country. Therefore, drug law enforcers will go after physicians treating patients in pain. These patients in pain then become the real victims of the zealous drug law enforcers.

There is in this country a "Painful Underground Railroad" consisting of people who have been denied painkiller medicine by doctors fearful of bureaucratic regulators. Fearing that they will lose their license or even go to prison, doctors across the country are generally unwilling to help people in extreme pain who need strong opiates or other pain relieving substances. Therefore, the "Painful Underground Railroad" consists of people in terrible pain who have been denied help and who travel anywhere at any cost to get relief from their horrible misery.

Medical journals have called the fear of prescribing pain killers "opiophobia". The consequence of this fear of the Drug Enforcement Administration or state regulators is suicide. Numerous patients who could have been helped have killed themselves or asked for physician assisted suicide because the pain they suffered is too much to bear. In the words of Dr. Sidney Schnoll who chairs the Division of Substance Abuse Medicine at the Medical College of Virginia: "We will go to great lengths to stop addiction-which, though certainly a problem, is dwarfed by the number of people who do not get adequate pain relief. So we will cause countless people to suffer in an effort to stop a few cases of addiction. I find that appalling."[29]

The undertreatment of pain by means of narcotics causes many patients to suffer so much that they wish for death. Dr. Russell Portenoy, director of analgesic studies at Memorial Sloan-Kettering Hospital in New York, told the New York Times: "The undertreatment of pain in hospitals is absolutely medieval........because physicians share the widespread social attitudes that these drugs are unacceptable......and many physicians fear sanctions against themselves if they prescribe these drugs."[30]

Recently, Texas and California adopted more humane provisions under their Pain Treatment Acts which now permit patients in pain to receive at least some relief. Nevertheless, the undertreatment of pain continues in the other 48 states as blind prejudice against all drugs has lead state boards of medicine to revoke the licenses of doctors who helped severely ill patients live with their pain. Of course, these boards make no provisions for the patients who are deprived of their doctor. Hence, patients who could no longer bear their pain have killed themselves even as the boards of medicine continued their witch hunts against the doctors helping them. [31]

It is therefore necessary that doctors of pharmacy become involved in the prescription of drugs for people in pain because those who hold such degrees are in a far better position to deal with the zealous drug law enforcers than are practicing physicians who cannot defend themselves.

Nevertheless, it cannot be overlooked that drug law enforcement is important because there are some pharmacists who use various methods to illegally tamper with the prescriptions they fill. These white collar crimes go almost unnoticed because, as we have already seen, pharmacists are given very high ratings by the public for honesty and integrity.[32]

Payne and Dabney have examined 292 cases of prescription fraud prosecuted by the Medicaid Fraud Control Units. Their research indicates that about 10% of all funds spent on health care in this country are lost to fraud and abuse. The consequences of health care fraud are several. First, the losses sustained by the health care system because of fraud means that some needed health care funds have been wasted and that some programs are therefore not funded at all or underfunded. Acts of prescription fraud also represent a possible physical threat to consumers. Severe illness and even death can result from the issuance of the wrong prescriptions. For example, a pharmacist substituted regular insulin for NPH insulin leading to the homicide of the patient.[33]

Most common among a number of frauds reported to the fraud control units is "generic drug substitution." This constituted 44.5% of all the fraud cases reported. 28.7 percent of cases reported dealt with accusations of "billing for non-existent prescription." Third of the list of frauds reported was "billing for prescriptions not ordered." That consisted of 19.9 percent of all fraud reported. Hence, over 93% of all types of pharmacy related fraud reported to the fraud control units were included in these three types of offenses. Nine other kinds of pharmacy fraud were also reported but their numbers are negligible.[34]

The distribution of non-sterile drugs is another form of dangerous offense for which some pharmacies have been prosecuted. For example, the State of Washington revoked the license held by For Your Health, Inc., a Kent, Washington pharmacy. This action was taken because the pharmacy chain distributed a non-sterile drug Magnesium – ATP and illegally manufactured the drug testosterone. This also led to a suit against the drug chain by the Drug Enforcement Agency and to a $5,000 fine. In New Jersey, Ambix Laboratories was shut down by a "consent decree of permanent injunction" because two of the firm's products were contaminated by bacteria and the laboratory facilities were unsanitary.[35]

Some would hold pharmacists alone responsible for filling dangerous prescriptions. Yet, pharmacists have to worry about the time needed to argue with insurers when that time could be spent counseling customers about their prescriptions. Others place some of the blame on insurance companies who force pharmacists to work twelve hours a day to build a higher volume and make up for lower prices. [36]

III

The idea that pharmacists need to make up for lower prices would seem a gross distortion to insurance companies and those many citizens who are not insured for drugs and who must pay for their prescriptions themselves. In fact, there are many who believe that drug prices are excessive because there is a plot to keep drug prices high. Instead, powerful buyers, such as HMOs and mail-order drug firms, are driving prices down. Big HMOs receive 25% discounts from drug manufacturers in exchange for a 100% increase in volume for some of their drugs. HMOs and mail-order drug sellers now take bids from manufacturers on all the similar drugs in any category and then put the lowest priced drug on a list of preferred drugs called formularies. Then they cajole doctors to prescribe the drugs on that list. The result is that overpriced drugs are not sold.

Medicaid patients are undoubtedly the biggest consumers of drugs in America. Because of the immense volume Medicaid buys each day, Medicaid has received a 15.7% discount since 1990. This discount is now also the maximum discount drug manufacturers are willing to offer large drug chains or other buyers. Therefore, while erstwhile large HMOs were receiving as much as a 40% discount from drug manufacturers, these HMOs must now pay more.

The effort of the Clinton administration to keep prices down is included in the so-called "Clinton Plan" for health care for all Americans. It would permit the Secretary of Health and Human Services to declare any drug too expensive with the right to demand a discount for more than 17 % usually given drug stores. If refused, the Secretary can then ban that drug from coverage under Medicare and other uses by Americans. [37]

Retail drug stores receive few if any discounts from wholesalers or manufacturers. This has led Rite Aid Corp. and nine other chains to sue the seven biggest drug manufacturers on the grounds that discounts given to HMOs and hospitals but not drug stores amounts to illegal price discrimination. Some examples cited by the drug chains are these: one hundred tablets of a potassium supplement cost a hospital $2.03. The same supplement is sold to drug stores for $27.31, a markup of 1,245%. "Inderal" is sold to HMOs and hospitals for $4.12. Drug stores buy this from American Home Products for $48.31. Numerous other examples can be reviewed here. [38]

Drug companies claim that their overall price increases averaged only 2.9% in 1996-97 and that this was the same as price increases in overall consumer prices. Drug manufacturers also argue that they must charge such immense prices because they need to pay for expensive research including attempts at manufacturing drugs which do not work. This costs the manufacturers a great deal of money which they then seek to recover by charging high prices to consumers. Furthermore, drug companies worry about the 17 year patent limit which many of their drugs reach each year and which then allow others to manufacture lower-priced generic substitutes. To overcome this problem some large drug manufacturers now develop their own generic substitutes as their

17 year patent monopolies ran out. This in turn has led to an examination of this practice by the Federal Trade Commission to see whether perpetuating a patent monopoly beyond its expiration violates the anti-trust laws. This is of great economic importance to the drug manufacturers as the market share of generics has risen from 21% in the 1980's to nearly 40% at the end of the '90's. [39]

This and numerous other examples demonstrate that making drugs has become one of the world's most lucrative industries. Recently, two large drug companies merged and became the second largest corporation on earth. Together, all drug manufacturers sell about $300 billion worth of drugs a year on which they earn about 30% or $90 billion. Because generic drugs can now compete with patented drugs the drug industry must now produce new drugs which can treat what was heretofore untreatable. Also, because the health maintenance organizations demand lower prices the drug industry must find drugs that are so much better than what was sold until now, that the new drug can supplant the old. Because it can take up to ten years from the registration of a new drug with the patent office until it appears on a pharmacist's shelf, drug manufacturers generally have far less protection than the patent laws allow. Patents run out after 17 years. Therefore it is possible that a drug will be protected only seven years or slightly longer. Meanwhile drug companies must do additional research at great expense in order to recoup the money invested in earlier research and to earn profits for shareholders. [40]

The giant pharmaceutical manufacturers are now facing a great deal of competition. So much so, that 50% of all the substances undergoing clinical tests in 1998 originate outside "big pharma" as the traditional drug firms are called in the industry. Therefore, the large companies are forced to increase their output by about 10% a year to stay abreast of the competition. To do so, the process of finding, testing and marketing new products by means of a new pharmaceutical technology is now under way which promises to do three things. First, increase the range of diseases treatable with drugs. Second, increase the precision and effectiveness of those drugs and third increase the ability to anticipate diseases instead of reacting to them. The idea of "predictive medicine" relies on the knowledge that in many cases illness can be foreseen and that better drugs can turn that knowledge into the ability to treat a person before the disease develops. This permits some pharmaceutical manufacturers to consider selling life-long health advice. [41]

A great stride towards "predictive medicine" was made in 1997 when Dr. Daniel Cohen of Paris, France made the first comprehensive map of all human chromosomes. The study of "genomics" permits pharmaceutical manufacturers to know in advance of producing a new drug what will cause side effects of a new drug and whether or not the new drug will have a poor response among patients. In view of the health maintenance organizations interest in saving money by any means it is certain that the HMOs will at once force the issue of pharmacogenomics. [42]

Driven by the need to reduce costs and competition, mergers of drug companies have now become commonplace throughout the world. These mergers have occurred mainly because of the entrance of managed care organizations into the prescription-drug market. The HMOs use two methods of monitoring the usage of drugs. The HMOs adopted lists of drugs compiled by physicians and pharmacists who compare the prices and benefits of various drugs. These lists are called "formularies." These lists were given physicians in an effort to limit the use of drugs to those appearing on the "formularies." The result has been that at the end of the "90s" prescriptions listed on "formularies" account for one half of all drug sales in the United States. The second method used by HMOs to monitor drug sales is the introduction of prescription benefit management. Pharmacists employed by these PBMs telephone doctors requesting that the doctors make substitutions of cheaper drugs for those already prescribed. Fearing that the HMOs will be drop them from the lists of approved physicians, doctors will do as told. In January 1998 the Food and Drug Administration proposed regulating the activities of prescription benefit managers to insure they provide doctors with accurate information. The FDA acted on the grounds that PBMs have given doctors false and biased information. The proposal would have P.B.Ms submit promotional material to the F.D.A. for an accuracy review. This proposal would be most important in monitoring the prescription benefit managements owned by drug manufacturers. [43]

Likewise, the Food and Drug Administration requires doctors to disclose any financial support from drug companies if they test new drugs or medical devices for such manufacturers. The F.D.A. must therefore be informed when doctors own a patent on a product they are studying or have more than $50,000 equity in a drug company at the time of their study or have received more than $50,000 in grants or equipment or fees from such a company. [44]

In their anxiety to control pharmaceutical research pharmaceutical manufacturers give large gifts to university researchers which universities cannot afford themselves. Such gifts include bio materials, laboratory equipment, trips and money. These "gifts", however, include agreements that the scientists test the company's product, that donated equipment not be shared and that all results derived from the research be reviewed by the drug manufacturer before publication. This gives manufacturers an opportunity to suppress findings they do not like. For example, Knoll Pharmaceutical suppressed a study showing that a drug they produced worked no better than a cheaper generic. The company then concealed the findings until a "public outcry" forced them to publish the work of Dr. Betty Dong, a University of California pharmacy professor. [45]

Prescription benefit management now also includes mail-order pharmacies that reduce costs of pharmaceuticals by eliminating the costs of running pharmacies. [46]

IV

Drug abuse is one of the most serious dysfunctions produced by American technology. According to sociological theory, a dysfunction is a consequence of social organization which reduces the capacity of the social system to survive or adapt. This contrasts with the meaning of a social function which refers to those aspects of social organization which contribute to the maintenance of society by means of social consensus. [47]

Because "a pill for every ill" is a common belief in America, heightened expectations concerning the efficacy of the health delivery system have reached beyond reality. Fostered by massive advertising campaigns designed to increase profits for drug manufacturers and sellers, many Americans have come to believe that all things are curable by means of pharmaceutics. It is thought by many that from over-the-counter products to physician's prescriptions all illness and discomfort can be eliminated by the use of drugs. Even the emotional tensions of everyday life are calmed by pills. Fifteen percent of Americans, or about 39 million people use tranquilizers to help them manage their daily affairs. This is also true in most European countries, notably Germany, France and England. [48]

There are those who believe that this level of drug use either promotes drug abuse or is *ipso facto* drug abuse. Using now the definition of drug abuse first proposed by the President's Advisory Commission on Narcotics and Drug Abuse this belief can be tested. According to that commission's report, drug abuse is the use of drugs under one of the following circumstances. First, that the drug is used in amounts creating a hazard to one's own health or that of the community. Second, that the drugs are obtained through illegal channels and third that the drug is taken on one's own initiative and not because of professional advice. [49]

Alcohol is undoubtedly the most abused drug in the United States. This is best understood by considering that the average American adult consumes 32 gallons of beer, 24.7 gallons of milk and 21.1 gallons of coffee each year. Some people do not drink any alcohol and are therefore excluded from this statistic. However, among those who do drink ten percent consume one half of all the alcohol consumed in this country.[50] Likewise, only a minority use drugs other than alcohol on a daily basis. Those who do so to excess and are called "drug addicts" can be helped by drug addiction treatments ranging from psychotherapy to the use of medication such as methadone.

Pharmacists have a role in the treatment of drug dependent citizens. Pharmacists work in methadone maintenance clinics where they are responsible for the preparation and dispensing of medication. In this position pharmacists keep precise records and are called upon by the staff of such clinics to consult concerning the pharmacology of drug therapy. Pharmacists are also asked by physicians in such clinics to arrive at a patient's dose and dose changes. In addition pharmacists can prevent adverse reactions to other pharmaceuticals taken by methadone treated patients. Because many drug addicts take a variety of drugs, pharmacists can explain the consequences of such abuse to patients in drug addiction treatment programs. Pharmacists also play a role on the state and federal level in addiction treatment programs. In that capacity pharmacists check program records to insure compliance with government regulations. Pharmacists also help in drug abuse prevention. This is done by identifying patients who visit several physicians to gain access to large quantities of a drug. Pharmacists can also offer physicians alternatives to the prescription of pain killers which often lead to the relapse of chemically dependent persons. Pharmacists can also identify fraudulent prescriptions used by addicts to gain drugs illegally. Finally, pharmacists can speak in schools and other community organizations in the hope of educating everyone concerning the dangers of drugs.[51]

These dangers are of course well known to pharmacists everywhere. Yet, this knowledge does not necessarily protect pharmacists from becoming drug abusers themselves. In 1982, the American Pharmaceutical Association publicly acknowledged that impairment by reason of alcohol and other drugs was a problem within its membership.[52]

The profession has therefore organized a pharmacy recovery network whose effort has been to deal with this danger by defining drug dependency as an illness and not a form of deviance. This avoids the moral condemnation of those who suffer drug dependency and substitutes humanitarian considerations leading to the rehabilitation of the pharmacist involved in drugs. The network is also active in avoiding the criminalization of drug addiction and its concomitant behavior, i.e., drug theft. Nevertheless, every state recovery program uses the threat of license revocation to coerce drug dependent pharmacists to sign treatment contracts. All this means that the entire profession-wide emphasis in dealing with drug dependent pharmacists is viewed within the medical model of social control.[53]

The danger of drug addiction by pharmacists is evidently related to the opportunities available to the profession. In addition, pharmacists suffer considerably more from emotional exhaustion, depersonalization and a sense of failure re personal accomplishments than is true of other professions. It is of interest to note in this connection that pharmacists working for health maintenance organizations rate their personal accomplishments higher than is true for "normative" pharmacists. Unlike so many other drug addicts, pharmacists who abuse drugs are seldom members of a drug sub-culture. Instead they are most likely to use excessive drugs alone and without the knowledge of anyone else.

The stress under which pharmacists must now work undoubtedly contributes to the illicit use of drugs in that profession. That stress includes the 12 hour days pharmacists must work in the chain pharmacies; the need to call physicians concerning similar and cheaper drugs than prescribed and as demanded by health maintenance organizations; the large volume of prescriptions which must be filled to compensate for the cheaper prices for which HMOs will compensate the pharmacy; the dependence on computers which fail regularly and create immense backlogs for which the pharmacist is responsible and the fact that the store manager is not a pharmacist but is nevertheless the "boss".

Added to all these problems is the need for accuracy in filling prescriptions lest the patient comes to harm and the pharmacist loses his license. It is also the duty of pharmacists to counsel customers concerning the use of their prescriptions. This counseling is federally mandated but is often impossible to achieve because of the great pressure under which pharmacists must work. Because older adults are more often consumers of health care services than younger people, pharmacists need to focus on this older population in their consultations.[54]

We have repeatedly said that non-adherence to prescribed medication is a widespread problem in the American health care system. This is particularly a problem among older adults. There are some older people who have hearing impairments or whose limited educational background makes it difficult for them to understand written information. Such clients need to be confronted with spoken instructions at a level they can understand. There are also clients whose foreign birth requires that they be given instructions in their native tongue or in simple English which they can comprehend. In such cases it may also facilitate communication if a friend or relative of the client with good English skills is present. Furthermore, it may facilitate communication with some ethnic minorities to know how conversation among them is initiated. Various cultures have different rules of politeness for initiating conversations. [55]

Immigrants to the United States may also be unable to understand the need to visit a doctor and a legitimate pharmacy when sick. In February 1998, the New York Times reported that a good number of Spanish speaking immigrants in the New York City area had visited pharmacies and not a doctor when sick. Some of the pharmacies thus involved gave the immigrants pharmaceuticals without a prescription. One outcome of such practices has been that some immigrants no longer respond to the basic antibiotics used to treat many kinds of infection. This is visible in the fact that 4% - 21% of patients living in various counties are resistant to penicillin which has been known to cure pneumonia and meningitis. [56]

It is evident from this brief review that the burdens placed on pharmacists during the decade ending in 1999 are so great that no one can meet all the requirements of government, health maintenance organizations, insurance companies, doctors and customer/ patients. It is also remarkable that the Clinton health care reforms were rejected by the public in 1994 on the grounds that they would lead to the establishment of a huge federal bureaucracy. That rejection has instead led to a private, giant bureaucracy which is impersonal and unresponsive to the needs of the sick. Power and greed and an utter lack of morals have led to this impasse. This assault on the health care system has indeed earned huge profits for the few although it has not resulted in an over-all decline of health care. In addition, the problems of the underinsured and the non-insured have been forgotten because the private health care bureaucracies need not answer to the electorate.

In the field of pharmacy several suggestions have been made concerning improvement for patients and pharmacists alike. These suggestions come from William A. Zellmer and were delivered to the annual meeting of the American Society of Health-System Pharmacists. Some of Zellmer's proposals are that ambulatory patients select a pharmacist, not a pharmacy; that pharmacists be taught to resist corporate edicts which undermine their ability to care for patients; that pharmacists recognize and honor outstanding pharmacists for their commitment to patients and that pharmacists, physicians and patients unite in improving the situation concerning patient care created by the new cost-cutting emphasis.

Summary

The drug industry has had great success in increasing life expectancy and alleviating pain and disease. Ethical drug research and distribution have been the main contribution of pharmacists in this process. In view of ever increasing knowledge in pharmacology and the need to assure themselves of a professional identity, pharmacy education has been lengthened to include the doctorate. This, together with the entrance of women into the profession has altered pharmacy considerably during the twenty years ending in 2000.

Government mandates have also changed pharmacy. This includes licensure and the introduction of mandatory counseling in both oral and written form. The effort of health maintenance organizations to reduce costs has led to greater pressure on pharmacists, longer hours and a reduction of independence. Pharmacists therefore face a great deal of stress in their work as they seek to improve their professional condition and protect their patients as well. These efforts are not confined to pharmacists. There are other professions involved in the health delivery system which also play a role in maintaining good health in America. Among these are dentists, optometrists, podiatrists and others whom we will meet in the next chapter.

NOTES

[1] Fielding H. Garrison, *History of Medicine,*   Philadelphia, W.B. Saunders, 1929, p. 22.

[2] Will Durant, *Ceasar and Christ,* New York, Simon and Schuster, 1944, pp. 502-503.

[3] John W. Wright, Ed., *The New York Times 1998 Almanac,* New York, Penguin Putnam Inc., 1997, pp. 396 and 484.

[4] Thomas R. Brown, Ed., *Handbook of Institutional Pharmacy Practice,* Bethesda, Md., American Society of Hospital Pharmacists, 1992.

[5] Bruce D. Weinstein and Amy Haddad, "The Ethics of Pharmaceutical Care," in: Calvin Knowlton and Richard Penna, Eds., *Pharmaceutical Care,* New York, Chapman and Hall, 1996, pp. 319-329.

[6] Calvin Knowlton and Richard Penna, *op.cit.,* pp. 34-43.

[7] William H. Honan, "Imperiled Species: 4 Year Degree in Pharmacy," *The New York Times,* December 17, 1997, p. B8.

[8] Bureau of Labor Statistics, "Occupational Employment Statistics, National Occupational and Wage Data," The Internet. *URL:http://stats.bls.gov/oes/national/oes66008.htm*

[9] Mickey C. Smith and David A. Knapp, "Pharmacy as a Profession, in: Smith and Knapp, *Pharmacy, Drugs and Medical Care,* Baltimore, Williams and Wilkins, 1992, p. 106..

[10] Fred Gable, "Community Pharmacy Practice," Chapter 7, *Opportunities in Pharmacy Careers,* Chicago, NTC Contemporary Publishing Co., 1997, p. 75.

[11] Beth B.Hess, Elizabeth W. Markson and Peter J. Stein, *Sociology(Fourth Edition)* New York, Macmillan Publishing Co., 1991, p. 179.

[12] Suzanne B. Levine, "The Pharmacist Factor," *Columbia Journalism Review,* Vol. 30, November-December 1991, p. 14.

[13] Gable, *op.cit.,*p. 78.

[14] Fredrick Nesbit, "Non-compliance With Psychotropic Drug Prescriptions," *American Journal of Psychiatry,* Vol. 151, No. 5, May 1994, p. 783.

[15] U.S. Department of Commerce, *Statistical Abstracts of the U.S.,* "Female Participation in Pharmacy," Washington, D.C., U.S. Government Printing Office, 1997.

[16] American Association of Colleges of Pharmacy, *Twenty Year Cross Sectional Study of Career Practice Patterns of Male and Female Pharmacists.* New York, American Association of Colleges of Pharmacy, 1990.

[17] John Manuel Andriote, "The 1998 Salary Survery," *Working Woman,* February, Vol.23, No.8, 1998, p. 46.

[18] P. A. Roberts, "Job satisfaction among U.S. pharmacists," *American Journal of Hospital Pharmacy,* Vol.40, 1983, pp. 391-399.

[19] Peter Keating, "Why You May Be Getting the Wrong Medicine," *Money,* Vol.26, June 1997, p. 143.

[20] *Op.cit.* pp.145-157.

[21] Diana L. Spore, Vincent Mor, Paul Larrat, Catherine Hawes and Jeffrey Hiris, "Inappropriate Drug Prescriptions for Elderly Residents of Board and Care Facilities," *American Journal of Public Health,* Vol.87, March 1997, pp. 404-409.

[22] No author, "Managing Medications," *Healthwatch,* #366, 1994, pp. 4-5.

[23] Nissa Simon, "How to Be Sure You're Not Getting the Wrong Medicine," *New Choices,* Vol.37, No. 9, November 1997, p. 70.

[24] Barbara A. Adamcik, H. Edward Ransford, Phillip R. Oppenheimer, Janice F. Brown, Pamela A. Eagan and Fred G. Weissman, "New Clinical Roles for Pharmacists: A Study of Role Expansion," *Social Science and Medicine,* Vol.22, No. 11, 1986, pp. 1187-1200.

[25] *Ibid.* p.1197.

[26] Teo Furtado, "The Over-the-Counter Culture," *Health,* Vol.6, No.1, February/March 1992, pp. 28-29.

[27] Maryann Napoli, "Why Prescription Drugs Can Cause New Problems Now," *New Choice,* Vol. 35, No. 3, April 1995, p. 49.

[28] Emile Durkheim, *Division of Labor in Society,* Trans. George Simpson, New York, Free Press, 1933. (1893)

[29] Jacob Sullum, "No Relief in Sight," *Reason,* Vol.28, No.8, January 1997, pp. 22-28.

[30] Russell Portenoy, "Physicians Said to Persist in Understanding Pain and Ignoring the Evidence," *The New York Times,* December 31, 1987, Sec. B. p.5.

[31] Sullum, op.cit. p. 28.

[32] John Taylor, "Medicaid Fraud Control," *F.B.I. Law Enforcement Bulletin,* Vol. 61, No. 10, 1992, pp. 17-20.

[33] Brian K. Payne and Dean Dabney, "Prescription Fraud: Characteristics, Consequences, and Influences," *Journal of Drug Issues,* Vol. 27, No. 4, Fall 1997, p. 808.

[34] *Ibid,* p. 810.

[35] Marian Segal, "Washington State Firm Prosecuted for Distributing Non-Sterile Drugs," *FDA Consumer,* Vol.28, No. 4, May 1994, p. 29.

[36] Susan Headden et.al., "Danger at the Drug Store," *U.S. News & World Report,* Vol.121, No.8, August 26, 1996, pp. 47-53.

[37] Shawn Tully, "The Plot to Keep Drug Pirces High," *Fortune,* Vol.28, No.16, December 27, 19993, p. 120.

[38] No author, "Can A 1,245% Markup on Drugs Really be Legal?" *Business Week,* #3343, November 1, 19993, p. 34.

[39] Catherine Yang, "The Drugmakers vs. the Trustbusters," *Business Week,* #3388, September 5, 1994, p. 67.

[40] No author, "The Pharmaceutical Industry," *The Economist,* Vol.346, February 21, 1998, p. 4.

[41] *Ibid.* p. 17.

[42] Lawrence M. Fisher, "Smoother Road From Lab to Sales," *New York Times,* February 25, 1998, p. D 1.

[43] No author, "U.S. Moves to Curb Some Drug Promotion," *New York Times,* Janaury 6, 1998, p. D11.

[44] Sheryl Gay Stolberg, "New Rules Will Force Doctors to Disclose Ties to Drug Industry," *New York Times,* February 3, 1998, p. A 12.

[45] Sheryl Gay Stolberg, "Gifts to Science Researchers Have Strings , Study Finds." *New York Times,* April 1, 1998, p. A 17.

[46] Anita M. McGahan, "Industry Structure and Competitive Advantage," *Harvard Business Review,* Vol.72, November-December 1994, pp. 115-124.

[47]Diana Kendall, *Sociology in Our Times,* New York, Wadsworth Publisihing Co., 1999, p. 14.

[48] Anthony C. Tommasello, "Drug Abuse," in: Mickey C. Smith and David A. Knapp, Eds., *Pharmacy, Drugs and Medical Care,* Baltimore, Williams and Wilkins, 1992, p. 77.

[49]*Ibid.,* p. 76.

[50] Charles F. Levinthal, *Drugs, Behavior and Modern Society,* Boston, Allyn and Bacon, 1996.

[51] T.J. Ives and C.C. Stults, "Pharmacy practice in a chemically-dependency treatment center," *American Journal of Hospital Pharmacy,* Vol. 47, 1990, pp. 1080-1083.

[52] Report of the American Pharmaceutical Association Policy Committee on Professional Affairs, *American Pharmacy,* Vol.22, 1982, pp. 368-380.

[53] Peter Conrad and Joseph W. Schneider, *Deviance and Medicalization ; From Badness to Sickness,* St. Louis, C.V. Mosby Co/, 1980.

[54] Peter P. Lamy, *Prescribing for the Elderly,* PSG Publishing, Littleton, Mass., 1980.

[55] Edward Sapir, *Culture, Language and Personality,* Berkeley, The University of California Press, 1961.

[56] Ian Fisher, "A New Health Risk for Immigrants," *The New York Times,* Febraury 2, 1998, p. B1.

Chapter IX

Health Delivery from Head to Foot: Dentistry, Optometry, Podiatry *et al*

I

Tooth decay and oral diseases are part of human history as evidenced by examining the skulls of Cro-Magnon man who lived 25,000 years ago in southern France. Early Egyptian papyrus written between 1700 and 1500 B.C.E. mentions diseases of the teeth as do Jewish sources such as Leviticus, Deuteronomy and Kings. That great encyclopedia of knowledge known to the Jews as the Talmud records that the third century Rabbi Eleazar mentions toothaches and their possible origin. In Talmud Shabbot we find discussions concerning the replacement of teeth by wooden, gold or silver substitutes and Talmud Bezah advises tooth ache sufferers to relieve their pain with vinegar.[1]

These Jewish practices were not unique. The Greek physicians Aesculapius (appr. 1300-1200 B.C.E.) and Hippocrates (460-377 B.C.E.) and the philosopher Aristotle (384-322 B.C.E.) wrote about tooth extraction and the diseases of the jaw and teeth. Aristotle is credited with being the first writer to deal with teeth in an extended manner. He examined teeth in relation to their comparative anatomy in his book translated into Latin as De Partibus Animalium or On the Parts of Animals. In that study "he compared the various dental apparatus of the then known species of animals." He describes the teeth of various animals and distinguishes between teeth and tusks or horns. Aristotle even recognized the relationship between dental caries and sweet food.[2]

Erasistratus of Cheos (335 –280 B.C.E.), one of the great anatomists of antiquity made recommendations for mouth disorders including one that seems bizarre today. To cure a tooth ache he recommended: "five berries of chrysocarpos to be beaten in oil of roses....then injected into the ear opposite the side affected."

Aurelius Cornelius Celsus, who lived in Rome (25 B.C.E.-50 C.E.) . wrote extensively on oral diseases as well as oral anatomy and dental surgery. There were numerous other Roman physicians, heavily influenced by their Jewish and Greek predecessors. Outstanding among them was Claudius Galenus, usually called Galen who lived from 131-201. His work was unquestioned in Europe until the 16th century. Despite his failure to distinguish human from animal teeth and the resulting distortions he made numerous important observations concerning the development of human teeth and the treatment of tooth inflammation. Jewish and Arab physicians greatly influenced medical and dental knowledge in Christian Europe. The major Jewish philosopher Maimonides, (Moses ben Maimon) (1135-1204) not only contributed immensely to knowledge of medicine and dentistry, but also translated into Latin and hence into European languages the many works on medicine produced by other Hebrew and Arabic writers.

The Middle ages saw self taught vagabonds extract teeth in the market places for a small fee. So called barber-surgeons also participated in the extraction of teeth, cutting hair, embalming and blood letting. It was in France, however, that we find the "father of modern dentistry," Pierre Fauchard (1678-1761) who wrote the first book on dentistry in a European language. Entitled *The Surgeon Dentist, A Treatise on Teeth*, this book describes the basic oral anatomy and function as well as signs and symptoms of oral pathology. John Hunter was the first to write books on dentistry in the English language as British dentists migrated to America in the 1700's. Here, Paul Revere constructed dentures from ivory, gold and silver of the kind worn by George Washington.

In the nineteenth century American dentistry gained a great deal from the initiation of nitrous oxide or laughing gas by the dentist, Dr. Horace Wells (1815-1848). The invention of the dental foot engine by Dr. Greene Vardiman Black (1831-1915) was also a product of the nineteenth century.[3]

The late nineteenth century and the early twentieth century have seen vast advances in dentistry. Periodontics, the treatment of oral disease, periodontology the need to cleanse the teeth and prevent disease, orthodontics or the straightening of teeth, oral surgery, and oral pathology were the earliest specialties in dentistry. Today (1999), prosthodontics or the restoration of missing teeth, pedeodontics, dealing with children's dental needs, dental public health, endodontics, operative dentistry, dental radiography and a number of other specialties are in vogue. In addition, the profession of dental hygienists, dental assistants and dental laboratory technicians have introduced a team support for the doctor of dentistry. All this has meant that the need for dental education at the university level has become as important to dentistry as it is to medicine and surgery. In fact, the level of dental education at the end of the 20th century is the same as that required of physicians, so that many of the classes offered by universities enroll students of dentistry, medicine and nursing.[4]

There are ninety nine schools of dentistry in the United States now enrolling approximately 4,000 students each year. This constitutes a 37% reduction in class sizes since 1978 when there were 6,300 dental students in this country. This reduction in dental students is not caused by lack of applicants but by the necessity of limiting class sizes because there are more dentists in America than are needed.[5]

This has led to the closing of some dental schools in the United States. The latest example of such a closing was the abandonment of dentistry by Northwestern University in 1996. Yet, there are those who now predict a critical shortage of dentists by 2005. Such a shortage would not occur if all applicants to dental schools could enter. However, dental professors, fearing an oversupply of dentists have reduced the number of dental students. In the four years ending in 1995 the number of applicants to dental schools in the United States rose by 51 percent. In that same period places in dental schools rose so little that there were 22 applicants for every seat in a dental school in 1996.[6]

In that year women constituted 36.4 percent of graduates of dental schools. One decade earlier, women dental graduates were only 22 percent of the class.

The consequence of this increasing interest of the female population in the practice of dentistry is that the number of professionally active female dentists rose from 3,777 in 1982 to 18,189 in 1996. This is an increase of 381.6 percent. During that same time period the percentage of male dentists rose only 9.8 percent.[7]

There is little doubt that the number of applicants to schools of dentistry is influenced by the high earnings available in that profession. According to the Journal of the American Dental Association, the mean net income of male dentists in 1997 was $121,640. For female dentists the mean net income that year was $95,410. Women in the profession earned 22% less than men mainly because women dentists were younger and had less experience than male dentists and because many of them worked part time so as to accommodate husbands and children. In addition, differences in income by gender are influenced by ownership, specialty, types of cases, fees charged and time spent on each procedure. It is significant that differences in income by gender remain even when these issues were eliminated from consideration.

This then raises the question of whether the feminization of dentistry and the lower income earned by women in the profession will reduce the number of applicants to dental schools.

Women have participated in dentistry for many years but only recently in great numbers. The first American woman to practice dentistry was Emily Jones. Jones did not attend a dental school but learned dentistry from her husband in the mid 1850's. The first woman to graduate from a dental schools was Lucy Hobbs who graduated in 1865. Until 1972 few women attended dental schools in America. Until that year they were only 1% of American dentists. Since 1972 the number of female dental graduates has risen to 16% of all American dentists (1999). In view of these numbers it is not surprising that there is now an American Association of Women Dentists who try to address all those issues which American women in all occupations face. These issues include child bearing at a time when women seek to devote themselves to career advancement as well.

It is noteworthy that one third of all female dentists had been dental hygienists and/or dental assistants. These occupations have always been attributed to women while the role of dentist has traditionally been attributed to men. This demonstrates that it is not sex but gender which determines occupational acceptance. Sex is biological, gender is social. The social construction of status - role have always determined the division of labor in all societies. Because status-roles are learned it is evident that the division of labor by sex is arbitrary and that men can re-negotiate the meaning of gender in each situation so that women can be seen as competent dentists, doctors or anything else of their choosing. Therefore it is not unreasonable to expect that men can enter the dental hygienist occupation and work for a woman dentist.[8]

There are approximately 153,000 active dentists in the United States. Another 29,000 dentists have abandoned the profession for another occupation or are retired. Because a large number of dentists moved through the system in the 1970's, over 23 percent of all American dentists were over 55 years of age in 1997. This number will rise to one third in 2005 and to 40% in 2010. Therefore a good number of retired dentists will face the same problem faced by so many retired Americans. That problem is the loss of professional activity and status, not income. It is therefore unfortunate and foolish that most states will not permit a retired dentist to volunteer his services to those who are too poor to pay unless the retired dentist takes re-licensing examinations in such retirement states as Florida and Arizona.[9]

There are over 148 thousand dental hygienists employed in the United States. Their mean annual income is $42,000 although 25% of dental hygienists earn more than $50,000. These dental hygienists perform dental prophylactic treatments commonly known as cleaning the teeth. There are also 231,000 dental assistants who help the dentist at the chair, set up the patient and the equipment, keep records and perform clerical tasks. These assistants are almost always women who earn a mean annual wage of $22,000.[10]

II

In February of 1997 the mass circulation magazine Reader's Digest headlined its front cover with the message that: "..........Dentists Rip Us Off." Using the common stereotype of dentist as sadist, the Digest depicts a dentist "hovering over a patient with the dreaded drill in hand." This inflammatory article sought to indict the profession as such and imply that dishonesty is the rule among dentists. The article was promptly answered by representatives of the profession who show that the complaints of the author of the Reader's Digest article, William Ecenbarger, labels as dishonesty what dentists call risk assessment. This means that there are so many variables associated with dental treatment that all dentists cannot agree or foresee which treatment will be successful, how long a treatment will protect the patient, how disease will progress without treatment or whether one treatment is better than another. Inconsistencies in dental treatment plans by several dentists are also related to aesthetics. There are dentists who recommend that someone close a gap between two teeth to improve the patient's appearance. Those who like this idea will accept it as a good suggestion while others may view such a suggestion as nothing more than an effort to make money. Furthermore, the accusation that dentists must be engaged in "rip offs" because they do not always agree on the treatment of a disease or disfigurement fails to understand that there are legitimate and honest differences in dentists beliefs concerning the outcomes of various possible treatments.[11]

In view of this attack on the integrity of the dental profession it is remarkable how much the public image of dentists has changed in America during the quarter century ending in 2000. For example, The New York Times Magazine recently published an article entitled "How the World Sees Us." This article shows that the "developing world" aspires to American technology including "even our teeth, gleaming, beveled, orthodontized into orderly white rows, are the envy of the world." [12]

Anyone who has traveled outside of North America will attest to the gross dental appearance of the majority of mankind. This is of course particularly visible among those who have reached middle age or old age. In the United States, by contrast, tooth loss is no longer the inevitable product of aging. Preventive and reconstructive dentistry have achieved that both functioning teeth and a good appearance are now commonplace among those who can afford to pay for these services. This means that the ancient, 5000 year tradition of dental extraction as a cure for dental pain is almost extinct in end-of-the-century America. Instead flossing the teeth and oral hygiene in general is "in" as visible in comic strips, movies, books and stories. Even a Barbie doll, called Dentist Barbie and dressed in white, has been introduced by toy makers.[13]

The consequences of these great changes in dental health are that dentists have attained a far higher prestige ranking at the end of the 20th century than their profession ever enjoyed at an earlier time. According to the National Opinion Research Center a national survey of 67 occupations listed by the NORC ranked dentists 6th in an array of 67 occupations relative to prestige. Sociologists have developed some detailed characteristics of occupational prestige. It suffices to understand that dentists rank consistently in the upper echelons of occupational prestige in the eyes of Americans.[14]

This considerable increase in the social honor accorded the profession by Americans was severely tested in 1991. In that year, Kimberly Bergalis accused her dentist, Dr. David Acer, of giving her deadly AIDS transmitted to her in 1987 when she was only 19 years old. This transmission of that deadly disease was not caused by sex, drugs or a blood transfusion. It was instead caused solely by the treatment Bergalis received from Dr. Acer. Acer also infected four other patients. Thereupon the Center for Disease Control in Atlanta, Ga., investigated how Dr. Acer infected five of his patients. Scientists from the CDC made every effort to find the means of infection but failed to prove how Dr. Acer's disease entered the bodies of his patients. The CDC scientists did prove however, that Acer was the source for each of the five patients' infection.[15]

The significance of the Bergalis case is that it shows that innocent people can be infected by AIDS. Therefore a flood of publicity accompanied Bergalis' statement that "I blame Dr. Acer and every single one of you bastards." Bergalis meant that Acer's disease was known, not only to him, but to health department officials and that nobody bothered to do anything to interfere with his continued practice of dentistry. If ever there was a violation of the Hippocratic Oath to "first, do no harm," then Dr. Acer surely violated that commitment.[16]

The transmission of AIDS from a dentist to a patient is extremely rare. There are many more cases on record with the Centers for Disease Control in which patients have infected their doctors with AIDS. Yet, on June 25, 1998 the Supreme Court agreed with a Federal Appeals

Court that dentists must treat patients with AIDS. That ruling was based on the "Americans with Disabilities Act," which provides that no one may be refused treatment by a licensed health care provider because of his disability. By defining AIDS as a disability, those who suffer from that disease are therefore covered by the act. The American Dental Association also tells its members that a patient's AIDS status is not a justification for refusal of treatment.[17]

The meaning of this Supreme Court Decision in Randon Bragdon vs. Sidney Abbott therefore places the risk of becoming infected by an AIDS patient upon the dentist or any other health care providers. This is a risk that evidently many dentists and doctors have already assumed in treating every kind of disease since the days of the bubonic plague in the fourteenth century.

Willingness to take risks for patients is undoubtedly a virtue all health deliverers must assume. This is one of the reasons that doctors, nurses and dentists are held in high regard by the public. Public trust in dentistry is evidently high as discovered by a study reported in the Journal of the American Dental Association. Accordingly, 85% of respondents in a university based research group study expressed trust in the dental profession. Despite some criticisms concerning failure by many dentists to lay out a treatment plan or discuss the cost of restorative dentistry in advance, that study revealed that 90% of respondents have a great deal of respect for the dental profession. A study by Consumer Report and quoted in the JADA concluded that more than 80% of respondents in that study thought that their dental work was good or very good.[18]

As we have seen, patients give dentists a vote of confidence as excellent providers. Nevertheless, this does not preclude that some patients have so little respect for their dentist and his employees that they engage in sexual harassment of the dental hygienist and others. As we have already seen with respect to the conduct of some patients of physicians and surgeons, there are those who violate common decency in the offices of health deliverers and additionally may make the doctor legally liable. This means that a patient who harasses a doctor's employee may thereby violate Title VII of the Civil Rights Act of 1964 and the Equal Employment Opportunity Commission's Guidelines on Discrimination Based on Sex. In addition a dentist – employer may also face liability for sexual harassment claims under state and local laws if he does not prevent such behavior by a patient against an employee of the dentist. It is important to keep in mind, in this connection, that claims of sexual harassment have now become so numerous that they are frequently used to gain money or to embarrass someone or to "get even" when there is no basis in fact for such claims.[19]

Patients can also create problems for dentists and themselves if they fail to keep appointments, forget their medication or behave badly in the waiting room towards other patients or the staff.[20]

In addition, dentists must contend with the continuing fear and anxiety concerning dentists and their treatments which persist among some patients, notably children. Dr. Lynn Baker-Ward, a psychologist, has investigated the dental anxiety phenomenon in children. She made a particular effort to discover whether or not there is a link between a mother's anxiety about dentistry and the anxiety of that mother's children concerning their own visit to the dentist. Surprisingly she found no connection. Instead she found that children who were anxious regarding any and all other aspects of their lives were also anxious about visits to the dentist even if their mother had no such anxiety.[21]

Dentists as well as other health care providers are forced to deal with a number of legal issues as a result of their business and profession. One legal issue faced by dentists refers to "restrictive covenants." Such "covenants" are contracts sometimes included in a partnership or employment agreement limiting the contracting parties from performing similar work for a period of time and within a certain geographic area. Among dentists the purpose of such "covenants" is to protect an owner or partner who has invested time, money and effort in a practice from taking patients away after the relationship is ended.

Another legal issue related to employment in a dentist's office is the concept of "at will employment." This refers to the right of an employer to terminate an employee and the right of an employee to leave at any time. Terminating an employee for opposing illegal activities is illegal. A dentist or anyone else using drugs to which an employee objects can be an example of violating public policy in that drug use can be illegal. Some states even have "wrongful discharge" laws which provide limits on when an employee can be fired.[22]

A third legal issue facing dentists to a far lesser extent than physicians is participation in managed care contracts. At the end of 1997 31% of dentists nationwide were participating in "managed care." In 1994, 29% of dentists participated in at least one such contract. Evidently then dentist participation in "managed care" has not increased much since 1994 nor is it as important an issue in dentistry as it is in medicine. It is significant that nearly 37% of female dentists were willing to participate in managed care contracts. Those dentists, whether male or female, who participated in managed care contracts earned an average of $110,000 while those not participating earned an average of $119,000 or 7.6% more than participants. The highest percentage of dentists participating in at least one managed care contract is found among those earning $50,000 per year or less while the highest number of dentists with no managed care contracts is found among those earning $121,000 or more. This difference is partially related to number of years of experience, size of practice and hours worked per week. However, it is obvious that those whose earnings are high will not permit outsiders to involve themselves in their dental practice while those earning little permit such involvement in the hope of attracting patients who are members of health maintenance organizations.[23]

Because HMOs seek to substitute cheaper treatments for expensive ones and because HMOs often refuse to "cover" treatment altogether, dentists who participate in "managed care" contracts may find that they are legally liable for injury to a patient because his insurance company refused to cover the costs of treatment. To protect himself from a malpractice charge caused by the refusal of an insurer to pay for the procedure dentists need to obtain the patients "informed consent" to conduct a different and cheaper procedure than that first recommended. It is of course recognized in both law and ethics that every patient has a right to determine what treatment he will be rendered. Therefore, lawyers are advising dentists to disclose to patients the nature of the recommended procedure; the material risks and benefits involved; the prognosis if the treatment is not undertaken and alternative treatment methods.[24]

III

Health care is provided in this country by a number of professions other than physician and dentist. Among these are opticians and optometrists. Neither should be confused with ophthalmologists who are physicians (M.D.s). Opticians cannot perform surgery nor treat eye disease and optometrists are now limited in the kind of treatment they can perform.

Opticians are technicians who make and fit eyeglasses and, in some jurisdictions, dispense contact lenses. Since they cannot prescribe corrective lenses nor diagnose disease opticians are licensed in only one half the states. In the other states anyone can claim to be an optician. There are more than 71,000 opticians in the United States earning a mean annual salary of $22,500. Most opticians are now working for large chain stores such as Lenscrafters and Pearle. There they design, measure, fit and adapt lenses to frames and measure customers for size of eyeglasses.

In July 1997 Consumer Reports reported that the going rate for eyeglass frames was then three times the wholesale cost, "or more."[25]

Optometrists earn a doctor of optometry degree from a four year college of optometry after earning a bachelor's degree from an accredited college or university. This means that optometrists have spent eight years in higher education. There they learn how to examine eyes, diagnose eye disease and prescribe glasses and contact lenses. Two-thirds of the states allow optometrists to prescribe drugs to treat eye disease. The average earnings of the 29,500 American optometrists are $80,000 although 24% earn a good deal more than that. Because that income is less than one half of the income of ophthalmologists managed care has of course favored that procedures which can be done by optometrists be done by them.[26]

A major dispute between ophthalmologists and optometrists concerns photorefractive keratectomy, a laser procedure that corrects nearsightedness by slightly flattening the cornea. This course of action will reduce the market for new glasses and contact lenses but will mean millions of dollars in fees for those doctors who perform this procedure. No one disputes that ophthalmologists, who are doctors of medicine and surgeons, are capable of performing this operation. Optometrists are now saying that they too should be allowed to do these keratectomies. Since this procedure costs between $1,800 and $2,300 it is obvious that a great deal of money is involved for those who have access to patients wanting this means of dealing with nearsightedness. Optometrists have succeeded more and more in convincing state legislatures that they should be allowed to gain the right to perform laser procedures. In this demand they have been supported by the health maintenance organizations. Idaho is one state in which the drive to allow optometrists the right to operate has succeeded. Other states considering such a move are Connecticut, Alaska, Colorado, New Jersey .California and Virginia. Ophthalmologists say that laser procedures are surgery which cannot and should not be performed by anyone not trained as a surgeon holding the degree of Doctor of Medicine.

The feud between ophthalmologists and optometrists is not new. In the 1970s ophthalmologists opposed the right of optometrists to use diagnostic drugs. Since then optometrists have obtained this right in 34 states, where they now treat glaucoma and other eye diseases.[27]

Optometrists and ophthalmologists have traditionally fitted and distributed contact lenses. Consumers had no choice, until recently, to use the lenses sold by these two professions. Now, however, contact lenses are sold by mail-order houses. To fight this competition, doctors, whether ophthalmologists or optometrists, have refused to release prescriptions to be filled by anyone other than themselves. In some states this is illegal. The practice has also led to lawsuits in that the State of Florida claims that some large optical manufacturers such as

Bausch and Lomb are involved in a conspiracy to shut new companies out of the replacement - lens business.[28]

Optometrists have recently entered the arena of "eye exercises." These "video gyms" claim to improve visual skills like focusing, peripheral vision and depth perception. To do this optometrists have installed high-tech, high blinking equipment designed to have the patient quicken reaction time or strengthen eye-hand co-ordination. Vision experts claim that this equipment and such methods as walking on a balance beam while reading a chart have significantly improved the performance of athletes in sports such as hockey, baseball and football. Medical doctors dispute these claims. In the words of Maria Therese Wegner-Aiello, M.D., a New York eye surgery specialist, "anyone who makes promises to improve your vision by working out your eye muscles should not be taken seriously."[29]

Serious however is the recently identified computer vision syndrome leading to such conditions as eye strain, blurred vision, and eye irritation. In extreme cases the constant use of a computer can bring on near-sightedness. Optometrists have therefore recommended that those using computers install filters in front of the computer screen to reduce the stress derived from glare and flicker. This area of eye care is the product of technology as are the developments in optometry used to defeat their consequences.[30]

IV

Another profession besides optometry which competes with doctors of medicine is podiatry. Podiatrists diagnose and treat diseases and deformities of the foot such as corns and bunions. They also perform some foot surgery. Podiatrists must have completed at least two years of undergraduate work in college. Many are college graduates. In addition podiatrists graduate from a four year school of podiatric medicine and hold the degree of Doctor of Podiatric Medicine. The mean income of the 14,000 podiatrists in the country is $85,000 annually although 27% earn more than $125,000 a year.

Bunion surgery is conducted by both orthopedic surgeons who are M.D.s and by podiatrists. This leads to the same conflict experienced by optometrists and ophthalmologists.

While some bunions are inherited it appears that the majority of these deformities occur because of the use of commercially made shoes. It is customary for Americans to squeeze their feet into tight shoes. This is true mostly of women who then run the risk of developing a swelling of the toe joint as well as the bursa, a fluid filled sac that protects the bones. Pointed shoes and high heels can also push the toe inward so that women are nine times more likely to suffer such a condition than men.

Orthopedic surgeons believe that podiatrists are not qualified to operate on patients affected by these problems because they may not do a hospital residency and because they make bunion surgery sound simple.[31]

In 1996 podiatrists became the first health deliverers to form a union. The purpose of organizing for collective bargaining was to deal with the managed care organizations who the union president said: "usurped" their profession and practices. Podiatrists feel particularly affected by the methods of the managed care organizations because orthopedists and dermatologists who are medical doctors compete with them for the patients available.

The new union has affiliated with the Office and Professional Employees International Union. Their purpose is to deal with the managed care organizations concerning capitation fees as well as doctors independence and judgment with particular reference to what doctors can tell patients.[32] An indication of the level of anger and frustration by podiatrists concerning managed care was best summarized by Dr. Louis Levine, president of the New York College of Podiatric Medicine. "This is indentured servitude for the American medical community," said Levine.[33]

In view of the formation of the podiatrists' union the American Medical Association has launched a study to discover how feasible it is for doctors to form unions.

V

Audiology is another profession which contributes to the health delivery system in the United States. Audiology is concerned with the "comprehensive diagnostic and rehabilitative services for all areas of auditory, vestibular, and related disorders."[34]

This definition of the professional responsibilties of audiologists was developed in 1996 by the American Speech-Language Hearing Association. This association holds that the practice of audiology includes 22 obligations. Among these are: interpreting test results that relate to disorders of human hearing. Examination of the ear canal so as to fit prosthetic devices. Supervision and conduct of newborn hearing screening programs. Dispensing hearing aids and other devices needed to alleviate the consequences of hearing loss. Audiological rehabilitation including speechreading, language development and counseling for patients with hearing loss. Rehabilitation of persons with balance disorders. Conduct of basic research to increase the knowledge base and fifteen others.[35]

In view of the aging of the American population it is to be anticipated that audiologists will be employed more and more among the old population. This geronotological care will be augmented by a greater and greater need for audiologists and speech therapists who can deal with the large number of immigrants now arriving in the United States from non-English speaking countries, particularly from Asia. Hence, multiculturalism and particularly gerontology will dominate the profession for years to come.

Currently there are 85,000 audiology and speech language pathology practitioners in the United States. It is estimated that this number will grow to 125,000 by 2005, an increase of 46% in six years. The median annual salary for those speech pathologists/audiologists practicing in the school system was $39,950 for nine months work in 1997. For those employed for 12 months a year the median salary was then $44,000. The consequences of this low pay are that too few students are willing to study audiology and speech pathology and that a considerable number of positions in this field remain vacant. [36]

VI

Alternative medicine includes all those approaches and techniques which are not taught in American medical schools but which are used by 34% of Americans. In a 1990 survey reported in the New England Journal of Medicine involving 1,539 respondents Eisenberg *et al* found that in the course of one year 13% had used relaxation techniques and 12% had visited a chiropractor. Massage and a number of other techniques had received the support of a lesser percentage of respondents. Only prayer and exercise were used by one quarter of the respondents. The survey also showed that patients visited alternative practitioners 425 million times. This is 40 million more times than these patients visited their primary care physician. These patients spent $13.7 billion on these alternative procedures. Ten billion, three hundred million dollars of this were paid by the patients themselves because it was not covered by any insurance.[37]

The popularity of alternative medicine can be tested by the increasing number of books and article in the popular literature dealing with alternative medicine. There are also more and more articles on alternative medicine in scientific journals. Therefore, the National Institute of Health established the Office of Alternative Medicine in 1992 in order to investigate the efficacy of alternative therapies. The Office of Alternative Medicines has divided alternative medicines into seven categories. Mind-Body Interventions are based on the well known inseperability of mind and body and the influence of social factors such as family and occupation to affect health and/or illness. In addition to various exercises, these mind-body interventions use support groups to deal with the feelings patients have about their illness. Bioelectromagnetic Therapies studies the relationship of living organisms to electromagnetic fields. These therapies include the use of electrical currents or magnetic fields to provide healing for bone fractures. It is claimed that this treatment diminishes pain and decreases anxiety. Alternative Systems of Medical Practice includes classical Chinese medicine of which acupuncture is the best known in the United States. It has been estimated that 12 million Americans rely on acupuncture to treat arthritis, nausea and pain. A panel convened by the National Institutes of Health has endorsed acupuncture as effective for those conditions. The panel also reported that acupuncture does not help with a number of other conditions tested. Partial success was also reported when acupuncture was used to reduce the pain associated with osteoarthritis. Patients tested did not, however, improve their mobility past an initial eight weeks.[38]

Similarly, the Norvatis Foundation reported that their panel on acupuncture also found "conclusive evidence that acupuncture is effective in easing dental pain, lower back pain, and nausea." In the areas of smoking cessation and weight loss the Norvatis Foundation found that acupuncture does not work.[39]

An additional study performed in Norway found that acupuncture can have adverse effects as serious as pneumothorax which is an accumulation of air in the pleural cavity. Fainting, local infections and increased pain were also encountered. Descriptions of acupuncture treatments by patients and physicians also conclude that this treatment works very well in some neighborhoods and some groups of people but not in other areas or with those too gullible to resist.[40]

Manual Healing Methods include osteopathic and chiropathic manipulations. These "hands-on" therapies are augmented by massage which does indeed alleviate lower back pain and enhance growth and development in low-weight babies. No doubt, chiropractic also improves the mood of the patient. However, there is no evidence that chiropractic can heal or cure anything other than discomfort. It cannot be used to treat serious illness or diseases derived from infections.[41]

Pharmacologic and Biologic Treatments are used by millions of Americans, particularly those whose disease cannot be cured by conventional means and which are life-threatening. Included in these treatments are so-called chelation therapy for cardiac patients, shark cartilage therapy for people with cancer and intravenous ozone therapy for those suffering from the human immunodeficiency virus. There are also patients who suffer from chronic pain associated with migraines or arthritis. Conventional medicine can do very little for those so affected leading many disillusioned sufferers to try the alternative. So far none of these alternative procedures has succeeded in lowering the death rate from the diseases so treated. The ten most common medical conditions which cause people to use unconventional therapy are back problems, arthritis, allergies, insomnia, sprains, headaches, high blood pressure, digestive problems, anxiety and depression.[42]

Herbal Medicine is yet another aspect of the alternative medicine scene. Many followers of this method of treatment believe that herbal medicines are safe and free from the side effects encountered so often as a result of high-tech intervention and the use of drugs. Despite these beliefs, adverse side effects have developed in connection with the use of herbal medicine while some treatments with these products have gone seriously wrong. Those who deal in this kind of therapy are not necessarily trained by anyone and are certainly not regulated by any state agency. Hence, anyone can claim to know how to treat patients by means of these alternative medicines. The annual market for herbal medicines has grown to $1.5 billion.[43]

Herbal medicines are used by Americans in all social strata including the educated and employed. Women are more likely to use herbal medicines than are men. Users of these medicines generally remain with their conventional physicians and combine these herbal medicines with those prescribed by their physicians.

Some of the plants used in herbal medicines are grown in the United States. Most are imported from around the world. There are also people who grow their own medicines in their herbal gardens. Many of the users combine these uses with such practices as naturopathy and meditation. These uses cannot be dismissed as nonsense because herbal medicines have always played a large role in the management of illness. Even now (1999), one quarter of the prescriptions written in the United States are for plant products.[44]

Herbal medicines contain pharmacologically active components. Nevertheless, the 1994 Dietary and Supplemental Health and Education Act permits herbal drugs to be placed into the same category as food supplements such as vitamins and minerals. Therefore, manufacturers can produce these drugs without proof of their safety or effects because there are so many regulatory loopholes attached to the minimal regulation affecting them.

In many cases the benefits of these medicines have been the result of the inclusion in the medicine of undisclosed anti-inflammatory agents and hormones. More important is the fact that these herbal medicines can cause a great deal of harm such as renal failure. Some patients have been poisoned by these substances because many of the imported herbal medicines are adulterated. Catherine Crone, M.D. and Thomas N. Wise, M.D. have published detailed tables showing adulterants found in herbal medicines, herbal medication toxicity and potential drug interactions. These tables indicate that there are some real hazards involved in taking these medicines. Chronic users are at particular risk in using these products as are pregnant women.[45]

Diet and Nutrition as means of preventing and curing disease have been used since the days of Hippocrates. In end-of-the-century America diet and nutrition as preventatives and cures for illness are becoming more widely used because many people believe that pollution, pesticides, herbicides and methods of food preparation are responsible for numerous chronic illnesses in Western man. Those who believe this like to point to indigenous peoples who are said to suffer from none of the diseases of Western technological societies.

Some of these dietary strategies are directed at a single disease. Others are directed at prevention of all diseases and become a way of life. There are numerous "diets" published mostly by doctors which promise all kinds of benefits. There is, for example, the Gerson diet consisting of raw foods and juices or the Scarsdale diet whose developer became best known for being a murder victim.

Physicians need to know and ought to know whether their patients are taking alternative medicines or diets. This is difficult to achieve because 72% of patients do not tell their doctors that they are taking an alternative medicine. In many cases this is not revealed because physicians frequently become defensive, dismissive and angry when the idea of alternative medicines is mentioned. Furthermore, many patients feel that their doctors have no interest in them as high-tech medicine turns patients into numbers. Alternative medicine is viewed by many patients as more human and more humane.[46]

VII

Alternative medicines, even those which have no scientific value, appear to have beneficial consequences in some cases. This phenomenon is known as the "placebo effect", derived from the Latin word placere which means "to please", placebo literally means "I shall please." Numerous experiments have shown that patients who are pleased with their medication will resist ill effects or symptoms because of the placebo they have taken. Generally a "placebo" is a sugar pill or anything without scientifically anticipated consequences. Some "placebos" do have or should have consequences which are defeated by the patient's beliefs. An example refers to an experiment in which researchers gave two groups of women "ipecac" used to induce vomiting. The women selected for the experiment all complained that they had bouts of nausea. Yet, the "ipecac" relieved their symptoms within one half hour. In another experiment the placebo pill caused stomach contractions or prevented them or had no effect at all depending entirely on what the patients were told before they took the placebo.[47]

Another use of the "placebo effect" was the dramatic use of this method when in 1960 some German surgeons told several angina pectoris, or strangulation of the chest patients that they would be given an operation which would relieve their pain. The surgeons only sliced the skin but did nothing more. The patients, believing in the success of the "operation" had no more pain.[48]

The "placebo effect" was of course the only means that primitive medicine before the 19th century had to cure anything. Evidently even the most absurd "cure" can promote the "placebo" effect. In the ancient world the phrase "post hoc ergo propter hoc," or "if it happened thereafter it must have happened for that reason," was readily believed. Today, however, the mystery of the "placebo effect" continues. It is of course not possible to heal a broken leg by means of "placebos." It has also been observed that "placebos" do not work unless the patient is fully conscious. A "placebo" given to an unconscious patient is useless. It ought to be understood, however, that all patients do not react favorably to "placebos", and that so far, no one has been able to discover a "placebo-prone personality."

The reason for this type of medical "success" among us is that 90% of all visits to doctors are for stress related conditions. These conditions are serious and real. Numerous studies have shown that anxiety, grief and marital disputes "undermine the body's immune system, making us vulnerable to illness." In fact there is now some evidence that optimism triggers healing processes while stress does the opposite. It is for this reason that people who pray are less likely to suffer cardiac arrest because prayer lowers blood pressure.[49]

The recognition of this relationship by the medical profession has led the Harvard University School of Medicine to offer a course in "Spirituality and Medicine." The intent of this course is to include the attitude of the patient and the doctor towards religion in the healing process. Dr. Herbert Benson of the Harvard Medical School faculty believes that one half of all stress - related visits to doctors could be avoided if the resources of religion were to be used with more efficiency than is the case now. Dr. Benson also estimates that 50 billion dollars could be saved annually by allowing religion to become a factor in reducing medical costs in this country.[50]

Although it remains fashionable among members of the healing professions to view religion as irrational thinking and a form of emotional confusion, the National Institute for Health Care Research has issued a bibliography concerning clinical analysis of spiritual themes. It is claimed that both women and men benefit from religion in that the death rate from tuberculosis as well as the death rate from circulatory diseases is reduced by 60 percent for both sexes. The explanation for these positive results concerning religious attendance lies first in behavior of those associated with religion. Religious belief reduces the rate of alcohol intake, drug use and addiction and stress related conduct such as adultery. Several studies have also shown that those who adhere to religious beliefs derive enough consolation and strength from religious conviction that their blood pressure is lower than that of those not affiliated with religion and that therefore their death rate is far lower as well.

Benson has shown that psychic stress, depression and fear, free cortisone and adrenaline and place the body into a state of emergency. These hormones, freely released over a long period of time, damage the body. Benson argues that prayer, the repetition of rituals and religious exercises create a relaxation response, reduced blood pressure, increases brain waves which are measurable in EEGs and thereby reduces insomnia, heart disturbances and other emotion induced difficulties.

Reliance on religion as a cure-all as promoted by some television preachers are of course gross exaggerations and sometimes exploitative. Nevertheless, the use of religion or any other means of attaining relaxation and a reduction of anxiety are proven means of preventing illness and helping in the recovery from disease.[51]

There are yet other means of preventing much illness. These means include exercise and nutrition. Although the need for both of these measures has been known for centuries there are millions of Americans who fail to give their attention to either of these preventatives. Others are very much concerned with both exercise and nutrition so that an entire exercise industry has arisen in the United States alongside of numerous commercial efforts to deal with overweight, poor eating habits and the introduction of safe food products.

The media are greatly concerned with the twin issues of exercise and nutrition as are schools. There can be no doubt that physical "work outs" and careful eating habits have a good deal to do with health delivery in this country. Therefore those issues shall be the content of our next chapter.

Summary

There are a number of health delivery systems outside of medicine which are of great importance to the American people. First among these is dentistry which has been known to even the most ancient civilizations. Jewish, Greek and Roman sources have been cited which deal with dentistry as then understood. Although early beliefs about dentistry seem bizarre today, the writers of treatises on dentistry were the founders of medical knowledge at least in the Western World.

Major advances in medical and dental knowledge had to wait until the 19th century. Even then, however, the removal of teeth to deal with pain was still very common. Only after the middle of the 20th century did dentistry become the high-tech profession it is today.

Optometry and allied fields as well as podiatry are challenging medicine as health care providers. All of these fields, including dentistry, are becoming feminized as more and more women enter areas at one time reserved only for men. In view of the need to deal with health maintenance organizations some of these providers have unionized or have threatened to do so.

There are a number of "alternative medicines" available in the United States today. These include herbal treatments, chiropracty and many others. There are also patients who benefit from the "placebo" effect and from religious belief in gaining recovery from illness.

Very important in preventing illness in the first place is exercise and nutrition. These means to maintaining health are the topics of the next chapter.

NOTES

[1] Milton B. Asbell, *Dentistry: A Historical Perspective*, Bryn Mawr, Pa., Dorrance & Co., 1988, pp. 14-16.

[2] *Ibid.* p. 19.

[3] *Ibid.*, p. 15.

[4] *Ibid.* pp. 140-150.

[5] Lawrence H. Meskin, "An Oversupply in the Offing?" *Journal of the American Dental Association*, Vol.128, July, 1997, p. 802.

[6] Joseph I. Shevenell, "Managed Care and Medicine," *Journal of the American Dental Association*, Vol.129, April 1998, p. 406.

[7] *Ibid.* p. 373.

[8] Dennis O. Kaldenberg, Anisa M. Zvonkovic and Boris W. Becker, "Women Dentists: The Social Construction of a Profession," in Joyce Tang and Earl Smith, Eds., *Women in the Professions*, Albany, N.Y., The SUNY Press, 1966, pp. 65-85.

[9] Lawrence H. Meskin, "What do Dentists do When They don't do Dentistry?" *Journal of the American Dental Association*, " Vol. 128, June 1997, p. 682.

[10] Bureau of Labor Statistics, "Occupational Employment Statistics," *The Internet.*

[11] Lawrence H. Meskin, "A Dental Rip-Off," *Journal of the American Dental Association*, Vol.128, March 1997, pp. 264-266.

[12] No author, "How the World Sees Us," *The New York Times Magazine*, Sec. 6, June 8, 1997, p. 37.

[13] Irwin D. Mandel, " The Image of Dentistry in Contemporary Culture," *Journal of the American Dental Association*, Vol.129, May 1998, pp. 607-613.

[14] William E. Thompson and Joseph V. Hickey, *Society in Focus: An Introduction to Sociology*, New York, Harper Collins College Publishers, 1994, p. 216.

[15] Joseph Palca, "CDC Closes the Case of the Florida Dentist," *Science*, Vol. 256, #5060, May 22, 1992, pp. 1130-1131.

[16] Jacob Weisberg, "The Accuser," *The New Republic*, Vol. 205, October 21, 19991, p.12.

[17] Linda Greenhous, "Ruling on Bias Law," *The New York Times*, June 26, 1998, p. A 1.

[18] Lawrence H. Meskin, "Patients First and Always," *Journal of the American Dental Association*, Vol.128, February 1997, p. 140.

[19] Peter M. Sfikas, "The Inappropriate Patient," *Journal of the American Dental Association*, Vol. 129, September 1998, pp. 1312-1315.

[20] Earl Lord, "Health Media Watch," *Journal of the American Dental Association,* Vol. 128, December 1997, p. 1640.
[21] Lynn Baker-Ward, "Into the Jaws of Anxiety," *Psychology Today,* Vol. 28, No. 4, July-August 1995, p. 10.
[22] Peter M. Sfikas, "Restrictive Covenants and At-Will Employment," *Journal of the American Dental Association,* Vol. 129, June 1998, pp. 772-774.
[23] James Bramson, Diane Noskin and Jon D. Ruesch, "Demographics and Practice Characteristics of Dentists Participating and Not Participating in Managed Care Plans," *Journal of the American Dental Association,* Vol 128, December 1997, pp. 1708-1714.
[24] Peter M. Sfikas, "Much Obliged," *Journal of the American Dental Assoication,* Vol.128, March 1997, pp. 370-373.
[25] No author, " Specs on Specs," *Consumer Reports,* Vol. 62, July 1997, pp.10-15.
[26] Jonathan Rabinowitz, "Optometrists Clash With Eye Surgeons over Laser Process," *The New York Times,* April 8, 1996, p. B5.
[27] *Ibid.* p. B6.
[28] Joseph Weber, "Contact Lenses: Focus on Open Markets," *Business Week,* January 13, 1997, p. 39.
[29] Cynthia Marks, "Eye Workouts That Don't Work," *Mademoiselle,* Vol. 95, November 1989, p. 142.
[30] Roberta Furger, "In Search of Relief for Tired, Aching Eyes," *PC World,* Vol. 11, No.2, February 1993, p. 29.
[31] Ann Renard, "The Bunion Wars," *Health,* Vol. 23, No.4, May 1991, p. 37.
[32] Steven Greenhouse, " Podiatrist to Form Nationwide Union; A Reply to H.M.Os." *The New York Times,* October 25, 1996, p. A1.
[33] *Ibid.,* p.B.2.
[34] Ad Hoc Committee on Scope of Practice in Audiology, "Scope of Practice in Audiology," *FT Magazine, ASHA,* Vol. 38, No. 2, Spring 1996, p. 12.
[35] *Ibid,* pp. 12-18.
[36] U.S. Bureau of Labor Statistics, Office of Employment Projections, November 1995.
[37] David Eisenberg *et al,* "Unconventional Medicine in the United States: Prevalence, Costs and Patterns of Use," *The New England Journal of Medicine,* Vol.328, 1993, pp. 246-252.
[38] No author, "Acupuncture Gives Knees a Lift," *Science News,* Vol. 145, No. 18, April 30, 1994, p. 319.
[39] Sara Abdulla, "Jury still out on aspects of acupuncture," The Lancet, Vol. 351, #9107, March 28, 1998, p. 962.

[40] Arne Johan Norheim, "Adverse effects of acupuncture," *The Lancet*, Vol. 345, June 17, 1995, p. 1576.

[41] Donald Krieger, "Therapeutic touch: the imprimatur of nursing," *American Journal of Nursing*, Vol. 75, 1975, pp. 784-787.

[42] Eisenberg, *op.cit.*, p.246.

[43] Rita Carter, "Holistic hazards," *New Scientist*, Vol. 151, No. 2938, July 13, 1996,p. 12.

[44] Robert J. Huxtable, "The harmful potential of herbal and other plant products," *Drug Safety*, Vol. 5, Suppl. 1, 1990, pp. 126-136.

[45] Catherine C. Crone and Thomas N. Wise, "Use of Herbal Medicines Among Consultation-Liaison Populations," *Psychosomatics*, Vol. 39, No. 1, January-February 1998, pp. 3-13.

[46] E. Ernst, "Complementary Medicine," *The Lancet*, Vol. 341, No. 8861, June 26, 1993, p. 1626.

[47] Peter Jaret, "Choose Treatments You Believe In," *Health*, Vol. 11, April 1997, pp. 99-100.

[48] Dieter E. Zimmer, "Placebo," *Die Zeit*, October 8, 1989, p. 58.

[49] *Ibid.*, p.100.

[50] Herbert Benson, *Timeless Healing: the Power and Biology of Belief*, New York, Simon and Schuster, 1997.

[51] Herbert Benson, *Your Maximum Mind*, New York, Times Books, 1987.

Chapter X

Patient, Heal Yourself: Exercise and Nutrition

I

In November 1993 the Centers for Disease Control and Prevention, the American College of Sports Medicine and the President's Council on Physical Fitness and Sports recommended that all persons over 18 years of age participate in moderate physical exercise for 30 minutes or more, at least five times a week.

This recommendation stems from epidemiological studies showing that even moderate physical exercise is associated with reduced risks of chronic diseases, morbidity and mortality and that only 22 percent of adults currently engage in leisure time activity at the levels recommended for health benefits.[1]

These benefits include a reduction of both systolic and diastolic blood pressure by an average of 10 mm Hg in persons with mild to moderate hypertension according to a position statement on physical activity, physical fitness and hypertension from the American College of Sports Medicine. To achieve this result the ACSM recommends physical exercise that uses large muscle activities three to five days per week for 20 to 60 minutes at an intensity of 50 to 85 percent Vo2 max. This means maximal oxygen consumption and refers to the maximum amount of oxygen the body can use; that is the amount of oxygen consumed during maximal physical activity.[2]

The ACSM statement also notes that physically active individuals have a lower risk of death than sedentary people (sedere=to sit; Lt.) because exercise also improves a number of other cardiovascular disease factors.[3]

Recognition of this fact has led to the introduction of corporate cardiovascular exercise programs in the United States. A long list of large, well known companies now participate in such programs including Arco, Boeing, Chase Manhattan, Exxon, Ford, Goodyear, Kimberly-Clark, Metropolitan Life, Pepsico, Rockwell, Western Electric, Xerox and many others. The incentives for these programs are reduced illness and absenteeism, less employee turnover and greater productivity.[4]

The effort to reduce health care spending has led the U.S. government into the same path. Over twenty years ago the "Forward Plan" of the U.S. Public Health Service included this statement: "Habitual inactivity is thought to contribute to hypertension, chronic fatigue, and resulting physical inefficiency, premature aging, poor musculature, and lack of flexibility which are the major causes of lower back pain and injury, mental tension, coronary heart disease and obesity." [5]

As the popularity of exercise has increased, commercial cardiovascular fitness centers have located in downtown areas of large American cities. These fitness centers seek to attract membership from the business community and do so with limited success. It has been estimated that 5% to 10% of workers in downtown office jobs participate in these programs before, during and after business hours. These fitness centers, also called "health clubs" provide a scientifically based program and are staffed by fitness specialists using "up-to-date" equipment. It has been estimated that about 18 million Americans are members of 12,000 American health clubs, whether commercial or voluntary such as the Jewish Community Centers and the Young Men's and Women's Christian Associations. These clubs provide employment for upward of 289,000 people. Because these clubs are open twelve to fourteen hours a day they generally have a work force of 50 of whom ten or fewer are full time. Hourly wages in health club employment for those not employed full time range from $6.00 an hour to $18.- an hour for specialty instructors. Full time employees are also poorly paid. A fitness director will earn about $25,000 a year and a general manager will earn from $40,000 to $45,000 annually. Among these employees are marketing and sales representatives who sell memberships and can expect approximately $25,000 or more, based on commission, a year. Generally only half of these employees are directly employed in fitness related work.[6]

Those who work in fitness related areas are required to be certified by one of the professional organizations in their field. These include the American Council on Exercise, the Aerobics and Fitness Association of America, the National Academy of Sports Medicine, the National Strength and Conditioning Association and the American College of

Sports Medicine. Such certification always includes a written examination in aid. In addition, competence in performing specific tasks is also required. Although a college education is not needed to take these certification examinations, health clubs increasingly demand a degree from those appointed to their staffs.[7]

Some universities also furnish adult fitness programs and cardiac rehabilitation facilities. Because universities already have physical resources and the expertise associated with their physical exercise physiology, exercise science and education departments, they would ideally be best suited to offer fitness programs to the public. This is theoretically true particularly since most colleges and universities also have a medical staff who can develop outstanding fitness programs. Unfortunately, most universities are so burdened with overwhelming bureaucracies that these resources frequently cannot be used because the various campus politicians have not been satisfied. These politicians include faculty committees, hosts of administrators, board members, students' representatives, medical personnel and others. It is of course true that almost all efforts within the academic community are enmeshed in these political obstacle courses so that anything done in "academia" is either slowed to the proverbial "snail's pace" or not done at all.[8]

In the event a university based fitness program does succeed then the most important resource a university based program can muster is its diversified faculty. This would include such sciences as anatomy, kinesiology and physiology, nutrition and weight training Even small colleges usually have faculty members who have specialized in a variety of sports and/or fitness techniques so that many are capable of dealing with cardiovascular disease prevention and intervention. The benefits of these cardio-vascular programs are evident. They increase functional capacity of the heart by providing maximal oxygen uptake, decrease resting and submaximal exercise heart rates and blood pressure and increase the heart's stroke volume. Body weight and percentage of body fat can also be reduced, particularly if exercise is combined with proper diet. This means that the risk of coronary artery disease is lessened by increased physical activity and proper nutrition. Furthermore, stress related behavior leading to anger, anxiety, depression and hostility is greatly reduced by exercise. It has also been observed that those who engage in regular exercise are less often associated with smoking, alcohol use and drug abuse. We have already seen that employee morale, efficiency and productivity are also improved by consistent health and fitness efforts.[9]

During the quarter century ending in 1999 numerous machines have been invented which are designed to defeat the inactivity which winter can impose on the residents of the northern part of the United States. Therefore exercise machines are sold to all those who want to remain at home but "work-out" just the same. Sometimes these machines are touted as a means of losing weight. This is so because these machines can assist in increasing metabolism and burn calories. The reason for exercise is to gain cardiovascular benefits which reduce the risk of high blood pressure, heart disease, diabetes and some cancers by reducing stress and tension. Exercise also slows the decline in muscle strength that disuse guarantees. In addition, weight bearing exercise is important to women because such exercise reduces the chances of suffering osteoporosis. Most important, exercise improves the emotional condition of those who do this and that in turn contributes immensely to good health.[10]

Research has discovered no superior exercise machines. In studies at numerous universities in various countries and American cities, using bikes, stair steppers, rowing machines and other devices, both women and men benefited from the use of any machines with similar outcomes. As Trevor Smith, editor of Running and FitNews writes, " ...there is one thing that all the studies have in common: they show that all exercise machines give physiological benefits. The choice becomes a matter of personal preference."[11]

Only a few "indoor athletes" would have the space and money to install an entire gymnasium in their house. At costs from $200 to $7,000 per machine only gymnasiums, whether commercial or community controlled can install twenty or more exercise machines. At the end of the decade (1999), these machines have become most versatile. For example, the Cybex Company makes an overhead press which weights 525 lbs. and allows the user to press up to 205 lbs. A "pull-down" is also available which permits the user to "pull down" up to 630 pounds. There is a "back-extension" machine which "works" the hip and lower back muscles. A so-called "ab crunch" provides a downward and forward motion for abdominal isolation and includes a weight stack up to 205lbs. . "Leg extension" and "leg curl" provide work for the lower part of the body and yet other machines get at every part of the user's body he wishes to involve. The point here is that a fully equipped gymnasium can provide machines which overlook nothing and provide physical exercise for every part of the body. Every few months new trainers are sold to the public. It is usually claimed that these machines, better than ever, can give the user the "work-out" he wants without the strain and exhaustion that normally accompany physical exercise. That is probably not possible. However, the number of choices a visitor to an up-to-date gymnasium has, insure that anyone can find a machine-produced exercise that he enjoys and will keep him motivated.[12]

Almost every month new machines are invented which are said to "adopt space technology." Most of these machines are "multiposition," so that mechanical arms and legs adjust around the user and prevent incorrect movements. The purpose of these machines is to reproduce almost any outdoor exercise such as cross-country skiing, running, rowing and such indoor sports as weight lifting. Most recently, inventor Michael Doane invented a swimming simulator which means that the user can "swim" on land.[13]

II

A large proportion of the American population is physically inactive. It is estimated that 30% of the population of North America participate in no exercise whatever and that approximately 50% of those who do join exercise programs drop out during the first 3 to 6 months.[14]

When researchers at the Center for Disease Control and Prevention compared data from 1988 to 1991 of the National Health and Nutrition Examination Survey III to findings of previous similar studies dating back to the 1960s they found that in the new sample 33.4% of participants were overweight. In that study, overweight was defined as body mass index values correlating with about 120% or more of desirable weight. In the 1976 to 1980 study only 25.4% of the participants were found to be overweight. Evidently then, the number of the overweight increased by eight percentage points between 1980 and 1991. The major reason cited in that study for this increase in overweight was sedentariness which is Latin for "sitting" too much.[15] This is true despite the recent publication by the surgeon general's office of a report entitled Physical Activity and Health which holds that even 30 minutes of moderate exercise each day can prevent heart diseases, lower the chances of diabetes and some cancers, relieve stress and depression and control weight. The Center for Disease Control has spent $10 million to alert the public to these dangers and benefits. "Sitting around can kill you as surely as smoking," commented Dr. Bess Marcus, professor of biomedicine at Brown University. Yet, two years after the publication of the surgeon general's report the state of American fitness is no better than before the report was issued.[16]

There are however a number of researchers including Dr. Paul D. Thompson who is associated with the American College of Sports Medicine who contend that the Center for Disease Control deliberately made recommendations concerning the value of a mere thirty minutes of exercise in order to please the public.[17]

This inactivity, mostly seen among women lies in the role that adult women must play in American culture. Unlike men, women are constantly driving children, shopping, running errands, and going to and from work. It has been repeatedly demonstrated that women carry a far greater burden within the family than is true of men and that therefore they have a good deal less time for leisure activities than men.[18]

A Gallup poll of 500 women concerning their exercise habits revealed that women are far less likely to exercise than is true of men. Women say that they don't have the time to exercise because they must go to work and that additional family responsibilities deprive them of all leisure time. Added to this handicap is the suburban sprawl. About one half of Americans live in suburbs which have no public transportation and where nothing is accessible without driving. Walking is impossible when distances are so great and time so short. Even the use of a bicycle is difficult if not dangerous among so many cars. Furthermore a large number of labor saving mechanical, electric and electronic devices make physical exertion almost unknown in the middle class home.

Amidst all these reasons for staying inactive it turns out that women and men who are unable to exercise because of their responsibilities nevertheless find time to go to movies, attend meetings, participate in community activities and attend school functions. Evidently, exercise is not a priority for these individuals. It is therefore also likely that many adults do not exercise because they know nothing about it, because gymnasiums seem like a foreign country to them and because they tried it and don't like it, whatever the reason. The fact that men are more likely than women to exercise lies also in the role difference of men and women. Men have been taught to be competitive, to exhibit physical prowess and that sports activity and masculinity go hand in glove.[19]

Since benefits of exercise can only be attained by those who do so regularly and who adhere to an exercise program for some time, the drop-out rate is significant. Dishman *et al* have isolated a number of factors which lead to adherence to physical exercise. Among these are: attitudes toward physical activity, self-perception, feeling of health responsibility and accessibility, convenience and proximity. Very important also is freedom from injury not only because an injured person cannot perform but also because injuries discourage participants and lead to refusal to continue. In addition, significant others made a great deal of difference in adherence. Participants whose spouses had a favorable attitude towards exercise were found to have considerably better adherence than those whose spouses had a neutral or negative attitude. In addition, friendship and a pleasant emotional atmosphere at the exercise site have a great deal to do with adherence.[20]

Numerous researchers have sought to discover the relationship between exercise and psychosocial health. This was demonstrated by a study carried out in a Finnish city where about one half of the old population practiced physical exercise. This study revealed that men carried out physical exercises more often than did women and that intensive practice of physical exercise was related to better self-rated health, a lower occurrence of depressive symptoms and self-rated meaningfulness of life. Both women and men exercised more if they rated their lives as meaningful while depressive symptoms were negatively associated with physical exercise. The study clearly showed that psychological well being is an important predictor of being able to carry out physical exercise at advanced ages. Furthermore, the relationship of physical exercise and psychological well being can be interpreted to be reciprocal. This relationship applies only to long term exercise, not to occasional efforts or short term performance.[21]

There are of course numerous additional studies of the relationship between physical exercise and emotional well being. The outcome of these studies can be summarized to yield these conclusions: First, exercise has a small beneficial effect on self-reported measures of anxiety. Second, exercise has a moderate beneficial effect on psychophysiological indices of anxiety. Third, psychophysiological reactivity to psychosocial stressors has a small to moderate negative association with aerobic fitness. Fourth, exercise has a moderate-to-large beneficial effect on depression. Fifth, exercise has shown a consistent relationship of moderate magnitude with measures of mood, self esteem, and other indices of psychological well being. Sixth, exercise has shown to be associated with positive changes in selected aspects of personality and psychological adjustment. Seventh, exercise may be associated with small-to-moderate beneficial effects for some aspects of cognitive functioning. Eighth, there is evidence of both pro-social and anti-social behavior associated with physical exercise. The anti-social behavior is related to excessive sports competition which can even become violent. Finally, some individuals are compulsive about exercise and that may be viewed as unhealthy.[22]

In 1976, William Glasser published a book he called Positive Addiction. In this book he introduced the view that one can be "addicted" to exercise although the word seems inappropriate in that connection when compared to alcohol, nicotine or drug addiction. Glasser claims that "addiction" can be good for the "addict" if it strengthens him. Glasser was particularly concerned with running as a "positive addiction," and claimed that persistent runners can benefit from "runner's high".[23]

Because running can become an "addiction", there are those who become so obsessed with that or some other exercise that they alter their daily schedules, continue to run when seriously injured, and neglect their responsibilities to their work, their home and their families. Like other "addictions," obsession with physical exercise can eliminate all other life choices so that the "addiction" becomes the controlling factor in the "addict's" life and not the other way around. Such negative outcomes are of course rare. A more serious threat for those who exercise is a possible iron deficiency. Writing in Medicine & Science, Connie Weaver claims that college age women who exercise, even moderately, may suffer from iron deficiency to the point of anemia. Such deficiencies can of course be rectified by eating supplemental meat and other foods. Her study was conducted at Purdue University and augmented by studies at the University of Florida and Penn State University.[24]

In 1977 Bandura *et al* hypothesized that an individual's level of confidence to engage in any specific behavior is significantly related to actual behavior. This is certainly true with respect to physical exercise. There are a good number of people who place so much importance on physical exercise that they will undertake it even when they are tired, drunk or in a bad mood.[25]

III

A considerable body of literature exists claiming that regular exercise has beneficial consequences because such activity reputedly slows aging and guards against a number of diseases and discomforts. Principally, however, it is claimed that exercise slows the aging process. The importance of that claim is underscored by the ever increasing age of the American population derived from the greater life span now achieved in the United States and other countries. The evidence for this claim is that in 1900 people over 65 constituted only 4 percent of the American population. In 1988 those over 65 had increased to 12.4 percent of the American population and is now approaching 13 percent (1999). In another thirty years the aged population will constitute 22 percent of all Americans.[26]

Life expectancy has evidently then increased since 1970. At that time life expectancy for women was 74.7 years and for men 67.1. In 1990 life expectancy for women was 78.8 years and for men 71.8 years. As a consequence, the population of the United States 65 years old or over numbers approximately 31 million or 12% and it is anticipated that by

2025 60 million senior citizens over 65 will constitute 20% of all Americans. Furthermore, the National Center for Health Statistics projected that between 10 and 18 million Americans will be over 85 years old by 2040.[27]

Heart disease affects the old much more than the middle aged or young and was the leading cause of death among Americans during the second half of the twentieth century. Therefore, the oft repeated claim that exercise helps prevent heart disease is worth examination.[28]

Researchers with considerable experience backed up by reliable studies have found such an effect. Golczewski has summarized the outcome of these studies and estimates that physically inactive persons have nearly 1.9 times the incidence of heart disease as the physically active. Truly astonishing is Golczewski's next comment that "this was not far different from the risk associated with high blood pressure (2.1), cigarette smoking (2.5), and high blood cholesterol (2.4)." A large epidemiological study concerning the effect of exercise on the overall death rate was reported in the New England Journal of Medicine in 1993. That study found that men who had been involved in moderate exercise programs "had a 23 percent lower overall death rate compared to those who did not."[29]

It has also been well documented that participation in a regular aerobic exercise program reduces the onset and risk factors associated with a number of serious diseases. It is less well known, in fact uncertain, to what extent exercise influences the immune function among the old. The limited evidence appears to indicate that diet, i.e., caloric restrictions have a far greater effect on the immune function than exercise.[30]

Because anti-aging is popular and lends itself to the development of business enterprises, there are a number of clinics in the United States who seek to make a profit from enrolling citizens in their anti-aging programs. Since the largest generation in the history of the United States is about to enter old age such programs indeed promise to be profitable, particularly when 61% of Americans say that they want to live a century. An example of such a program is "Cenegenics," a term derived from the Greek and indicating "new" developments (in the field of aging.) Such programs are not new. For years wealthy persons have traveled to such places as Palm Springs, California and visited so-called "Life Extension Institutes" to ingest various hormones or "anti-aging supplements." Such treatment has always appeared to be on the fringes of good medical practice. Yet, most recently, a 1,500 member American Academy of Antiaging Medicine has been organized and has issued certification in that specialty. The sum of their approach to anti-aging is first to ask the old to continue to use their intellectual abilities.

The belief that mental acuity must decline with old age has been contradicted by experience so often that it cannot be maintained any longer. It is of course true that those who do not use their mental functions will lose them sooner than those who use them. It is evidently also important to avoid stress which not only takes its toll on the body but also on the mind. This means that tension relieving routines can be of great help and exercise is surely one of these routines.[31]

A recent study by the Cooper Institute for Aerobics Research in Dallas, Texas found that thin people who were not physically fit were three times as likely to die young as heavy people who exercised regularly. This finding and others has led some experts to claim that the medical risks of inactivity have been mistaken for obesity-related risks. Even the chances of developing breast cancer have been associated with exercise. A study reported in the journal Health claims that women who work out vigorously were nearly 40 percent less likely to develop breast cancer than those who do nothing.[32]

That exercise has a beneficial effect on arthritis or inflammation of the joints can easily be ascertained by asking any of those 156,000 Americans who suffer from that disease and exercise regularly. This new emphasis on exercise is visible by noting that in 1993 only 62,000 Americans participated in such exercises. The prevalence of arthritis is great. It has been estimated that one half of the 60 million Americans with that disease are 65 years old or over. Arthritis is the chief cause of disability in the United States as it limits everyday activities such as dressing, climbing stairs and walking.

Results of the "Fitness Arthritis and Seniors Trial", an 18 month study of arthritis in 365 senior citizens, concluded that those who participated in regular exercise showed significant improvements in tests of physical performance such as increased range of motion in joints, climbing stairs, getting in and out of cars or lifting and carrying ten pounds or more. This means that both aerobic activity and strengthening exercises are of benefit to arthritis sufferers.[33]

Improvement in sleep quality among older adults is another benefit of physical exercise for older adults. In a randomized controlled trial of 16 weeks duration King *et al* discovered that participation in a physical activity program is related to improvements in rated sleep quality in older adults. The results of this study showed that it takes more than 8 weeks to gain greater sleep duration and sleep efficiency, which refers to the feeling of being rested on awakening in the morning.[34]

There is also some evidence that regular physical exercise may protect against Alzheimer's disease. Dr. Arthur L. Smith, a neurologist and his colleagues at Case Western Reserve University conducted a study of the effects of physical activity and concluded that "healthy individuals reported significantly more physical activity over four decades than those with Alzheimer's disease." The study by Dr. Smith *et al* involved 126 persons diagnosed with Alzheimer's disease and 315 healthy controls. Fifty five men and seventy one women were included in that study.[35]

Bess Marcus, *et al*, examined the effects of physical exercise on smoking relapse. Twenty previously sedentary female smokers were randomly assigned so smoking cessation lectures plus exercise. Exercise treatment included three weekly supervised exercise sessions. In addition health/wellness lectures were included in the treatment of these smokers. Compared to a number of similar studies the results show that exercise does not significantly affect smoking cessation if compared to groups who were subject only to lectures and non-exercise contacts. However, those who exercised were more likely to remain abstinent if they did cease smoking than those who did not exercise.[36]

Although it may sound "far-fetched," a study by audiologists Helaine Alessio and Kathleen Hutchinson discovered a link between fitness and hearing. It was found that those who exercised regularly five times each week lost only 7 decibels of hearing as compared to 15 decibels for those who did not exercise, in an experiment in which the researchers played a 105 decibel sound into the subjects' ears. Although all the volunteers regained their hearing within a day or two the researchers concluded that over time such short-term damage can affect hearing loss permanently. It is now estimated that over 10 million Americans suffer from noise induced hearing loss and that that number is increasing rapidly. The researchers found that cardiovascular conditioning makes the heart beat more strongly which in turn increases the amount of blood that pumps through the capillaries. Regular exercise also increases the production of cell-repairing proteins and therefore protects ears from noise damage.[37]

In addition to some of the physical consequences of exercise just reviewed it is noteworthy that regular exercise also has some psychological and social benefits. If exercise is a means of preserving one's health then it also serves to maintain control of ones affairs among those whose age may well result in losing autonomy to younger children and other care-givers. This means that exercise prevents the dependency of the old on the young with all the negative consequences of that status-role reversal. Exercise leads to more self-confidence and therefore improves self-evaluation which, in the long run, permits the old more independence than is usual among those who lack self-confidence.[38]

"Exercise can banish the blues," according to Kenneth Fox, senior lecturer in physical education at the University of Exeter. Using a pooled analysis of 104 studies including 3,000 subjects Fox found that exercise significantly reduced anxiety and depression, especially among the old. This is no doubt the outcome of such "feelgood" factors as distraction from worries and the opportunity to mix with people. Reporting in The New Scientist, Fox says that there is now convincing evidence that exercise "is effective as part of a treatment programme for people with moderate-to-mild-depression, high stress levels, and those requiring rehabilitation from some forms of addictions, such as alcoholism."[39]

Chronic abuse of alcohol is directly related to a number of debilitating consequences including adverse effects on the immune function in abusers. A good estimate of these consequences is however affected by such factors as nutritional status, stress, depression and other drug use. Chronic abuse of alcohol is also related to an increased mortality rate, cardiovascular and liver abnormalities including cirrhosis and acute hepatitis. Therefore an effort has been made to discover whether or not there is any effect of exercise on impaired immune function in substance abusers. The answer is that there is no such effect. "In the alcohol abuser," say Blank and Meadows, "chronic, endurance type exercises cannot restore the functional capacity of cells or enhance cell surveillance." Moreover, increased exercise participation and physical fitness are not associated with a decline in alcohol abuse. On the contrary. Alcohol and drug use are barriers to participation in regular exercise programs in high school and elsewhere.[40]

The scientific justification for vigorous exercise is far from being obvious. Only an at least superficial understanding of cardiac functions leads one to recognize that the heart is responsible for blood flow and that every cell in the body needs blood in order to survive. Since all blood in the body passes through the chambers of the heart the ability of the coronary network to provide the heart with peak amounts of blood is vital. Therefore, the coronary network must be regularly challenged to maintain that ability. Since an increased demand for blood causes the heart to work harder the key to creating that demand is physical activity and that is exercise.[41]

Researchers know that the body's natural ability to dissolve blood clots increases during exercise but diminishes immediately afterwards. Yet, a study by Dr. John R. Stratton found that in a 6 month exercise program those who exercise regularly "have a clot dissolver circulating in their blood in the resting state and therefore are less likely to form unwanted clots in the vessels of the heart and brain."[42]

The Center for Disease Control has concluded that inactivity contributes to more than one third of the 500,000 annual heart disease related deaths in the United States. Exercise, on the other hand, boosts blood volume and consumes triglyceride fats. These fats have been linked to an increased risk of heart attack. Exercise also lowers blood pressure. Dr. Linda Pescatello found that even moderate exercise for 30 minutes leads to an immediate reduction of 6 to 10 millimeters of mercury lasting for 13 hours.[43]

It would seem evident from this discussion that exercise must lead to greater longevity than would normally be expected if those who exercise are compared to those who do not exercise. Lamb therefore advances the hypothesis that "higher levels of physical activity in men living in technologically advanced countries are significantly associated with reduced all-cause and selected cause specific mortality rates."[44]

Pfaffenbarger *et al* found that if middle aged men have been habitually active or become active they are more likely to reach old age than if they had remained sedentary. For example, men who hold sedentary jobs but who expand more than 2,000 kcal/wk or calories per week during leisure time have a life expectancy 2.51 years longer than similar men who expand less than 500 calories per week. The difference in life expectancy between those who exercise and those who do not decreases with age.

Exercise is not only related to a reduction of cardiovascular diseases, it also has an effect on non-insulin dependent diabetes. A study of University of Pennsylvania alumni concluded that every increase of 500 kcal of energy expenditure per week was associated with a 6% lower incidence of non-insulin dependent diabetes.

Osteoporosis is the outcome of a decrease of bone mass in old age. Osteoporosis is also associated with inactivity. Exercise reverses that because habitual physical weight bearing exercise is instrumental in preventing osteoporosis. This assertion is the outcome of reviewing a number of studies concerning bone density.[45]

Nutrition is also related to exercise in older adults as is obesity, a Latin word which means "eat away" and which is thought to cause or exacerbate heart disease, stroke, diabetes, gout, osteoarthritis, impaired social functioning, reduced economic performance and prejudice together with discrimination.

IV

It has been estimated that over one third of the American population is afflicted by obesity. In view of the list of disabilities, diseases and dysfunctions which obesity brings with it, it would appear easy to combat this problem by simply eating less and properly. If that were so, then obesity would not be one of the major American public health problems which it has been for some years and is today (1999).[46]

A definition of obesity depends in part on knowing the optimal weight any person can accommodate at his height. This means of measurement leads to some controversy as to what constitutes excessive weight since people of the same height may have a larger or smaller bone structure. A number of methods have been used to find a "desirable" weight for height and gender. The federal department of Health and Human Services has defined an "obese" person as one who exceeds "desirable" weight by 20% or more. The "desirable" weight used by Health and Human Services is either the 1959 or 1983 weight table developed by the Metropolitan Insurance Co.. According to the 1983 table, a 5.7" man should weigh between 140 and 152 pounds and a woman of the same height should weigh between 133 and 147 pounds. A man 6ft. tall should weigh 155-169 pounds according to the Metropolitan table while a 5.10" woman should weigh between 142 and 156 pounds.[47]

Body Mass Index is another means of determining overweight and is defined as truncal circumference. Evidently there are several ways by which obesity can be determined. The reason for this is that the location of extra fat in the body makes a difference. Some obese persons carry their extra fat around their hips. Others are exceedingly fat in their middle section, carrying a "tire" around their abdomen. The thighs can also be the principal location for extra fat leading to "pear" obesity. Numerous methods of a scientific nature have now been developed to determine the exact degree of obesity among the American population. These methods lead to the conclusion that demography, personality, genetics and environment are all "risk factors" in becoming overweight.[48]

Epidemiological studies have shown that industrialized nations and affluent communities in developing countries exhibit the most obesity. In the United States, overweight occurs most often in the Northeast and Midwest and affects women and blacks more than men and whites. In the U.S., low economic status is also associated with obesity so that there is an inverse relationship between economic status and weight.

Personal factors determining overweight become visible in childhood. A study by Braddon showed that 33% of adults who were overweight at age 36 or more were already overweight at age seven and 63% were overweight by age fourteen. Evidently, then, the early prevention of obesity may be of critical importance in preventing adult obesity. This is also true of smoking. Smokers weigh less than non-smokers, which may be a recommendation to smoke but is evidently offset by the unhealthy consequences of nicotine intake.[49]

Child bearing and menopause are also related to weight gain alone because maternal body fat, gained during pregnancy, is not altogether lost in the postpartum period. Lactation also promotes fat mobilization particularly if lactation is accompanied by the consumption of a high fat diet and a lack of physical activity.[50]

One of the most discussed issues concerning obesity is the genetic issue. In animals the evidence that obesity can be inherited is overwhelming. In humans the connection to genetic transmission is not so clear although several studies have demonstrated that body fat mass is subject to significant familial transmission. Nevertheless, environmental factors are favored by most investigators as being responsible for overweight in humans.[51]

Whether obesity is genetic or promoted by the environment does not alter the indisputable fact that there must have been surplus energy available to those who suffer from fat disposition. Therefore, aerobic exercise and dieting are essential in order to deal with the obesity problem. Weight loss, whatever its origin, has some important benefits which are immediately apparent. In diabetic persons weight loss may reduce their need for insulin. Such weight loss can be influenced by exercise. However, the principal and most essential means of obesity intervention must be dieting. This emphatic statement can be supported by the results of four national surveys which have shown that dieting is a component of weight loss in 84% of women and 77% of men. Unsupervised dieting and even some commercial dieting programs can be dangerous because some diets omit vitamins and minerals which are essential to the body. The best method of achieving weight reduction is a combination of exercise and dieting. Studies of Boston policemen have shown that subjects who continued to exercise after cessation of dieting tended to maintain their weight loss while those who ceased exercising tended to regain all the weight lost earlier. This then demonstrates that initial loss of weight is dependent more on diet than on exercise but that a permanent result is more dependent on exercise than on diet.[52]

Now, the effort to burn more calories, even when not "working-out" in a gymnasium has become most popular. The word "metabolism" meaning to "throw a change", is mainly used in advertising this effort. The premise here is that an exercise regimen will allow everyone to use up more calories not only during "workouts" but around the clock. It has therefore been estimated by some researchers that the carryover from aerobic exercises is about 15 percent. Others have claimed that the "carryover" is negligible and that an increase in metabolism is so small that it cannot be measured. This dispute may well be the outcome of a natural condition, muscle loss, which affects all humans with advancing age. Beginning with our mid-twenties we lose about one third of one percent of muscle by weight each year throughout our life. Therefore, a decrease in calories burned is also certain throughout any life time. Someone burning 1,900 calories at age 30 will only burn 1,672 calories a day at age 70. That means that 228 calories a day will have to be cut from the diet of those having reached age 70 or they will see fat accumulate in their thighs, bellies and chests. There are of course individual differences which dictate the optimum weight and diet for every person depending at least on sex.[53]

Therefore, Linda Hamilton, a doctor and a professional dancer, recommends that optimal weight for women can be attained by taking in 1,400 to 1,600 calories a day. For men she recommends an intake of 1,600 to 1,800 calories. Since the average American dietary intake runs from 2,200 to 2,500 calories a day it evidently takes a great deal of discipline for most Americans to reach the optimum. That discipline is of course easier to achieve if the food intake is distributed over the whole day.

Hamilton further recommends that female dancers eat between 1,200 and 1,500 mg of calcium each day while male dancers eat 800 to 1,000 mg of calcium daily. To retain a sufficient amount of calcium Hamilton advises that plant based foods are a good source of calcium but are hard for the body to absorb. Dairy products are of course more easily absorbed but cause losses of calcium because of their high protein content.[54]

These recommendations presume an athletic life style which is certainly achieved by professional dancers. The average American is of course neither a dancer nor an athlete. On the contrary. Considering that a third of all Americans are overweight it might be assumed that at least that third of Americans would be willing to diet. While no one can say with certainty how many Americans really stay on a diet, a study by Drewnowski *et al* found that among a random sample of high school graduates only 4% of those contacted were dieting. This study found that even among men who wished to lose weight the prevalence of dieting was only 4%. Drewnowski attributes this lack of interest in dieting to the prevalence of satisfaction with body image among men in contrast to women who, in the study by Drewnowski, were a great deal more dissatisfied with their body image. Hence women contacted in the Drewnowski study dieted more than men while men, unwilling to diet, exercised more than women.[55]

The Cooper Institute for Aerobic Research in Dallas has initiated a study called "Project Alive." This study sought to compare two methods of getting 235 sedentary men and women moving. Half the participants were asked to "work out" in a gym for 30 minutes at least three times a week. The other half met once a week in small groups to discuss how to integrate physical activity into their lives without going to any gym. The conclusion of this comparison is that "lifestyle activities" provide benefits similar to those attained by going to a "gym." Both groups, it was found, burned about 150 extra calories each day and showed similar improvements in blood pressure, body composition and cholesterol profile.[56]

It should be obvious from the foregoing that "Americans cannot expect to reach realistic health goals until diet and exercise are merged into one behavior", according to Dr. Steven Blair, who is director of epidemiology and clinical applications at the Cooper Institute. Blair demonstrates that nutrition advice and restrictive recommendations do not work unless strengthened by physical activity. This means that exercise and diet are interdependent behaviors, work together (synergistic effects) and must be considered together. Several findings were presented by Blair as a consequence of an interdisciplinary colloquium held in Dallas in 1995. These findings are: 1. Diet and physical activity have complementary beneficial effects on the major chronic diseases affecting the US population, including heart disease, hypertension, diabetes, hyperlipidemia, obesity, some cancers and osteoporosis. Diet and physical activity also affect normal growth and "healthy" aging. 2. Therefore, every American adult should exercise 30 minutes or more every day. 3. *Regular* physical exercise improves nutrition utilization and allows intake of an increased amount of food. 4. Benefits from merging diet and activity are attainable throughout life. There are several more recommendations all of which underlined the need for regular, moderate physical activity.

A test of these hypotheses was conducted by the Cooper Institute in 1995. That test followed 10,000 men aged 60 or older who received two fitness tests over a five year period. During a 5 year follow up after the second fitness test, 223 of the men had died. The death rate for men who were physically unfit at both examinations was 122 per 10,000. The death rate for men who were initially unfit, but who improved and were at least moderately fit at the second test was 68 per 10,000. This constitutes a 44% decline in death between those who exercised and those who did not. A better argument for exercise can hardly be made.

Based on the knowledge here reviewed some schools have now adopted the Fit for Life program which seeks to include physical education, health education and nutrition. Students who enroll in this program in their school also volunteer at least 5 hours a week outside class in a wellness or fitness center. They also engage in community sponsored events such as an annual Marathon. Others supervise skating parties by grade school children and design and deliver lessons on nutrition to children in the grades. In addition to classroom instruction and instruction in bench aerobics, students in the Fit for Life program are also taught how to measure blood pressure, understand heart rates, calculate calories consumed and learn the fundamentals of weight control. Nutritional information, using the food "pyramid" is taught to those enrolled in Fit for Life.[57] This program also includes a drug prevention unit which is incorporated into this course. It is hoped that the early exposure of children to the need for exercise and nutrition will give them a life long commitment to these values after they reach adulthood. This may defeat the claim of so many people that they have no time for exercise. Yet, an accumulation of ten minutes of exercise three times a day by walking, cycling or running ought to be possible for anyone.[58]

V

Exercise also has emotional benefits. As we have already seen, anxiety and depression seem to be alleviated by exercise. Nevertheless, there are those who dispute the frequently held belief that depression and anxiety are relieved in direct proportion to the intensity of the exercise. At the University of Georgia researchers reviewed dozens of studies looking for a link between workout intensity and mood. That review found that "changes in stress levels after a workout were the same whether volunteers did light, moderate or strenuous exercise." This does not mean that those who exercise are less anxious and stressed than those who do not exercise. It means only that the intensity of the exercise is not related to the degree in mood alteration.[59]

Those who conducted that study believe that "working-out" has the same effect on the emotions as sitting in a quiet room or using standard relaxation techniques. It is of course possible that the repetitive motions, the change in activities and the interpersonal interaction in gymnasiums contribute more to the psychological consequences of exercise than the physical activity itself.

Page and Tucker studied the relationship between emotional health and exercise by investigating the emotional consequences of exercise among adolescents. The results of that investigation were that adolescents who did not exercise or did so rarely scored higher on each measure of psychological discomfort such as loneliness, shyness and hopelessness than did adolescents who exercised frequently.[60]

The reasons for these findings include that exercise and physical activity is often performed within social groups so that those who already have friends and belong to clubs or teams are unlikely to feel much psychological discomfort. In addition it is easily seen that those who lack social skills and are not members of any group or team have a tendency to withdraw and thereby become involved in that cycle of rejection, withdrawal, loneliness, rejection etc. which never ends throughout the rejectee's lifetime. American culture rewards physical prowess and penalizes failure to be competent in sports. Therefore, those who cannot perform have reason to feel rejected. It is furthermore possible that those who appear to have shed some of their psychosocial stress because of exercise are only temporarily relieved of their emotional pain which returns soon after the exercise is over.[61]

It may well be that emotional pain is more common than any other illness in the United States at the end of the 20th century. That this is so can be judged by the huge tranquilizer pill consumption in this country every day. That consumption of pills and drugs adds to the cost of health care in America is well known and has already been discussed. From the sociological point of view the widespread use of pills to deal with all our health needs contributes to the sick role which constitutes a form of deviance and is treated as such in American society. That sick role includes the view that those who are sick, for any reason, are not responsible for their condition; that those who are sick are temporarily exempt from their normal obligations; that those who are sick must get well and that those who are sick are obliged to get competent help from the medical profession to hasten their recovery. [62]

That help is generally only available in the doctor's office or in the hospital. It is therefore the hospital which shall be the topic of our next chapter.

Summary

Only 22% of American adults engage in regular exercise. Such exercise has numerous benefits particularly for the cardiovascular system. There are therefore numerous health clubs in this country which promote cardiovascular programs. These are generally staffed by professional employees and are designed to reduce stress and anxiety. It is claimed that regular exercise and dieting slows the aging process and reduces the chances of suffering numerous diseases and disabilities.

Obesity is one of these disabilities. Therefore the major finding of this chapter is that dieting and exercise must go together in order to increase cardiovascular endurance, increase heart function and capacity and thereby insure long term benefits from either strategy.

NOTES

[1] No author, "Recommendations on Physical Exercise," *The American Family Physician*, Vol. 48, No. 6, November, 1993, pp. 1168.

[2] David F. Tver and Howard F. Hunt, *Encyclopedic Dictionary of Sports Medicine*, New York, Chapman and Hall, 1986, p. 232.

[3] No author, "Physical Activity and Hypertentension," *The American Family Physician*, Vol. 48, No. 8, December, 1993, p. 1561.

[4] Richard C. Day and Robert C. Cantu, "Corporate Fitness," in Robert C. Cantu, Editor, *The Exercising Adult*, New York, Macmillan Publishing Co., 1987, p. 31.

[5] U.S. Public Health Service, *Forward Plan for 1977-1981*, Washington, D.C., Department of Health, Education and Welfare, 1977, p. 108.

[6] Kathleeen Green, "Leading the Life: Jobs in Health Clubs," *Occupational Outlook Quarterly*, Vol. 39, No. 2, Summer 1995, pp. 15-22. See also: Bureau of Labor Statistics, *National Occupational Employment Statistics*, October 28, 1998.

[7] *Ibid*, p.20.

[8] Gerhard Falk, *The Life of the Academic Professional*, Lewiston, N.Y., The Edwin Mellen Press, 1990, pp. 113-147.

[9] Thomas Manfredi, W. Jay Gillespie and Karen S. Congdon, "University-based cardiac rehabilitation and adult fitness programs," in: Day and Cantu, op.cit. pp. 43-61.

[10] Trevor Smith, "Which is the Best Exercise Machine?" *Consumer's Research Magazine*, Vol. 80, No. 12, December 1997, p. 21.

[11] *Ibid.*, p. 23.

[12] Joseph Alper, "The Machine of Your Dreams," *Health*, Vol.12, No.7, October, 1998, pp. 38-42.

[13] James Braham, "Fitness Machines Adopt Space Technology," *Machine Design*, Vol. 67, No. 8, April 20, 1995, p. 29.

[14] Bess H. Marcus, Cheryl A. Eaton, Joseph S. Rossi and Lisa L. Harlow, " Self-Efficacy, Decision-Making and Stages of Change: An Integrative Model of Physical Exercise," *Journal of Applied Social Psychology*, Vol. 24, No. 6, March 1994, p. 489.

[15] No author, "America's Getting Fatter," *American Journal of Nursing*, Vol.94, September 1994, p. 9.

[16] Michael Mason, "Why we don't exercise," *Health*, Vol.12, No. 5, July-August 1998, p. 66.

[17] Lynn Rossellini, "How far should you go to stay fit?", *U.S. News and World Report*, November 10, 1997,p.95.

[18] Gerhard Falk, *Sex, Gender and Social Change: The Great Revolution*, Lanham, Md., The University Press of America, 1998, pp. 255-262.

[19] Mason, *op.cit.*, p. 69.

[20] Francis Heinzelman and R.W. Bagley, "Response to physical activity programs and their effects on health behavior," *Public Health Reports*, Vol. 85, , 1970, pp. 905-911.

[21] J. M. Ruuskanen and I. Ruoppila, "Physical Activity and Psychological Well-being among People Aged 65 to 84 Years," *Age and Aging*, Vol.24, No. 4, July 1995, pp. 292-296.

[22] Stuart Biddle, "Exercise and Psychosocial Health," *Research Quarterly for Exercise and Health*, Vol. 66, No.4, 1995, pp. 292-297.

[23] William Glasser, *Positive Addiction*, New York, Harper and Row, 1976.

[24] K.M. Reese, "Women who exercise run risk of iron deficiency," *Chemical and Engineering News*, Vol. 73, November 27, 1995, p. 52.

[25] Albert Bandura, "Self-efficacy; Toward a unifying theory of behavioral change," *Psychological Review*,
Vol. 84, 1977, pp. 191-215.

[26] Ursula Adler Falk and Gerhard Falk, *Ageism, the Aged and Aging in America*, Springfield, Ill., Charles C. Thomas, Publishers, 1997, pp. 246-253.

[27] David R. Lamb, *Perspectives in Exercise Science and Sports Medicine*, Carmel, Ind., Cooper Publishing Group, 1995, p. 2.

[28] William C. Cockerham, *Medical Sociology* (7th Ed.), Englewood Cliffs, N.J., Prentice-Hall, Inc., 1998.

[29] James A. Golcsewski, *Aging: Strategies for Maintaining Good Health and Extending Life*, Jefferson, N.C., Mc Farland & Co., Inc, Publishers, 1998, p. 68.

[30] Robert S. Mazzeo, "Exercise, Immunity and Aging," in: Robert Goetz, Ed., *Exercise, Immunity and Aging*, New York, CRC Publishers, 1996, pp. 199-203.

[31] Susan V. Seligson, "Anti-Aging Comes of Age," *Health*, Vol.12, No.3, April 1998, p. 64.

[32] *Ibid.*, p. 66.

[33] Walter Ettinger et.al., "A Randomized Trial Comparing Aerobic Exercies and Resistance Exercise with a Health Education Program in Older Adults with Knee Osteoarthritis-The Fitness Arthritis and Seniors Trial" *Journal of the American Medical Association*, Vol. 277, No. 1, January 1, 1997, pp. 25-31.

[34] Abby C. King, Roy F. Oman, Glenn S. Brassington, Donald L. Bliwise and William L. Haskell, "Moderate-Intensity Exercise and

Self-rated Quality of Sleep in Older Adults," *Journal of the American Medical Association,* Vol. 277, No.1, January 1, 1977, pp. 32-37.

[35] Arthur L. Smith, "Regular physical exercise may protect against Alzheimer's disease," *Geriatrics,* Vol. 53, No. 6, June 1998, pp. 94-95.

[36] Bess H. Marcus, Anna E. Albright, Raymond S. Niaura, Elaine R. Taylor, Laurey R. Simkin, Susan I. Feder, David B.Abrams, and Paul D. Thompson, "Exercise Enhances The Maintenance of Smoking Cessation in Women," *Addictive Behaviors,* Vol. 20, No. 1, January-February 1995, pp. 87-92.

[37] No author, "Tone Your Thighs, Tune Your Ears," *Health,* Vol.8, P. 14, October 1994, p. 15.

[38] Patrick E. Fontane, " Exercise, Fitness and Feeling Well," *American Behavioral Scientist,* Vol.39, No.3, January 1996, p. 288.

[39] Debora MacKenzie, "Life getting you down? Go and work up a sweat," *New Scientist,* Vol. 143, No. 1942, September 10, 1994, p. 9.

[40] Sally E. Blank and Gary G. Meadows, in: Ira Wolinsky, Editor, *Nutrition in Exercise and Sport,* Boca Roran, CRC Press, 1998, p. 217.

[41] Mair Zamir, "Secrets of the Heart," *The Sciences,* Vol.36, No.5, September-October 1996, pp. 26-31.

[42] Keith Thompson, "Exercise boosts body's clot-busting ability," *The Physician and Sports Medicine,* Vol.18, No. 3, March 1990, p. 43.

[43] Marcia Barinage, "How Exercise Works Its Magic," *Science,* Vol.276, May 30, 1967, p. 1325.

[44] David R. Lamb, *Perspectives in Exercise Science and Sports Medicine,* Carmel, Ind., Cooper Publishing Group, 1995, p. 13.

[45] Ibid, p. 17.

[46] Paul H. Lachance, "Human Obesity," *Food Technology,* Vol.48, No.2, February 1994, p. 127.

[47] J.E. Manson, M.J. Stampfer, C.H. Hennekens, and W.C. Willet, "Body weight and longevity," *Journal of the American Medical Association,* Vol.257, 1987, pp. 353-358.

[48] Lachance, *op.cit.,* p.128.

[49] F.E.M. Braddon, B. Rodgers, M.E.J. Wadsworth, and J.M.C. Davies, "Onset of Obesity in a 36 Year Birth Cohort Study." British Medical Journal, Vol.293, 1986, pp. 299-303.

[50] C.L. Ley, B. Lee and J.C. Stevenson, "Sex and Menopause associated Changes in Body Fat Distribution." *American Journal of Clinical Nutrition,* Vol. 55, 1992, pp. 950-954.

[51] C. Bouchard and L. Perusse, " Heredity and Body Fat," *Annual Review of Nutrition,* Vol.8, 1988, pp. 259-277.

[52] Pavlou, K.N., Krey, S., and Steffee, W.P., "Exercise as an adjunct to weight loss and maintenance in moderately obese subjects," *American Journal of Clinical Nutrition,* Vol. 49, 1989, pp. 1115-1123.
[53] David Sharp, "Give Your Metabolism a Lift," *Health,* Vol.12, No. 2, March 1998, p. 32.
[54] Linda Hamilton, "A Sensible Approach to Weight Loss," *Dance Magazine,* Vol.71, November 1997, pp. 63-65.
[55] Adam Drewnowski, Candace L. Kurth and Dean D. Krahn, "Effects of Body Image on Dieting, Exercise and Anabolic Steroid Use in Adolescent Males," *International Journal of Eating Disorders,* Vol. 17, No. 4, May 1995, pp. 381-385.
[56] Carol Krucoff, "Can't Get To The Gym? Activate Your Life!" *The Saturday Evening Post,* Vol. 270. No. 1, January/February 1998, p. 26.
[57] Lana Hawhee Shuck, "Fit for Life: An Integrated, Holistic Approach to Health," *Contemporary Education,* Vol. 69, No.3, Spring 1998, 157-158.
[58] Steven N. Blair, "Diet and Activity: The Synergistic Merger," *Nutrition Today,* Vol. 30, No.3, May/June 1995, pp. 108-111.
[59] Peter Jaret, "You Don't Have to Sweat to Reduce Your Stress," *Health,* November/ December 1995, pp. 83-88.
[60] Randy M. Page and Larry A. Tucker, "Psychosocial Discomfort and Exercise Frequency: An Epidemiological Study of Adolescents," *Adolescence,* Vol.29, No. 113, Spring 1994, pp. 183-191.
[61] *Ibid.,* p.189.
[62] Talcott Parsons, *The Social System,* New York., The Free Press, 1951, pp. 436-439.

Chapter XI

The Hospital Establishment

I

An institution or establishment exists first and foremost to provide services for its members. Therefore the hospital meets the first criterion of an institution. A second function of any institution is to replace its members whenever they leave for any reason. Surely, the hospital fulfills that criterion since no hospital is dependent for its existence on any one person or group of persons. All can and are continuously replaced. Thirdly, a hospital is an institution because hospitals pass knowledge from one generation to the next. Hospitals teach medicine and teach about the means of dealing with patients. Hospitals, like all institutions, provide order. This means that hospital personnel decide who is to be admitted and who is discharged and how treatment shall proceed. Finally, hospitals, like all institutions, provide a sense of purpose to their consumers (patients) and their providers (all their personnel).[1]

One more function of all institutions is to segregate the population. This is true of those labeled sick and who are segregated in hospitals, military personnel who are segregated in camps, some of the old who are segregated in nursing homes and, most of all, children who are segregated in schools. These institutions are of course all open to visits and scrutiny by outsiders as there is a continuous movement in and out of hospitals, nursing homes, schools and military camps by both the institutionalized and visitors. There are also total institutions such as prisons and mental hospitals which differ from all other institutions in that they do no permit the kind of interaction possible in the normal institution. These institutions are voluntary although schools, which are not voluntary, do not meet the characteristics of a total institution. The total institution isolates people from the rest of society for a distinct period of time during which the isolated people come under the total control of officials who govern these institutions. Most important is that those who enter a total institution are stripped of their former selves and depersonalized, as Goffman has shown.[2]

In part, this depersonalization is also imposed on hospital patients although the degree to which this can be done is far less than is true of a nursing home, prison or psychiatric institution. The similarities are nevertheless striking. First, patients who enter a hospital are given an identification number, usually carried around the wrist. Another means of depersonalizing hospital patients is to call them by their first names. Hospital clerks and clerks in doctors' offices generally use this device as a means of humiliating the patient since the use of first names is normally restricted to close relatives and friends or to little children. By using a patient's first name the adult is infantilized and deprived of his autonomy. This enhances the hospital clerk's sense of self importance and creates a wall of segregation between the medical staff always called, deferentially "doctor", and the patient. Another device for the reduction of the patients' status to that of an object is the demand that the patient wear pajamas or a hospital gown. These gowns are generally open in the back so as to create embarrassment for the patient. Even those who wear pajamas and other means of covering themselves are nevertheless deprived of their normal social standing as the hospital employees take control of the patient's body. No doubt there is nothing more humiliating than to lose control of one's body. This is an experience which more than any other device deprives hospital patients of their individuality, sense of worth, self direction and autonomy. Anyone who must subject himself to the invasion of his physical being by strangers who happen to be employed in a hospital, nursing home or other institution is reduced to the status of a non-person and converted from a subject to that of an object. It is precisely this conversion to the condition of an object which serves the purposes of hospital employees best because objects do not interfere in the routines of the institution but are as docile as farm animals.

Outside of a hospital one's own body is a private matter. Normally, we take care not to expose private parts of our body in public and to relegate all bodily care to the private sphere. Even talking about intimate parts of the body is generally prohibited by social convention as is "passing gas" or scratching oneself in pubic areas. Therefore, even the sick try to hide their discomfort.

In a hospital the patient's body becomes open to public inspection. In the hospital setting, doctors, nurses and all kinds of personnel examine and manipulate the patient or at least his body. From technicians to surgeons, health workers expose the body of the patient, insert needles and tubes into it and discuss all of this openly in front of visitors and other patients.[3]

The hospital environment itself increases the discomfort of the patient. Hospitals are confining, the rooms are small, must be shared with strangers and are often noisy, untidy, poorly ventilated and unpleasant. All this creates a situation for the hospital patient which deprives him of his life-long social status and role and forces him to accept a role wholly different from the one he is accustomed to play in the course of his normal life routines.

Sociologists refer to the condition of the hospital patient as "role exit." This means that the patient is forced to relinquish his social role which has constituted his self-identity and assume the new identity of patient. This is both difficult and painful and needs to be given some consideration by the hospital staff.[4]

To the hospital staff, patients are objects. This is true not only because of the extensive use of technology in the treatment of patients but also because of the distinct social differences between hospital staff and patients. This is particularly visible in large hospitals. There the staff is generally young and the patients old. Young nurses and doctors "lord it over" whole floors of patients old enough to be their grandparents. Many of the patients have no education while the staff must be educated. Ethnic differences add to the discomfort as Catholic nurses and Jewish doctors treat Protestant patients and vice versa. Many patients in large hospitals are poor while doctors are frequently wealthy and nurses have a secure income.

Even more disastrous for the patient is the technologically cold fashion by which patients are confronted in our hospitals. To doctors, patients are objects having a technically defined illness. To the patient there is a great deal of fear and little understanding of the procedures facing him. Instead, the patients feel alienated from the hospital and view the hospital workers as uninterested in their needs.

Hospital workers generally view the complaints of patients as trivial "whining." To them, open hospital gowns, too many blood samples and constant traffic in and out of the patients rooms are not worth their attention. Yet, the patient suffers more from the treatment received in the hospital than the disease treated by the doctor. The patient, on arriving at the hospital, becomes a "case" and is at once dehumanized. This is particularly so for those needing surgery. Made unconscious by an anesthetic, the patient is reduced to the position of a turkey in a butcher shop. This is particularly evident when the patient is used as a learning experience for medical students or when the patient is used as a research object.[5]

About one half of all patients will not cooperate with the staff and actively resist their hospital regimen. The reason for this resistance is that many patients regard their medical treatment as "unwanted, intrusive, disruptive and the manner in which it is given, presumptuous."[6]

Non-compliance with medical authority is viewed by some hospital staff as an unwarranted audacity. This is particularly the case if the hospital authority belong to that group who are convinced that the wishes of the patient are unimportant and deviant. Some hospital staff seek to control patients in a number of ways to insure that patients make no demands on them and keep quiet, no matter what procedure they may have suffered. Drugs are the best means of controlling patients since a drugged patient can hardly ask any questions or confront the staff. Withholding information also serves to control patients. Nurses are constantly faced with questions they may not be able or allowed to answer so that deception of patients is sometimes used to deal with patients' questions.

All of these methods are finally designed to insure that the medical staff have power over the patient. Since any medical observation of any person will always produce some problem, some deviance, some illness, some potential abnormality it can be shown that medical examinations actually produce illness where there was none.[7]

Because these considerations have been ignored for so long, Patients' Rights organizations have recently sought to provide patients with some means of maintaining their dignity and sense of self worth while hospitalized. These "patient's rights" became an issue in the mid-1960's when civil rights, welfare rights, women's rights and student's rights were fought over in the streets and became a permanent part of American civil liberties. Until then, hospitals literally trampled on the rights of patients who are frightened, sick and physically naked and utterly powerless.

In 1966 Mt. Sinai Hospital in New York became the first to introduce a patient representative who was to intervene on behalf of the patient. By 1972 a national organization of patient representatives had emerged and by 1973 the National Society for Patient Representatives and Consumer Affairs had developed an NSPRCA "Code of Ethics."[8]

Patient representatives help patients become active participants in their own care. In that status they explain hospital policies and procedures that patients question. They intervene in disputes among patients, families and staff and investigate complaints on behalf of patients so that the patient does not become the center of the conflict. The role of the patient representative becomes particularly acute in connection with dying patients. Even room assignments can become the province of the patient representative. The patient's representative can cross all administrative lines and interact with employees at every level thereby also saving the hospital from lawsuits.[9]

Finally, patient representatives can help patients understand and use the Patient Bill of Rights proposed by the American Hospital Association and now commonly posted in every hospital in America. According to that Bill of Rights the patient has the right to considerate and respectful care, and to information concerning his diagnosis, treatment and prognosis. The patient, according to that Bill of Rights, is also entitled to know the identity of all who treat him and to privacy and confidentiality. Financial considerations are also to be explained to every patient as he has the right to participate in decision making concerning his illness. There are also a number of other "rights" enjoyed by the hospital patient.[10]

It is certain that Congress will consider federal legislation to insure "patient protection" in hospitals. Therefore, the American Hospital Association is making an effort to bring about a private, "voluntary patient protection" policy. This is promoted "in the hope of defeating a bill sponsored by Sen. Edward Kennedy and Rep. John Dingell intended to allow beneficiaries to sue hospitals and health plans and employees to "blow the whistle" on hospital management.[11]

II

The first hospitals in the western world, as the word indicates, were hosts or receivers of guests and were intended to receive pilgrims to Middle Eastern holy places. Some hospitals were established directly after the Council of Nicea in 325 C.E.. Thereafter, an order of knights who called themselves the Hospitalers assumed responsibility for the building and maintenance of these resting places. Today there exists in Paris a hospital called the Hotel Dieu which was established in 600. That hospital was evidently the first true medical center in that "it embraced many of the activities necessary to care for the sick."[12]

At the beginning of the 12th century some 200 hospitals were established in England to deal with a large number of leprosy patients who had contracted that disease during the crusades.

The first American general hospital was built by the Quakers, who opened their hospital in Philadelphia in 1751 in order to care for those among the sick whose home conditions would not allow treatment. A few other hospitals were also established in the 18th century and more came into being in the 19th century. These hospitals were used only by the poor so that as late as 1909 the Massachusetts General Hospital in Boston still cared only for the poor and physicians were not allowed to charge for their services there.

The death rate in these hospitals was very high particularly because they were centers of epidemics and contained all the horrors of operations without anesthetics other than alcohol. It was only with the discovery of ether by the dentist W.T.G. Morton in 1846 that operations became more bearable, leading to a dramatic increase in surgery throughout the United States.

Even then, however, American hospitals were "undifferentiated welfare institutions" used almost entirely by poor immigrants, unmarried mothers and others who were dependent on public assistance. Every "respectable " citizen avoided hospitals because there was really no medical reason for entering a hospital. In case of illness Americans usually relied on home-remedies and did not call a physician. When doctors were called, they dealt with their patients at home and that included accident victims.

Hospitals were dangerous places in the nineteenth century and before because they caused infections or sepsis which is merely a Greek word for rotten. Hence the word anti-septic so commonly used now.

Prior to the use of technology as applied in hospitals, doctors not only treated the disease as best they could, but they also practiced "family medicine" in the sense of dealing with the patient's whole environment.

Hospitals in these early years were almost entirely voluntary and dependent on charitable contributions of the rich to the poor. The donors did not expect to ever enter a hospital themselves. Instead, applicants for hospital treatment were those who could not pay anything and whose "good moral character" was attested by someone with important social connections or someone with a great deal of money. This meant that laymen, and not doctors, controlled who would be admitted to a hospital. Consequently the hospital patient, until the 20th century was stigmatized and viewed as unworthy. Paternalism and authoritarianism such as is described in Dickens', novels greeted the hospital patient.

Physicians practiced in hospitals gratuitously. This, however, was not charity. Doctors spent only a few hours in a hospital each week in order to learn and then gain high fees for knowledge acquired from the poor by servicing the rich who were paying for the support of the hospital's patients in the first place. Furthermore, many physicians were themselves the products of the upper class and had studied in Europe, particularly in Germany, to gain a better knowledge of their profession and to secure a sufficient reputation for themselves.

In the late 19th century, the American middle class began to use the hospital for its surgery needs as more and more men, and some women, left their families to live as "bachelors" on their own. Deprived of family care, these single people went to hospitals when in need of care. Similarly, more and more people became old at the end of the 19th century and they too needed to enter hospitals after their spouses had died.

In addition to these reasons, hospitals became more and more useful to Americans as the size of the family shrank because of birth control and the establishment of "conjugal" one generation families. These smaller families are not equipped to deal with illness at home particularly because both men and women work and there is little space in which to isolate or care for the sick.[13]

Finally, in the latter part of the 19th century, following the work of Pasteur and Lister in bacteriology and antiseptic surgery, hospitals began to lose their reputation as only a place to die and became known as places where one might get well. Then, with the discovery of sulfa drugs in the mid 1930s and penicillin in the 1940s surgery without infection became possible. After the close of World War II in 1945 American medical technology expanded quickly until that technology included such amazing achievements as the production of artificial kidneys, hearts and other organs.

Since 1966, when the U.S. government instituted Medicaid and Medicare legislation the introduction of a large number of bureaucratic agencies into hospital affairs has become commonplace. There are now 40 federal agencies, 96 state agencies 18 city and county agencies and 10 voluntary, quasi-public groups regulating 109 functions within our hospitals.[14]

The introduction of these programs meant the near end of the segregated black hospitals in this country. Thus, between 1961 and 1988 49 black hospitals in the U.S. closed while a large number of others consolidated or merged with white hospitals. The reasons for the abandonment of these black hospitals was of course the integration movement of the 1960s and the introduction of government funds into the larger white hospitals with the attendant requirement to end all racial segregation.[15]

Today, (1999) there are 6,201 hospitals in the United States. These hospitals accommodate 1,061,688 beds and admitted 33,307,152 patients in 1997. Among them, 24,338,194 operations were performed in one year. On any one day during the year 684, 875 Americans are hospitalized amounting to a total hospitalization of 250,193,842 hospital days. Hospitals received 505,454,608 outpatient visits in 1997 of which 97,552, 005 or 19% were emergencies. Meanwhile, 3,790,678 newcomers were born in American hospitals in 1997 constituting 95% of all American births.[16]

American hospitals employ 3,728,000 persons and spend $350.1 billion per year. This means that the average cost of accommodating one inpatient per day in American non-government hospitals was $1,005.45 in 1996.[17]

By 1998 a 1.2% decline in hospital admissions occurred in the United States. Admissions of patients under age 65 dropped one percent and admissions of patients over 65 declined 1.5 percent. Outpatient visits increased by 6.1 percent in 1998 while the length of stay for patients over 65 dropped from 6.5 days to 6.4 days. Total income of hospitals increased by 3.2 percent in 1998 and that increase was mainly due to increases in outpatient revenue.[18]

In view of the large expenditures incurred by American hospitals the compensation of hospital administrators is also very large. Thus, the median income of chief executive officers of American hospitals was $185,300 in 1998. The chief medical officers of American hospitals earned $197,800 that year while other executives earned at least $91,000 annually. Hospital executives received an average of 7.5% increases in 1997 while nurses were increased by only 2.1% in that same year. Evidently, the biggest gains in compensation in hospital employment have gone to those already earning the most and who are furthest removed from the purpose of a hospital, i.e., patient care.[19]

All of this highlights the mounting economic pressures placed on hospitals and the entire health care system in the United States by the discrepancy between costs and public expectations. Nationally, the United States spends $1 trillion a year on health care which constitutes about 15% of gross national product but will rise to 20% of gross national product in 2002. This means that one of every seven dollars spent in the United States is spent on health care and that hospital expenditures amount to 40% thereof.

Despite this large income, hospitals are faced with a number of economic pressures at the end of the century. These pressures are the result of social change and cannot be addressed by blaming anyone. First among these pressures are the increasing number of cost effective specialty clinics and doctors offices which provide a much more personal and quality care than is true of impersonal hospital clinics. Second, the overall aging of the U.S. population has led to an ever increasing number of old hospital patients who have multiple complaints and who are admitted mainly because they are unable to care for themselves. Third, younger patients now admitted to hospitals often suffer such serious illnesses as cancer and AIDS or accident related injuries.

It is expensive to treat these patients, many of whom are underinsured or have no health insurance whatever. It has been repeatedly estimated that 41 million or 18% of Americans under age 65 are have no hospital insurance so that uncompensated care is now a growing part of hospital expenditures. In addition, new technology costs more and more as patients demand better and better diagnostic capabilities.

All of these pressures are not under the control of hospitals. However, administrative costs certainly are under hospital control and it is in this area that more and more money is being spent each year. Today, administrative costs use up 20% of hospital expenditures. Nurses spend almost half their time writing in patients charts rather than caring for the patient at hand and lengths of stay are extended because test results are delayed or medical records are missing.[20]

Meanwhile numerous surveys of American patients find that only one in ten patients are satisfied with their hospital experience because of the impersonality, inconvenience and lack of consideration for the needs of the patient on the part of hospital staff.

One consequence of this almost universal dissatisfaction with American hospitals has been the introduction of the "for-profit" hospital. These hospitals are generally owned and operated by private corporations seeking to earn a profit. By means of mergers and acquisitions of not-for-profit hospitals these corporations are growing ever faster in this country. It is to be anticipated therefore that in a few years there will be only about 3,500 hospitals in the United States. The others will have to shut down as they fail to compete with the for-profit hospitals which will render a far better service to each patient but will also pay taxes. This does not mean that there will be no community hospitals. It does mean however, that there will be intense competition for patients with several results. Among these will be that the focus of cost will be even greater than it is now. Health care programs that do not produce income will be eliminated. More and more tax-exempt hospitals will consolidate to meet the competition from "for profits." There will be a "bifurcation" of hospitals with the best doctors and others choosing to work in the wealthy "for profit" hospitals, which accept only the best paying patients, even as community hospital patients will be treated with lesser expertise, lesser technology and lesser care. Finally all hospitals will seek to cater to the wishes of employers and health maintenance organizations.[21]

"For–profit" hospitals and health maintenance organizations claim that profits are by no means bad for health care. They argue that controlling costs does not sacrifice quality but that the "fee-for-service" system meant that a third of all tests given and operations performed were unnecessary and were performed only to make doctors rich. They further say that there is little difference between "for-profit" hospitals and non-profit hospitals because all need to attract customers, keep costs down and avoid inefficiency.[22]

Despite these claims, several states have passed bills which made it illegal to sell a not-for- profit hospital to a for-profit one. Those who promote such legislation say that "for-profits" will either reduce service to patients or raise costs unnecessarily for the sole purpose of maintaining their profit.[23]

Examples of such "takeovers" of public hospitals by private corporations can be found all over the United States. One such example is the privatization of the University of Cincinnati hospital, which is being challenged now by the city of Cincinnati on the grounds that the hospital's charitable mission is not being preserved by the Health Alliance chain which bought it. Health Alliance was accused by the City of Cincinnati of being unwilling to service those not insured and of engaging in unfair labor practices towards the hospital's employees. Similarly, two major hospital systems in Texas are considering merging thereby anticipating revenues of $2.6 billion.[24]

One of the methods designed to reduce hospitalization costs has been the institution of 494 diagnosis related groups (DRGs) used by the Medicare Prospective Payment System. These DRGs are lists of diseases or disorders. Each of theses diseases or disorders has been given a number by the Medicare bureaucracy and attached to a flat amount of money Medicare will pay for treatment of that disorder or disease. The money is subject to capitation, a term used by insurance companies concerning the lump sum they pay any hospital for the treatment of a disease for each day the patients spends in the hospital. Evidently, it is in the interest of the hospital to discharge patients as soon as possible so that the hospital can keep the difference between the money given them for the care of the patient and the actual cost. In sum, the shorter the hospital stay of any patient, the more the earnings of the hospital. The longer the hospital stay, the less the profit. Obviously, then, capitation and DRGs together have reduced hospitalization costs even if these reductions are often made at the expense of the patient.[25]

Another consequence of the DRG system is that physicians are no longer in charge of the patient. Instead, accountants and business managers decide the fate of patients by evaluating the success of a surgeon by the speed with which his patients are discharged from the hospital without returning within thirty days. The business calculation behind this method of evaluating doctors is that a "good" doctor moves his patients out of the hospital before the capitation money runs out while a doctor who performs poorly is one whose patients stay too long to allow the hospital to make a substantial profit or whose patient return to the hospital so soon that their new complaint is related to the previous stay. This entire method of allowing business graduates to evaluate the work of physicians may seem preposterous to some, but is justified by the business community as being necessary in order to make a profit. It must be evident to the reader that this method must result in the early discharge of some patients who cannot survive outside the hospital or who must be readmitted in the immediate future.

The temptation to discharge the patient too soon or to give him substandard care is a matter of ethics. Therefore, the American College of Healthcare Executives has developed a "Code of Ethics". This code has been devised with the fundamental objective to "enhance the overall quality of life, dignity and well-being of every individual needing health care services; and to create a more equitable, accessible, effective and efficient healthcare system." Included in the code is a good deal of admonition concerning the relegation of financial concerns to a secondary consideration with respect to patients whose health is viewed as the first consideration. Even a minimal acquaintance with hospital administration at the end of the 20th century reveals that the priorities of hospital executives and health care managers are the reverse.[26]

III

It is no exaggeration to say that the public sees hospitals as cold, frightening and uncaring places. This is in part true because anyone would fear medical diagnosis and treatment. Nevertheless, the need to create a more caring system for patients and for staff members is very great at the end of the century.

This need has been increased as technology expands because constant changes make dealing with health care more and more impersonal and remote. Therefore, some hospitals have introduced recreational therapy, humor, massage therapy, music therapy, guided imagery, and visualization to help patients in regaining soundness of body, mind and spirit. The role of religion is also more integrated into hospital routine where "patient centered" care is considered important.[27]

"Patient-centered" care cannot be attained under the circumstances which hospitals and doctors must now face with their patients. This is true because of the ever greater encroachment of health care organizations on the hospitals and their doctors. Dr. Ira Kodner, speaking to the Annual Meeting of the American Society of Colon and Rectal Surgeons, likened the current demands made on doctors by HMOs to the demands made on German doctors by the Nazi government in the 1930s and 1940s.

Dr. Kodner, quoting Dr. Denton Cooley, showed that patients resent the high cost and increasingly impersonal nature of hospital treatment.

Dr. Kodner believes that the so-called "protection" of the public from unscrupulous physicians and the "run-away" cost of medical care is the "marching order" of managed care just as similar orders were issued by the Nazi government sixty years ago. Dr. Cooley said in that connection that "...laws should be enacted to hold administrators of health care organizations accountable for the undercare of patients."

Dr. Kodner went on to say that excellence of hospital care is now rationed with easy access for the well-off and difficult access for the sick and old. The consequences of all this are that "patients spend more time ....completing paper work than actually seeing their doctor." Even the label has changed. Patients are now called "consumers" by the HMOs which tends to depersonalize hospital care even more. Kodner not only decries the destruction of the erstwhile doctor/patient relationship but also the assault of the business mentality on the professional integrity of doctors and hospitals. That integrity is assaulted because the doctors have now been placed into a dilemma. That is, to either earn a reasonable income and keep their jobs by rationing the amount of money that may be spent on a patient's recovery or face unemployment. Kodner shows that like the German doctors under the Nazis, American doctors are compromising their values and regard for human rights because they need their income and their jobs.[28]

The questions raised by Dr. Kodner include "Should we (physicians) remain silent if dialysis is denied to the elderly? Are we prepared to accept the reality of a two-tiered system in which the wealthy receive care and the poor are denied? Should we continue to comply with the for-profit health care systems that make a millionaire a month out of venture capitalists and simultaneously drain money away from patient care and medical research?" These and other questions can only be answered if all hospital management everywhere were to unite and face these threatening issues together. That unity must at least include the following ground: 1. Medicine and nursing must not be diverted from their primary tasks: the relief of suffering, the preservation and treatment of illness and the promotion of health. 2. Pursuit of corporate profit and personal fortune have no place in caregiving, 3. permit members of health care plans to sue them directly for harm caused at the direction of such plans 4. a patient's right to a physician must not be curtailed and 5. access to health care must be the right of all." Finally, in the words of Dr. Ira Kodner, health care administrators should be told "you eat because I work."[29]

It is now of course obvious that hospitals can only insure that these five objectives are met if they change. These changes are already taking place and include first of all hospital mergers. These are taking place at a rapid rate both in the United States and Canada. This has led to a great deal of consternation in many communities as witnessed by the uproar that occurred when the board of mangers at a Lewiston N.Y. hospital sought to merge with and close a Niagara Falls, N.Y. hospital even though these two communities adjoin each other. The evidence for this emotional involvement in our hospitals are the millions of dollars annually contributed in the form of charitable donations by citizens in every American and Canadian community. Hospital closures appear to many so-called policy makers as an attractive money saving device. However, as the population of the U.S. and Canada ages, such closures will have terrible consequences for the aging populations of both countries because an ever older population will require an ever larger share of the Gross Domestic Product. Currently, the United States spends over 12% of its Gross Domestic Product on health care. The question that must be answered is: "How much more money can we spend on health care without neglecting everything else we need and must do?"[30]

Hospital patients, now called "consumers" by health maintenance organizations are changing hospitals rapidly. Today (1999) patients are frequently well educated and demanding. Among these demands are the oft repeated insistence on holistic medicine which deals with the emotional as well as physical aspects of illness and demands that each patient be treated with respect as a person, and not only as an object of this or that procedure.

The other side of the demands now made on hospitals is the need for patients to participate in holding down health care costs. For example, patients need to call their family doctor instead of going to an expensive emergency room. On the other hand, that decision may well be the result of the doctor showing anger and upset if he is called at night or at other inconvenient times. Patients need also to understand that hospitals cannot grant anyone immortality by using "heroic" measures and expensive technology when there is no hope of keeping a patient alive.

American hospitals are not only facing these challenges but are also competing with one another in attracting patients without arousing the ire of the health maintenance organizations and insurance companies. In short, hospitals need to fight for patients even as they must reduce or at least maintain costs.

The best way to do that is to treat patients with concern and kindness and to abandon the old viewpoint that the patient is merely a piece of meat upon which an operation shall now be performed. It costs nothing to be friendly and pleasant and to leave each patient with his self-respect intact. Hospitals will gain more adherents from treating patients as important people than insisting that a patient has no rights.

Such improvement between staff and patients at any hospital depends largely on the "morale" of the hospital staff. Staff can hardly be pleasant to patients if they don't feel appreciated and are not secure in their jobs. Therefore it is vital that doctors and others working in a hospital must be secure in sharing their honest opinion with bosses and administrators without being penalized. Security and a pleasant environment for those who work in a hospital go a long way toward a pleasant atmosphere for patients who, in any event, are frightened and upset over their illness and the procedures they face.[31]

However, the exact opposite is now happening at American hospitals. For example, in September of 1998 a Waterbury, Connecticut 367 bed hospital announced elimination of 150 full time positions because the hospital faces a $1 million loss as admissions dropped from 13,797 in 1997 to an anticipated 12,787 in 1998 and further reductions to 12, 400 in 1999.[32]

Likewise, New Britain General Hospital eliminated 112 positions in September of 1998 when changes in reimbursement for the Medicare and Medicaid programs cost the hospital $10.2 million.[33]

The need to reduce costs, the subsequent insecurity of the staff and the effect this has on patients creates a true dilemma for hospitals. As we have just seen, community hospitals need now to compete with for-profit hospitals who treat their patients far better than community hospitals because any business needs to treat the customer with kindness and courtesy if it hopes to make a profit and attract "repeat business." The dilemma for community hospitals is to ensure similar treatment for their "consumer-patients" even as downsizing affects the staff adversely.

IV

Nurses are particularly affected by the consequences of downsizing. Yet, nursing is without doubt the most critical factor in patient care in hospitals and in patient outcomes. Therefore it is reasonable to consider the effect that layoffs of RNs in hospitals have had on patient care. Hospitals, seeking to save money, have resorted to staff substitutions by replacing registered nurses with lesser trained personnel or with employees who have no nursing training whatever. This is occurring precisely at a time when the increasing complexity of hospital inpatient caseloads calls for more skilled nursing care.

Nursing represents the largest department in any hospital constituting around 40 percent of full time equivalent personnel and 30 percent of any hospital budget. Therefore, nursing has become the principal target of cost reduction efforts by hospital management.[34]

To make it possible to care for patients even as registered nurses are not hired or eliminated, hospitals have now appointed nurse assistants to perform a good deal of the care to be delivered to patients. These nurse assistants generally work under the supervision of one registered nurse so that registered nurses must now increasingly display management and supervisory skills. Registered nurses are now also assuming the role of case manager as "care teams" take on the responsibility for the patient in the hospital and after he has been discharged. The purpose of this reorganization of nursing is to save money and to span the boundaries between inpatient, ambulatory and community nursing. Major savings are achieved by all of these devices but particularly by the use of the so-called ancillary (anculus Latin=servant) personnel. Therefore the training of such personnel becomes a serious issue with reference to patient care. In California, for example, 99 percent of ancillary personnel have less than 120 hours of training. Only 20 percent of American hospitals require a high school diploma for appointment into an ancillary position and 88 percent of hospitals provide less than 40 hours of instruction time for those newly appointed.

Registered nurses are of course concerned that these changes have already resulted in a reduction of quality of care for patients. This may well be the case. However, there is not now (1999) a comprehensive study concerning the effects of ratios of RNs per bed on patient outcomes. It would therefore be of great help to hospital managers and patients if such a study could be provided particularly since there are those who claim that the reorganization of hospitals as indicated has actually improved patient outcomes.[35]

While there is no study concerning the effects of RNs per bed on patient outcomes, several studies have been made concerning the overall effects of hospital downsizing on surviving staff. These studies indicate first that before 1995 many hospitals had occupancy rates as high as 90% while four years later occupancy rates in many hospitals are only 50%. This decline in occupancy rates is therefore the main reason for the reduction in staff faced by nurses and others.[36]

These policies have already led to the loss of 750,000 new jobs. A survey by the American Nurses Association has shown that 60% of hospitals in all states reported layoffs of nurses. On a personal level, such layoffs create grief and anxiety not only among those deprived of their livelihood, but also among those still surviving on the staff.[37]

Several studies have shown that downsizing is traumatic for all nurses involved. A whole list of emotional consequences of the downsizing experience for nurses have been recorded by Noer who coined the word "survivor syndrome" and included distrust, fear, insecurity, depression, guilt and betrayal as only some of the emotions produced by these policies. Evidently, the morale of the survivors is greatly affected by downsizing. In addition, the work load of survivors increases as others are laid off so that that pressure and the need to do work for which many of the "survivors" have not been trained makes those still on the job unhappy and overworked. The effect on patients should be obvious.[38]

It is of course unlikely that any of these practices will be needed or will continue for much longer. Already it is evident that from now on only the most acutely ill persons will be admitted to any American hospital, there to be treated with the most sophisticated technological devices. This is another way of saying that hospitals will become large critical care units while everyone else will be placed in a sub-acute care unit or nursing home. Therefore, these nursing homes and sub-acute care units will look very much like yesterdays hospital. This will therefore mean that "when the current frenzy to restructure slows down the rate of increasingly ill patients in hospitals will necessitate even higher nurse-patient ratios."[39]

It has been argued that hospital staff are the hospital and it can easily be shown that nurses are the staff. This will become even more evident as increases in technology and a very high level of patient understanding will require nurses with more and more skill and hence more and more training.[40]

V

It should not be overlooked that the current interest in reducing the nursing staff must take into account the sporadic and volatile demand made on nurses in the course of a week or even a day. Emergency rooms are the best example of the hour-by-hour fluctuation to which the staff is subject. Yet, all units of a hospital find that patients will arrive unannounced at any time and on any day. Therefore, a unit may have 30 patients one day, 15 the next and 35 the day thereafter. A laboratory in a hospital may find that half their tests must be done between 7 a.m. and 10 a.m. and the other half are done all day.

Nurses must of course rely on various centralized services to help care for patients. This centralization leads to a great deal of waste and "orchestration" which deprives patients of nursing time and it appears, could be better achieved if support services were decentralized. "...Service centralization is akin to repairing a car's engine inside the garage but keeping the necessary tools and parts in various other areas outside the garage."[41]

More specifically, it is certain that on any one day almost all patients need one or more of the centralized services of the hospital. As a result "a multitude of hospital employees are continually occupied with the required process related orchestration–an accompanying flurry of scheduling, coordination, walking and writing activities." One result of all this activity is the employment of numerous "schedulers", "coordinators" and "dispatchers" who cost a great deal of money. Huge computer transactions are also necessary to deal with all these process-related activities.

For patients, the outcome of this centralization of services is that their treatment is dependent on the convenience of the centralized staff and not on the needs of the patient. Centralization also results in the constant moving of patients from one part of the hospital to another, thereby imposing on the patient the indignity of being shuttled around the hospital in his open-backed gown and parked in some corridor to await transfer.

Doctors are also inconvenienced by centralization as they must wait for laboratory results before making their next decision. Patients and doctors must also wait to use a respirator or some other device so that the patient has to stay in the hospital longer than would be needed if the delays did not impose these limitations on both doctors and patients.

Finally, it seems a tremendous waste to impose so many narrow job definitions on hospitals. This results in a great amount of idle time on the part of support staff, particularly clerks. For example, a central transport department clerk will sit idle because all requests have been handled and the hospital mandates this waste of money and time because the clerks job description does not allow her to do anything else even if it must be done. In short, the more the compartmentalization, the less the flexibility of each hospital employee and the greater the waste. Such waste is of course equally great in other departments. For example, a Housekeeper I may clean tile in a public area but not carpets, which is the job of a Housekeeper II. Therefore, a messy spill on a carpet will wait to be cleaned until a Housekeeper II is available even as a Housekeeper I sits around with nothing to do. In sum, hospitals could save a great deal of money, provide better patient care and relieve some of their worst economic pressures if they would change from extreme fragmentation and an unreasonable division of labor to a more efficient method of letting the same person do many things provided she is competent to do them.[42]

In view of the reduction of hospital occupancy the competition for patient volume in American hospitals has become "extraordinarily ferocious." This is particularly true in densely populated areas which have numerous hospitals all trying to survive the problems already outlined. Emergency departments are particularly involved in maintaining a competitive edge for their hospital because many people judge a hospital's efficiency only on the treatment they receive in a crisis situation in an emergency room, or ER.

That judgment may also be called "patient satisfaction" and depends on the amount of time it takes for a patient to be treated in an emergency. Other than accidents, heart attacks are the most common reason for visiting an emergency room.

Overloook Hospital in Summit, N.J. has been a leader in making emergency room visits more efficient and has won the "Best Practice" award of the Health Care Financing Administration and the American Gold Standard by the Health Care Advisory Board. One reason for naming Overlook Hospital is that the median time from the arrival to the treatment of patients was reduced from 70 minutes in 1993 to 15 minutes in 1997. This reduction in time was achieved at the Overlook Hospital Emergency department by organizing a horizontally integrated system. This new approach led to more collaboration as departmentalization decreased and people who once shared little information and seldom worked together were now working as a team.

The hospital then tracked patient satisfaction and found that the overall emergency department satisfaction score delivered by patients rose from 77.5 during the first quarter of 1996 to 86.6 during the last quarter of 1998. This increase in patient satisfaction was achieved by reducing the time to administer antibiotics to patients with pneumonia, neutropenia and fever; using bedside patient registration and reducing time to analyze x-rays from 71 minutes in 1996 to 30 minutes in 1997.[43]

All of these efforts underscore the competition which hospitals now try to meet not only by giving patients and their families more satisfaction but also by advertising. For example, Johns Hopkins Hospital, located in Baltimore, MD and one of the most established hospitals in the country, now resorts to advertising its services in New York City.[44]

Eli Ginzberg has shown that the most important changes in hospital operations now occurring are: "The increasing emphasis of both private and public sector payers on moderating the steep rises in their annual premium rates across the enrollment spectrum and the rapid expansion of 'managed care'." This method of saving money depends on assigning enrollees (patients) to designated "primary care physicians" who then authorize referrals to specialists and/or hospital care. This does indeed save money. It also jeopardizes the patients because primary care physicians cannot send very many patients to specialists or to the hospital without losing their standing as "provider" for a health maintenance organization. Fearing loss of the income that is associated with being a "provider", primary physicians try to do everything themselves, which can be disastrous for the patient.

Ginzberg next points to the development of alternative lower cost treatment sites from home care to so called "sub-acute" beds in some hospitals and the loss of freedom by patients to choose their own specialists or their own hospital. Managed-care plans send patients to those hospitals which are the cheapest even if the hospital is not equipped to deal with the patients complaint. Ginzberg further shows that hospitals are now associating with one another for the purpose of purchasing supplies. Such associations give groups more buying power and allows them to share some technological improvements such as the growth of new and larger ambulatory (walk in) facilities which therefore provide each hospital with more income.[45]

These, and many other changes in hospital utilization, management and care are already under way so that the depersonalization of medical treatment is now assured. It is questionable how long the public, i.e. the consumer of health care, will tolerate this reduction of each person to a number or less.

Looking at all this close up and as it affects the daily routine of a hospital we see that included in such a routine is the army of hospital workers who arrive each morning to staff the numerous positions needed to keep patients alive or at least treat their pain. From dealing with hopeless cancer to heart "trouble" and lung congestion to accident victims who come into hospitals at all hours and need immediate attention to the arrival of a newborn, hospitals are tremendously busy at all times. Someone brings a child who has passed out in school. Even as doctors try to discover why the child has fainted, someone else is brought into the ER because he had so severe a motor-cycle accident that 17 people work on him right away. Meanwhile, in another area of the hospital a cancerous breast is removed from a woman who would otherwise die within that month.

As all this proceeds, medical students are learning their new profession. They are told how to interview a new patient and deal with the emotional aspects of patient-doctor relationships. Pathology, meanwhile, deals with tissue from cadavers as learning devices derived from patients who have just died from pulmonary hypertension, lupus and a heart attack. Even as that death engulfs the grieving family a baby is born in that same hospital.

During all these procedures, thousands of light bulbs are used and need to be replaced. Thousands of pounds of dirty linen are cleaned involving a truly astronomical detergent bill, thousands of beds are "made" by housekeepers, thousands of rest rooms are cleaned, innumerable telephone lines are constantly busy, as the pharmacy dispenses huge amounts of doses to patients. Millions of syringes, gloves, suture needles and gowns are used annually and on a 24 hour basis as some doctors work to exhaustion in shifts from 29 to 34 hours.[46] This then, is the reality of the American hospital.

Summary

Hospitals, like all institutions, fulfill assigned functions in American society. Hospitals, were terribly infected "holes in the wall" before the discovery of penicillin. Patients, then and now, are forced to accept "role exit". Some patients in some hospitals become infected or are otherwise poorly treated. Some patients complain that they are treated like an object and not a person. These complaints have led to the "Patient's Bill of Rights" and to the establishment of patient representatives."

There has been a great increase of hospital use since the 19th century because of the invention of new "wonder drugs". As government has become more and more involved in health care, a great medical bureaucracy has developed. Patients are seldom satisfied with all this as the development of hospital mergers and the consolidation of other health facilities is occurring at an ever faster pace.

Those hospitalized for serious physical ailments will want to use the entire "high tech" approach to their problem. There are, however, patients in our hospitals who have no physical problem. We call these patients "mentally ill". It is the province of the next chapter to discuss such hospitals and review their past, present and future in America.

NOTES

[1] Diana Kendall, *Sociology in Our Times*, New York, Wadsworth Publishing Co., 1999, p. 109.

[2] Erving Goffman, *Asylums, Essays on the Social Situation of Mental Patients and Other Inmates*, Chicago, Aldine Press, 1961.

[3] Anselm Strauss, Shizuko Fagerhaugh, Barbara Suczek and Carolyn Wiener, *Social Organization of Medical Work*, Chicago, University of Chicago Press, 1985, p. 106.

[4] Helen R.F. Ebaugh, *Becoming an Ex: The Process of Role Exit*, Chicago, University of Chicago Press, 1988.

[5] Daniel F. Chambliss, *The Patient as Object*, Chicago, The University of Chicago Press, 1996, p. 127-133.

[6] Irving K. Zola, *Socio-Medical Inquiries*, Philadelphia, Temple University Press, 1983, pp. 216-217.

[7] Chambliss, *op.cit.*, pp. 148-149.

[8] Lawrence R. Phillips, *In the Name of the Patient: Consumer Advocacy of Health Care*, Chicago, American Hospital Association, 1995, p. 2.

[9] *Ibid.*, pp. 2-1.

[10] *Ibid.*, p. A2.

[11] Eric Weissenstein, "No PARCA required," *Modern Healthcare*, Vol.28, No. 15, April 13, 1998, p. 8.

[12] Donald Snook, Jr., *Hospitals, What They Are and How They Work*, Rockville, MD., Aspen Systems Corp., 1981, p.3.

[13] Morris J. Vogel, "The Transformation of the American Hospital, 1850-1920," in: Susan Reverby and David Rosner, Eds., *Health Care in America*, Philadelphia, Temple University Press, 1979, pp. 105-116.

[14] *Ibid.* p.6.

[15] Mitchell F. Rice and Woodrow Jones Jr., *Public Policy and the Black Hospital*, Westport, Conn., Greenwood Press, 1994, pp. 101-107.

[16] No Author, "U.S. Registered Hospitals: Utilization, Personnel, and Finances," in *1998 Hospital Statistics*, Chicago, Healthcare Infosource, Inc., 1998, p. 4.

[17] *Ibid.*, p.2.

[18] No Author, "Hospital Pulse," *Hospital and Health Networks*, October 20, 1998, p. 40.

[19] Sandra Yingling and S.J. Bolster, "Banking on Bonuses: 1998 Salary Survey," *Hospital and Health Networks*, Vol.72, No.17, September 5, 1998, pp. 24-27.

[20] William J. Leander, *Patients First*, Chicago, Health Administration Press, 1996, pp. 3-4.

[21] Sandy Lutz and E. Preston Gee, *The For-Profit health Care Revolution*, Chicago, Irwin, 1996, p. 171.

[22] No author, "For-profit medicine," *The Economist*, Vol.344, No. 5, August 2, 1997, p. 16.

[23] Deanna Bellandi, *"For-profits get a break" Modern Health Care*, April 13, 1998, p. 20.

[24] Mary Chris Jaklevic, "Cincinnati fights to take back control of hospital," *Modern Health Care*, Vol.28, No. 15, April 13, 1998, p. 24.

[25] No author, *Profiles of U.S. Hospitals*. HCIA, Inc. Baltimore, 1995, p. 755.

[26] Duncan Neuhauser, "American College of Healthcare Executives Code of Ethics," in Anthony R. Kovner and Duncan Neuhauser, Eds., *Health Services Management*, Ann Arbor, Health Administration Press, 1990, p. 56.

[27] Mickey L. Parsons and Carolyn L. Murdaugh, *Patient –Centered Care-A Model for Restrucering*, Gaithersburg, MD., Aspen Publications, 1994, p. 605-608.

[28] Ira Kodner, "The Patient-Doctor Relationship," *Vital Speeches*, Vol.64, No. 22, September 1, 1998, pp. 695-698.

[29] *Ibid*, p. 697.

[30] Nancy Cybulski, Jo-anne Marr, Isabel Milton and Dalton Truthwaite, *Reinventing Hospitals*, Mc Leod Publications, Toronto, 1997, p. 4.

[31] *Ibid,.*, pp. 25-26.

[32] No author, ."Hospital Cuts Jobs," *The New York Times*, Friday, September 4, 1998, p. B8.

[33] No author, *The New York Times*, Friday, September 4, 1998, p. B10.

[34] Gooloo S. Wunderlich, Frank S. Sloan and Carolyn K. Davis, *Nursing Staff in Hospitals and Nursing Homes*, Washington D.C., National Academy Press, 1996, p. 94.

[35] *Ibid.,*p. 102.

[36] T.F. Moore, "Rightsizing: Living with the new reality," *Healthcare Financial Management*, Vol. 48, No.9, 1994, pp. 49-53.

[37] Thomas Begany, "Layoffs: Targeting RNs." RN, Vol 57, No. 7, 994, pp. 37-38.

[38] David Noer, *Healing the wounds: Overcoming the trauma of layoffs and revitalizing downsized organizations*. San Francisco, Jossey-Bass, Inc., 1993.

[39] L.H. Aiken, "Transformation of the Nursing Work Force," *Nursing Outlook*, Vol.43, 1995, p. 201.

[40] Maryann F. Fralic, "How Is Demand for Registered Nurses in Hospital Settings Changing?" in Edward O'Neil and Janet Coffman Eds., San Francisco, Jossey-Bass, Inc., 1998, p. 68.

[41] Leander, *op.cit.*pp. 17-29.

[42] *Ibid.*, pp 3-29.

[43] Brad Stratton, "Overlook Hospital Emergency Department: Meeting the Competition with Quality," *Quality Progess,* Vol. 31, No.10, October 1998, p. 41.

[44] Eli Ginzberg, *Tomorrow's Hospital,* New Haven, Yale University Press, 1996, p. 129.

[45] *Ibid.*, pp. 128-142.

[46] Nicole M. Christian, "Hospital Fined for Overwork of Residents," *The New York Times,* August 21,1998, p. P6.

Chapter XII

Extra-ordinary Measures: The Mental Hospital

I

Between 1955 and 1998 the number of state hospital beds for citizens deemed "mentally ill" dropped from 339 per capita to 41. This loss of hospital beds was achieved by the closing of state mental hospital facilities during the past four decades. These closings are particularly dramatic because during those same four decades the number of Americans who are in need of professional treatment for mental disorders has risen so high that psychiatric disorders are the leading cause of hospitalization for men between the ages of fifteen and forty-four.[1]

The principal reason for this hospitalization is the excessive use of drugs, including alcohol, by a large number of Americans. Because so many Americans use substances that can clearly be defined as the causes of mental illness, our jails and prisons are filled with patients whose crime may well have to do with the use and sale of controlled substances but who are in need of mental health care, not prison.

The evidence for the shifting of mental health care from state hospitals to the penal system can be viewed by inspecting the prison statistics of the U.S. Department of Justice for 1997. There were over 1.2 million prisoners under Federal or State jurisdiction in that year. In 1997 state prisons operated at 15% to 24% above capacity and Federal prisons operated at 19% above capacity even as 23% of state prisoners and 60% of federal prisoners were incarcerated on drug offenses.[2]

As Torrey has written: "Quietly but steadily, jails and prisons are replacing public mental hospitals as the primary purveyors of public psychiatric services for individuals with serious mental illnesses in the United States."[3]

The incarceration of mental patients in jails and prisons can be seen nationwide. For example, in the San Diego County jail 14% of the 4572 male inmates and 25% of the 687 female inmates were on psychiatric medication on March 30, 1995 as then reported by the San Diego Union Tribune.[4] In King County, Seattle, Washington 160 out of 2000 inmates were found mentally ill on any given date so that that jail has become King County's largest mental institution. In Travis County, Austin, Texas 14% of jail inmates were said to be seriously mentally ill. In Miami, Florida the Dade County jail usually houses 350 people with serious mental illness and in Los Angeles 3,300 out of 21,000 inmates require mental health services every day.

Of the over 2 million Americans held in American jails or prisons or on parole about 8% or more than 162 thousand, are mentally ill. That would be about twice the number of mentally ill persons than are now in state mental hospitals on any one day. Mentally ill people are frequently abused by other prisoners, many of whom have no patience with mentally unstable and even bizarre behavior.

Some of the mentally ill in jails and prisons have not been charged with anything. They are being kept in these lock-ups only because the county has no other facility in which to keep them. These people are generally awaiting a bed in one of the state mental health facilities but have not been successful. The majority of the mentally ill in jails have been charged with minor offenses such as the man in Florida who refused to leave a motel that "God has given me."[5]

This shift of psychiatric care out of public mental hospitals at the end of the twentieth century constitutes the last of several phases in the treatment of mental patients in the United States. The first of these phases began in 1790, at the beginning of this republic, when Philippe Pinel, a French psychiatrist, and William Tuke, a British reformer conceived of an institution for mentally ill citizens they called an "asylum" or a retreat where the disturbed patient could recuperate under "wise guidance".[6]

Such a retreat was added to the Pennsylvania Hospital dating from an earlier time. Then, beginning in 1813 a number of institutions for "mentally disturbed" patients were established in several states where 85% of patients recovered in three to nine months. Only 15% became custodial patients.

In the 1840's this country first saw mass immigration arrive here from Europe. This is best understood if we consider that in 1840 the population of the United States was 17, 069,453 and that in 1850 it had risen to 23,191,876 i.e. an increase of 36%. These numbers overwhelmed the privately supported asylums so that, under the leadership of Dorothea Dix, public "mental hospitals" were established in 28 of the then existing 33 states.

In 1832 the first publicly funded hospital for the mentally ill in America was built in Massachusetts. This was called the Worcester Lunatic Asylum and represented the first separation of the well-off from the indigent mental patients as private money continued to support the former and local taxes now supported the latter. Thereafter, the public and the private systems developed differently.[7]

Shortly, however, this and similar hospitals became overcrowded. Then, treatment gave way to mere custodial care as the cost of supporting these institutions became unbearable for local communities. Numerous abuses of mental patients were documented by Dorothea Dix and others so that the New York State Legislature passed the New York State Care Act in 1890. This act shifted the cost of operating mental hospitals from local communities to the state. Such laws were subsequently passed in all states so that by 1910 the number of psychiatric hospitals rose from 200 in 1875 to over 4,000 nationwide. Likewise, the number of patients increased by 240 percent between 1903 and 1950 even though the American population only doubled during those years.[8]

Between 1875 and 1950 it was popularly believed that mental illness is incurable and that custodial care is the only means of dealing with it. However, in 1908 Clifford Beers published his very influential book *A Mind That Found Itself*. That book led to the foundation of scientific psychiatry under the leadership of Adolf Myer and the development of the mental hygiene movement with the founding of the National Committee for Mental Hygiene. That committee influenced the establishment of hospitals for the mentally ill which were dedicated to acute treatment rather than only custodial care. The committee also involved university psychiatry departments in these hospitals. The mental hygiene movement also supported alternative institutions such as child guidance clinics and outpatient facilities to deal with a variety of emotional problems in the American population.[9]

The mental hygiene movement and the experience of psychiatry during World War II led to the establishment of 1,200 American outpatient clinics for psychiatric patients by 1955. Before 1940 there were none. This growth was greatly influenced by the Mental Health Services Act of 1946 designed to help veterans of the second world war. Consequently, 25,000 community based psychiatrists practiced in the United States in 1975. New hospitals for the mentally ill were constructed in record numbers at the expense of the federal taxpayer as private insurance funds became available to support psychiatric care.

After 1960, however, deinstitutionalization became popular as the community mental health center began to take its place under the influence of "social psychiatry".

New York once more became the first to respond to this new movement with legislation when in 1954 that state enacted the Community Mental Health Services Act providing expansion of outpatient treatment. These measures were also adopted by other states so that by 1977 there were only 160,000 residents of mental hospitals in the nation. This represented a decline of 71% from 559,000 residents in 1955.

As the resident population of mental hospitals decreased and outpatient treatment increased, the cost of treating mental illness also increased. In 1993, the National Advisory Mental Health Council estimated that cost at $148 billion a year.[10]

In the main this cost represents expenditures incurred by community-based alternatives to mental hospitals. The closing of state supported mental hospitals is of course commanded by the large proportion of state budgets which are devoted to the care and treatment of the mentally ill. In New York State, six percent of the budget for 1997-1998 was spent on mental health. This despite the fact that the earnings of mental health workers also called psychiatric technicians are quite low. These 77,000 technicians were at one time called "attendants". Their earnings range mainly between $12,000 and $24,000 per year although 23% of such technicians earn between $24,000 and $33,000.[11]

Critics of mental hospitals argue that these facilities provide poor treatment not only because well trained people are unwilling to work for such low wages but also because the deteriorating physical plants cost too much to maintain even as those costs prevent the further development of community based treatment programs.[12]

Therefore, closing state hospitals has become a universal effort in all states of the union particularly since state mental hospitals cannot collect Medicaid reimbursement for patients eighteen to sixty-four.[13]

In an effort to reduce the number of residents in state mental hospitals, many seriously mentally ill people have been placed in nursing homes during the past thirty years despite the 1987 Omnibus Budget Reconciliation Act which prohibits placements in nursing homes of people with diagnoses of mental illness unless there is a clear need for nursing care. It is this last provision which makes almost all mentally ill people eligible for nursing homes and thereby again facilitates closing mental hospitals.

Becker has summarized the factors influencing decisions to close state mental hospitals. According to Becker these factors are: legislative receptiveness to change; economic impact on the community; union power; the economic interests of public mental health administrators; consensus among various interest groups; the availability of community alternatives to public mental hospitals; the expectation of funding of community based mental health agencies by the state and the federal government and the ability of other agencies to deal with dangerous persons among the mentally ill. [14]

Dangerous persons are of course those who commit violent acts before and after admission to a psychiatric facility. Several studies, beginning in the 1970's, have demonstrated that roughly 10% to 14% of patients admitted to psychiatric hospitals had attacked someone just before admission. A recent study by Tardiff *et al* demonstrated that female patients were as violent as male patients and that the characteristics of the violent attacks were the same for both sexes. These characteristics were that violence was often directed at family members; that over one third of the attacks resulted in physical injury and that friends, caregivers and even casual acquaintances could be targets of such attacks. Ninety percent of such attacks occurred outside of institutions.

The motive for such attacks may vary. However, the increased incidence of violence among female patients is undoubtedly related to an increase in substance abuse with particular reference to cocaine. There is a good deal of evidence also, that polysubstance abuse increases the risk of violence beyond that of using only a single substance such as cocaine. [15]

II

Because some psychiatric patients are violent while many are involved in the use of controlled substances the closing of public state-run mental institutions in recent years has given rise to numerous private, for-profit mental health care organizations. These private psychiatric institutions and out-patient clinics generally treat patients who are insured by Medicaid, Medicare and CHAMPUS, which is an acronym for Civilian Health and Medical Program and refers to care furnished by the federal government to former members of the armed services and their families.

Admissions of children and adolescents to these private psychiatric institutions have increased dramatically in the last decades of the 2oth century. Thus, the National Institute of Mental Health reports that in recent years admissions of people younger than 18 to private hospitals increased by 60 percent even as admissions to public hospitals declined.

Justification for this great increase in child and adolescent admissions to these psychiatric institutions usually include the argument that children and adolescents with serious mental disorders constitute a serious threat of harm to others and themselves. Yet, a thorough review of national surveys shows that fewer than one third of juveniles admitted for inpatient mental health treatment were diagnosed with acute mental disorders such as psychosis, serious depression or organic disorder associated with a need for psychiatric hospitalization.[16]

In addition, a study by Kiesler and others has shown that inpatient care is not superior to some type community based care. In addition, Kiesler *et al* showed that out-patient care is 40% less expensive than in patient care. Furthermore, a number of community-based, family-centered programs have been developed which have proven successful in treating children and adolescents while avoiding the stigma of inpatient mental health admission.[17]

In many psychiatric institutions, both private and public, children are locked alone into rooms for long periods of time. The arguments in favor of this practice are that such "seclusion" serves to remove disruptive inpatients and protect others. Further, it has been argued that seclusion of children is a re-socializing mechanism. Yet, the New York State Office of Mental Health does not allow "seclusion" as a form of therapeutic intervention. According to OMH directives, "seclusion" can only be used if it can be shown that "seclusion" is necessary to prevent serious injury to anyone. Even then, a physicians order must be written for each "seclusion" although in an emergency, temporary seclusion is allowed without such an order.[18]

It needs little imagination to recognize that anyone, locked away alone, will feel a terrible sense of helplessness and despair. Because so many children, adolescents and adults who suffer psychiatric illness were the victims of beatings and other abuse it is not surprising that seclusion is particularly problematic for individuals who have been so abused. In fact, it appears that "seclusion" is yet another form of abuse related much more to the convenience of the staff than the needs of the patient. Inspection alone reveals the relationship between duration and frequency of "seclusion" and staff/patient ratios.[19]

Not only such measures as "seclusion" but admission to mental hospitals are often unnecessary. For that reason the Juvenile Justice and Delinquency Prevention Act of 1974 prohibited states from placing dependent or neglected youths and status offenders in secure facilities such as prisons, jails, detention centers or juvenile training schools. Thereupon, some families resorted to private institutionalization because their children were rebellious or disruptive at home.[20]

Another reason for the overuse of psychiatric hospitalization of children and youths has been the refusal of most private insurance companies to pay for outpatient mental health services although many of them will pay for inpatient hospitalization. Furthermore, private practitioners will not usually see uninsured, poor patients nor will Medicaid pay for anything but prediagnosed mental disorders.

A third reason for the over-institutionalization of adolescents and children in psychiatric facilities was the Supreme Court decision in Parham v. J.R. of 1979. That decision reduced the civil rights of children with reference to involuntary commitment by allowing parental discretion together with a statement from an admitting physician as sufficient to admit a minor. Consequently, no state gives children the protection afforded adults who are involuntarily committed.[21]

Finally, the rise of investor owned for-profit hospital chains has resulted in aggressive marketing techniques by these corporations. These techniques are designed to fill their beds but are not necessarily in the best interest of their patients. These corporations market through the use of television, radio, newspaper and magazine ads promising to "fix anything." They also provide "free" mental health training for teachers in the hope of developing relationships for future referrals. These investor-owned corporations also incur higher costs than public institutions and therefore charge more and collect more money than public hospitals.[22]

Because many physicians and others believe that a good number of children, adolescents and adults have been hospitalized in psychiatric institutions without good and sufficient reason, the Select Committee on Children, Youth and Families of the House of Representatives recently held hearings on that issue. These hearings included testimony from investigators for the committee who testified that "thousands of adolescents, children and adults have been hospitalized for psychiatric care that they really didn't need. They found hospitals that hired bounty hunters to almost kidnap patients."[23]

According to that testimony psychiatrists were pressured by hospitals to alter diagnoses to increase hospital profits. Also, hospital representatives went to schools and promised "kickbacks" to counselors for referring students who had mental health insurance and who would then be hospitalized until their insurance ran out. Bonuses were paid to employees to keep the beds filled. Because military personnel and their families receive mental health benefits they have become particular targets of private, for-profit hospitals.

One example of such abuses was provided by Senator Mike Moncrief, Chairman of the Texas Senate Interim Committee on Health and Human Services. He described the case of an adolescent boy who was "apprehended at his grandparents home in Austin, Texas by employees of a private security firm." Seized by employees of the firm who pretended to be police, the boy was sent to a psychiatric hospital for a substance abuse problem he did not have. He was released only after the intervention of a state senator and an order from a judge. Investigators found other citizens who were held against their will by psychiatric hospitals after they voluntarily sought treatment for such conditions as back pain or eating disorders. Evidently, these conditions all cured "miraculously" the day their insurance ran out.

The "Select Committee" of the House also heard considerable evidence of overbilling and overcharging by private psychiatric hospitals. The director of the fraud division of the department of insurance of New Jersey, Louis Parisi testified to the committee that "health care fraud is a $16 billion to $80 billion industry." [24]

Managed care and utilization review have of course changed this dismal situation a good deal during the past several years. Long term care had already been reduced drastically as we have seen so that most insurance companies allowed only 28-30 days in-patient coverage before managed care became popular. Now, managed care is "doled out bit-by-bit a few days at a time" and depends on convincing the reviewers that hospitalization is medically necessary. [25]

In those private and public institutions which are not seeking to hospitalize anyone unnecessarily a good deal of planning is necessary before admission can proceed. In such hospitals admission procedures often seem unnecessarily delayed as families and referring sources usually act only when a crisis is upon them. These delays are produced because responsible hospital staff will evaluate a potential patient on an "out-patient" basis. This should include discussion of whether the facility provides the service needed and what eventual outcome of hospitalization is expected.

Good and sufficient treatment in an institution should include family meetings, individual psychotherapy, group meetings, psychological testing, medication and, in case of children and adolescents, school and educational achievements. Brunstetter has shown that "hospitalization should be used sparingly-for reasons other than just financial ones." Further, he writes, that in most instances more can be accomplished with a short-term hospital experience aimed at laying a sound foundation for outpatient treatment. Psychiatric hospitals have always had the same purposes. These are safety, removal from a stressful situation, evaluation and diagnosis, medication and treatment, all in the interest of restoration of self-esteem. Evidently, most individuals who enter mental hospital suffer from a self-defeating state of mind. The purpose of intervention by hospital staff therefore should be the promotion on the part of the patient of a feeling of worth and value as a person. No doubt there are many people who can benefit a great deal from reassurance and support even during a short stay in a positive and warm, personal environment in a psychiatric facility.[26]

Although the number of long term residents in mental hospitals has been greatly reduced there are nevertheless numerous Americans still in need of such services.

III

The number of managed health care plans in America has increased from 174 in 1976 to 550 in 1998. This means that in 1998 fifty-eight million people were enrolled in HMOs and another 82 million were in other types of managed health care plans.[27]

Therefore it is evident that psychiatric services are now as much under the constraints imposed by managed care as are all medical services available to Americans. As is true in other areas of health care delivery the health maintenance organizations rely on capitated health care programs as a means of reducing costs. Generally this means that insurers are now limiting inpatient psychiatric stays to 30 days with the result that there has been a significant decline in inpatient psychiatric use.[28]

Another result of the penetration of psychiatric care by health maintenance organizations has been the reduction in the number of public mental hospital beds over the past several decades and the increasing use of general hospitals as the primary source of acute inpatient psychiatric care. This means that non-profit general hospitals continue to constitute the largest component in the psychiatric hospital system despite the recent expansion of investor owned psychiatric facilities. However, a number of municipalities, notably New York City, seek to sell their municipal hospitals to private investors in the belief that the private sector is providing equivalent services and can fulfill the same responsibilities with greater effectiveness and efficiency. This belief has been challenged by a study conducted by Olfson and Mechanic and reported in the American Journal of Psychiatry. Using the National Hospital Discharge Survey, Olfson and Mechanic found that public hospitals are much more willing and likely to treat the poor, the disadvantaged and the uninsured than is true of private non-profit hospitals and proprietary hospitals. Their study shows that 39.1% of psychiatric patients in public hospitals were uninsured. Only 12.7% of such patients in proprietary hospitals were uninsured and 15.6% of patients in private non-profit hospitals were uninsured. It is therefore clear that localities cannot close inpatient psychiatric units on the assumption that non-profit and proprietary hospitals will service the uninsured and poor population. Proprietary psychiatric hospitals now serve mostly well-insured and less severely ill populations than non-profit hospitals. Patients in both proprietary and non-profit hospitals are also better insured than is true of public hospital patients.[29]

These many changes from the traditional long-term in-patient mental hospital system to the current short-term treatment system has led to a major debate between the psychotherapy profession and third party payers as to the treatment of individuals with persistent mental illness. That debate centers on those who defend the health maintenance organizations and who argue that capitated payments make costs of psychiatric hospitalization predictable without any proven reduction in quality or client satisfaction. Their opinion is based on the view that for now "health care reform is dead." This view is supported by the failure of the Clinton proposals of 1994 to be legislated by congress so that health care in the United States is now a commodity and not a right. Since fee for service is also dead and Medicaid is nearly finished as well, states are now enrolling their Medicaid clients into prepaid HMOs. Hence, publicly funded mental health services are becoming capitated systems as well. This has led to a reduction in the growth of health care expenditures as enrollment in prepaid systems is now growing by ten percent each year. Consequently it is becoming difficult to distinguish between private and public sectors because managed care enterprises are becoming heavily involved with the Medicaid population while community mental health programs are seeking commercial contracts.[30]

On the other side of the argument are those detractors of health maintenance organizations who argue that the concept of "medical necessity" will reduce effective care for those who need it the most. That argument rests on the claim that states which fund HMOs in place of community mental health centers are making the same mistake already made with de -institutionalization. That claim is that funding HMOs will again lead to a reduction of access to hospital or residential care. [31]

That access is contingent on the 5,498 mental health facilities available in the United States in 1997. Of these, only 273 were state or county psychiatric hospitals. 162 were Veterans Administration psychiatric units in veterans hospitals, 1,616 were part of general hospitals, 972 were private psychiatric facilities and the others were "free standing" outpatient organizations.[32]

These 2,475 "free standing" outpatient psychiatric clinics as well as other psychiatric facilities are available as crisis units and therefore reduce the need for the traditional inpatient beds. A study by Ash and Galletly compared the effects of brief hospitalization with standard hospitalization and found that "brief hospitalization was often preferable to longer term hospitalization." "Preferable" here means that the Ash and Galletly study found that brief hospitalization patients spent significantly less time as inpatients during a two year follow up period and showed less psychopathology and impairment in role functioning than long term hospitalized psychiatric patients.[33]

Ash and Galletly further contend with Breslow *et al* that the majority of patients admitted to short stay beds in a psychiatric emergency service showed significant improvement and did not require transfer to long term care. Such patients were mostly diagnosed as schizophrenic or suffering from "personality disorders" associated with suicidality and substance abuse. Furthermore, Ash and Galletly found that the presence of a crisis unit in a psychiatric facility enables the main psychiatric services to develop inpatient programs for their particular patient group without the demands of frequent crisis admissions.[34]

The introduction of mobile psychiatric crisis intervention is yet another means by which long term psychiatric hospitalization can be avoided. While several countries, notably the Netherlands, Italy and Great Britain have had mobile psychiatric crisis intervention since the 1920's this method is hardly known in the United States. Yet, it has been said of this service in Amsterdam that "one psychiatrist in this service is more effective than the whole personnel of a 50-bed ward."[35]

Recently, the city and county of Kalamazoo, Michigan initiated a similar program in mobile psychiatric intervention. Using a 24 hour on-site crisis intervention team including a psychiatrist, Kalamazoo experienced a dramatic decline in state hospital admissions compared to two previous years. Moreover, it was found, that as soon as the mobile crisis intervention team was withdrawn there was a sharp increase in admissions to the state hospital. This then demonstrates that the traditional, expensive, long term hospitalization method of treating mental illness is largely unnecessary and too expensive. A review of the literature reveals that many people with major mental illnesses can be treated safely and effectively with substantially less expense in settings that provide the essential functions of a hospital without some of the nonessential functions that carry high operating costs. Therefore, the effective utilization of an alternative to hospitalization depends on an effective crisis service and on an adequate hospital backup if needed.[36]

This is not to say that there are not some who do need long term hospitalization. However there are a number of mentally ill people who can be accommodated in a few hospitals or psychiatric units in general hospitals designed for the purpose of treating them on a long term basis.[37]

Before World War II there were only 37 general hospitals out of approximately 4,000 who had psychiatric units. After that war, psychiatric units in general hospitals developed considerably and reached their peak in 1970 when there were 690 such units in this country. This development was caused by the support given general hospitals by the National Institute of Mental Health in training psychiatrists and by the inclusion of mental illness under both Medicare and Medicaid in 1965. During the thirty four years after 1965 this trend was reversed as community mental health centers largely took the place of the general hospital psychiatric wards.[38]

Three reasons for that shift can be discerned. The first is economic as the cost of psychiatric treatment was shifted from the states to the federal government. The second is ideological in that the desire to treat the patient in a setting in which there is a maximum of freedom is widespread among professionals. Finally, politics dictates that government money is shifted away from inpatient to outpatient services. This shift has been made possible because such new medications as clozapine and tegretol are now available. In addition, family intervention is practiced widely as major advances in diagnosis and therapy have important implications for hospital treatment. The findings of numerous studies concerning long-term/short-term hospitalization for schizophrenia show that patients with three to sixty day hospitalization do no worse than patients with longer hospitalization, with particular reference to the risk of re-hospitalization over eighteen to twenty four months.[39]

Because so many studies have shown that longer hospitalization has no greater benefits than shorter treatment, inpatient psychiatric care has been subject to utilization management by managed care insurers. Utilization management is a cost-containment strategy. A study by Wickizer *et al* found that on average only about one third of the number of days initially requested by psychotherapists were approved by utilization managers. This was much more common in cases diagnosed as drug or alcohol dependency than in other cases. Wickizer *et al* also found that managed care made no distinction concerning individual differences at the initial request. Thus, almost all of the 2,265 cases reviewed by them show that the same number of days of treatment were approved at time of admission no matter what the diagnosis although after admission some patients were granted longer stays than others. Longer stays in any facility require a considerable amount of "paper work" by physicians and the nursing staff so that the burden of obtaining approval substantially increased the costs of utilization management, through lost nursing and physician time spent on filling out papers instead of attending to patients. It should also be noted that restrictions on in-patients increases the costs of out-patient care. Therefore, the savings imposed by managed care utilization review are not nearly as great as insurers believe or say they believe.[40]

IV

The cost of psychiatric hospitalization is very much influenced by its success since those who fail to gain from such hospitalization are most likely to enter the "revolving door" of readmission at periodic intervals. This is evident because the social "climate" in a hospital can lengthen or shorten a patient's stay and has a direct effect on his ability to stay out of the hospital after discharge. The phrase "social climate" refers to the "personality" of a setting or environment such as a family, a workplace or a treatment program. Specifically, "social climate" involves the needs of every person and the degree to which the social environment can fulfill these needs.[41]

One example of the "social climate" and its effect on patients is disagreement among staff concerning a patient's treatment. It appears that where there is such disagreement, the conflict among the staff has a direct effect on the hyperactivity of patients, which is increased as disagreements proceed and decreased once such conflict has been settled. Fiscal constraints are also part of the "social climate" and often generate low staff morale. That low morale has a further effect on the patients in the care of the staff. A third and very important example of the influence of "social climate" on psychiatric patients is the ability of any patient to adapt to the custodial situation in which the patient is confined, often against his will. Goffman called custodial facilities "total institutions" and succeeded in influencing generations of sociologists, psychiatrists and patients' rights advocates concerning the conditions in mental hospitals. Goffman's study concerning the social situation of mental patients in St. Elizabeths' Hospital in Washington, D.C. was written in the mid-1950's. At that time Goffman worked as assistant to the athletic director at that hospital and was therefore in a position to gather ethnographic data on the social life of patients in that hospital.[42]

A "total institution", according to Goffman, is one which separates inmates from outsiders and thereby delivers the inmate into the total control of the institutional management, be that a prison, a camp or a hospital. The central feature of a "total institution" is that all activities of the inmate take place in the same environment, including work, sleep, recreation and eating. Everything occurs under the eyes of the same authority and all activities, throughout the day, are scheduled without attention to human needs or the wishes of the individual. In a "total institution" a great social distance develops between inmates and staff who seek to destroy the inmates old "self" and create a new "self". Dispossessed and stripped of his former identity, the inmate is humiliated and abused. The final outcome of the depersonalization of the inmates by the staff is the adoption of the staff point-of-view by the inmates. This Goffman calls the "moral career" of mental patients. The first step in this "moral career" says Goffman is the realization by mental patients that they have been deserted by society and are now subject to any mortifying experience imposed by the staff. This includes restrictions on freedom, the loss of self-esteem, the recognition by each patient that he is nothing more than a mental case and a failure. According to Goffman, the staff inflicts on the patient the notion that the patient has behaved badly on the outside and must change his conduct if he wants to get discharged and function again among other people. Goffman also viewed psychiatry as poorly equipped to deal with mental patients because psychiatrists did not understand that behavior seen on a hospital ward differs from behavior elsewhere, that psychiatrists usually see those patients who need help the least and that patients on hospital wards tend to reject the services offered by psychiatrists. Goffman's work has been very influential in creating an image of mental hospitals in the view of the public. The scathing criticism of psychiatry and mental hospitals included in Goffman's book was influential in leading to the deinstitutionalization of thousands of patients.[43]

In the same year in which Goffman published Asylums (1961), the psychiatrist Thomas S. Szasz published The Myth of Mental Illness. That book denies that psychiatry is a branch of medicine and calls psychiatric treatment and mental illness a "double impersonation." Szasz means that mental patients who impersonate the sick role are called "hysterics" because they impersonate illness. Likewise, argues Szasz, physicians who say that they can treat such an "illness" are impersonating physicians and "play the role of the medical therapist."[44]

In a later book, entitled A Lexicon of Lunacy, Szasz argues that "Since there are no mental diseases, there can be no treatments for them." From this view Szasz concludes that the policy of involuntary hospitalization should be prevented by law. "In a free society," says Szasz, " bodily and personal self-ownership is a basic human right." Furthermore, argues Szasz, there is no line of demarcation between self injurious behavior due to mental illness and self injurious behavior not due to mental illness. Szasz also objects to the well-known argument by psychiatrists that they need to protect "insane" persons from the danger they pose to others and themselves. He claims that the psychiatric argument that they, the psychiatrists, liberate the patient from his illness is hypocrisy. He views involuntary psychiatric intervention as enslavement and writes that psychiatric coercion is not treatment but torture. Therefore, Szasz would have us all sign a Psychiatric Will, similar to a "Last Will and Testament" designed to constitute a contract between the potential psychiatric patient and the potential psychiatrist refusing or permitting involuntary hospitalization or refusing or permitting the use of drugs etc. Szasz, too, was very influential in reducing the use of mental hospitals as he concluded that the psychiatrists' power should earn "our condemnation and rejection."[45]

Condemnation of psychiatric hospitals and especially involuntary commitment does not come only from Goffman and Szasz.. It also comes from former patients such as Vic Stevenson who described his experiences in a psychiatric facility in the 1990's to the psychologist Jerome Carson. This account includes a discussion of violence by staff upon patients and by patients upon each other and upon the staff.[46]

Detractors of psychiatric institutions will find such accounts as corroboration of their beliefs. There are those, however, who say that psychiatric hospitals can succeed if they rest on some basic tenets including these: that the psychiatric ward is a social network with its own subculture influenced by staff and patients alike; that the staff can and will make an effort to identify the underlying social processes; that the staff directs these social processes so as to facilitate a positive response to the whole treatment program for psychiatric inpatients.[47]

Such lofty pronouncements need to be confronted with the reality that few mental hospital attendants can understand any of these goals, that the turnover among staff and among patients is so high that these constant personnel changes defeat the effort to achieve such goals *ipso facto* and that violence or the possibility of violence exists in all psychiatric institutions at all times.

Interpersonal conflict is of course not limited to psychiatric institutions. On the contrary, it is very common and is usually resolved through verbal means. Likewise, in psychiatric institutions such conflict needs to be resolved in a non-physical fashion. Therefore, early detection of conflict within the psychiatric community is of the greatest importance. Such early detection depends on prompt and amiable conflict resolution within the staff and on the open admission that there is conflict between patients when that does occur. Nothing is more ominous than denial that conflict exists. Such denial permits conflict to go unattended and can lead to a serious "collective explosion." Normally, conflict is resolved by democratic means. In a psychiatric hospital, however, the staff governs in an autocratic fashion because staff have the power to discharge and otherwise discipline individual patients. This is of course the certain outcome of psychiatric hospitalization which means that the individual is unable to cope with the responsibilities of daily life and has therefore entrusted his welfare to others. Patients who have a tendency to commit violence and who have exhibited violent conduct will test the limits of staff indulgence as do so many people in so many social situations anywhere. In psychiatric settings, as anywhere else, assaults are preceded by visible signs of anger and/or potential violence. Such signs include seizing another patient's belongings, making threatening gestures, verbal abuse and finally assault. In such situations the psychiatric staff can use such methods as isolation and restraint by use of seclusion which is called "the hole" when used in prisons. Restraint, as for example the use of handcuffs by police, is also used outside of psychiatric hospitals. Before such extreme measures are used on a patient who threatens to harm himself or others, several less confining methods can be used to reduce tension and avoid assault. These methods includes meeting with individuals involved in conflict; separating patients involved in conflict and restricting the level of participation of conflicting patients in the activities of the hospital. All of these measures are of course less successful in a psychiatric milieu than elsewhere precisely because antisocial people suffering from severe personality disorders are incarcerated in such hospitals so as to segregate them from the "normal" community.[48]

In view of the real possibility that some psychiatric patients may be violent in situations that would not provoke violence among "normal" people it seems unlikely that the advice of Thomas Szasz to deinstitutionalize everyone will be ever be universally applied. This is also true of patients who abuse drugs and alcohol and who are most likely to be "revolving door" patients. However, Sangueneti *et al* found that although drug use and alcohol use are most frequent among those rehospitalized, the "primary psychiatric diagnosis, and not drug or alcohol use, is the critical determinant of hospitalization." Therefore they concluded that "treatment for alcoholism and substance abuse will not in itself decrease the number of admissions to acute psychiatric inpatient units."[49]

Hence it is reasonable to speculate that it is the policy of deinstitutionalization which is itself responsible for the high incidence of "revolving door" patients because some former patients are unable, for emotional reasons, to deal with life on the outside for very long. According to a study by Haywood etc. al., money problems, housing problems and failure to comply with community treatment are also involved. These researchers discovered that alcohol/drug problems and medication non-compliance are the chief causes of rehospitalization and that these problems affect depressed patients more than any others.[50]

In a study of 255 patients Lyons *et al* found that 38% of patients were readmitted to psychiatric hospitals within a six months period after discharge. Patients readmitted were more disturbed in their behavior than were those who remained outside the hospital. Readmitted patients in the Lyons study were less likely to be engaged in leisure time activities than those not readmitted. The Lyons study and several others all found that patients with schizophrenia were more likely to be readmitted than those not suffering from that disability.[51]

V

Work with schizophrenic patients is therefore inevitably part of employment in a psychiatric hospital. Therefore it is vitally important to consider how the staff can function adequately in a psychiatric setting. Few studies have been made of this issue. However, Corrigan, Holmes and Luchins investigated "burn out" among state hospital psychiatric staff. They found that such "burn-out" is significantly associated with generalized anxiety, low self esteem and self doubt. Consequences of "burn-out" are a high rate of absenteeism, the development of significant health problems and difficulty in dealing with patients.

Corrigan *et al* found that staff members with large and satisfactory collegial support suffer burnout less frequently than those without such support. Similarly, a friendly and supportive attitude by management reduced "burn-out." With reference to the Maslach Burnout Inventory, it is precisely depersonalization which has considerable influence on "burn-out" together with emotional exhaustion and a lack of personal accomplishments. In the Corrigan study "burn out" was correlated with high anxiety and with poor health and with a negative job attitude. That same study found that support from colleagues and interested peers reduced the risk of "burn out" and that this was even more true among staff who perceived administrators as helpful and supportive.[52]

Therefore administrators of psychiatric facilities need to be well acquainted with a knowledge of group theory upon which so much work with inpatients in psychiatric hospitals depends. All administrators need to deal with decision making, the distribution of information and, most important, the ability to induce a positive and cooperative attitude among staff and inmates. Innumerable studies of management have shown that merely giving orders is a useless and even counter-productive method of administration and management. According to Barnard who wrote the classic study of executive functions over sixty years ago, an order given is not necessarily an order obeyed. Barnard promoted the acceptance theory of authority to the effect that organizations are cooperative systems. This means that informal networks, more than authoritative structures, serve as a means of communication and cohesion among individuals. This can be observed in any organization and certainly in psychiatric institutions where workers engage in any behavior which will support their own needs, particularly if there is a lack of congruence between the demands of the organization and the needs of the worker.[53]

A number of theories of management have been proposed over the years since Taylor first developed the "science" of management. These theories included Max Weber's classical organization theory, behavioral management theory as initially developed by Roethlisberger and Dickson at the Hawthorne Plant of the General Electric Co. and the work of Philip Zimbardo which demonstrated that prison violence (and hence hospital violence) is rooted in the social character of the institution itself and not in the personalities of the staff or the inmates.[54]

If it can be kept in mind that the social character of the institution and not any one person or persons is most likely responsible for violence or other problems in a psychiatric setting then the need for administrators to assign "blame" will at least be diminished. Reducing the assignment of "blame" will permit a much more open work environment in which administrators can elicit the cooperation of staff by gaining cooperation instead of demanding cooperation without success. It needs to be repeated here that authority can hardly succeed in a mental hospital but that staff cooperation can and does succeed.

The truth is that a hospital's formal structure does not truly reveal how decisions are made and how authority is managed. Informal structures, not formal charts of organization, are the key to understanding any organization, be that an army, a university, or a mental hospital. Such characteristics as race, gender, ethnicity and religion generally have far more influence on the decision making process than formal lines of authority. Yet, precisely these attributes are hidden and seldom mentioned and even denied. Therefore, the experienced mental hospital administrator will recognize what is happening "behind" the formal structure.[55]

In recent years, with the advent of managed care, the formal structure and the formal goals of mental hospitals have been even more challenged than ever before because the staffs of all hospitals and particularly the staffs at state mental hospitals has been forced to spend an extraordinary amount of time on paperwork which hardly helps the patient and seems unproductive to many. A study conducted by Corrigan, Hess and Garman found that the average psychologist working at one of 12 midwestern state hospitals reported that one quarter of his work consists of providing documentation other than work reflecting the psychologists expertise. That means that the paperwork here mentioned does not include filling out test forms or writing up test batteries. These psychologists also agreed that those with lesser formal training, holding the master's degree, did the same work as those holding a doctorate. Therefore, administrators need to examine whether spending large amounts of time on paperwork and little time on patient treatment is an effective way to use highly trained psychologists in mental hospitals.[56]

Unreasonably high case loads are an additional impediment to effective clinical work with patients. Thus, some physicians face case loads of up to 50 in acute care settings and long-term caseloads in the hundreds. Pelonero *et al* have demonstrated that the average time these large caseloads allow a therapist to spend with each patient is 19.1 minutes or less. Anyone can recognize that this lack of attention to the needs of the hospitalized patient almost dooms the organization to failure if it is believed that mental hospitals should and can provide more than just custodial care. [57]

Mental hospitals have generally been isolated from the community and have seldom functioned in a continuum with other psychiatric services. Hence, patients who leave a psychiatric hospital are rarely connected to that hospital after their discharge and must therefore live in two worlds even as they feel they do not belong to either. Sociologists have called such people "marginal men" referring to persons who simultaneously share the life of two different groups. Such marginality results in stigmatization. Here a stigma is defined as a sign or a social attribute that so devalues a person's social identity that it disqualifies that person from social acceptance.[58]

It is this stigmatization which causes a good number of former mental hospital patients to fail in the community and to be forced to return to the hospital. Therefore, hospital aftercare needs to involve the family of the erstwhile patient and show them the advisability of not holding very high expectations as to the patient's posthospital performance. Furthermore, families need to know that repeated hospitalization will probably do the patient more harm than good. This may be a hard lesson to learn because many families run out of patience with the bizarre conduct of those suffering from acute emotional disturbance. In addition there are more and more Americans who have become victims of Alzheimer's disease, affecting almost only the old. As the average age of the American population rises, old age symptoms also increase. More and more Americans are therefore faced with the need to deal with these old age phenomena, including all kinds of emotional and mental disturbances. Now, more than 5% of Americans over the age of 65 are living in nursing homes. That percentage increases with advancing age. Nursing homes house not only the old. There are people who spend a limited amount of time in nursing homes because they need to recover from a serious operation or because they have become the victims of an accident. Therefore we shall next discuss the over 13,000 nursing homes now operating in the United States who are serving more than 1.7 million people a year.[59]

Summary

The closing of state mental hospitals has come at a time when there is an increase in drug use so that the need for treatment for the emotionally ill is greater than ever. Therefore, jails and prisons are now being used to compensate for some of the beds no longer available in mental hospitals. These mental hospitals have existed ever since the founding of the American republic and have undergone several phases of organization and use during the past two hundred years.

A good number of the patients in psychiatric institutions are children brought there by parents who could not deal with their children's rebelliousness or substance abuse. In view of the pressures placed on psychiatric institutions by government policies and managed care, some private hospitals have resorted to such "white collar" crimes as overbilling and confining young people against their will.

Brief hospitalization has taken the place of long term care. This appears to cut costs somewhat, although the "revolving door" in mental hospitals has admitted numerous patients several times at a considerable cost. Both Erving Goffman and Thomas Scacz have written books attacking state mental hospitals. Such hospitals house a good number of violent persons who need to be controlled by the administration with the help of the staff. Mental hospital patients carry a stigma which also attaches to those who are mentally ill by reason of old age. That stigma carries over to nursing homes which shall be the topic of our next chapter.

NOTES

[1] Ronald C. Kessler, "Lifetime and 12 Month Prevalence of DSM-III-R Psychiatric Disorders in the United States: Results of the National Comorbidity Survey." *Journal of the American Medical Association*, Vol. 271, March 2, 1994, p. 654 D.

[2] U.S. Department of Justice, Bureau of Justice Statistics, "Prison Statistics," November 22, 1998, p. 1.

[3] E. Fuller Torrey, "Jails and Prisons-America's New Mental Hospitals," *Americna Journal of Public Health*, Vol. 85, No. 12, December 1995, p .1611.

[4] Cahrles Rother, "For jails and the mentally ill, a sentence of growing stress," *San Diego Union Tribune*, March 30, 1995.

[5] Torrey, *op.cit.*, p. 1612.

[6] John P. Docherty, "Two Hundred Years of Inpatient Psychiatry," in: John P. Docherty, Editor, *Inpatient Psychiatry in the 1990's.* San Francisco, Jossey-Bass, 1994, pp. 5-6.

[7] Albert Deutsch, *The Mentally Ill in America: A History of their Care and Treatment from Colonial Times.* New York, Columbia University Press, 1937.

[8] J.P. Morrissey and H.H. Goldman, "Cycles of Reform in the Care of the Chronically Mentally Ill," *Hospital and Community Psychiatry*, Vol. 35, 1984, pp. 785-793.

[9] Docherty, *op.cit.*, p.9.

[10] *Ibid.*, p.12.

[11] Bureau of Labor Statistics, "National Occupational and Wage Data," December 8, 1998, p. 1.

[12] Fred W. Becker, "The Politics of Closing State Mental Hospitals: A Case of Increasing Policy Gridlock," *Community Mental Health Journal*, Vol. 29, No. 2, April a993, p.103.

[13] Charles C. Feis, C.T. Mobray and Paul J. Chamberlain, " Serving the chronic mentally ill in state and coammunity hospitals," *Community Mental Health Journal*, vol.26, 1990, pp. 221-232. vol.26,

[14] Becker, *op.cit.* p.

[15] Kenneth Tardiff, Peter M. Marzuk, Andrew C. Leon, Laura Portera and Cindy Weiner, "Violence by Patients Admitted to a Private Psychiatric Hospital," *American Journal of Psychiatry*, Vol. 154, No. 1, January 1997, p.88.

[16] Mary Keegan Eamon, "Institutionalizing Children and Adolescents in Private Psychiatric Hospitals," *Social Work*, Vol.39, No. 5, September 1994, pp. 588-594.

[17] C.A. Kiesler, "Public and professional myths about mental hospitalization," *American Psychologist*, Vol. 37, 1982, pp. 1323-1339.
[18] New York State Office of Mental Health, *OMH Report of the Task Force on Restraint and Seclusion*, Albany, N.Y. 1993.
[19] Kathleen A. Earle and Sandra L. Forquer, " Use of Seclusion with Chidren and Adolescents in Public Psychiatric Hospitals," *American Journal of Orthopsychiatry*, Vol.65, No.2, April 1995, pp. 238-244.
[20] 42 U.S.C. 5601.
[21] L.A. Weithorn, "Mental hospitalization of troublesome youth: An analysis of skyrocketing admission rates," *Stanford Law Review*, Vol. 40, 1988, pp. 773-838.
[22] Eamon, *op.cit.* p. 592.
[23] Select Committee on Children, Youth, and Families. House of Representatives. One Hundred Second Cogamess, Second Session, "Psychiatric Treatment Bilks the System and Betrays our Trust," U.S. Government Printing Office, 1992.
[24] *Ibid.* p.45..
[25] Richard W. Brunstetter, *Adolescents in Psychiatric Hospitals*, Springfield, Illinois, Charles C. Thomas, 1998, p. 33.
[26] *Ibid.* p.37.
[27] John W. Wright, Editor, *The New York Times 1998 Almanac*, The New York Times, N.Y. 1997, p. 383.
[28] Richard Frank, Donald Salkever and Samuel Sharfstein, "A new look at rising mental health insurance costs," *Health Affairs*, Vol. 10, 1991, pp. 116-123.
[29] Mark Olfson and David Mechanic, "Mental Disorders in Public, Private Nonprofit and Proprietary General Hospitals," *American Journal of Psychiatry*, Vol. 153, No.12, December 1996, pp. 1613-1619.
[30] Bentson H. McFarland, "Ending the Millenium," *Community Mental Health Journal*, Vol.32, No.3, June 1996, pp. 219-220.
[31] R. Thomas Riggs, "HMOs and the Seriously Mentally Ill-A View from the Trenches," *Community Mental Health Journal*, Vol. 32, No.3, June 1996, pp. 213-217.
[32] "Mental Health Facilities: Summary by Type of Facility," *117th Statistical Abstract of the United States 1997*, Table 205.
[33] David Ash and Cherrie Galletly, "Crisis Beds: The Interface Between the Hospital and the Community,"
International Journal of Social Psychiatry, Vol.43, No.3, Autumn 1997, pp. 193-198.

[34] Richard E. Breslow, B.I. Klinger and B.J. Erickson, "Crisis hospitalization on a psychiatric emergency service," *General Hospital Psychiatry*, Vol.15, 1993, pp. 307-315.

[35] Harold Miller, "The Health Service in Amsterdam," *International Journal of Social Psychiatry*, Vol.2, 1956-1957, p.145.

[36] William H. Sledge, et.al. "Day Hospital/Crisis Respite Care Versus Inpatient Care, Part II: Service Utilitzation and Costs, *American Journal of Psychiatry*, Vol. 153, No.8, August 1996, p.1074.

[37] Georges R. Reding and Michael Raphelson, "Around-the-Clock Mobile Psychiatric Intervention: Another Effective Alternative to Psychiatric Hospitalization," *Community Mental Health Journal*, Vol.31, No.2, April 1995, pp179-187.

[38] Charles A. Kiesler and Celeste Simpkins, *Hospitaization for Mental and Other Disorders*, New York, Plenum Press, 1993, pp.22-23.

[39] Ira D. Gluck, "Unbundling the Function of an Inpatient Unit," in: John P. Doherty, Ed., *Inpatient Psychiatry in the 1990s*. San Franciso, Jossey-Bass, 1994, p. 38.

[40] Thomas M. Wickizer, Daniel Lessler and Karen M. Travis, "Controlling Inpatient Psychiatric Utilization Through Managed Care," *American Journal of Psychiatry*, Vol.153, No. 3, March, 1996, pp. 339-345.

[41] Rudolf H. Moos, *Evaluating Treatment Environments*, New Brunswick, N.J., Rutgers University Press, 1997, p.24.

[42] Ervin Goffman, *Asylums: Essays on the Social Situation of Mental Patients and Other Inmates*. New York, Doubleday-Anchor, 1961.

[43] Raymond M. Weinstein, "Goffman's *Asylums* and the Total Institution Model of Mental Hospitals," *Psychiatry*, Vol., 57, No. 4, November 1994, pp. 348-367.

[44] Thomas S. Szacz, *The Myth of Mental Illness*, New York, Dell Publishing Co., 1961, p. 306.

[45] Thomas S. Szacz, *A Lexicon of Lunacy*, New Brunswick,N.J., Transaction Publishers, 1993, pp. 159-183.

[46] Vic Stevenson and Jerome Carson, "The Pastoral Myth of the Mental Hosptial: A Personal Account," *International Journal of Social Psychiatry*, Vol.41, No.2, Summmer, 1995, pp. 147-151.

[47] Manoel W. Penna, "The Effects of the Milieu on Assaults," in:John R. Lion and William H. Reid, Eds, *Assaults Within Psychiatric Facilities*, New York, Grune and Stratton, 1983, p. 299.

[48] *Ibid.*, p.305.

[49] Vincenzo Sanguineti, Stephen Samuel, Stephen L. Schwartz and Mary Robeson, "Retrospective Study of 2,200 Involuntary Psychiatric

Admissions and Radmissions," *American Journal of Psychiatry*, Vol.153, No.3, March 1996, pp. 392-396.

[50] Thomas W. Haywood, Howard M. Kravitz, Linda S. Grossman, James L. Cavanaugh, John M. Davis and Dan A. Lewis, "Predicting the "Revolving Door" Phenomenon Among Patients With Schizophrenia, Schizoaffective, and Affective Disorders," *American Journal of Psychiatry*, Vol. 152, No. 6, June 1995, pp. 856-851.

[51] Cathy Owen, Valerie Rutherford, Michael Jones, Christopher Tennant and Andrew Smallman, "Psychiatric Rehospitalization Following Hospital Discharge,", *Community Mental Health Journal*, Vol.33, No. 1, February 1997, pp. 13-24.

[52] Patrick W. Corrigan, E. Paul Homes and Daniel Luchens, " Burn-out and Collegial Support in State Psychiatric Hospital Staff," *Journal of Clinical Psychology*, Vol.51, No.5, September, 1995, pp. 703-710.

[53] Chester Barnard, *The Functions of the Executive*, Cambridge, Harvard University Press, 1938.

[54] Max Weber, *Economy and Society*, Berkeley, The University of California Press, 1978. See also: Frederick J. Roethlisberger and William J. Dickson, *Management and the Worker*, Cambridge, Harvard University Press, 1939 and Philip G. Zimbardo, "Pathology of Imprisonment," *Society*, Vol.9, April 1972, pp. 4-8.

[55] John A. Talbott, Robert E. Hales and Stuart L. Keill, *Textbook of administrative psychiatry*, Washington, D.C., American Psychiatric Press, 1992, pp. 3-30.

[56] Patrick W Corrigan, Larry Hess and Andrew N. Garman, "Results of a Job analysis of Psychologists Working in State Hospitals," *Journal of Clinical Psychology*, Vol. 54, No.1, 1998, pp. 11-18.

[57] Anthony L. Pelonero, Richard L. Elliot, Jack W. Barber and Al Best, "Physician Caseload at Public Mental Institutions," *American Journal of Psychiatry*, Vol. 153, No.3, March 1996, pp. 429-431.

[58] Erving Goffman, *Stigma: Notes on the Management of Spoiled Identity*,Englewood Cliffs, N.J., Prentice Hall, 1963.

[59] William Michaux, *The First Year Out*, Baltimore, Johns Hopkins University Press, 1969, pp. 153-160.

Chapter XIII

The American Nursing Home

I

There are 21,000 nursing homes in the United States. These "homes" care for more than 1.8 million Americans each year. This large number of patients is derived primarily from our ever increasing life expectancy. Although the phrase "life expectancy" refers to the number of years a new-born infant is expected to live, it is salient to underscore here that at this writing (1999) the average length of life in the United States is 76 years. Since an American who is that old can expect to live yet another 11 years it is evident that the needs of old age must be addressed in this country by furnishing 35 million, or 12.6 percent of the U.S. population the help this population needs.

There are now about 4.3 million Americans over age 85 and among these, 72,000 people who have reached age 100 or more. It is noteworthy that there are only 70 men for every one hundred women in the segment of the population now over age 65. Hence, the number using nursing home care is ever rising as those over age 65 have a 44% chance of spending time in a nursing home. Of course, not all nursing home patients are of an advanced age. Accidents, strokes and a variety of operations lead some younger folks to recuperate in nursing homes. Nevertheless, the vast preponderance of nursing home patients are there for the rest of their lives so that the nursing home is truly the final station before the grave for many Americans.[1]

The cost of nursing home care is about $74 billion each year. Fifty-eight percent of that cost is paid by Medicare and Medicaid, i.e., the taxpayer. Personal savings and social security benefits pay the other 42 percent. Included in that cost are considerable expenditures for salaries. Thus, 62% of nursing home administrators earn $33,000 to over $125,000 a year. Nursing home aides, orderlies and attendants generally earn between $12,000 and $21,000 annually. This becomes so very expensive because nursing homes need to be staffed 24 hours a day on every single day throughout the year by 1.3 million full time equivalent personnel. In addition, like hospitals, nursing home utilities and other expenses continue at all times as well. [2]

As a consequence the average cost of nursing home care was $41,000 per year in 1997. There were at that time many nursing homes which charged a great deal more than that. Hoping to avoid such expenditures, many senior citizens have given their assets to their children so that Medicaid, i.e., the taxpayer, would pay their nursing home bills for them. Medicaid is a state-run health subsidy for the poor. According to the law governing Medicaid eligibility, a senior citizen can give his assets to adult children or anyone else but must then wait three years from the time of that disposition of the assets until he applies for Medicaid. Because this law is so difficult to enforce the director of the Health Care Finance Administration which administers Medicaid seeks to have this law repealed.[3]

It should also be noted here that the states which help pay the bills for most patients in nursing homes demand repayment of nursing-home costs paid by Medicaid after the patient has died. To collect such repayments, states will put liens on the homes of deceased Medicaid patients even if their children continue to live there. Some states make claims against other property of the deceased including bank accounts. Each State runs its own Medicaid program so that these "pay-back" requirements differ from state to state.[4]

Medicaid pays nursing home operators about $82 per day compared to the $125 per day now charged private pay patients. This constitutes a difference of 66% and led at least one large corporate nursing home chain to evict its Medicaid patients until the State of Kentucky fined that nursing home operator $260,000. Some states, notably California and Tennessee, have laws prohibiting the eviction of nursing home residents. Senator Bob Graham of Florida has announced his intention of seeking federal legislation to prohibit the eviction of Medicaid patients from nursing homes and to force those homes who participate in the higher rate Medicare program to accept Medicaid patients.[5]

Although the number of nursing home patients increased rapidly before 1985, the National Nursing Home Survey of 1995 found that during the decade then ending the number of nursing home residents had risen only 4%. Residents of nursing homes are predominantly white and 72% of nursing home residents are female. The number of nursing homes had decreased 13% between 1985 and 1995 while the number of beds had increased 9%. During that same decade, 1985-

1995, the population of the United States aged 65 or older grew eighteen percent.

Most nursing homes, i.e., 66% are operated for profit. There is however, a shift from proprietary homes to corporate, chain nursing homes which now constitute over half of all nursing homes in the United States.[6] This growth in corporate operated chain nursing homes is not only progressing because proprietary homes are selling out to corporate operators but because several of the large chains have merged to form a few super-chain corporate nursing home owners. For example, in June of 1998 Health Care and Retirement Corporation acquired Manor Care Inc. for stock then valued at $2.36 billion "thus creating the largest and most profitable company in its industry." The new company will have about 295 nursing homes, 76 outpatient clinics, 116 rehabilitation centers and 47 "assisted care facilities" located in 32 states.[7]

These mergers were in part dictated by necessity as more stringent Medicare reimbursement policies took effect on July 1, 1998 as a consequence of the passage by Congress of the Balanced Budget Act of 1997. Prior to July 1998 Medicare paid nursing home operators on the basis of nursing care costs. Now, Medicare pays a per diem fee. Medicare now also penalizes hospitals for discharging patients too quickly. Since many of those so discharged were sent directly to nursing homes, this shift in policy decreases the number of applicants for nursing home beds.

In an effort to reduce spending for home health care Medicare has undertaken to reduce payments for care at home by $16 billion during the five years ending in 2003. These cuts have led to considerable losses for the biggest home health care corporations. Medicare is also seeking to save $9.5 billion from changes in skilled nursing payments. That program cost the taxpayer $12.2 billion in 1997 and constituted 10% of the nursing home industry's income that year.[8]

The Health Care Financing Administration which administers both Medicaid and Medicare spends $30 billion a year on nursing home care. This permits that government agency to deal with the many complaints concerning sub-standard nursing homes found all over this country as incorporated into a report by the General Accounting Office and submitted to the Senate Special Committee on Aging in the summer of 1997. The purpose of that report was to assess compliance with the rules adopted by Congress in 1995 following these complaints. These rules are to be enforced by the states. Included in the report is the recommendation that a national registry be established listing employees convicted of abusing nursing home residents and requiring facilities to conduct criminal background check on potential employees.

This recommendation came about as it was revealed that people with histories of serious criminal conduct were given jobs as caregivers for the old. Patient advocates have long complained of crimes against the nursing home residents. Chief among these crimes is theft. In a questionnaire included in a study by the sociologist Diana Harris, ten percent of nursing home workers say that they saw nursing home workers steal jewelry, money and other items from residents. In a similar study carried out in Texas it turned out that one half of the male employees of one nursing home had arrest records and one quarter had felony convictions.[9]

Now, several states have adopted tough laws which permit inspectors to level criminal prosecution and fraud charges on nursing home owners, including national chains for neglecting patients and overcharging the government for care not given. For example, in Michigan the attorney general brought charges against Horizon/CMS Health Care Corp. for tolerating avoidable bed sores and failing to provide adequate nutrition. In addition the corporation is accused of destroying medical records to hide incidents adversely affecting their patients. In Philadelphia the government alleges that the needs of several diabetic patients were neglected in one facility and that in another home a patient was scalded to death. Federal law requires that health care providers convicted of crimes related to patient abuse and neglect be expelled from Medicare and Medicaid for five years. Two thirds of nursing home revenue is derived from those two programs so that the financial losses for those so convicted are likely to put such homes out of business.[10]

Not only government agencies, but juries in civil cases have given punitive damages to patients who have been injured or neglected in nursing homes. An example is the more than $70 million awarded a patient in one of the Beverly Enterprises nursing homes in California who broke her hip as a result of negligence on the part of nursing home employees. Beverly Enterprises owns 569 facilities nationwide. Likewise, the family of Charles Barnes, a dementia patient, was awarded $6.2 million by a Florida jury after he drowned in a pond because he had left the nursing home undetected. Other allegations against nursing homes involve sexual assaults, beatings and gross neglect.[11]

In view of these allegations and conditions in some nursing homes together with the widespread wish of many old Americans to stay in their own homes or at least avoid incarceration in a nursing facility, home care has become an ever more acceptable alternative to nursing homes.

In addition to these wishes, the cost of nursing home care makes it impossible for many senior citizens to even consider entering a nursing home. Those who seek to rely on Medicare for nursing home residence soon find that they must pay a $760.- deductible fee themselves and that thereafter they are fully covered for only 60 days. Medicare also pays all expenses of a hospital stay up to 20 days.

Home care is also covered by Medicare although it is restricted to those who are "homebound" and in need of intermittent care that only a licensed nurse can provide. Medicare also covers dialysis machines, wheelchairs, respirators, and other equipment as long as a doctor certifies that the equipment is medically necessary. Medicare also pays for home health aides who help bathe, dress and feed a patient. These combined services may be used for 35 hours a week for a two month benefit period which a doctor can renew indefinitely. Generally, doctors allow patients to have these benefits for 25 hours a week. Therefore, the very sick who need around-the-clock care must be able to spend $1,500.- per week as home health aides earn $7 to $15 per hour and nurses receive from $20 to $60 an hour. These benefits do not apply to that 10% of patients who suffer from Alzheimer's disease because that disease leaves the patient in good physical condition even as the brain of an Alzheimer's patient degenerates.[12]

Because the cost of Medicare is so high even as so many Americans cannot afford nursing home care themselves, Congress appointed a National Bipartisan Commission of the Future of Medicare as mandated by the Balanced Budget Act of 1997. That commission is dealing with projected income rates and cost rates for the hospital insurance program under Medicare in an effort to balance income and outlays until the year 2010. That mission was achieved by the Balanced Budget Act of 1997 but needs far more consideration because the number of beneficiaries will increase more rapidly than the labor force after 2010, particularly because after 2010 life expectancy will deplete the hospital insurance trust fund as it is now funded.[13]

II

It has been estimated that slightly more than one third of the population of the United States will be admitted to a nursing home at some time during their lives.[14]

It is therefore of interest to know what motivates so many Americans to enter a nursing home. First among the factors motivating Americans to enter such a "home" is their health status. Medical conditions such as cancer, stroke, fracture or neurological impairment increase the chances of entering a nursing home considerably. Hence, the more severe the impairment the greater the chances of admission to a nursing home. Among those whose impairments interfere with activities of daily living, such a dressing, toileting, taking medication, meal preparation and eating, the odds of entering a nursing home are three times greater than among those without such impairments

Likewise, old people with moderate to severe cognitive impairment, even without activities-of-daily-living-impairment were three times more likely to be admitted to a nursing home than old people without cognitive impairment. Evidently, those who suffer both kinds of impairment are even more likely to enter a nursing home.[15]

There were more than 4 million Americans age 85 or more in 1998. These are now the fastest growing segment of our population and among them there are some who have reached 100. These very old people are almost all in nursing homes because they are unable to take care of themselves. This means that these very old people are usually incontinent and often suffer from dementia or cognitive impairment. Therefore, extreme old age is another reason for entering a nursing home.[16]

Relationships to other people are also important in promoting entry into a nursing home. Those living alone are more likely to be admitted to a nursing home than those living with others. For men, the absence of a spouse is strongly related to admission to a nursing home. Contact with children or other family members does not reduce the chances of male admissions to a nursing home. Women, however, are less likely than men to enter a nursing home if they have contact with at least one family member, whether a spouse, a child or someone else. The reason for the reduction of admissions to nursing homes for those old people who have contact with a family member is that such family are likely to help the old with social support and physical tasks and often furnish the old with a place to live.[17]

Loneliness is yet another reason for entering a nursing home. Loneliness should not be confused with being alone. It is entirely possible for some people to be surrounded by family and friends and yet feel lonely. There are others who are indeed alone in that they live alone and have been single for years and yet do not feel lonely. Loneliness has been defined as "an unpleasant and distressing experience that is caused by the subjective assessment that one or more aspects of one's relationship with others are unsatisfactory." It appears therefore that intimate relationships have a lot more to do with loneliness than frequency of visits or 'phone calls.[18]

There are therefore some old people who seek to avoid the feeling of loneliness by entering a nursing home with the expectation of enjoying the companionship of others in the home. Because loneliness can lead to depression and depression can mimic dementia it is possible that some patients will be seen as demented when in fact their condition is caused by depression. Relatives may well conclude that an old person among them can no longer take care of himself because depression increases the burden on the care-givers of the old. If such care-givers feel they cannot or will not deal with the patients depression, the likelihood of entering a nursing home increases. Loneliness is of course also associated with deterioration of physical health.

Therefore, those who live in rural areas where fewer services are available are less likely to be receiving assistance from a care provider than are urban dwellers concerning the same disabilities. Although rural areas have fewer services than urban areas, this is not true of nursing homes. On the contrary. Research has shown that rural areas have a larger number of nursing home beds than urban areas, per capita, and that a larger proportion of non-metropolitan elders reside in rural long-term facilities than is true of such urban facilities.[19]

Because of the underdevelopment of in-home and community based services to the old in rural areas the ability of rural residents to maintain their independence is diminished and therefore the rural old are more dependent on nursing homes at an earlier age than is true of urban dwellers.[20]

A second reason for the entrance of rural dwellers into nursing homes at an earlier age than is true of urban dwellers is that the isolation of the urban nursing home resident is much greater than is true of rural nursing home residents. Because the boundary between the community and its nursing homes is much more permeable in rural areas than in urban settings, rural people have a more positive attitude towards nursing homes than do city people. In fact, rural people are much more likely to include nursing home residents in their community activities than is true of city residents so that this inclusion alone permits more rural aged and nursing home residents to make a successful nursing home adjustment.[21]

This means that although aging is a predictable and inevitable process there are some who can minimize the negative effects of the aging process and can therefore undergo "successful aging" as contrasted to "usual aging." A considerable body of research supports the common observation that those who remain productive at any age are far more likely to undergo "successful" aging in that they remain involved in various activities and continue to have control over their lives than those who are not productive. This observation also applies to nursing home residents. Therefore it is not surprising that nursing homes which permit residents more control over something will be more successful in managing residents who are depressed, confused or combative. Even so simple a task as caring for a plant or deciding when to watch a movie "have been shown to have a dramatic effect on residents' psychosocial adjustment by improving their sense of control."[22]

III

Whatever the reasons for entering a nursing home may be, the principal concern of patients as well as their relatives with respect to nursing home care is the well being of those who must live in a nursing home. An immense literature had developed concerning nursing home living and that indicates that the prospect of having to live in a nursing home is very much on the mind of millions of Americans even as their parents and grandparents are already residents there.

It is for that reason that the Omnibus Budget Reconciliation Act of 1990 included a "Resident Assessment Instrument" designed to measure satisfaction of nursing home residents with their nursing home. To enforce this provision, research nurses have been employed. These research nurses visit nursing facilities for 4 days. While on the premises, research nurses collect data through interviews with residents, interviews with multiple shifts of staff caregivers and through review of medical records, including physicians' orders, treatment plans, nursing progress notes and medication records. The assessments of nursing homes by research nurses includes investigation into the use of physical restraints and psychotropic drug use and behavior management of patients. "Behavior management" refers to managing physical and/or verbal aggression by some patients or dealing with socially inappropriate behavior such as smearing feces, disrobing, yelling or pacing or resisting nursing care.[23]

It has been estimated that 86% of patients suffering from dementia engage in such disruptive behavior. Since all nursing home patients do not suffer from dementia only 43% of all nursing home residents engage in disruptive conduct. Nevertheless, "a consistent picture emerges of frequent and troublesome behaviors among many residents in nursing homes." Disruptive behavior has been defined by Beck *et al* as behavior which endangers the resident and others and/or behavior which is stressful, frightening or frustrating to residents, caregivers or others and/or behavior which is socially unacceptable or isolating.[24]

Traditionally, nursing homes have used physical restraints and anti-psychotic drugs to deal with such conduct. These methods, however, are no longer acceptable to state inspectors because they have frequent negative consequences for the patient/resident. Among these negative consequences are increased disorientation from sedating drugs and injuries due to physical restraints. In addition, nursing homes using drugs and restraints can easily become the targets of additional legislation and yet more regulatory enforcement as well as a bad reputation in the community. Therefore nursing homes have reduced the use of these methods and have instead incorporated behavioral management training into certification and continuing education programs for registered nurses, licensed practical nurses and nursing assistants. This approach to behavioral problems by nursing home residents has been recommended by a number of experts in gerontology and is summed up in a letter to the New York Times written by Dr. Leslie S. Libow who is chief of medical services at the Jewish Home & Hospital for Aged in New York City. Writes Dr. Libow, "…"no external approach, including legislation or enforcement, will have a lasting impact. It is only change from within each nursing home and the nursing home industry that will improve the quality of care."[25]

Therefore behavioral skills training can achieve a great deal more than restraints of any kind. Such behavioral skills training consists of a 5-hour in-service and subsequent on-the-job training. The content of such training includes (1) identifying factors in the environment that can affect resident behavior (2) identifying antecedents, behaviors and consequences (3) communications skills (4) positive reinforcement procedures (5) distraction and diversion techniques. If such a curriculum can be successfully taught and absorbed by the staff it can nearly eliminate the use of restraints both physical and chemical, as disruptive behavior can then be kept at a minimum.[26]

Such behavior is the product of the kind of agitation also visible among prisoners and others who have been incarcerated. Nursing homes, however, are not prisons so that there is a substantial public interest in the well being of nursing home residents as manifested by a good deal of external monitoring of such homes. This is particularly true because there has been such a great federal investment in nursing home care. When, in the 1960's the nursing home industry suddenly expanded, that period was marked by a good deal of exploitation and several major "nursing home scandals." The consequences of these "scandals" were a string of regulations, both federal, state and local. The purpose of these regulations was to measure the process that indicates whether the right things were done with sufficient skill to assure successful outcomes. Outcomes in terms of nursing home residents can also be called measures of quality of life. Such measures would include residents satisfaction with care, services and the living environment as well as cost. It should be obvious that it is much easier to make every effort to provide all of these conditions than to deal with legal challenges and expensive litigation. One of the advantages of government regulation of nursing homes is therefore that the inspectors and regulators prevent a good deal of litigation as they critique the nursing homes and thereby improve the chances of acceptable outcomes for the patients and the nursing home.

It is of course understood that most residents of nursing homes suffer from serious chronic problems which *ipso facto* imply deterioration and possibly death. Nevertheless, improvement is possible for at least some patients in a number of areas such as mobility, better cognition, less pain and discomfort, increased social activities and satisfactory social relationships. [27]

Mansfield and Werner have demonstrated that improvement can be achieved and how an enhanced environment inside a nursing home can have positive effects on residents who suffer anxiety. Some of those who have an anxiety problem pace or wander the corridors of the nursing homes incessantly. To deal with this behavior, Mansfield and Werner installed murals depicting nature scenes on the walls of nursing home corridors. They added artificial plants and trees, and tape recorded nature sounds such as the song of birds. In addition, Mansfield and Werner hung wall posters of persons familiar to the residents such as Albert Einstein and President Kennedy. Scenes depicting family life and classical music were also provided. All of this led to some decreases in agitated behavior, including pacing or wandering as well as exit seeking and trespassing into the rooms of other patients. [28]

The failure of some patients to recognize their own room is frequently related to Alzheimer's disease, a deterioration of the brain first described by the German neuropathologist Alois Alzheimer in 1906. Because there are now some 4 million Americans with Alzheimer's disease, two thirds of nursing home patients are victims of that disease. In addition there are some other form of dementia. To those whose who are so afflicted the "look-alike" rooms in nursing homes can easily get confused when the room of each patient looks just like that of his neighbors. Because so many nursing home residents suffer from dementia, "special care units" represent the fastest growing part of the nursing home business. Such units have tripled since 1991, reaching a capacity of 120,000 beds at the end of 1998. While such units can deliver better care than traditional nursing homes, the Alzheimer's Association has concluded that these special units " may too often be an expensive marketing technique that segregates memory impaired residents but fails to provide for their special needs."[29]

Dementia is not the only condition that leads to agitated behavior. Cruise *et al* have shown that much anxiety can be related to sleep disruption. Such sleep disruption is common in nursing homes because staff make incontinence care rounds every two hours throughout the night. Loud sounds and light changes also contribute to sleep disruption in nursing homes as staff talk in normal conversational voices, pull privacy curtains around beds and turn on room lights. Cruise *et al* say that "we do not believe that nursing home staff are even remotely aware of the importance of sleep or of the problem that residents have with sleep." [30]

Hopelessness and the loss of the ability to direct daily life are additional reasons for developing anxiety and feelings of isolation among nursing home residents. To counter these problems some nursing homes have resorted to the so-called "wellness groups". These groups of demented patients are given a sense of accomplishment and fulfillment by allowing each group to introduce its members and leaders, stating goals of each group session, presenting demonstrations, participating in group exercises and summarizing session activities. These groups have helped patients whose agitated behavior included those with a history of physical aggression, verbal abuse or continuous wandering. According to Lantz *et al* these groups are much more helpful than the traditional effort to "control" patients' behaviors because patients enrolled in such groups take an active part in their own healing and thereby reduce the distress symptoms associated with agitation.[31]

"Family Stories Workshops" are another method used by some nursing homes to deal with patients suffering dementia of any kind. The methods employed in these "workshops" involve family members of dementia residents who assist nursing home staff in personalizing resident care. This means that caregivers can develop life stories of the residents and recount them to staff providing the care. The results are that such life story events reduce strife between caregivers and family members and prevent the resentment some staff feel for families whose concern is sometimes interpreted as "intrusion." These family stories workshops also indicate to the staff that the patients are treatable and that they can interact meaningfully. Evidently, the manner in which staff view patients affects the fashion by which staff treat patients. [32]

Such treatment is sometimes less than should be expected. Despite the effort of outside monitors, both private and public, to insure the well being of nursing home residents, numerous "horror stories" concerning the neglect and abuse of nursing home patients continue to agitate the public. In October of 1997, seven years after the passage of the Omnibus Budget Reconciliation Act and six years after Congress passed the Patient Self-determination Act of 1991, a "special investigation" discovered nursing homes in which no one attended to the needs of sick and very old patients for hours. Accordingly, "senior citizens in nursing homes are at far greater risk of death from neglect than their loved one often imagine." That investigation also revealed that the Texas attorney general has filed 50 lawsuits against nursing homes for neglect. Bad hygiene, inattention to frail residents and incompetent staff were all cited as reasons for the conviction of a nursing home owner on fraud charges in Detroit. In California, Palo Alto attorney Von Packard found that 7% of all deaths in nursing homes were caused by "utter neglect" meaning lack of food and water, bed sores and other preventable ailments. Packard found a number of deaths of nursing home patients were caused by malnutrition. It can therefore be speculated that "if the rest of America's 1.6 million nursing home residents are dying of such causes at the same rate as those living in California then 35,000 Americans are dying a premature death or in unnecessary pain." Since the taxpayer spends more than $45 billion a year on nursing homes through Medicaid and Medicare neglect and mistreatment of nursing home residents constitutes fraud. In Philadelphia, David Hoffman, an assistant U.S. attorney sued Geriatric and Medical Companies, Inc. for allowing patients to suffer festering bed sores "eating away the flesh" of nursing home patients. Innumerable other violations of nursing home residents occur at all times. However, inspections of nursing homes seem to have little effect on the treatment residents receive. This is so because the government fined only 2% of nursing homes inspected despite the failure of two thirds of nursing homes to pass the inspections randomly undertaken. This means that of the 15,000 nursing homes inspected by state inspectors each year, 10,000 are in violation of nursing home regulations but are never penalized. It is the obligation of the federal Health Care Financing Administration to enforce its own regulations and fine nursing homes cited by state inspectors. In 1997, one in every three nursing homes inspected in the U.S. was cited for neglect. At that time state inspectors recommended that these nursing homes be barred from collecting money for new patients. However, only 228 of these nursing homes were fined at all by the Health Care Financing Administration, and these paid only 65% of the fines first levied.[33]

Some nursing homes have been accused of abusing patients. Others have been accused of financial irregularities and of Medicare and/or Medicaid fraud. Fraud is defined as "obtaining or attempting to obtain payments by dishonest means with intent, knowledge and willingness." Such fraud may consist of billing for services not provided; incorrect reporting of diagnoses or procedures to get a higher payment; billing for covered services when non-covered services were provided and "kickbacks", bribes and rebates. There is a whole additional catalogue of fraud and abuse committed by some nursing homes. Therefore, President Clinton, in July of 1998, announced a new drive to cut nursing home abuses. Included in that announcement were steps leading to an improvement in the quality of care for nursing home patients. The effort here was to reduce the number of cases of nursing home residents complaining of bed sores, dehydration and nutrition problems.[34]

One of the complaints against some of these nursing homes was that ten years after the passage of the Nursing Home Reform Act of 1987, there were still some nursing homes who were using physical restraints prohibited by that law. That act states in part that "residents have the right to be free from any physical or chemical restraint imposed for purposes of discipline or convenience and not required to treat the resident's medical symptoms." [35]

Many nursing homes resist this limitation on restraints because this would increase the total cost of care in American nursing homes by $1 billion. This explains why the use of restraints have declined by only 4% from 25% in 1977 to 21% in 1996. Castle *et al*, have studied these practices and found that many patients could not sustain the normal activities of daily living and that others showed on a cognitive performance scale that they needed restraints to make their lives possible. This means that nursing homes must have extensive resources to implement the provisions of the nursing home reform act.[36]

Therefore it would seem reasonable to expect that nursing homes who are members of a chain would be more likely to be restraint free than those not members of chains. This expectation is based on the assumption that chain nursing homes achieve economics not available to those who operate singly. It is certainly true that the purchasing of equipment and supplies is less expensive for chains than for others and that the savings the chains attain can then be used for other purposes. Castle and Fogel have investigated this issue and found that restraint free nursing homes have higher rates of RNs per resident than is true of those who use restraints. Lower occupancy rates are also associated with a reduction of restraints for nursing home residents. Despite all this, Castle and Fogel found that chain nursing homes are less likely to be free of restraints than other nursing homes. Therefore it is reasonable to assume that the desire for more profit reduces the inclination of chain nursing homes to be restraint free. This is true because a high staff-to-patient ratio is associated with reductions in restraints. Furthermore, facilities with a high proportion of Alzheimer special care units are less likely to be restraint free than those with fewer demented patients. There are now some facilities who have adopted devices not formally determined by regulators to be restraints such as belts with Velcro fasteners which many residents cannot open. Such belts have the same effect as restraints prohibited by the Nursing

Home Reform Act but are not included in the regulations derived from that law.

In sum, restraint free nursing homes care for physically less impaired patients; they are more likely to be not-for-profit; they are generally smaller, low occupancy nursing homes not belonging to chains and they are more likely to be located in urban than in rural areas.[37]

IV

The Patient Self-Determination Act was first implemented in 1991. The purpose of that act was to insure that patients' written advance directives be honored. The act requires that patients be informed under state law to participate in their medical decision making and to issue written advance directives. Nevertheless, the majority of long term care providers do not have advance directives concerning their wishes in case of impending death. In fact, only 10% of nursing home patients have issued advance directives as to whether to be hospitalized "in extremis" or when to cease making "heroic efforts" to save their lives. These directives are generally called "do not resuscitate order". Research has shown that the majority of old persons do not desire resuscitation.[38]

Prior to the 1991 implementation of the Patient Self-Determination Act, nursing homes participating in Medicare or Medicaid programs were mandated to use the Resident Assessment Instrument of the federal government in October of 1990. That instrument seeks to assess all residents at time of admission, annually and after any significant change in the residents' status. As a consequence, nursing homes were induced to institute innovations reflecting the outcome of these resident assessments. These innovations included computerizing the nursing home facilities, exchanging ideas at professional meetings, acquiring new medical equipment, creating new opportunities for patient self-expression etc.. Castle and Holl also report that more highly educated managers are more likely to adopt innovations which they then explained to others working there. Those managers who have a good education are also more likely to exchange ideas at professional meetings than those who have less education. Indications are that merely belonging to a professional association does not mean that the member will be exposed to new ideas through personal contacts. Evidently, educated managers are far more likely to talk to others and discover what innovations there are. Personal contacts, not ideas found in publications, are most effective in providing managers with new methods of treatment and maintenance of nursing home residents.

The study by Castle and Holl revealed a strong relationship between the adoption of such innovations in nursing homes and the length of employment of a nursing home manager. They found that managers with longer tenures are more likely to engage in innovative behavior because long tenure legitimizes the adoption of innovations more than short-term management control. In fact, the employment stability of nursing home administrators is a significant factor influencing the quality of care provided to patients in nursing homes.

That employment stability is in turn dependent on the right of managers to make decisions and to exercise a considerable degree of autonomy. The ever growing number of nursing homes owned by chains make such managerial control less and less likely and therefore contributes to the nearly 25% turnover in nursing home administrators occurring every year in the United States.[39] This then indicates that corporate owners need to give consideration to the damage which a high rate of administrative turnover inflicts on any nursing home as it reduces staff morale and incurs high costs for recruitment, relocation orientation and training of new employees.[4041]

There is a considerable literature concerning human resource management which plainly indicates that employee retention is related to job satisfaction and commitment to the organization. Therefore, open communication as well as recognition of performance and accomplishments is very important. Pay equity and promotional opportunities are also related to employee retention as is job satisfaction. Such job satisfaction depends on such factors as value congruence, ethical compatibility and, most of all, the expectation that the skills and abilities of a professional employee are recognized and used. Such recognition is best achieved by permitting professional employees to participate in decision making.

Decision making in nursing homes generally involves registered nurses because the primary health care needs of nursing home residents are for nursing care. Therefore, most managers of nursing homes rely on the decisions made by nurses for advice, not only concerning patient care, but also concerning organization-level administrative matters. This is also true because nurses are often the only professionals in nursing homes. This is not to say that social workers and doctors are not also on the staff of every nursing home. However, many nursing home social workers do not hold the M.S.W. degree certifying their professional status while the doctors who do visit nursing home patients are seldom available for more than cursory information.[42]

In fact, a study by Katz, *et al* has shown that only one fourth of all American physicians are involved with nursing home patients and one third of physicians in the primary care disciplines reported caring for nursing home patients. According to Katz *et al*, even those who do have a nursing home practice spend two hours or less per week in a nursing home. Family practitioners are most likely to be involved with a nursing home, followed by internists and general practitioners. Only 15% of specialists contacted by Katz *et al* said that they spent any time in a nursing home.

Because the number of physicians with nursing home involvement is so low, the Residency Review Committee of Family Practice and Internal Medicine has recommended mandated nursing home rotations and a significant expansion of geriatrics in medical school curriculums.[43]

Meanwhile, much of the work with patients in nursing homes is carried by nursing home social workers. Traditionally, a social worker has been someone who holds a Masters Degree in Social Work generally called an M.S.W.. More recently, those who have earned the B.S.W. degree in only four years are also called social workers. These social workers are responsible for dealing with the aforementioned behavior disorders including depression, dementia and the social factors associated with aging. Included in the social workers' methods are personality assessments, behavioral interventions, family and group therapy. By these means, social workers, more than anyone else, prevent the need for using chemical or physical restraints.

In addition to the social work methods already mentioned, social workers contact outsiders, whether family or professionals, on behalf of each patients. Social workers make appointments for patients, call family members and encourage them to visit, act as mediators between patients and family and others and are generally advocates for resident/ patients when and where needed. This advocacy is essential in preserving self-determination for nursing home residents. For example, social workers will ask patients whether or not they wish cardiopulmonary resuscitation if needed. Physicians do that also. However, a study by Berger and Mejerovitz revealed that doctors often assume that patients who have rejected cardiopulmonary resuscitation are therefore equally uninterested in other kinds of intervention. Yet, the evidence indicates that patients who do not want CPR are nevertheless interested in mechanical ventilatory support. This example emphasizes the importance of holding specific discussions with each patient concerning his wishes. That is one of the principal tasks of social workers in nursing home settings. Usually, the preferences of impaired, institutionalized patients are unknown, particularly when family members are not available or not interested.[44]

The work of social workers in nursing homes is made much more difficult because so much time of the social worker must be spent on doing "paper work" demanded by state investigators. Much of this documentation is repetitious and meaningless and prevents the social worker from dealing with, even speaking to the residents. Most of the employees who do the work labeled "social work" in nursing homes are not trained in social work but have a degree in anything at all. This permits these employees to deal with the paper work required, even if they have no interpersonal skills and no means of dealing with the needs of the residents. These nursing home employees are called "social work assistants". They have to deal with as many as 175 residents, a task impossible to fulfill.

Some nursing homes also employ a social work consultant. The consultant is an M.S.W. who visits the nursing home once a week and reputedly deals with patients who need the help of someone with experience and advanced education. It is however, unlikely that a social work consultant will indeed see patients. It is far more likely that the social work consultant will also be caught up in the paper work demanded by the "surveyors" who visit the nursing homes sporadically for the state in which they are located.[45]

V

Allied to nursing homes is the recent development in assisted living facilities, which range from renovated private homes to high-rise apartment buildings operated on the grounds of a nursing home. The concept of assisted living refers to an effort to give both care and autonomy to residents too healthy for a skilled nursing facility and yet no longer able to live on their own.

Residents of assisted living facilities have a private room or apartment but eat in a communal setting. They generally receive help with such daily tasks as dressing, cleaning and laundry. Usually, assisted living facilities also provide transportation to medical appointments and shopping and social activities. Nearly 70% of residents in ALFs require help with dispensing medication. Over 64% need help with bathing, 46% need help with dressing and about a third need help with toileting.

The average stay of a resident in an ALF is 28 months. This limited tenure is the result of the high morality rate in assisted living facilities. Nearly 31% of the residents die within two to three years after arrival. Thirty six percent require a skilled nursing home and over 12% require a hospital. The remainder may have left the ALF for a number of reasons.

Ninety percent of assisted living facilities are private pay and cost as much as $4,000 per month although there are some which cost only

$2,000 per month. The remaining ten percent are covered by Supplemental Security Income, Social Security Block Grants or other entitlement programs. Forty two percent of all facilities receive state program assistance for residents. There are also several states which are considering Medicaid waiver programs concerning ALF. These 30,000 facilities now house about 750,000 residents, two numbers which are increasing all the time.

The average age of residents in assisted living facilities is 83 with an average annual income of $28,100. The average per diem cost of an assisted living facility was $71 in 1998 while the average cost of a skilled nursing facility was $111 that year.[46]

Evidently, then, this economic efficiency coincides with the overwhelming preference people have to stay out of traditional nursing homes. Because this segment of care for the old is growing so fast, a number of major corporations, including the Marriott hotel chain, have entered the assisted living business.[47]

There are several other options some senior citizens use to elude the traditional nursing home. Assisted Independent Living is an option offered by private businesses, public agencies, civic groups and non-profit and religious organizations. The effort here is to offer companionship and support for those living independently. Included are adult care programs, senior centers, meals on wheels, transportation services and telephone reassurance services. Costs for these services range from $500.-per week. Adult day care averages $30.- per day and companion services average about $10.- per hour. Live-in homemakers receive between $100 and $400 per week. Another means of escaping the traditional nursing home is home health care. This is generally useful following a hospital stay. It includes discharge planning, medical supervision, in-home care and rehabilitation services. These services can be covered by Medicaid and/or Medicare if authorized by a physician. Visits by a registered nurse cost $83-$90.- per visit. A home health aide costs $30.- per hour. Continuing-care Retirement Communities charge entrance fees ranging from $5,000.- to $300,000 but are not always required. Housing ranges from $60,000 to $90,000 per year for a typical one-bedroom unit and is normally limited to individuals with an annual income of $40,000.- or more. These communities are best described as residential communities with a health care component. These communities offer different levels of care thereby guaranteeing that residents are not uprooted every time their needs change.[48]

Summary

Nearly two million Americans receive nursing home care every year. This is related to an ever-increasing life expectancy at a cost of $74 billion annually and is heavily supported by the government/taxpayer through Medicare and Medicaid. Most nursing homes are "for-profit" and are merging more and more into corporate chain enterprises.

Over the years there has been a good deal of complaint concerning neglect and abuse of nursing home patients. Nevertheless, many old people enter nursing homes because of illness, loneliness, lack of community services and/or dementia,. The number of patients suffering from dementia is increasing as life expectancy increases. This has led to a good deal of behavior problems among nursing home patients countered by nursing homes with the use of restraints. However, the Nursing Home Reform Act and the Patient Self-determination Act have prohibited restraints so that changes in programs and methods are called for to reduce behavior problems. These changes are dependent on administrators as well as nurses and social workers who constitute the professional staff in most nursing homes. Alternatives to nursing homes are assisted living facilities, assisted independent living, and continuing care retirement communities.

NOTES

[1] John W. Wright, Ed. *The New York Times Almanac,* New York, Penguin Putnam, Inc., 1998, pp. 275-277 and pp. 380-382.

[2] Bureau of Labor Statistics, *1996 National Occupational Employment Wage Date,* 1998.

[3] Kelly D. Smith, "How seniors can give away assets without fear of landing in jail," *Money,* Vol.26, No. 6, June 1997, p. 24.

[4] Melinda D. Wilcox, "Will Nursing Home Bills Haunt Your Estate?" *Kiplinger's Personal Finance Magazine,* Vol.52, No. 4, April 1998, pp. 115-118.

[5] Michael Moss and Chris Adams, "Evictees Relish Nursing Homes' Reversal," *Wall Street Journal,* May 21, 1998, pp. B1 and B12.

[6] National Center for Health Statistics, *An Overview of Nursing Homes and their Current Residents:The 1995 National Nursing Home Survery,* Hyattsville, MD., 1997.

[7] James P. Miller, "Health Care & Retirement to Buy Manor Care," *The Wall Street Journal,* June 11, 1998, pp. A3 and A8. See also: The New York Times, June 11, 1998, p. D2.

[8] Milt Freudenheim, "New Medicare Rules: Winners and Losers," *The New York Times,* July 4, 1998, p.D2.

[9] Michael Moss, "Many Elders Receive Care at Criminals' Hands," *The Wall Street Journal,* March 18, 1998, p. B1 and B 14.

[10] Michael Moss, "Criminal Probes Target Abusive Nursing Homes," *The Wall Street Journal,* May 28, 1996, pp. B1 and B15.

[11] Michael Moss, "Nursing Homes Get Punished by Irate Jurors," *The Wall Street Journal,* March 6, 1998, pp. B1 and B8.

[12] Alexandra Alger, "Nursing home or home nursing?" *Forbes,* Vol. 159, No. 6, March 24, 1997, p. 160.

[13] John Foster, "The Financial Status of Medicare," *Public Health Reports,* Vol. 113, No. 2, March/April 1998, p. 117.

[14] Paul Kemper and Charles M. Murtaugh, "Lifetime use of nursing home care." *New England Journal of Medicine,* Vol.324, 1991, p. 595.

[15] Allan Jette, Laurence G. Branch, Lynn A. Sleeper, Henry Feldman and Lisa M. Sullivan, "High Risk Profile for Nursing Home Admission," *The Gerontoloigst,* Vol.32, No.5, October 1992, pp. 634-640.

[16] Linda Saslow, "Living to be 100: Anger, Arthritis and Occasional Joy," *The New York Times,* May 3, 1998, Sec. XIV, LI,1. and p 4.

[17] Victor L. Greene and John I. Ondrich, " Risk factors for nursing home admissions and exits: A discrete-time hazard approach." *Journal of Gerontology: Social Sciences,* Vol.45, 1990, pp. S250-S258.

[18] Letitia A Peplau and Daniel D. Perlman, *Loneliness, A sourcebook of current theory, research and therapy.* New York, Wiley, 1982.

[19] U.S. Bureau of the Census: 1990 census of the population. General population characteristics. United States. Washington D.C. U.S. Government Printing Office, 1992.

[20] Chuck W. Peek, Raymond T. Coward, Gary R. Lee and Barbara A. Zsembik, "The Influence of Community Context on the Preference of Older Adults for Entering a Nursing Home," *The Gerontologist,* Vol.37, No.4, August 1997, pp. 533-542.

[21] *Ibid.*p. 534.

[22] John Rodin, "Aging and health: Effects of the sense of control." *Science,* Vol.233, 1986, pp. 1272-1276.

[23] Catherine Hawes, *et al,* "The OBRA-87 Nursing Home Regulations and Implementation of the Resident Assessment Instrument: Effect on Process Quality." *Journal of the American Geriatrics Society,* Vol. 45, No. 8, August 1997, pp. 977-985.

[24] Cornelia Beck, et.al., "Correlates of Disruptive Behavior in Severely Cognitively Impaired Nursing Home Residents," *The Gerontologist,* Vol.38, No.2, April, 1998, pp. 189-198.

[25] Leslie S. Libow, "Nursing Home Care," *The New York Times,* August 5, 1998, p. A22.

[26] Alan B. Stevens, et.al. "Teaching and Maintaining Behavior Management Skills With Nursing Assistants in a Nursing Home," *The Gerontologist,* Vol.38, No. 3, June 1998, pp. 379-384.

[27] Robert L. Kane, "Assuring Quality in Nursing Home Care," *Journal of the American Geriatric Society,* Vol.46, No. 2, February, 1998, pp. 232-237.

[28] Jiska Cohen Mansfield and Perla Weiner, "The Effects of an Enhanced Environment on Nursing Home Residents Who Pace," *The Gerontolgist,* Vol.38, No.2, April 1998, pp. 199-208.

[29] Joseph P. Shapiro, "Comfort and Care," *U.S. News & World Report,* Vol. 122. No. 21, June 2, 1997, p. 66.

[30] Patrice A. Cruise *et al* "The Nighttime Environment and Incontinence Care Practices in Nursing Homes," *Journal of the American Geriatrics Society,* Vol. 46, No. 2, February 1998, pp. 181-186.

[31] Melinda Lantz, Eric N. Buchalter and Lucia McBee, "The Wellness Group: A Novel Intervention for Coping With Disruptive Behavior in Elderly Nursing Home Residents," *The Gerontoloigst,* Vol.37, No.4, August 1997, pp. 551-556.

[32] Kenneth Hepburn, et.al., "The Family Stories Workshop: Stories for Those Who cannot Remember." *The Gerontologist,* Vol. 37, No.6, December, 1997, pp. 827-832.
[33] Mark Thompson, "Neglect," *Time,* Vol. 150, No. 17, October 27, 1997, pp. 34-38.
[34] George E. Pataki, *Operation Restore Trust,* Medicare, Binghamton, N.Y. 1998.
[35] Omnibus Budget Reconciliation Act of 1987. Public Law 100-203, Subtitle C. The Nursing Home Reform Act. 42 U.S.C. 1395i -3 (a)-(h) (Medicare); 13966r (a) –(h) (Medicaid).
[36] Nicholas G. Castle, Barry Fogel and Vincent Mor, "Risk Factors for Physical Restraint Use in Nursing Homes: Pre-and Post Implementation of the Nursing Home Reform Act," *The Gerontologist,* Vol. 27, No.6, December 1997.
[37] *Ibid.,* p.187.
[38] Joan M. Teno, *et al,* "Changes in Advance Care Planning in Nursing Homes Before and After the Patient Self-Determination Act: Report of a 10-State Survey," *Journal of the American Geriatric Society,* Vol.45, No. 8, August 1997, pp. 939-944.
[39] John Gilbert, "Administrators on the move," *McKnight's Long Term News,* Vol. 17, No. 10, 1996, p.1.
[40] Peter A. Weil and P.A. Kimball, "A model of voluntary turnover of hospital CEOs." *Hospital and Health Services Administration,* Vol.40, 1995, pp. 362-385.
[41]
[42] Ruth Anderson and Reuben R. McDaniel, Jr., "Intensity of Registered Nurse Participation in Nursing Home Decision Making," *The Gerontologist,* Vol. 38, No.1, February, `1998, pp; 90-100.
[43] Paul R. Katz, Jurgis Karuza, John Kolassa and Alan Hutson, "Medical Practice with Nursing Home Residents: Results from the National Physician Professional Activities Census," *Journal of the American Geriatrics Society,* Vol.45, No. 8, August 1997, pp. 911-917.
[44] Jeffrey T. Berger and Deborah Majerovitz, "Stability of Preferences for Treatment Among Nursing Home Residents," *The Gerontologist,* Vol.38, No.2, April 1998, pp. 217-223.
[45] Ursula Adler, *A Critical Study of the American Nursing Home,* Lewsiton, N.Y., The Edwin Mellen Press, 1991, pp. 187-189.
[46] Gemma M. Tarlach, "Explosion in Assisted Living Means New Opportunities" *Drug Topics,* vol. 142, No. 4, February 1998, p.70.
[47] Linda T. Barton, "A Shoulder To Lean On: Assisted Living In The U.S.", *American Demographics,*
Vol. 19, No.7, July 1997, pp. 45-51.

[48] *Ibid.* p. 48.

Bibliography

Books

Ackley, Dana C., *Breaking Free of Managed Care*, New York, The Guilford Press, 1997.

Adler, Ursula, *A Critical Study of the American Nursing Home*, Lewiston, N.Y., The Edwin Mellen Press, 1991.

Allan Guttmacher Institute, *Sex and America's Teenagers*, New York, The Institute, 1994.

American Medical Association, *Physicians Characteristics and Distribution in the U.S. 1997-1998*, Chicago, 1998.

American Medical Association, *Socioeconomic Characteristics of Medical Practice*, Chicago, American Medical Association, 1993.

American Medical Association/Specialty Society, *Medical Liability Project Fact Sheets*. Chicago, AMA/Specialty Society, 1992.

Annas, G., "Baby Fae: the 'anything goes' school of human experimentation" in G. Annas , *Judging Medicine*, Clifton, N.J., Humana Press, 1988.

Asbell, Milton B., *Dentistry: A Historical Perspective*, Bryn Mawr, Pa., Dorrance & Co., 1988.

Barkan, Steven E., *Criminology: A Sociological Understanding*, Upper Saddle River, N.J., Prentice Hall, 1997.

Barnard, Chester, *The Functions of the Executive*, Cambridge, Harvard University Press, 1938.

Benson, Herbert, *Timeless Healing: the Power and Biology of Belief*, New York, Simon and Schuster, 1997.

Benson, Herbert, *Your Maximum Mind*, New York, Times Books, 1987.

Blank, Sally E., and Gary G. Meadows, in: Ira Wolinsky, Editor, *Nutrition in Exercise and Sport,* Boca Roran, CRC Press, 1998, p. 217.

Block, Thomas, *Milestones in Microbiology,* Washington, American Society for Microbiology, 1975.

Brown, Thomas R., Ed., *Handbook of Institutional Pharmacy Practice,* Bethesda, Md., American Society of Hospital Pharmacists, 1992.

Brumberg, Joan Jacobs, *Fasting Girls: The Emergence of Anorexia Nervosa as a Modern Disease,* Cambridge, Mass., Harvard University Press, 1988.

Brunstetter, Richard W., *Adolescents in Psychiatric Hospitals,* Springfield, Illinois, Charles C. Thomas, 1998, p. 33.

Bureau of Labor Statistics, *1996 National Occupational Employment Wage Date,* 1998

Campbell, Alastair, Grant Gillett and D. Gareth Jones, *Practical Medical Ethics,* New York, Oxford University Press, 1992.

Campion, Frank D., *The AMA and U.S. Health Policy since 1940,* Chicago, Chicago Review Press, 1984.

Cassedy, James H., *Medicine in America: A Short History,* Baltimore, The Johns Hopkins Press, 1991.

Chambliss, Daniel F., *The Patient as Object,* Chicago, The University of Chicago Press, 1996.

Cherney, Alison, *The Capitation and Risk Sharing Guidebook,* Chicago, Irwin Professional Publishing, 1996.

Citizens Commission on Graduate Medical Education, *The Graduate Education of Physicians,* Chicago, The American Medical Association, 1966.

Cockerham, William C., *Medical Sociology* (7th Ed.), Englewood Cliffs, N.J., Prentice-Hall, Inc., 1998.

Coile, Jr. Russell C., *The New Medicine: Reshaping Medical Practice and Health Care Management,* Rockville, MD, Aspen Publishers, 1990.

Conrad, Peter and Joseph W. Schneider, *Deviance and Medicalization; From Badness to Sickness,* St. Louis, C.V. Mosby Co/, 1980

Coombs, Robert H., *Mastering Medicine: Professional Socialization in Medical School,* New York, The Free Press, 1978.

Corcoran ,Kevin, and Vikki Vandiver, *Maneuvering the Maze of Managed Care,* The Free Press, New York, 1996.

Council on Graduate Medical Education, *Fourth Report: Recommendations to Improve Access to Health Care through*

Physicians Workforce Reform. Rockville, Md., U.S. Department of Health and Human Services, 1994.

Cybulski, Nancy Jo-anne Marr, Isabel Milton and Dalton Truthwaite, *Reinventing Hospitals,* Mc Leod Publications, Toronto, 1997.

Day,Richard C. and Robert C. Cantu, "Corporate Fitness," in Robert C. Cantu, Editor, *The Exercising Adult,* New York, Macmillan Publishing Co., 1987, p. 31.

Del Veccio Good, Mary-Jo, *American Medicine: A Quest for Competence,* Berkeley, The University of California Press, 1995.

Deutsch, Albert, *The Mentally Ill in America: A History of their Care and Treatment from Colonial Times.* New York, Columbia University Press, 1937.

Docherty, John P., "Two Hundred Years of Inpatient Psychiatry," in: John P. Docherty, Editor, *Inpatient Psychiatry in the 1990's.* San Francisco, Jossey-Bass, 1994, pp. 5-6.

Dossey, Larry, *Space, Time & Medicine,* New Science Library, Boston, 1982.

Duffy, John, *From Humors to Medical Science: A History of American Medicine,* 2nd Ed., Urbana, The University of Illinois Press, 1993.

Durant, Will, *Ceasar and Christ,* New York, Simon and Schuster, 1944.

Durkheim, Emile, *Division of Labor in Society,* Trans. George Simpson, New York, Free Press, 1933. (1893)

Ebaugh, Helen R.F,. *Becoming an Ex: The Process of Role Exit,* Chicago, University of Chicago Press, 1988.

Ennis, Maeve and J. Gredis Gudzinskas, "The effect of accidents and litigation on doctors," in: Charles Vincent, Maeve Ennis, Robert J. Audley, Eds., *Medical Accidents,* New York, Oxford University Press, 1993, p.167.

Erickson, Beth M., *Helping Men Change; The Role of the Female Therapist,* Newbury Park, Cal., Sage Pulicatons, 1993.

Falck, Hans S., *Social Work: The Membership Perspective,* New York, Springer Publishing Co., 1988,

Falk, Gerhard, *The Life of the Academic Professional,* Lewiston, N.Y., The Edwin Mellen Press, 1990,.

Falk, Gerhard, *A Study of Social Change in Six American Institutions,* Lewiston, NY., The Edwin Mellen Press, 1993.

Falk, Gerhard, *Sex, Gender and Social Change,* The *Great Revolution,* Lanham, New York, Oxford, The University Press of America, 1998.

Falk, Isidore, Sydney C. Rufus Rorem and Martha D. Ring, *The Costs of Medical Care,* Chicago, The University of Chicago Press, 1933.

336   *Hippocrates Assailed: The American Health Delivery System*

Falk, Ursula Adler and Gerhard Falk, *Ageism, the Aged and Aging in America*, Springfield, Ill., Charles C. Thomas, Publishers, 1997.

Flexner, Abraham, *Medical Education: A Comparative Study*, New York, Macmillan, 1925.

Forssmann, Werner, *Experiments on Myself: Memoirs of a Surgeon in Germany*, New York, St. Martin's Press, 1974.

Fralic, Maryann F., "How Is Demand for Registered Nurses in Hospital Settings Changing?" in Edward O'Neil and Janet Coffman Eds., San Francisco, Jossey-Bass, Inc., 1998, p. 68.

Fredericks, Marcel A. and Paul Mundy, *The Making of a Physician*, Chicago, Loyola University Press, 1976.

Freidson, Elliott *Professionalism Reborn: Theory, Prophecy and Policy*, Chicago, The University of Chicago Press, 1994.

Freud, Sigmund and Joseph Breuer, "Studies in Hysteria," in James Strachey, Editor and Translator, Sigmund Freud, *The Complete Psychological Works*, Vol. 2, New York, Norton, 1976.

Fuchs, Victor R. *Who Shall Live?*, New York, Basic Books, 1974.

Funkenstein, Daniel H. *Medical Students, Medical Schools and Society During Five Eras: Factors Affecting the Career Choices of Physicians*, Cambridge, MA., Ballinger Publishing Co., 1878.

Garrison, Fielding H., *History of Medicine*, Philadelphia, W.B. Saunders, 1929.

Gelhorn, Walter, *Individual Freedom and Government Restraints*, Baton Rouge, Louisiana State University Press.

Ginzberg, Eli, *Tomorrow's Hospital*, New Haven, Yale University Press, 1996,.

Ginzburg, E. M. Ostrow and A.B. Durka, *The Economics of Medical Education*, New York, Josiah Macy Foundation, 1993.

Glasser, William, *Positive Addiction*, New York, Harper and Row, 1976.

Gleitman, Henry, *Psychology*, Second Edition, New York, W.W. Norton & Co., 1986.

Gluck, Ira D., "Unbundling the Function of an Inpatient Unit," in: John P. Doherty, Ed., *Inpatient Psychiatry in the 1990s.* San Franciso, Jossey-Bass, 1994, p. 38.

Goffman, Ervin, *Asylums: Essays on the Social Situation of Mental Patients and Other Inmates.* New York, Doubleday-Anchor, 1961.

Goffman, Ervin, *Stigma: Notes on the Management of Spoiled Identity*, Englewood Cliffs, N.J., Prentice Hall, 1963.

Golcsewski, James A., *Aging: Strategies for Maintaining Good Health and Extending Life*, Jefferson, N.C., Mc Farland & Co., Inc, Publishers, 1998.

Goldstein Arnold P., and Howard N. Higginbotham, "Relationship Enhancement Methods". In: F.H. Kanfer and Arnold P. Goldstein, Eds., *Helping People Change*, Elmsford, N.Y., The Pergamon Press, 1991.

Grosch William N. and David C. Olson, *When Helping Starts to Hurt*, New York, W.W. Norton & Co., 1994.

Henry, William J., John H. Sims, and S. Lee Spray, *The Fifth Profession: Becoming a Psychiatrist*, San Francisco, Jossey- Bass, 1971.

Hess, Beth B., Elizabeth W. Markson and Peter J. Stein, *Sociology(Fourth Edition)* New York, Macmillan Publishing Co., 1991.

Hummer, Patricia M. *The Decade of Elusive Promise, Professional Women in the United States,1920-1930*. Ann Arbor, Research Press, 1976.

Jardine, Nichlas "The laboratory revolution in medicine as rhetorical and aesthetic accomplishment." in: Andrew Cunningham and Perry Williams, Eds., *The Laboratory Revolution in Medicine*, New York, Cambridge University Press, 1992, p. 304.

Kaldenberg, Dennis O., Anisa M. Zvonkovic and Boris W. Becker, "Women Dentists: The Social Construction of a Profession," in Joyce Tang and Earl Smith, Eds., *Women in the Professions*, Albany, N.Y., The SUNY Press, 1966.

Kalisch, Philip A. and Beatrice Kalisch, *The Advance of American Nursing*, 3rd Edition, Philadelphia J.B.

Kant, Immanuel, *Fundamental Principles of the Metaphysics of Morals*, T.K. Abbott, Translator, Bobbs Merrill, Indianapolis 1949.The German version of this book is: *Grundlegung zur Metaphysik der Sitten.*.

Kaplan, Robert M., *The Hippocratic Predicament*, New York, The Academic Press, 1993.

Katz, Jay, *The Silent World of Doctor and Patient*, New York, The Free Press, 1984.

Kendall, Diana, *Sociology in Our Times*, New York, Wadsworth Publisihing Co., 1999.

Kendall, Fred Gable, *Opportunities in Pharmacy Careers*, Chicago, NTC Contemporary Publishing Co., 1997.

Kiesler, Charles A. and Celeste Simpkins, *Hospitalization for Mental and Other Disorders*, New York, Plenum Press, 1993.

King, Glenn W., *Statistical Abstracts of the United States 1997*, Washington, D.C., The Bureau of the Census, 1998.

Kramer, Peter, *Listening to Prozac: A psychiatrist explores anti-depressant drugs and the remaking of the self.* New York, Penguin Books, 1994.

Lamb, David R., *Perspectives in Exercise Science and Sports Medicine,* Carmel, Ind., Cooper Publishing Group, 1995.

Lamy, Peter P., *Prescribing for the Elderly,* PSG Publishing, Littleton, Mass., 1980.

Leander, William J., *Patients First,* Chicago, Health Administration Press, 1996.

Levinthal, Charles F., *Drugs, Behavior and Modern Society,* Boston, Allyn and Bacon, 1996.

Lindberg, Janice B., Mary Love Hunter and Ann Z. Kruszewski, *Introduction to Nursing,* Philadelphia, Lipppincott-Raven Publishers, 1998.

Lutz, Sandy and E. Preston Gee, *The For-Profit health Care Revolution,* Chicago, Irwin, 1996.

Manfredi, Thomas, W. Jay Gillespie and Karen S. Congdon, "University-based cardiac rehabilitation and adult fitness programs," in: Day and Cantu, op.cit. pp. 43-61.

Marshall, Thomas H., *Class, citizenship and social development,* New York, Doubleday, 1965.

Marston, Robert Q. and R. M. Jones, *The Science of Medical Practice: Medical Practice in Transition,* Princeton, The Robert Wood Johnson Foundation, 1992.

Maslach, Christine, *Burnout-The Cost of Caring.* Enblewood Cliffs, N.J., Prentice-Hall, 1982.

Mazzeo, Robert S., "Exercise, Immunity and Aging," in: Robert Goetz, Ed., *Exercise, Immunity and Aging,* New York, CRC Publishers, 1996, pp. 199-203.

Mead, George H., *Mind, Self and Society,* Chicago, University of Chicago Press, 1934.

Michaux, William, *The First Year Out,* Baltimore, Johns Hopkins University Press, 1969.

Moos, Rudolf H., *Evaluating Treatment Environments,* New Brunswick, N.J., Rutgers University Press, 1997.

Morantz-Sanchez, Regina Markell, *Sympathy and Science: Women Physicians in American Medicine,* New York, Oxford University Press, 1985.

Morone, James, *The Democratic Wish,* New York, Basic Books, 1990.

National Opinion Research Center, *Cumulative Codebook: General Social Surveys.* Chicago, 1991.

New York State Office of Mental Health, *OMH Report of the Task Force on Restraint and Seclusion,* Albany, N.Y. 1993.

No Author, Editorial, "Routine Practice," *The Bosotn Medical and Surgical Journal*, Vol.108, January 11, 1883, p. 827, in Charles E. Rosenberg, *The Care of Strangers: The Rise of America's Hospital System*, NY, Basic Books, 1987.

No author, *Profiles of U.S. Hospitals*. HCIA, Inc. Baltimore, 1995. National Center for Health Statistics, *An Overview of Nursing Homes and their Current Residents: The 1995 National Nursing Home Survery*, Hyattsvile, MD 1997.

No Author, "U.S. Registered Hospitals: Utilization, Personnel, and Finances," in *1998 Hospital Statistics*, Chicago, Healthcare Infosource, Inc., 1998, p. 4.

Noer, David, *Healing the wounds: Overcoming the trauma of layoffs and revitalizing downsized organizations.* San Francisco, Jossey-Bass, Inc., 1993.

Numbers, Ronald L. *Almost Persuaded*, Baltimore, The Johns Hopkins University Press, 1978.

Ogburn, William F., "Culture Lag as Theory," in William F. Ogburn, *On Culture and Social Change*, Chicago, University of Chicago Press, 1964, pp. 86-95.

Osborne, Liz, *Resolving Patient Complaints*, Gaithersburg, MD., Aspen Publishers, Inc., 1995.

Outka, George, "Social Justice and equal access to health care," in Stephen Lammers, ed., *On Moral Medicine*, Grand Rapids, William B. Erdmans Publishing, 1987.

Parsons, Mickey L. and Carolyn L. Murdaugh, *Patient –Centered Care-A Model for Restrucering*, Gaithersburg, MD., Aspen Publications, 1994..

Parsons, Talcott *The Social System*, New York., The Free Press, 1951.

Pataki, George E., *Operation Restore Trust*, Medicare, Binghamton, N.Y. 1998.

Pellegrino, Edmund D. "The Reconciliation of Technology and Humanism: A Flexnerian Task 75 Years Later, in *Flexner, 75 Years Later: A Current Commentary on Medical Education*, New York, University Press of America, 1987.

Pellegrino, Edmund D. "The Sociocultural Impact of Twentieth Century Therapeutics" in Morris J. Vogel and Charles Rosenberg, Eds., *The Therapeutic Revolution*, Philadelphia, The University of Pennsylvania Press, 1979.

Penna, Manoel W. "The Effects of the Milieu on Assaults," in:John R. Lion and William H. Reid, Eds,

Peplau, Letitia A and Daniel D. Perlman, *Loneliness, A sourcebook of current theory, research and therapy.* New York, Wiley, 1982.

Phillips, Lawrence R., *In the Name of the Patient: Consumer Advocacy of Health Care*, Chicago, American Hospital Association, 1995.

Pope, Kenneth S. Janet L. Sonne and Jean Holroyd, *Sexual Feelings in Psychotherapy*, Washington, D.C., American Psychological Association, 1993.

Rice, Mitchell F. and Woodrow Jones Jr., *Public Policy and the Black Hospital*, Westport, Conn., Greenwood Press, 1994.

Roberts, Joan J. and Thetis M. Group, *Feminism in Nursing*, Westport, Con. Praeger, 1995.

Rosenberg, Charles E., *The Care of Strangers: The Rise of America's Hospital System*, New York, Basic Books, 1987.

Rosenthal, Elisabeth, "Young Doctors Find Specialist Jobs Hard to Get," *The New York Times*, April 15, 1995, Sec. I, p. 1

Roethlisberger, Frederick J. and William J. Dickson, *Management and the Worker*, Cambridge, Harvard University Press, 1939.

Rosenberg, Charles E., " The Therapeutic Revolution: Medicine, Meaning and Social Change in Nineteenth Century America," in Morris J. Vogel, Ed., *The Therapeutic Revolution*, Philadlephia, The University of Pennsylvania Press, 1970.

Ryack, Elton, *Professional Power and American Medicine*, Cleveland and New York, The World Publishing Co., 1967.

Sapir, Edward, *Culture, Language and Personality*, Berkeley, The University of California Press, 1961.

Schlesinger, Jr., Arthur M., *The Coming of the New Deal*, Bosotn, Houghton Mifflin Co., 1959.

Sinclair, William J., *Semmelweiss; His Life and His Doctrines*, The University Press, Manchester, 1909.

Smith, Mickey C. and David A. Knapp, "Pharmacy as a Profession," in: Smith and Knapp, *Pharmacy, Drugs and Medical Care*, Baltimore, Williams and Wilkins, 1992, p. 106..

Snook, Jr., Donald, *Hospitals, What They Are and How They Work*, Rockville, MD., Aspen Systems Corp., 1981.

Society for the Right to Die, "The Physician and the Hopelessly Ill Patient," New York, *Society for the Right to Die*, 1985, p.87.

Starr, Paul, *The Social Transformation of American Medicine*, New York, Basic Books, 1982.

*Statistical Abstract of the United States 1997,*Washington, D.C. 1998, Table 205.

Strauss, Anselm Shizuko Fagerhaugh, Barbara Suczek and Carolyn Wiener, *Social Organization of Medical Work*, Chicago, University of Chicago Press, 1985.

Sydenstricker, Edgar and Isidore S. Falk, *Preliminary Reports,* Washington, D.C., Committee on Economic Security, 1934.

Szacz, Thomas S., *A Lexicon of Lunacy,* New Brunswick,N.J., Transaction Publishers, 1993.

Szacz, Thomas S., *The Myth of Mental Illness,* New York, Dell Publishing Co., 1961.

Talbott, John A., Robert E. Hales and Stuart L. Keill, *Textbook of administrative psychiatry,* Washington, D.C., American Psychiatric Press, 1992.

Thomas Maeder, *Children of Psychiatrists and other Psychotherapists,* New York, Harper & Row, 1989.

Thompson, William E. and Joseph V. Hickey, *Society in Focus: An Introduction to Sociology,* New York, Harper Collins College Publishers, 1994.

Tommasello, Anthony C., "Drug Abuse," in Mickey C. Smith and David A. Knapp, Eds., *Pharmacy, Drugs and Medical Care,* Baltimore, Williams and Wilkins, 1992.

Tönnies, Ferdinand, *Communiy and Society, (Gemeinschaft und Gesellschaft),* Charles P. Loomis, Translator, New York, American Book Co., 1940.

Tyler. David F., and Howard F. Hunt, *Encyclopedic Dictionary of Sports Medicine,* New York, Chapman and Hall, 1986.

U.S. Department of Justice, Bureau of Justice Statistics, *Prison Statistics,* November 22, 1998, p. 1.

Valberg, L.S., M.A. Gonyea, D.G. Sinclair and J.Wade, *Planning the Future Academic Medical Center.* Ottawa, Canadian Medical Association, 1994.

Vogel, Morris J., "The Transformation of the American Hospital, 1850-1920," in: Susan Reverby and David Rosner, Eds., *Health Care in America,* Philadelphia, Temple University Press, 1979, pp. 105-116.

Weber, Max, *Economy and Society,* Berkeley, The University of California Press, 1978.

Weber, Max, *The Protestant Ethic and the Spirit of Capitalism,* Talcott Parsons, Trans., New York, Scribner, 1956.

Weinstein, Bruce D. and Amy Haddad, "The Ethics of Pharmaceutical Care," in: Calvin Knowlton and Richard Penna, Eds., *Pharmaceutical Care,* New York, Chapman and Hall, 1996, pp. 319-329.

Weisse, Allen B., *Conversations in Medicine: The Story of Twentieth Century American Medicine in the Words of Those Who Created It,* New York, New York University Press, 1984.

Weissenstein, Eric, "No PARCA required," *Modern Healthcare,* Vol.28, No. 15, April 13, 1998.

Wigmore, J.H. *Evidence,* 3rd Ed., Boston, Little, Brown, 1961.

Wunderlich, Gooloo S., Frank S. Sloan and Carolyn K. Davis, *Nursing Staff in Hospitals and Nursing Homes,* Washington D.C., National Academy Press, 1996.

Zola, Irving K., *Socio-Medical Inquiries,* Philadelphia, Temple University Press, 1983.

Journals

Abdulla, Sara "Jury still out on aspects of acupuncture," *The Lancet,* Vol. 351, #9107, March 28, 1998, p. 962.

Ad Hoc Committee on Scope of Practice in Audiology, "Scope of Practice in Audiology," *FT Magazine, ASHA,* Vol. 38, No. 2, Spring 1996, p. 12.

Adamcik, Barbara A., H. Edward Ransford, Phillip R. Oppenheimer, Janice F. Brown, Pamela A. Eagan and Fred G. Weissman, "New Clinical Roles for Pharmacists: A Study of Role Expansion," *Social Science and Medicine,* Vol.22, No. 11, 1986, pp. 1187-1200.

Aiken, Lorraine, "Transformation of the nursing workforce," *Nursing Outlook,* Vol.43, No.5, 1995, pp. 201-209.

Alger, Alexandra, "Nursing home or home nursing?" *Forbes,* Vol. 159, No. 6, March 24, 1997, p. 160.

Allen, Karen, and Jim Blascovich, "Effects of Music on Cardiovascular Reactivity Among Surgeons," *JAMA,* September 21, 1994, p. 882.

Alper, Joseph, "The Machine of Your Dreams," *Health,* Vol.12, No.7, October, 1998, pp. 38-42.

Altman, David and Jordan J. Cohen, "Problems and Promises: The Potential Impact of Graduate Medical Education Reform," *The Milbank Quarterly,* Vol. 72, No. 4, December 1994, pp. 719-722.

Amado, Rivka-Grundstein, "Values education: a new direction for medical education," *Journal of Medical Ethics,* Vol.21, No. 3, June 1995, pp. 174-178.

Anders, Robert L., "Targeting Male Students," *Nurse Educator,* Vol. 18, No.2, March/April, 1993, p. 4.

Anderson, Carole A., "Nurses to Recommend Provider Mix in Shortage Areas," *Public Health Reports,* Vol. 113, No. 1, January/February 1998, p. 1132

Anderson, Ruth R. and Reuben A. McDaniel, Jr., "Intensity of Registered Nurse Participation in Nursing Home Decision

Making," *The Gerontologist,* Vol.38, No.1, February 1998, pp. 90-100.

Andriote, John Manuel, "The 1998 Salary Survery," *Working Woman,* February 1998, p.45.

Andriote, John Manuel, "The 1998 Salary Survery," *Working Woman,* February,1998, p.46.

Ash, David and Cherrie Galletly, "Crisis Beds: The Interface Between the Hospital and the Community,"

Aspy, David N., Cheryl B. Aspy and Patricia M. Quinby, "What Doctors Can Teach Teachers about Problem-Based Learning," *Educational Leadership,* Vol. 50m No.7, April 1993, p. 22.

Ayanian, John Z., "The Prospect of Sweeping Reform in Graduate Medical Education," *The Milbank Quarterly,* Vol. 72, No. 4, December 1994, p. 705.

Baker-Ward, Lynn, "Into the Jaws of Anxiety," *Psychology Today,* Vol. 28, No. 4, July-August 1995, p. 10.

Bandura, Albert, "Self-efficacy; Toward a unifying theory of behavioral change," *Psychological Review,*

Barinage, Marcia S., "How Exercise Works Its Magic," *Science,* Vol.276, May 30, 1967, p. 1325.

Barney, Joseph A., Janet Fredericks, Marcel Fredericks and Patricia Robinson, "Internalization of Professional Attitudes of Physicians: Implications for Health Care," *Education,* Vol. 117, No. 4, Summer 1997, pp. 530-539.

Barton, Linda T., "A Shoulder To Lean On: Assisted Living In The U.S.", *American Demographics,* Vol. 19, No.7, July 1997, pp. 45-51.

Barzansky, Barbara, Harry S. Jonas and Sylvia I. Etzel, "Educational Programs in U.S. Medical Schools, 1997-1998," *Journal of the American Medical Association,* Vol.280, No.9, Septembr 2, 1998, p. 805.

Beck, Cheryl Tatano, "Nursing Students' Experiences Caring for Dying Patients," *Journal of Nursing Education,* Vol. 36, No.9, November 1997, pp. 408-415.

Beck, Cornelia, "Correlates of Disruptive Behavior in Severely Cognitively Impaired Nursing Home Residents," *The Gerontologist,* Vol.38, No.2, April, 1998, pp. 189-198.

Begany, Thomas, "Layoffs: Targeting RNs." RN, Vol 57, No. 7, 994, pp. 37-38.

Bellandi, Deanna, *"For-profits get a break" Modern Health Care,* April 13, 1998, p. 20.

Berger, Jeffrey T., and Deborah Majerovitz, "Stability of Preferences for Treatment Among Nursing Home Residents," *The Gerontologist*, Vol.38, No.2, April 1998, pp. 217-223.

Biddle, Stuart, "Exercise and Psychosocial Health," *Research Quarterly for Exercise and Health*, Vol. 66, No.4, 1995, pp. 292-297.

Blair, Steven N., "Diet and Activity: The Synergistic Merger," *Nutrition Today*, Vol. 30, No.3, May/June 1995, pp. 108-111.

Blizzard, Peter J., "International Standards in Medical Education or National Standards/Primary Health Care-Which Direction?" *Social Science and Medicine*, Vol. 33, No. 10, 1991, pp. 1168-1169.

Boland, Arthur L., "Our Qualifications as Orthopaedic Surgeons to be Team Physicians," *The American Journal of Sports Medicine*, Vol. 24, No.6, November/December 1996, p. 712.

Bouchard, C. and L. Perusse, " Heredity and Body Fat," *Annual Review of Nutrition*, Vol.8, 1988, pp. 259-277.

Braham, James, "Fitness Machines Adopt Space Technology," *Machine Design*, Vol. 67, No. 8, April 20, 1995, p. 29.

Bramson, James, Diane Noskin and Jon D. Ruesch, "Demographics and Practice Characteristics of Dentists Participating and Not Participating in Managed Care Plans," *Journal of the American Dental Association*, Vol 128, December 1997, pp. 1708-1714.

Breo, Dennis L., "Two surgeons who dared are still chasing their dreams," *JAMA*, Vol. 262, No. 20, November 24, 1989, 2904.

Breslow, Richard E., B.I. Klinger and B.J. Erickson, "Crisis hospitalization on a psychiatric emergency service," *General Hospital Psychiatry*, Vol.15, 1993, pp. 307-315.

Brieger, Gert H. "Why the University-based Medical School Should Survive: A Histroical Perspective"

Brink, Susan and Nancy Shute, "Are HMOs the right prescription?" U.S. News and World Report, October 13, 1997, p. 60-64.

Brown, Phyllida, "Dentists and surgeons in the U.S. face compulsory HIV testing. *The New Scientist*, Vol. 129, No. 1753, January 26, 1998, p.21.

Brown, Susan and Dorothy Grimes, "Who's number one in primary care, RNs or MDs ?" *RN*, Vol.59, No. 4, April, 1996, p. 16

Buerhaus, Peter I. and Douglas O. Staiger, "Future of the Nurse Labor Market According to Executives in High-Managed Care Areas of the United States," *Image: Journal of Nursing Scholarship*, Vol. 29, No. 4, Fourth Quarter, 1997, pp. 313-318.

Bundren, Lee Ann, "State Consumer Fraud Legislation Applied to Health Care Industry," *The Journal of Legal Medicine*, Vol. 16, No. 1, March 1995, p. 159.

Burg, Brad, "What Jobs are out there now? Which jobs will there be tomorrow?" *Medical Economics*, September 25, 1995, pp. 171-174.

Campbell, Paulette Walker, "U.S. Will Pay Teaching Hospitals to Reduce the Number of Residents They Train," *The Chronicle of Higher Education*, Vol. XLIV, Number 2, September 5, 1997, p. A 51.

Campbell, Paulette Walker, "Senators Are Dubious of House Plan to Suspend Audits of Teaching Hospitals," *The Chronicle of Higher Education*, Vol. XLIV, No.10, October 31, 1997, p. A45.

Carmel, Sara and Seymour M. Glick, "Compassionate-Empathic Physicians." *Social Science and Medicine*, Vol. 43, No. 8, October 1996, pp. 1253-1261.

Carter, Rita, "Holistic hazards," *New Scientist*, Vol. 151, No. 2938, July 13, 1996,p. 12.

Cassell, Joan, "The Woman in the Surgeon's Body: Understanding Difference," *American Anthropologist*, Vol. 98, No.1, pp. 41-53.

Castle, Nicholas G., Barry Fogel and Vincent Mor, "Risk Factors for Physical Restraint Use in Nursing Homes: Pre-and Post Implementation of the Nursing Home Reform Act," *The Gerontologist*, Vol. 27, No.6, December 1997.

Cheifitz, D.I. and J.C. Salloway, "Patterns of Mental Health Services Provided by HMOs." *American Psychologist*, Vol. 39,1984, pp. 495-502.

Coady, N.F. and C. S. Wolgien, "Good therapists' views of how they are helpful," *Clinical Social Work Journal*, Vol.24, No. 3, 1996, pp. 311-322.

Conviser, Richard, Margaret J. Rotondo and Mark Loveless, "Predicting the Effect of the Oregon Health Plan on Medicaid Coverage for Outpatients with HIV," *American Journal of Public Health*, Vol. 84, No.12, December 1994, pp. 1994-1995.

Cook, Circe, " Reflections on the Health Care Team: My Experiences in an Interdisciplinary Program." JAMA, Vol.277, No.13, April 2, 1997, p.1091.

Cornwell III, Edward E., David Jacobs, Mark Walker, Lenworth Jacobs, John Porter and Arthur Fleming, "National Medical Association Surgical Position Paper on Violence Prevention," *JAMA*, Vol.273, No. 22, June 14, 1995, pp. 1788-1789.

Corrigan, Patrick W., Larry Hess and Andrew N. Garman, "Results of a Job analysis of Psychologists Working in State Hospitals," *Journal of Clinical Psychology*, Vol. 54, No.1, 1998, pp. 11-18.

Corrigan, Patrick W., E. Paul Homes and Daniel Luchens, " Burn-out and Collegial Support in State Psychiatric Hospital Staff," *Journal of Clinical Psychology*, Vol.51, No.5, September, 1995, pp. 703-710.

Cromley, Janet, "When Your Doctor is a Nurse," *Good Housekeeping*, Vol. 225, No.2, August 1997, pp. 145-146.

Crone, Catherine C. and Thomas N. Wise, "Use of Herbal Medicines Among Consultation-Liaison Populations," *Psychosomatics*, Vol. 39, No. 1, January-February 1998, pp. 3-13.

Cruise, Patrice A., "The Nighttime Environment and Incontinence Care Practices in Nursing Homes," *Journal of the American Geriatrics Society*, Vol. 46, No. 2, February 1998, pp. 181-186.

Cutchin, Malcolm P., "Community And Self: Concepts for Rural Physician Integration and Retention," *Social Science and Medicine*, Vol. 44, No. 11, June 1997, p. 1661.

Daugherty, Steven R, "Learning, Satisfaction and Mistreatment During Medical Internship," *Journal of the American Medical Association*, Vol.279, No. 15, April 15, 1998, pp. 1194-1199.

Davis-Martin, Shirley, "Research on Males in Nursing," *Journal of Nursing Education*, Vol. 23, No. 4, April 1984, pp. 162-164.

DeLeon, Patrick H., Diane K. Kjervik, Alan G. Kraut and Gary R. Vanden Bos, "Psychology and Nursing: A Natural Alliance, *American Psychologist*, Vol.40, No. 11, November 1985, p. 1153.

deMayo, Robert A ., "Patient Sexual Behavior and Sexual Harassment: A National Survey of Female Psyhologists," *Professional Psychology: Research and Practice*, Vol.28, No. 1, February 1997, pp. 58-62.

Drew, Edward B. "The Health Syndicate: Washington's Noble Conspirators," *The Atlantic* Vol. 220, No. 75, December 1967.

Drewnowski, Adam, Candace L. Kurth and Dean D. Krahn, "Effects of Body Image on Dieting, Exercise and Anabolic Stereoid Use in Adolescent Males," *International Journal of Eating Disorders*, Vol. 17, No. 4, May 1995, pp. 381-385.

Eamon, Mary Keegan, "Institutionalizing Children and Adolescents in Private Psychiatric Hospitals," *Social Work*, Vol.39, No. 5, September 1994, pp. 588-594.

Earle, Kathleen A. and Sandra L. Forquer, " Use of Seclusion with Chidren and Adolescents in Public Psychiatric Hospitals," *American Journal of Orthopsychiatry*, Vol.65, No.2, April 1995, pp. 238-244.

Ebert, Robert H., "Medical Education at the Peak of the Era of Experimental Medicine," *Daedalus,* Vol. 112, No.5, Spring, 1986, pp.76-77.

Edwards, Jana K. and Jenniger M. Bess, "Developing Effectiveness in the Therapeutic Use of Self," *Clinical Social Work Journal,* Vol.26, No.1, Spring 1998, p. 90.

Eisenberg, David, "Unconventional Medicine in the United States: Prevalence, Costs and Patterns of Use," *The New England Journal of Medicine,* Vol.328, 1993, pp. 246-252.

Eisler, Peter, "Care, control at center of unique labor dispute," *USA Today,* December 7, 1998, p. 1.

Elam, Carol L., Edwin D. Taylor and E. Nelson Strother, Jr., "Preparing for Medical School and the Medical Profession: Advice to Advisors" *National Academic Advising Association Journal,* Vol. 16, No. 2, Fall 1996 p. 34.

Englehardt, H. T., Jr., "National health care policy: the moral issues." *American College of Surgeons Bulletin,* Vol. 78, No. 4, pp. 10-14.

Ernst, E., "Complementary Medicine," *The Lancet,* Vol. 341, No. 8861, June 26, 1993, p. 1626.

Ettinger, Walter, "A Randomized Trial Comparing Aerobic Exercies and Resistance Exercise with a Health Education Program in Older Adults with Knee Osteoarthritis-The Fitness Arthritis and Seniors Trial" *Journal of the American Medical Association,* Vol. 277, No. 1, January 1, 1997, pp. 25-31.

Evans, H. and C.A. Fergason, "Medical unversities and academic health centers: lessons of history," *Academic Medicine,* Vol. 71, 1996, pp. 1141-1142.

Falk, L.A., B. Page and W. Vesper, "Human values and medical education: From the perspective of health care delivery," *Journal of Medical Education,* Vol. 48, 1973, pp. 152-157.

Feis, Charles C., C.T. Mobray and Paul J. Chamberlain, " Serving the chronic mentally ill in state and community hospitals," *Community Mental Health Journal,* vol.26, 1990, pp. 221-232.

Fink , David and Annemarie Franczyk, "Area HMOs", *Business First of Buffalo,* May 19, 1997, p. 58.

Fontane, Patrick E., " Exercise, Fitness and Feeling Well," *American Behavioral Scientist,* Vol. 39, No.3, January 1996, p. 288.

Foster, John, "The Financial Status of Medicare," *Public Health Reports,* Vol. 113, No. 2, March/April 1998, p. 117.

Fox, Nicholas J., "Postmodernism, rationality and the evaluation of health care," *The Sociological Review,* Vol. 39, No. 4, November 1991, p.725.

Frank, Richard, Donald Salkever and Samuel Sharfstein, "A new look at rising mental health insurance costs," *Health Affairs*, Vol. 10, 1991, pp. 116-123.

Friedman, Maurice, "Buber's Philosophy As the Basis for Dialogical Psychotherapy and Contextual Therapy," *Journal of Humanistic Psychology*, Vol. 38, No. 1, Winter 1998, pp. 25-40.

Furger, Roberta, "In Search of Relief for Tired, Aching Eyes," *PC World*, Vol. 11, No.2, February 1993, p. 29.

Furtado, Teo, "The Over-the-Counter Culture," *Health*, Vol.6, No.1, February/March 1992, pp. 28-29.

Galbraith, Michael, "Attracting Men to Nursing: What Will They Find Important in Their Career?" *Journal of Nursing Education*, Vol. 30, No.4, April 1991, pp. 182-186.

Garfein, Jennifer L., "The Patient's Perspective," *JAMA*, Vol.275, No. 17, May 1, 1996, p. 1371.

Gilbert, John, "Administrators on the move," *McKnight's Long Term News*, Vol. 17, No. 10, 1996, p.1.

Gillon, Raanon, "Case studies and medical education," *Journal of Medical Ethics*, Vol.22, No. 1, February 1996, pp. 3-4.

Glaser, Ronald J., "The Doctor Is Not In," *Harper's Magazine*, Vol. 296, No. 1774, March 1998.

Glick, Shimon M., "The teaching of medical ethics to medical students," *Journal of medical ethics*. Vol. 20, No. 4, December 1994, p. 241.

Golden, Valerie and Barry A. Farber, "Therapists as Parents: Is It Good for the Children?" *Professional Psychology: Research and Practice*, Vol.29, No.2, March 1998, pp. 135-139.

Gordon, Suzanne, "The Quality of Mercy," *The Atlantic Monthly*, Vol. 279, No. 2, February,1979 p.81.

Green, Kathleeen, "Leading the Life: Jobs in Health Clubs," *Occupational Outlook Quarterly*, Vol. 39, No. 2, Summer 1995, pp. 15-22. See also: Bureau of Labor Statistics, *National Occupational Employment Statistics*, October 28, 1998.

Greenblatt, Morris and Paul Rodenhauser, "Mental health administration: Changes and challenges." *Administration and Policy in Mental Health*, Vol. 31, 1993, pp. 97-100.

Greene, Victor L. and John I. Ondrich, " Risk factors for nursing home admissions and exits: A discrete-time hazard approach." *Journal of Gerontology: Social Sciences*, Vol.45, 1990, pp. S250-S258.

Gruber, Jonathan, Kathleen Adams and Joseph P. Newhouse, "Physician Fee Policy and Medicaid Program Costs," *The Journal of Human Resources*, Vol. 32, No. 4, Fall 1997, p. 634.

Hall, John C. and Cameron Platell, "Half-life of truth in surgical literature," *The Lancet,* Vol.350, December 13, 1997, p. 1752.

Hamilton, Linda, "A Sensible Approach to Weight Loss," *Dance Magazine,* Vol.71, November 1997, pp. 63-65.

Hanft, Robert, "National Health Expenditures," 1950-1965" *Social Security Bulletin,* Vol. 30, No. 3, February 1967.

Harmon, Susan M. and Jerry B. Vannatta, "Senior medical students learn as simulated patients," *Medical Teacher,* Vol. 17, No. 1, March 1995, p. 31.

Hart, Daniel and Alice Park, "Too Big a Heart," *Time, Special Issue,* Vol. 150, No. 19, Fall 1997, pp. 35-37.

Hartz, Arthur J., Jose S . Pulido and Evelyn M. Kuhn, "Are the Best Coronary Artery Bypass Surgeons Identified by Physician Surveys?" *American Journal of Public Health,* Vol. 87, No. 10, October 1997, p. 1645.

Haspel, Katherine S. and Linda M. Jorgenson, "Legislative Action Regarding Therapist Sexual Misconduct: An Overview", *Professional Psychology, Research and Practice,* Vol.28, No.1, February 1997, pp.63-72

Hawes, Catherine *et al,* "The OBRA-87 Nursing Home Regulations and Implementation of the Resident Assessment Instrument: Effect on Process Quality." *Journal of the American Geriatrics Society,* Vol. 45, No. 8, August 1997, pp. 977-985.

Hawkins, Clifford, "Changing Doctor-Patient Relationships: The Causes," *Contemporary Review,* Vol.25, No. 1484, September 1989, p. 146.

Haywood, Thomas W., Howard M. Kravitz, Linda S. Grossman, James L. Cavanaugh, John M. Davis and Dan A. Lewis, "Predicting the "Revolving Door" Phenomenon Among Patients With Schizophrenia, Schizoaffective, and Affective Disorders," *American Journal of Psychiatry,* Vol. 152, No. 6, June 1995, pp. 856-851.

Headden, Susan, "Danger at the Drug Store," *U.S. News & World Report,* Vol.121, No.8, August 26, 1996, pp. 47-53.

Heimlich, Henry, "Advances in Medical Education," *Resource Video,* Physicians Committee for Responsible Medicine, 1997.

Helmlinger, Connie, "ANA Hails Landmark Law as Nursing Victory," *AJN* Vol. 97, No. 10, October 1997, p. 16.

Hepburn, Kenneth, "The Family Stories Workshop: Stories for Those Who cannot Remember." *The Gerontologist,* Vol. 37, No.6, December, 1997, pp. 827-832.

Heymann, Stanley J., "Patients in Research: Not just subjects, but partners." *Science,* Vol. 269, pp. 797-798.

Hogan, Mary, Franklin J. Eppig and Daniel R. Waldo, "Access to Physicians," *Health Care Financing*

Holmes, Oliver Wendell, "The Contagiousness of Puerperal Fever," *New England Quarterly Journal for Medicine and Surgery*, in *Medical Classics*, Vol. 1, No. 3, November 1936, p. 213.

Humphreys, Keith, "Clinical Psychologists and Psychotherapists," *American Psychologist*, Vol. 51, No.3, March 1996, p. 190.

Hunt, Gerard J., and Jeffrey Sobal, "Teaching Medical Sociology in Medical Schools," *Teaching Sociology*, Vol. 18, No. 3, July 1990, p. 320.

Hunter, Lauren and Vanda Lops, "Certified Nurse Midwives," JAMA, Vol. 277, No.13, April 2, 1997, p. 1095.

Hunter, Kathryn M., "Eating the Curriculum," *Academic Medicine*, Vol.72, No. 3, March 1997, p. 169.

Huxtable, Robert J., "The harmful potential of herbal and other plant products," *Drug Safety*, Vol. 5, Suppl. 1, 1990, pp. 126-136.

Ives, T.J. and C.C. Stults, "Pharmacy practice in a chemically-dependency treatment center," *American Journal of Hospital Pharmacy*, Vol. 47, 1990, pp. 1080-1083.

Jack, David B., "Robot surgeons: never mind the cost, feel the quality," *The Lancet*, Vol.348, No. 9035, October 26, 1996, p. 1160.

Jaklevic, Mary Chris, "Cincinnati fights to take back control of hospital," *Modern Health Care*, Vol.28, No. 15, April 13, 1998, p. 24.

Jaret, Peter, "Choose Treatments You Believe In," *Health*, Vol. 11, April 1997, pp. 99-100.

Jaret, Peter, "You Don't Have to Sweat to Reduce Your Stress," *Health*, November/ December 1995, pp. 83-88.

Jette, Allan, Laurence G. Branch, Lynn A. Sleeper, Henry Feldman and Lisa M. Sullivan, "High Risk Profile for Nursing Home Admission," *The Gerontoloigst*, Vol.32, No.5, October 1992, pp. 634-640.

Joel, Lucille A., "Your License to Practice," American Journal of Nursing, Vol.95, No. 11, November 1995, p. 7.

Jolly, P., Jolinn, L., Krakower, J.K. , Beran, R.L., " Review of U.S. Medical School Finances 1993-1994" *Journal of the American Medical Association*, Vol. 268, 1992. pp.1149-1155.

Jones, Robert F. and David Korn, "On the Cost of Educating a Medical Student," *Academic Medicine*, Vol. 72, No.3, March 1997, pp. 201-208.

Judd, Marmor, "Letter to the Editor," *Psychiatric News*, March 18, 1994, pp.22-23.

Kalis, Lisa, "Salary Report," *Working Woman*, Vol.22, No.1, January 1997, pp. 31-33 and 69-76.

Kalis, Lisa, "Salary Report," *Working Woman*, Vol.23, No.2, February 1998, pp. 39-41.

Kane, Robert L., "Assuring Quality in Nursing Home Care," *Journal of the American Geriatric Society*, Vol.46, No. 2, February, 1998, pp. 232-237.

Katz, Paul R., Jurgis Karuza, John Kolassa and Alan Hutson, "Medical Practice with Nursing Home Residents: Results from the National Physician Professional Activities Census," *Journal of the American Geriatrics Society*, Vol.45, No. 8, August 1997, pp. 911-917.

Keating, Peter, "Why You May Be Getting the Wrong Medicine," *Money*, Vol.26, June 1997, p. 143.

Keepnews, David, "New Opportunities and Challenges for APRNs." *AJN* Vol. 98, No.1, January 1998, pp. 46-52.

Kelly, Carole, "Surveyeing Public Health Nurses' Continuing Education Needs: Collaboration of Practice and Academia," *The Journal of Continuing Education in Nursing*, Vol. 25, No3, May-June 1997, pp. 115-123.

Kessler, Ronald C., "Lifetime and 12 Month Prevalence of DSM-III-R Psychiatric Disorders in the United States: Results of the National Comorbidity Survey." *Journal of the American Medical Association*, Vol. 271, March 2, 1994, p. 654 D.

Kemper, Paul and Charles M. Murtaugh, "Lifetime use of nursing home care." *New England Journal of Medicine*, Vol.324, 1991, p. 595.

Kenyon, Virginia, *et al*, "Clinical competencies for community health nurses," *Public Health Nursing*, Vol. 7, No. 1, 1990, pp. 33-39.

Kiesler, C.A. "Public and professional myths about mental hospitalization," *American Psychologist*, Vol. 37, 1982, pp. 1323-1339.

Kindig, J.A., J.M. Cultice and F. Mullan, "The Elusive Generalist Physician: Can We Reach a 50% Goal?" *Journal of the American Medical Association*, Vol. 270, 1993, pp. 1069-1073.

King, Abby C., Roy F. Oman, Glenn S. Brassington, Donald L. Bliwise and William L. Haskell, "Moderate-Intensity Exercise and Self-rated Quality of Sleep in Older Adults," *Journal of the American Medical Association*, Vol. 277, No.1, January 1, 1977, pp. 32-37.

Knox, Richard, "Drug Resistant Virus has AIDS Implications," *The Boston Globe*, February 1, 1989.

Kodner, Ira, "The Patient-Doctor Relationship," *Vital Speeches,* Vol.64, No. 22, September 1, 1998, pp. 695-698.

Kreiger, Lloyd M., "Cardiac Surgery Performance Reports," *The New England Journal of Medicine,* Vol. 336, No. 6, February 6, 1997, p. 442.

Krey, S., Pavlou, K.N., and Steffee, W.P., "Exercise as an adjunct to weight loss and maintenance in moderately obese subjects," *American Journal of Clinical Nutrition,* Vol. 49, 1989, pp. 1115-1123.

Krieger, Donald, "Therapeutic touch: the imprimatur of nursing," *American Journal of Nursing,* Vol. 75, 1975, pp. 784-787.

Krucoff, Carol, "Can't Get To The Gym? Activate Your Life!" *The Saturday Evening Post,* Vol. 270. No. 1, January/February 1998, p. 26.

Lachance, Paul H., "Human Obesity," *Food Technology,* Vol.48, No.2, February 1994, p. 127.

Lantz, Melinda, Eric N. Buchalter and Lucia McBee, "The Wellness Group: A Novel Intervention for Coping With Disruptive Behavior in Elderly Nursing Home Residents," *The Gerontoloigst,* Vol.37, No.4, August 1997, pp. 551-556.

Leavitt, Judith Walzer, "Medicine in Context: A Review Essay of the History of Medicine," *American Historical Review,* Vol. 95, No. 5. December 1990, p.1473.

Lemonick, Michael D., "The Tumor War," in *Heroes of Medicine,* Edward L. Jamieson and Barrett Seman, Eds. New York, Time Special Issue, Vol. 150, No. 19, Fall 1997, pp. 46-48.

Levine, Suzanne B., "The Pharmacist Factor," *Columbia Journalism Review,* Vol. 30, November-December 1991, p. 14.

Ley, C.L., B. Lee and J.C. Stevenson, "Sex and Menopause associated Changes in Body Fat Distribution." *American Journal of Clinical Nutrition,* Vol. 55, 1992, pp. 950-954.

Lord, Earl "Health Media Watch," *Journal of the American Dental Association,* Vol. 128, December 1997, p. 1640.

Lovell, M.C. "The politics of medical deception: challenging the trajectory of history" *Advances in Nursing Science,* Vol. 2, No. 3, 1980, pp. 73-86.

MacKenzie, Debora, "Life getting you down? Go and work up a sweat," *New Scientist,* Vol. 143, No. 1942, September 10, 1994, p. 9.

Mahoney, Michael J., "Psychotherapists Personal Problems and Self-Care Patterns," *Professional Psychology: Research and Practice,* Vol.28, No.1, February 1997, pp. 14-16.

Mandel, Irwin D., " The Image of Dentistry in Contemporary Culture," *Journal of the American Dental Association,* Vol.129, May 1998, pp. 607-613.

Mangan, Katherine S., "Some Medical and Nursing Schools Declare a Truce and Start to Work Together," *The Chronicle of Higher Education,* Vol. XLIV, #17, December 19, 1997, p. 8.

Mansfield, Jiska Cohen and Perla Weiner, "The Effects of an Enhanced Environment on Nursing Home Residents Who Pace," *The Gerontolgist,* Vol.38, No.2, April 1998, pp. 199-208.

Manson, J.E., M.J. Stampfer, C.H. Hennekens, and W.C. Willet, "Body weight and longevity," *Journal of the American Medical Association,* Vol.257, 1987, pp. 353-358.

Marcus, Bess H., Cheryl A. Eaton, Joseph S. Rossi and Lisa L. Harlow, " Self-Efficacy, Decision-Making and Stages of Change: An Integrative Model of Physical Exercise," *Journal of Applied Social Psychology,* Vol. 24, No. 6, March 1994, p. 489. .

Marcus, Bess H., Anna E. Albright, Raymond S. Niaura, Elaine R. Taylor, Laurey R. Simkin, Susan I. Feder, David B.Abrams, and Paul D. Thompson, "Exercise Enhances The Maintenance of Smoking Margolese, Howard C. "Engaging in Psychotherapy with the Orthodox Jew," *American Journal of Psychotherapy,* Vol. 52, No. 1, Winter 1998, pp. 37-53.

Marjoribanks, Timothy, Mary-Jo Delvecchio Good, Ann G. Lawthers and Lynn M. Peterson, "Physicians' Discourses on Malpractice and the Meaning of Medical Malpractice," *Journal of Health and Social Behavior,* Vol. 37, June 1996, pp. 163-178.

Marks, Cynthia, "Eye Workouts That Don't Work," *Mademoiselle,* Vol. 95, November 1989, p. 142.

Mason, Michael, "Why we don't exercise," *Health,* Vol.12, No. 5, July-August 1998, p. 66.

McClendon, B., Jerald Robert M. Politzer, Evelyn Christian and Enrique S. Fernandez, "Downsizing the Physician Work Force," *Public Health Reports,* Vol.112. #3, May/June 1997, p.235.

McFarland, Bentson H., "Ending the Millenium," *Community Mental Health Journal,* Vol.32, No.3, June 1996, pp. 219-220.

McGahan, Anita M., "Industry Structure and Competitive Advantage," *Harvard Business Review,* Vol.72.

Mc Gregor, Alan, "Sentenced for homicide," *The Lancet,* Vol.342, No. 8871, September 4, 1993, p.610.

McKinlay John B. and J.D. Stoeckle, "Corporization and the social transformation of doctoring," *The International Journal of Health Services,* Vol. 18, 1988, pp. 191-205.

McKinlay, John B., Deborah A Potter and Henry Feldman, "Non-Medical Influences on Medical Decision Making, " *Social Science and Medicine*, Vol.42, No. 5, March 1996, p 773.

McLeod, S.M. and H.N. McCullough, "Social Science Education as a Component of Medical Training," *Social Science and Medicine*, Vol.39, No. 9, 1994, p. 1367.

McMenamin, Brigid, "Crusader," *Forbes*, March 9, 1998, p. 102.

Meredith, Philip, "Patient Satisfaction With Communication in General Surgery: Problems of Measurement and Improvement." *Social Science and Medicine*, Vol.37, No. 5, September, 1993, p. 591.

Meskin, Lawrence H., "A Dental Rip-Off," *Journal of the American Dental Association*, Vol.128, March 1997, pp. 264-266.

Meskin, Lawrence H., "An Oversupply in the Offing?" *Journal of the American Dental Association*, Vol.128, July, 1997, p. 802.

Meskin, Lawrence H., "What do Dentists do When They don't do Dentistry?" *Journal of the American Dental Association*, " Vol. 128, June 1997, p. 682.

Meskin, Lawrence H., "Patients First and Always," *Journal of the American Dental Association*, Vol.128, February 1997, p. 140.

Meyer, Katherine A., "An Educational Program to Prepare Acute Care Nurses for a Transition to Home Health Care Nursing," *The Journal of Continuing Education in Nursing*, Vol.28, No. 3, May/June 1987, pp,124-129.

Miles, H.S., "Informed demands for non-beneficial medical treatment." *The New England Journal of Medicine,*" Vol. 325, 1991, pp. 512-515.

Miller, Harold "The Health Service in Amsterdam," *International Journal of Social Psychiatry*, Vol.2, 1956-1957, p.145.

Moore, Art "Hospice Care Hijacked," *Christianity Today*, Vol.42, No.3, March 2, 1998, pp. 38-41. .

Moore, T.F., "Rightsizing: Living with the new reality," *Healthcare Financial Management*, Vol. 48, No.9, 1994, pp. 49-53.

Morreim, E. Haavi, "Redefining Quality by Reassigning Responsibility," *American Journal of Law and Medicine*, Vol. XX, No. 1 and 2, Summer 1994, p. 86.

Morrissey, J.P. and H.H. Goldman, "Cycles of Reform in the Care of the Chronically Mentally Ill," *Hospital and Community Psychiatry*, Vol. 35, 1984, pp. 785-793.

Muller, Stanley, "Physicians for the Twenty- First Century: Report of the Project Panel on the General Professional Education of the Physician and College Preparation for Medicine," *Journal of Medical Education*, Vol. 59, Part 2, 1984.

No author, "How the World Sees Us," *The New York Times Magazine*, Sec. 6, June 8, 1997, p. 37.

No author, "Managed Care," *Medical Economics*, Vol.75, No. 22, November 9, 1998, p. 24.

No author, "Managing Medications," *Healthwatch*, #366, 1994, pp. 4-5.

No author, "Mishap in the Operating Room," *The Economist*, Vol. 344, No. 8028, August 2, 1997, p.48.

No author, "Nevada Supreme Court Overturns Discipline of Neurosurgeon," *JADA*, Vol.124, June 1993, pp. 116-117.

No author, "Physical Activity and Hypertension," *The American Family Physician*, Vol. 48, No. 8, December, 1993, p. 1561.

No author, "Recommendations on Physical Exercise," *The American Family Physician*, Vol. 48, No. 6, November, 1993, pp. 1168.

No author, "Skullduggery," *Scientific American*, Vol. 262, No. 6, June 1990, p. 34.

No author, "The Pharmaceutical Industry," *The Economist*, Vol.346, February 21, 1998, p. 4.

No author, "Tone Your Thighs, Tune Your Ears," *Health*, Vol.8, P. 14, October 1994, p. 15.

Noren, Jay, "A National Physician Workforce Policy, " *Public Health Reports*, Vol. 112, No. 3, May/June 1997, pp. 219-221.

Norheim, Arne Johan, "Adverse effects of acupuncture," *The Lancet*, Vol. 345, June 17, 1995, p. 15762

Okasha, Ahmed, "The Future of Medical Education and Teaching: A Psychiatric Perspective," *American Journal of Psychiatry*, Vol 154, No. 6, June 1997, p. 80.

Payne, Brian K. and Dean Dabney, "Prescription Fraud: Characteristics, Consequences, and Influences,"

Olfson, Mark and David Mechanic, "Mental Disorders in Public, Private Nonprofit and Proprietary

Onion, Carl W.R. and Peter D. Slade, "Depth of information processing and memory facts," *Medical Teacher*, Vol. 17,No.3, 1995, p. 307.

Oransky, Ivan and Jay Varma, "Nonphysicians Clinicians and the Future of Medicine," *JAMA*, Vol.277,

Owen, Cathy Valerie Rutherford, Michael Jones, Christopher Tennant and Andrew Smallman, "Psychiatric

Rehospitalization Following Hospital Discharge,", *Community Mental Health Journal*, Vol.33, No. 1, February 1997, pp. 13-24.

Page, Randy M. and Larry A. Tucker, "Psychosocial Discomfort and Exercise Frequency: An Epidemiological Study of Adolescents," *Adolescence*, Vol.29, No. 113, Spring 1994, pp. 183-191.

Nadelson, C., "Medical Education: A Commentary oɪ Contemporary Issues," *American Journal of Psych* No. 7, July 1996, Festschrift Supplement, p. 3.

Nadelson, C., "Ethics, empathy and gender in health (*Journal of Psychiatry,* Vol 150, No. 9, 1993, p. 130

Nagelkerk, Jean, Patricia M. Ritola and Patty J. Vaɪ Informatics: The Trend of the Future,"

Napoli, Maryann, "Why Prescription Drugs Can Cause Now," *New Choice,* Vol. 35, No. 3, April 1995, p. ∠

National Association of Social Workers, "Caplan Addɪ Care and Ethics," *Update,* Vol. 22, No. 5, Novembɩ

Nesbit, Fredrick, "Non-compliance With Psycɪ Prescriptions," *American Journal of Psychiatry,* V May 1994, p. 783.

Neuhauser, Duncan, "American College of Healthc Code of Ethics," in Anthony R. Kovner and Dunɩ Eds., *Health Services Management,* Ann Administration Press, 1990, p. 56.

No author, *The Economist, Vol. 338, No. 7957,* March 34-35

No author, "New Doctor Roles for 21st Century" Newsletter Edition, Volume 118, No. 2531, August

No author, "Patients and Consumers: Wants and Needɪ Vol. 1, 1961, pp. 927-928.

No author, "The Hippocratic Oath: A Basis for Ɲ Standards," JAMA The Journal of the Ame Association, Vol. 264, No. 17, pg.2311.

No author, " Specs on Specs," *Consumer Reports,* Vol. pp.10-15.

No author, "Acupuncture Gives Knees a Lift," *Scien* 145, No. 18, April 30, 1994, p. 319.

No author, "America's Getting Fatter," *American Jourɪ* Vol.94, September 1994, p. 9.

No author, "Can A 1,245% Markup on Drugs Real *Business Week,* #3343, November 1, 19993, p. 34.

No author, "Clear and Present Danger," *Nursing,* Vɩ September, 1995, p. 9.

No Author, "Court Says Surgeon Should Have Discloseɩ *JAMA,* Vol.124, May 1993, p. 165.

No author, "For- profit medicine," *The Economist,* V August 2, 1997, p. 16.

No author, "Hospital Pulse," *Hospital and Health Netɪ* 20, 1998, p. 40.

Palca, Joseph, "CDC Closes the Case of the Florida Dentist," *Science,* Vol. 256, #5060, May 22, 1992, pp. 1130-1131.

Parker, Malcolm, "Autonomy, problem-based learning, and the teaching of medical ethics," *Journal of Medical Ethics,* Vol.21, No. 5, October 1995, pp. 305-310.

Paterson, Barbara L., "The Negotiated Order of Clinical Teaching," *Journal of Nursing Education,* Vol.36, No. 5, May 1997, pp. 197-205.

Peek, Chuck W., Raymond T. Coward, Gary R. Lee and Barbara A. Zsembik, "The Influence of Community Context on the Preference of Older Adults for Entering a Nursing Home," *The Gerontologist,* Vol.37, No.4, August 1997, pp.533-542.

Peeno, Linda, "What is the value of a voice?" U.S..News and World Report, Vol. 129, No.9, March, 1998, p.40

Pelonero, Anthony L., Richard L. Elliot, Jack W. Barber and Al Best, "Physician Caseload at Public Mental Institutions," *American Journal of Psychiatry,* Vol. 153, No.3, March 1996, pp. 429-431.

Pescosolido, Bernice A., "Teaching Medical Sociology through Film: Theoretical Perspectives and Practical Tools," *Teaching Sociology,* Vol. 18, No. 3, July 1990, p. 340.

Reding, R. and Michael Raphelson, "Around-the-Clock Mobile Psychiatric Intervention: Another Effective Alternative to Psychiatric Hospitalization," *Community Mental Health Journal,* Vol.31, No.2, April 1995, pp179-187.

Reese, K.M., "Women who exercise run risk of iron deficiency," *Chemical and Engineering News,* Vol. 73, November 27, 1995, p. 52.

Reilly, Thomas W., Steven B. Clauser and David K. Baugh, "Trends in Medical Payments and Utilization 1975-1989," *Health Care Finance Review Annual Supplement,* 1990, pp. 15-33.

Relman, Albert S., "The Future of medical practice," *Health Affairs,* Vol. 2, 1983, pp. 5-19.

Remley Jr , T. Theodore P., Barbara Herlihy, and Scott B. Herlihy, "The U.S. Supreme Court Decision in *Jaffe v. Redmond*: Implications for Counselors." *Journal of Counseling and Development,* January/February 1997, Vol. 75, pp. 213.

Renard, Ann, "The Bunion Wars," *Health,* Vol. 23, No.4, May 1991, p. 37.

Richmond, Julius B. and Rashi Fein, "The Health Care Mess," *JAMA,* Vol. 273, No.1, January 4, 1994.

Riggs, R. Thomas, "HMOs and the Seriously Mentally Ill-A View from the Trenches," *Community Mental Health Journal,* Vol. 32, No.3, June 1996, pp. 213-217.

Roberts, P. A., "Job satisfaction among U.S. pharmacists," *American Journal of Hospital Pharmacy,* Vol.40, 1983, pp. 391-399.

Rodin, John, "Aging and health: Effects of the sense of control." *Science,* Vol.233, 1986, pp. 1272-1276.

Roe, Benson B., "The UCR Boondoggle: A Death Knell for private Practice?" *New England Journal of Medicine,* v. 305, July 2, 1981, pp. 41-45.

Rossellini, Lynn R, "How far should you go to stay fit?", *U.S. News and World Report,* November 10, 1997,p.95.

Rothman, David J., "The Public Presentation of Blue Cross, 1935-1965". *Journal of Health Politics,* U.S. Congress 1964:28

Ruhlman, Lori B., "A Bridge, A Hand, A Guide," *Health Care News of Central New York,* Vol.6, No. 7, July1998, p. 1.

Ruuskanen J. M. and I. Ruoppila, "Physical Activity and Psychological Well-being among People Aged 65 to 84 Years," *Age and Aging,* Vol.24, No. 4, July 1995, pp. 292-296.

Sand, Margaret and Susan P. Phillips, "A Qualitative Study of Sexual Harassment of Female Doctors by Patients," *Social Science and Medicine,* Vol. 45, No.5, September 1997, pp. 669-667.

Sanguineti, Vincenzo, Stephen Samuel, Stephen L. Schwartz and Mary Robeson, "Retrospective Study of 2,200 Involuntary Psychiatric Admissions and Readmissions," *American Journal of Psychiatry,* Vol.153, No.3, March 1996, pp. 392-396.

Savitz, Sean I., "The Pivotal Role of Harvey Cushing in the Birth of Modern Neurosurgery," *JAMA,* Vol.278, No. 13, October 1, 1997, p. 1119.

Schücklenk, Udo, "The Inferiority Complex of Primary Care Physicians," *Hastings Center Report,* Vol. 27, No. 6, November/December 1997, p. 51.

Segal, Marian, "Washington State Firm Prosecuted for Distributing Non-Sterile Drugs," *FDA Consumer,* Vol.28, No. 4, May 1994, p. 29.

Seligson, Susan V., "Anti-Aging Comes of Age," *Health,* Vol.12, No.3, April 1998, p. 64.

Selingo, Jeffrey, "Suit Seeks to Halt Audits of Teaching Hospitals," *The Chronicle of Higher Education,* Vol. 44, November 7, 1997, p. A 34.

Sfikas, Peter M., "Much Obliged," *Journal of the American Dental Association,* Vol.128, March 1997, pp. 370-373.

Sfikas, Peter M., "Restrictive Covenants and At-Will Employment," *Journal of the American Dental Association,* Vol. 129, June 1998, pp. 772-774.

Sfikas, Peter M., "The Inappropriate Patient," *Journal of the American Dental Association*, Vol. 129, September 1998, pp. 1312-1315.

Shapiro, Joseph P., "Comfort and Care," *U.S. News & World Report*, Vol. 122. No. 21, June 2,

Sharp, David, "Give Your Metabolism a Lift," *Health*, Vol.12, No. 2, March 1998, p. 32.

Sherman, Deborah Witt, "Correlates of Death Anxiety in Nurses Who Provide AIDS Care," *Omega*, Vol. 34, No.2, 1996-1997, pp. 117-136.

Sherrod, Roy A., "The Role of the Nurse Educator: When the Obstetrical Nursing Student is Male," *Journal of Nursing Education*, Vol.28, No.8, October 1989, pp. 377-379.

Sherry, Paul, Robert Teschendorf, Silas Anderson and Frank Guzman, "Ethical beliefs and behaviors of college counseling center professionals," *Journal of College Student Development*, Vol.32, 1991, pp. 350-359.

Shevenell, Joseph I., "Managed Care and Medicine," *Journal of the American Dental Association*, Vol.129, April 1998, p. 406.

Showalter, Mark H., "Physicians Cost Shifting Behavior: Medicaid versus other patients." *Contemporary Economic Policy*, Vol.15, April 1997,p.83.

Shuck, Lana Hawhee, "Fit for Life: An Integrated, Holistic Approach to Health," *Contemporary Education*, Vol. 69, No.3, Spring 1998, 157-158.

Shute, Nancy, "A surge in graduate programs for nurses," *U.S. News and World Report*, March 2, 1998, p. 89.

Simmons, P. and Cavanaugh, S., "Relationships among childhood parental care, professional school climate and nursing student caring ability," *Journal of Professional Nursing*, Vol. 12, 1996, pp. 373-381.

Simon, Carol J., David Dranove and William D. White, "The Impact of Managed Care on the Physician Market Place, *Public Health Reports*, Vol. 112, No 3, May 6, 1997, pp. 222-230.

Simon, Nissa, "How to Be Sure You're Not Getting the Wrong Medicine," *New Choices*, Vol.37, No. 9, November 1997, p. 70.

Simpson, K.H., "The development of a clinical ethics consultation service in a community hospital," *Journal of Clinical Ethics*, Vol.3, No.2, 1992, pp. 124-130.

Sledge, William H., "Day Hospital/Crisis Respite Care Versus Inpatient Care, Part II: Service Utilitzation and Costs, *American Journal of Psychiatry*, Vol. 153, No.8, August 1996, p.1074.

Smith, Arthur L., "Regular physical exercise may protect against Alzheimer's disease," *Geriatrics*, Vol. 53, No. 6, June 1998, pp. 94-95.

Smith, Kelly D., "How seniors can give away assets without fear of landing in jail," *Money*, Vol.26, No. 6, June 1997, p. 24.

Smith, Trevor, "Which is the Best Exercise Machine?" *Consumer's Research Magazine*, Vol. 80, No. 12, December 1997, p. 21.

Snadden, David and Donald Mowat, "Community-based curriculum development: what does it really mean?" *Medcial Teacher*, Vol. 17, No.3, September 1995, pp. 298-302.

Sonneck, Gernot and Renate Wagner, "Suicide and Burnout of Physicians," *Omega*, Vol. 33, No. 3, December 1996, pp.255-257.

Sperry, Len and Harry Prosen, "Contemporary Ethical Dilemmas in Psychotherapy," *American Journal of Psychotherapy*, Vol. 52, No.1, Winter1998, pp. 54-65.

Spitz, Henry I., "The Effect of Mental Health Care on Group Psychotherapy: Treatment, Training, and Therapist-Morale Issues, *International Journal of Group Psychotherapy*, Vol. 47, No.1, Summer 1997, p. 28.

Spore, Diana L., Vincent Mor, Paul Larrat, Catherine Hawes and Jeffrey Hiris, "Inappropriate Drug Prescriptions for Elderly Residents of Board and Care Facilities," *American Journal of Public Health*, Vol.87, March 1997, pp. 404-409.

Stamler, Lynette Leeseberg and Barbara Thomas, "Patient Stories: A Way to Enhance Continuing Education," *Journal of Continuing Education in Nursing*, Vol. 28, No. 2, March/April 1997, pp. 64-68.

Steubert, Helen J., "Male Nursing Students' Perception of Clinical Experience," *Nurse Educator*, Vol. 19, No.5, September-October 1994, pp. 28-32.

Stevens, Alan B. *et al*, "Teaching and Maintaining Behavior Management Skills With Nursing Assistants in a Nursing Home," *The Gerontologist*, Vol.38, No. 3, June 1998, pp. 379-384.

Stevenson, Vic and Jerome Carson, "The Pastoral Myth of the Mental Hosptial: A Personal Account," *International Journal of Social Psychiatry*, Vol.41, No.2, Summmer, 1995, pp. 147-151

Stratton, Brad, "Overlook Hospital Emergency Department: Meeting the Competition with Quality," *Quality Progess*, Vol. 31, No.10, October 1998, p. 41..

Strupp, Hans, "The therapist's theoretical orientation: an overrated variable," *Pschotherapy: Theory, Research and Practice*, Vol. 15, No. 4, April 1978, pp. 314-317.

Stuck, E. and H. U. Aronow, "A trial of annual in-home comprehensive geriatric assessments for elderly people living in the community," *New England Journal of Medicine,* Vol. 333, No. 18, 1995, p. 1184.

Sullum, Jacob, "No Relief in Sight," *Reason,* Vol.28, No.8, January 1997, pp. 22-28.

Sulmasy, Daniel P. and Eric S. Marx, " Ethics education for medical house officers: long term improvements in knowledge and confidence," *Journal of Medical Ethics,* Vol. 23, 1997, pp. 88-92.

Swanson, David B., Geoffrey R. Norman and Robert L. Linn, "Performance Based Assessment: Lessons from the Health Professions," *Educational Researcher,* Vol.24, No.5, June-July 1995, p. 6.

Tancredi, L. and J. Barondess, "The Problem of Defensive Medicine," *Science,* Vol.200, 1978, pp. 879-893.

Tardiff, Kenneth, Peter M. Marzuk, Andrew C. Leon, Laura Portera and Cindy Weiner, "Violence by Patients Admitted to a Private Psychiatric Hospital," *American Journal of Psychiatry,* Vol. 154, No. 1, January 1997, p.88.

Teno, Joan M. *et al,* "Changes in Advance Care Planning in Nursing Homes Before and After the Patient Self-Determination Act: Report of a 10-State Survey," *Journal of the American Geriatric Society,* Vol.45, No. 8, August 1997, pp. 939-944.

Teri, L., "Effects of sex and sex-role style on clinical judgment." *Sex Roles,* Vol.8, No. 6, pp. 639-649.

Thelander, Hulda, "Opportunities for Medical Women," *Journal of the American Medical Women's Association,* Vol. 3, February 1948, p, 67.

Thomas, Sally and Gale Hume, "Delegation Competencies: Beginning Practitioners' Reflections," *Nurse Educator,* Vol. 23, No. 1, January-February 1998, p. 38.

Thomas, Lewis, "AIDS: An Unknown Distance to Go, " *Scientific American,* Vol. 259, 1988, p. 152.

Thomas, Lewis, "On the Science and Technology of Medicine," *Daedalus,* Winter, 1977, pp. 37-38.

Thompson, Keith, "Exercise boosts body's clot-busting ability," *The Physician and Sports Medicine,* Vol.18, No. 3, March 1990, p. 43.

Thompson, Mark, "Neglect," *Time,* Vol. 150, No. 17, October 27, 1997, pp. 34-38.

Tomes, Nancy, "Oral History in the History of Medicine," *The Journal of American History,* Vol. 78, No. 2, September 1991, p. 609

Torrey, E. Fuller, "Jails and Prisons-America's New Mental Hospitals," *American Journal of Public Health,* Vol. 85, No. 12, December 1995, p.1611.

Treasure, Tom, "Where did I go wrong?" The Lancet, Vol. 344, August 13, 1994, pp. 419-420.

Troyen, Brennan, "Quality of Clinical Ethics Consultation," *Quality Review Bulletin,* Vol. 18, 1992, p.4.

Truman, Esau G., "The Evangelical Christian in Psychotherapy," *American Journal of Psychotherapy,*

Tully, Shawn, "The Plot to Keep Drug Pirces High," *Fortune,* Vol.28, No.16, December 27, 19993, p. 120.

Twemlow, Stuart W., "Exploitation of Patients: Themes in the Psychopathology of their Therapist" *American Journal of Psychotherapy,* Vol.51, No.3, Summer 1997, p. 359.

Udvarhelyi, I., Steven Terry Roseborough, Richard Lofgren, Nicole Lurie, and Arnold M. Epstein, "Teaching Status and Resource Use for Patients with Acute Myocardial Infarction: A new look at the indirect costs of graduate medical education." *American Journal of Public Health,* Vol 80, No. 9, September 1990, pp. 1099-1100.

Utiger, Robert D., "Praise Reform and Start the Litigation," *The New England Journal of Medicine,* Vol. 329, No. 23, December 2, 1993.

Vassar, Mary J. and Kenneth W. Kizer, "Hospitalizations for Firearm-Related Injuries," *JAMA,* Vol.275, No. 22, June 12, 1996, pp. 1734-1739.

Vaughan, Jeanette, "Is There Really Racism in Nursing?" Journal of Nursing Education, Vol. 36, No. 3, March 1997, pp. 135-139.

Vendecreek, Larry, Deborah Frankowski and Susan Ayres, "Use of the Threat Index with Family Members Waiting during Surgery," *Death Studies,* Vol.18, No.6, 1994, pp. 641-647.

Voelker, Rebecca, "Surgeons Offer 'New Lease' After Domestic Abuse," *JAMA,* Vol.274, No. 20, November 22/29, 1995, p. 1573.

Wallace, Andrew G., "Educating Tomorrow's Doctors: The Thing That Really Matters Is that We Care," *Academic Medicine,* Vol.72, No. 4, April 1997, pp. 253-258.

Wallace, Marquis Earl, "Private Practice, A Nationwide Study," *Social Work,* Vol. 27, 1982, pp. 262-267.

Weber, Joseph, "Contact Lenses: Focus on Open Markets," *Business Week,* January 13, 1997, p. 39.

Weil, Peter A. and P.A. Kimball, "A model of voluntary turnover of hospital CEOs." *Hospital and Health Services Administration,* Vol.40, 1995, pp. 362-385.

Weinberg, Alvin W., "Biomedical Policy: LBJ's Query Leads to an Illuminating Conference," *Science,* Vol. 154, November 1966, p. 619.

Weiner, Jay, "Forecasting the effect of health reform on U.S. physician workforce requirement," *Journal of the American Medical Association,* Vol. 272, 1994, pp.222-230.

Weinstein, Raymond M., "Goffman's *Asylums* and the Total Institution Model of Mental Hospitals," *Psychiatry,* Vol., 57, No. 4, November 1994, pp. 348-367.

Weinstein, Leonard, "Malpractice-the syndrome of the '80's." *Obstetrics and Gynecology,* Vol. 72, 1988, pp. 130-135.

Weisberg, Jacob, "The Accuser," *The New Republic,* Vol. 205, October 21, 19991, p.12.

Weisman, Avery D., "The Physician in Retirement: Transition and Opportunity," *Psychiatry,* Vol. 59, No. 3, Fall 1996, p. 300.

Wells, K.B., "The behavioral sciences in medical education and practice." *Journal of the American Medical Association,* Vol.60, 1985, pp. 493-495.

White, Kerr L. "General Practice in the United States," *The Journal of Medical Education,* XXXIX, April 1964, pp.337-338.

White, L.A. "Mental hospitalization of troublesome youth: An analysis of skyrocketing admission rates," *Stanford Law Review,* Vol. 40, 1988, pp. 773-838.

Whitford, David, "Now the Doctors Want a Union," *Fortune,* Vol. 136, No. 11, December 8, 1996, p. 32.

Wickizer, Thomas M., Daniel Lessler and Karen M. Travis, "Controlling Inpatient Psychiatric Utilization Through Managed Care," *American Journal of Psychiatry,* Vol.153, No. 3, March, 1996, pp. 339-345.

Wilcox, Melinda D., "Will Nursing Home Bills Haunt Your Estate?" *Kiplinger's Personal Finance Magazine,* Vol.52, No. 4, April 1998, pp. 115-118.

Wilson-Silver, Melanie H., "Patients' Rights in England and the United States of America: *The Patient's Charter* and the New Jersey Patient Bill of Rights: a comparison." *Journal of Medical Ethics,* Vol.23, 1997, pp. 213-220.

Wolf, Susan M., "Quality Assessment of Ethics in Health Care: The Accountability Revolution," *American Journal of Law and Medicine,* Vol. XX, No. 1, Summer 1994, p. 105.

Yang, Catherine "The Drugmakers vs. the Trustbusters," *Business Week,* #3388, September 5, 1994, p. 67.

Yingling, Sandra and S.J. Bolster, "Banking on Bonuses: 1998 Salary Survey," *Hospital and Health Networks,* Vol.72, No.17, September 5, 1998, pp. 24-27.

Zamir, Mair, "Secrets of the Heart," *The Sciences,* Vol.36, No.5, September-October 1996, pp. 26-31.

Zimbardo, Philip G., "Pathology of Imprisonment," *Society,* Vol.9, April 1972, pp. 4-8.

Newspapers

Alvarez, Lizette, "Nasty, Costly Battle Shapes Up Over Changing Managed Care," *The New York Times,* June 3, 1998, p. A21.

Anders, George and Ron Winslow, "Turn for the Worse: HMOs' Woes Reflect Conflicting Demands of American Public," *The Wall Street Journal,* Vol. 122, Sec. A, December 22, 1997, p. 1.

Associated Press, "Doctors' Reliance on Technology Is Bringing House Calls to an End," *The New York Times,* December 18, 1997, p. A22.

Associated Press, "Syracuse nursing students seek lawyer in administrative mix-up," *The Buffalo News,* August 11, 1998, p. A-4.

Chartrand, Sabra, "Why is this Surgeon Suing?" *The New York Times,* June 8, 1995, pp. D1-5.

Christian, Nicole M., "Hospital Fined for Overwork of Residents," *The New York Times,* August 21,1998, p. P6.

Davis, Henry L., "State suspends top Buffalo heart surgeon over conduct," *The Buffalo News,* August 19, 1998, p. A 1.

Eichenwald, Kurt, "Some in Congress Seek to Curb Inquiry Into Fraudulent Billing by Teaching Hospitals," *The New York Times,* Thursday, July 3, 1997, p. A 14.

Farquhar, Larissa Mac "Andrew Weil, Shaman, M.D.," *The New York Times Magazine,* August 24, 1997, pp.30-31.

Fisher, Jan, " Plastic Surgery, Unsupervised, Leads to a Fine for a Hospital, " *The New York Times,* December 19, 1997, p. B1.

Fisher, Lawrence M., "Smoother Road From Lab to Sales," *New York Times,* February 25, 1998, p. D 1.

Fisher, Ian, "A New Health Risk for Immigrants," *The New York Times,* Febraury 2, 1998, p. B1.

Freudenheim, Milt, "As Insurers Cut Fees, Doctors Shift to Elective Procedures, " *The New York Times,* November 17, 1996, p. 24.

Freudenheim, Milt, "Insurers Tighten Rules and Reduce Fees for Doctors," *The New York Times,* June 28, 1998, p. 1.

Freudenheim, Milt, "Nurses Treading on Doctor's Turf," *The New York Times,* Nov. 2, 1997, Sec. 4, p. 5.

Freudenheim, Milt, "New Medicare Rules: Winners and Losers," *The New York Times,* July 4, 1998, p.D2.

Galant, Debra, Organized Medicine: Dr. Anthony Tonzola Thinks a Doctor's Union Is the Way to Keep H.M.O.'s From Calling All the Shots," *The New York Times,* January 25, 1997, Sect. XII, p.41.

Gilbert, Susan, "Forget About Bedside Manners, Some Doctors Have No Manners," *The New York Times,* December 23, 1997, p.F7.

Goldman, Alan J., "Commentary," *The Los Angeles Times,* January 21, 1996, p. B5.

Grady, Denise, "Doctors Urged to Admit Mistakes," *The New York Times,,* December 9, 1997, p. F 9.

Greenhouse, Linda, "Living to be 100: Anger, Arthritis and Occasional Joy," *The New York Times,* May 3, 1998, Sec. XIV, LI,1. and p 4.

Greenhouse, Linda "Ruling on Bias Law," *The New York Times,* June 26, 1998, p. A 1.

Greenhouse, Steven, " Podiatrist to Form Nationwide Union; A Reply to H.M.Os." *The New York Times,* October 25, 1996, p. A1.

Hilzenrath, David S., "Some HMO's get tight-fisted about paying bills," *The Buffalo News,* March 31, 1998, p. E 2.

Honan, William H., "Imperiled Species: 4 Year Degree in Pharmacy," *The New York Times,* December 17, 1997, p. B8.

Jaschik, Scott, "Health - Care Changes Would Transform Medical-School Financing and Curricula," *The New York Times,* Vol 40, September 29, 1993, p. A24.

Jeffrey, Nancy Ann, "New Threat for HMO's: Doctor Discipline Boards," *The Wall Street Journal,*

Kilborn, Peter T., "Nurses Get New Role in Patient Protection," *The New York Times,* March 26, 1998, p. A 14.

Krauthammer, Charles, "We're losing our experienced doctors," *The Buffalo News,* January 12, 1998, p. C3.

Lambert, Bruce, "Picture This: Big Smiles After Surgery," *The New York Times,* October 18, 1997, p. B1.

Leary, Warren E., "The Whole Body Catalogue," *The New York Times,* July 8, 1997, Sec.C, pp. 1-6

Libow, Leslie S., "Nursing Home Care," *The New York Times,* August 5, 1998, p. A22.

McGinley, Lurie, "U.S. Health Costs Are Expected to Double by 2007," *The Wall Street Journal,* September 15, 1998, p. A2.

Miller, James P., "Health Care & Retirement to Buy Manor Care," *The Wall Street Journal*, June 11, 1998, pp. A3 and A8. See also: The New York Times, June 11, 1998, p. D2.

Moss, Michael and Chris Adams, "Evictees Relish Nursing Homes' Reversal," *Wall Street Journal*, May 21, 1998, pp. B1 and B12.

Moss, Michael, "Criminal Probes Target Abusive Nursing Homes," *The Wall Street Journal*, May 28, 1996, pp. B1 and B15.

Moss, Michael, "Many Elders Receive Care at Criminals' Hands," *The Wall Street Journal*, March 18, 1998, p. B1 and B 14.

Moss, Michael, "Nursing Homes Get Punished by Irate Jurors," *The Wall Street Journal*, March 6, 1998, pp. B1 and B8.

No author, "Hospital Cuts Jobs," *The New York Times*, Friday, September 4, 1998, p. B8.

No author, "Brain Surgeon Who Made a Mistake Is Reinstated," *The New York Times*, October 4, 1995, p. C 4.

No author, "Centers Suggested for High –Risk Surgery," *The New York Times*, January 19,1995, p. 13A

No author, "U.S. Moves to Curb Some Drug Promotion," *New York Times*, Janaury 6, 1998, p. D11.

No author, "Union aims to organize physicians," *Buffalo News*, March 2, 1999, p.A1.

No author, *The New York Times*, Friday, September 4, 1998, p. B10.

O'Neill, Edward H., "Academic Health Centers Must Begin Reforms Now," *The New York Times*, Vol. 40, September 8m, 1993, p. A 48.

Pear, Robert, "Panel Endorses Alternative To President's Health Plan," *The New York Times*, March 24, 1994, p. A 18.

Pear, Robert, "Panel Finds Medicare Costs Are Underestimated by U.S.'" *The New York Times*, June 3, 1998, p. A 21.

Portenoy, Russell, "Physicians Said to Persist in Understanding Pain and Ignoring the Evidence," *The New York Times*, December 31, 1987, Sec. B. p.5.

Rabinowitz, Jonathan, "Optometrists Clash With Eye Surgeons over Laser Process," *The New York Times*, April 8, 1996, p. B5.

Riordan, Teresa, "Patents: New legislation seeks to exclude surgical procedures from patent protection," *The New York Times*, March 6, 1995, p. D2.

Robinson, Jody, "I'm a Doctor, Not a Paper Pusher," *The Wall Street Journal*, April 1, 1998, p. A18.

Rosenthal, Elisabeth, "Post-Surgery Deaths Prompt Inquiry at a Queens Hospital," *The New York Times,*

Rother, Charles "For jails and the mentally ill, a sentence of growing stress," *San Diego Union Tribune*, March 30, 1995.

Saslow, Linda, "When Insurers Deem That Surgery Is Purely Cosmetic," *The New York Times*, November 23, 1997, p. 14.

Singer, Penny, "Grant Helps to Ready Primary Care Doctors," *The New York Times*, Vol. XIV, WC p. 10.

Spalato, Mark V., "Nurses, Beware," *The New York Times, October 5, 1997*, Sec. IV, p. 14:6.

Stolberg, Sheryl Gay, "New Rules Will Force Doctors to Disclose Ties to Drug Industry," *New York Times*, February 3, 1998, p. A 12.

Stolberg, Sheryl Gay, "Gifts to Science Researchers Have Strings , Study Finds." *New York Times*, April 1, 1998, p. A 17.

Weizel, Richard, "A Test of Mettle in a Real-Life E.R.," *The New York Times*, July 27, 1997, Sec.13, p8.

Zimmer, Dieter E., "Placebo," *Die Zeit*, October 8, 1989, p. 58.

Documents

Alan J. Mishler vs. The State of Nevada Board of Medical Examiners, #22397. 849 P.2d P. 291.

American Pharmaceutical Association Policy Committee on Professional Affairs, *American Pharmacy*, Vol.22, 1982, pp. 368-380.

American Association of Colleges of Nursing, Baccalaureate nursing education for the future: Defining the essential elements. Washington, D.C., 1997.

American Association of Colleges of Pharmacy, *Twenty Year Cross Sectional Study of Career Practice Patterns of Male and Female Pharmacists*. New York, American Association of Colleges of Pharmacy, 1990.

Bureau of Labor Statistics, "National Occupational and Wage Data," December 8, 1998, p. 1.

Bureau of Labor Statistics, "Occupational Employment Statistics, National Occupational and Wage Data," The Internet. *URL:http://stats.bls.gov/oes/national/oes66008.htm*

Bureau of Labor Statistics, "Occupational Employment Statistics," *The Internet*.

Bureau of Labor Statistics, *Occupational Employment Statistics*, March 12, 1998, Table # 32502..

Bureau of Labor Statistics, *op. cit.*, March 12, 1998 table #32505

Bureau of Labor Statistics, Washington, D.C., *Occupational Employment Statistics*, 1998.

Bureau of the Census, *Population projections of the United States by age, sex, race and Hispanic origin:1995-2050. Current Population Reports P25-1130* Washington, D.C., Government Printing Office, 1996.

Center for Disease Control, The National Institute of Mental Health, Suicide Rates in the United States, 1995.

Duncan-Poitier, Johanna, *You Have the Right to Competent Professional Services,* Brochure issued by The New York State Education Department, Albany, N.Y. (No Year) p. 3.

F.B.I. Law Enforcement Bulletin, Vol. 61, No. 10, 1992, pp. 17-20.

Harvard Medical Practice Study, *Patients, doctors and lawyers: medical injury, malpractice litigation and patient compensation in New York State,* Report of the HMPC, New York, 1990

Hippocratic Oath.

Jaffe v. Redmond et al 1996, WL 315841 (U.S. June 13, 1996).

Omnibus Budget Reconciliation Act of 1987. Public Law 100-203, Subtitle C. The Nursing Home Reform Act. 42 U.S.C. 1395i -3 (a)-(h) (Medicare); 13966r (a) –(h) (Medicaid).

Select Committee on Children, Youth, and Families. House of Representatives. One Hundred Second Cognress, Second Session, "Psychiatric Treatment Bilks the System and Betrays our Trust," U.S. Government Printing Office, 1992.

State University of New York - University at Buffalo, *Graduate Professional Class Schedule,* Buffalo, New York, Fall 1998, pp. 66-67.

The Association of American Medical Colleges, *American Medical School Admission Requirements, 49th Edition,* Washington, D.C., 1998.

442 U.S.C. 5601.

U.S. Bureau of Labor Statistics, Office of Employment Projections, November 1995.

U.S. Bureau of the Census: 1990 census of the population. General population characteristics. United States. Washington D.C. U.S. Government Printing Office, 1992.

U.S. Department of Commerce, *Statistical Abstracts of the U.S.* Washington, D.C., U.S. Government Printing Office, 1997.

U.S. Public Health Service, *Forward Plan for 1977-1981,* Washington, D.C., Department of Health, Education and Welfare, 1977, p. 108.

Reference Works

Johnson, Otto Ed., *Information Please Almanac,* New York, Houghton Mifflin Co. New York 1997.

Wright, John W. Ed. *The New York Times Almanac,* New York, Penguin Putnam, Inc., 1998.

"Man-made Cures," in *The Random House Encyclopedia,* James Mitchell, Editor, New York, Random House, 1990.

Index

About the Author

Gerhard Falk is the author of more than forty journal articles and eight books including *Sex, Gender and Social Change,* (University Press 1998); *Ageism, the Aged and Aging in America*-with Ursula Falk (Charles C. Thomas, Inc. 1997); *American Judaism in Transition* (University Press 1995); *Murder-An Analysis of Its Forms, Conditions and Causes* (Mc Farland & Co., Inc., Inc. 1990) etc. Dr. Falk is also the recipient of the State University of New York Chancellor's Award for Excellence in Teaching.